American
Buildings
and Their
Architects

This book is the fourth one in a four-volume work which, under the general title of *American Buildings and their Architects,* provides an architectural analysis and evaluation of American buildings from colonial times to about 1960. The first two volumes, by William H. Pierson, Jr., proceed from the earliest settlements to the Chicago World's Fair. The final two volumes, written by William H. Jordy, concentrate on buildings in the late nineteenth century to the 1960s.

WILLIAM H. JORDY studied at Bard college and New York University before receiving his Ph.D. at Yale University. He first taught at Yale and then joined the faculty of Brown University, where he is currently Professor of Fine Arts. He was a Guggenheim Fellow in 1954, and served as advisor on nineteenth-century architecture for the Carnegie Foundation study *Arts of the United States.* Mr. Jordy's writings include *Henry Adams: Scientific Historian* and *Montgomery Schuyler: "American Architecture and Other Writings* (edited with Ralph Coe), as well as articles in journals such as the *Journal of the Society of Architectural Historians,* the *Architectural Review* and *Architectural Forum.*

American Buildings and Their Architects

VOLUME 5

THE IMPACT OF EUROPEAN MODERNISM IN THE MID-TWENTIETH CENTURY

William H. Jordy

OXFORD UNIVERSITY PRESS
New York   Oxford

Oxford University Press

Oxford   New York   Toronto
Delhi   Bombay   Calcutta   Madras   Karachi
Petaling Jaya   Singapore   Hong Kong   Tokyo
Nairobi   Dar es Salaam   Cape Town
Melbourne   Auckland

and associated companies in
Beirut   Berlin   Ibadan   Nicosia

Printed in the United States of America

TO THE MEMORY OF
GRANT MILLER
PROMISE LOST TO VIOLENCE

Contents

List of Illustrations

xi

Acknowledgments

For prefatory remarks on the nature and intent of this volume, see the introductory remarks in the preceding one, *American Buildings and Their Architects: Progressive and Academic Ideals at the Turn of the Twentieth Century.*

It remains to thank those who have given me special assistance with the essays in this volume. With respect to Rockefeller Center, Wallace Harrison, one of its principal designers, and Caroline Hood, director of public relations for the Center, have been exceedingly helpful. Regarding the Philadelphia Saving Fund Society Building: I am grateful for the interviews, and the comments on early drafts provided by William Lescaze, Louis McAllister, and E. W. Bolton, Jr., on the architectural side of the project, and by Donaldson Cresswell and Isaac W. Roberts, on the institutional side. Conversations with Robert A. M. Stern have also been illuminating. Marcel Breuer very kindly read and commented (sometimes critically) on my discussion of the Ferry Cooperative House, as did Thomas McCormick at a time when he was a member of the history of art faculty at Vassar College. The staff of Mies van der Rohe, especially Peter Carter, was helpful on Mies' buildings. Philip Johnson gave counsel on the Seagram Building. On the Guggenheim Museum, both Thomas M. Messer, director when this was written, and James Johnson Sweeney, former director, read and criticized the manuscript. In respect to the architectural and engineering aspects of the Guggenheim, I especially appreciate the cooperation of Professor Mendel Glickman, consulting engineer for most of the building, of William H. Short, Wright's supervisor on the project, and of George N. Cohen, contractor for the building. For an interview concerning the Richards Medical Research Building, I am grateful to Louis I. Kahn.

Marcel Breuer and the *Architectural Record* have granted me permission to cite at considerable length from the architect's remarks published in Peter Blake, *Marcel Breuer, Architect and Designer.* Louis Kahn and *Progressive Architecture* in one instance, Kahn and *Architectural Forum* (Time-Life, Inc.) in the other, have done the same for extensive citations from Jan C. Rowan, "Wanting To Be, The Philadelphia School," *Progressive Architecture* (April 1961), and from Walter McQuade, "Architect Louis Kahn and His Strong-Boned Structures," *Architectural Forum* (October 1957). Of course I am equally grateful to the authors and publishers of those books and articles cited more sparingly, to the photographers and other sources for pictorial material named in the List of Illustrations, and to the draftsmen and other assistants mentioned in the preface to *American Buildings and Their Architects: Progressive and Academic Ideals at the Turn of the Twentieth Century.*

Three of these chapters have been previously published, but with considerable differences: Chapter 2, on the Philadelphia Saving Fund Society Building, in the *Journal of the Society of Architectural Historians;* Chapter 4, on 860 Lake Shore Drive and the Seagram Building, and also Chapter 6, on the Richards Medical Research Building, in the *Architectural Review.* For permitting their appearance here in altered form, I thank both of these publications.

William H. Jordy

Providence, Rhode Island, 1970

American
Buildings
and Their
Architects

CHAPTER I

Rockefeller Center and Corporate Urbanism

In the great city of our age there will be a civic center, a public place which, like the agora of Athens, the Roman forum, and the medieval cathedral square, will be community focus and popular concourse. What it will be like in spatial organization and plastic treatment may be largely foreseen in a recent great urban development—Rockefeller Center in New York City.
SIGFRIED GIEDION, Space, Time and Architecture, 1941

Already in New York Rockefeller Center affirms to the world the dignity of the new times . . . just as the skyscraper of Howe and Lescaze [the Philadelphia Saving Fund Society Building] does in Philadelphia.
. . .
The secret of such a success lies in the flawless and rigorous division of responsibilities among technicians grouped in a team. *Everything is planned synchronously and synthetically at the beginning of the job. Such constructions have a perfect and faultless life.*
LE CORBUSIER, When the Cathedrals Were White, 1947, his account of a visit to the United States

A PLACE IN PLACELESSNESS

Nationally, even internationally, Rockefeller Center is famous as an outstanding venture by private enterprise in large-scale commercial building with momentous urban consequences. For New York City its plaza has created a badly needed focus not only for the fashionable Fifth Avenue shopping area, but for the entire city as well.

Like most American cities, New York has provided for pedestrian space in its commercial area with treeless sidewalks of minimal width and with occasional (very occasional) landscaped squares. Historically, these landscaped squares have been anti-urban in quality. In keeping with the native hatred of cities, they have been principally designed to provide escape, or at least respite, from what has been regarded as a defective mode of existence. Around a few of these parks, during a particular period, some cardinal activity of the city has become concentrated, and such a park has flourished briefly as a square at the center of things. Thus, at the turn of the century, the park at Madison Square was a place of withdrawal suddenly transformed into a place of intense activity as well. Here at 23rd Street, where the diagonal of Broadway crosses Fifth Avenue and where Madison Avenue originates a block away—with the park in the middle—there was once a focus of shopping. Some notable monuments of the period also clustered around this Square: McKim, Mead & White's Madison Square Garden (completed in 1890); their Madison Square Presbyterian Church (1903–6); Le Brun & Sons' tower addition to the Metropolitan Life Insurance Company (1905–9); and D. H. Burnham & Company's Fuller Building (1901–3), popularly known as the Flatiron Building because it was squeezed into the wedge-shaped site made by the crossing of Broadway and Fifth Avenue.* By 1900, fashionable stores—in a momentous switch from Broadway—were already leapfrogging northward up Fifth Avenue, making it a shopping street well into the forties. With the "longevity" peculiar to most New York real estate, the buildings around Madison Square by McKim, Mead & White have been razed. The Garden, with its fanciful tower inspired by the Giralda and its pergolaed roof top for dining and dancing (where White met his sensational death), disappeared in 1925; the "Byzantine" dome of the Presbyterian Church, briefly a splendor of the city, went to the wreckers as early as 1918, its site spared from commerce for barely a decade. Although still a busy park, Madison Square is no longer what it was. It serves its district, but has faded as a landmark sufficiently prominent to attract tourists.

The notable example of a park having consistently maintained a dual character as a place for relaxation and a place of bustle at the center of distinctive activity is City Hall Park (Figs. 1, 2). As this is written plans are underway for a grandiose mall north of City Hall which will link this building with other governmental structures, some existing, others to be erected on redeveloped land near by. With one

* Illustrated in *American Buildings and Their Architects: Progressive and Academic Ideals at the Turn of the Twentieth Century*, fig. 40.

FIGURE 1. *City Hall Park, New York. The City Hall* (1802–12), *begun and largely designed by Joseph-François Mangin, completed with some changes by John McComb, Jr., is in the center background. The base of McKim, Mead & White's Municipal Building* (*completed* 1908) *barely shows in the upper right corner. Behind City Hall, the roof of the City Court Building indicates part of the site of the forthcoming mall which will be surrounded by new civic and commercial buildings.*

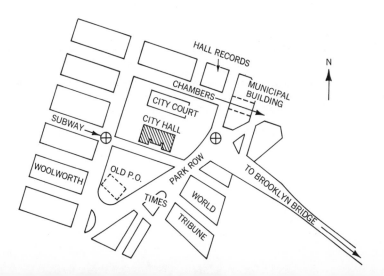

important exception, these plans (tentative in the mid-sixties†) will not substantially alter the Park (south of City Hall) or change the existing relationship of the Park to its environs. The Park provides for the display of the petite elegance of Mangin and McComb's Neoclassic City Hall (1802–12) by setting it apart from its surroundings, much as a showcase isolates an architectural model. This function of the Park, together with its situation, makes it an admirable example of a landscaped area of modest dimensions which serves at once as a setting for a landmark, as a place of respite, and as a network of pathways to destinations all around its perimeter. Rather, we should say it possesses this kind of potential, for its half-hearted landscaping and flaccidly skewed axiality cry for decisive form, one which is more purposefully adjusted to the buildings and activities of the area. Yet, even if conventional in design and somewhat scrubby in upkeep, it is at least a comfortable, and comforting, space, being as frequented for these reasons as for the convenience of its pedestrian criss-cross. One index to the formality of the proposed revamping is that it promises to eliminate the paths altogether; to make the entire area into lawn and trees—a place to look at, not to walk in; to make it, in effect, an obstacle to walk around.

Some years ago the activity of City Hall Park was even more intense than now. In the northeast corner, the approach to James and Washington Roebling's famed Brooklyn Bridge (1867–73), now curlicued with the usual ramping, brings Long Island traffic to the cluster of government offices and courts. This complex is dominated by McKim, Mead & White's Municipal Building (completed 1908), in which the ancient imperiousness of the Roman arch at the base of the building, providing a tunnel for Chambers Street, is joined to the modern imperiousness of the skyscraper above. Beside the causeway to the Bridge, along the eastern edge of the Park, three skyscrapers known as Newspaper Row once housed the *World*, the *Tribune*‡ and the *Times*. To the south, directly opposite City Hall, Alfred Mullet's old central post office (1869–78) illegally encroached on the Park as the most prominent

---

† This scheme by Edward Stone and Eggers & Higgins consists of a tall skyscraper shaft for municipal services behind City Hall, with a depressed mall linking the two. An extensive area around the mall will be lined with rows of trees. The old intricacy of movement promises to disappear in the pompous scale and formality of the projected scheme. See *Progressive Architecture*, January 1965, pp. 180–83, which outlines the vexed history of proposals for replanning the area. Its defects notwithstanding, the scheme as of 1965 is at least the best solution in the series.

‡ Illustrated in *American Buildings and Their Architects: Progressive and Academic Ideals at the Turn of the Twentieth Century*, fig. 1.

4

FIGURE 2. *City Hall Park, looking toward Cass Gilbert's Woolworth Build-ing, 1911–13.*

mansarded building in the city, until its demolition in 1939. Along the western edge of the Park, Cass Gilbert's Neo-Gothic Woolworth Building (1911–13) still dominates a line of office buildings (Fig. 2). It stood for years as the tallest building in the world and, as such, a tourist landmark. (Its observation floor was eventually closed owing to midtown competition, partly from its successor to the title, the Empire State Building,* and partly from Rockefeller Center.) To these sources of attraction within the wall of offices and stores around City Hall Park, add the flanking stations for convergent subway lines. All in all, the Park is worth a visit from anyone who would see the role of the landscaped square (crude though this one is in many respects) in an intensely urban situation.

Rewarding as it may be to students of urban spaces, few of them would select City Hall Park as a major symbol of the city, and almost no outsider would. The gathering places that have come to symbolize Manhattan have depended less on municipal sponsorship than on private enterprise. Prior to the building of Rockefeller Center in the 1930's, three were especially prominent. Of these, Times Square was perhaps preëminent. Still a potent symbol of the frenetic vitality of the city, it has in recent years lost much of its luster, becoming excessively honkytonk, although talk of upgrading is perennial. As for its future, nothing with so many people and so many lights is heading toward obscurity.

Wall Street is another such symbol. A focus of pedestrian activity within the city, the Street (or rather the financial district of which it is the heart) has been reinforced by a cluster of open spaces in the vicinity. The first of these was the plaza of Skidmore, Owings & Merrill's Chase Manhattan Bank (1955–64) in the block bounded by Nassau, Liberty, Williams, and Pine Streets. However welcome this irregular pedestrian space may be amidst the density of surrounding building, and embellished as it is by a sunken stone garden by Isamu Noguchi, it is curiously empty of activity. A restaurant—and one not excessively deluxe—in part of the ground floor of the bank, with an outdoor café for warm weather, might bring life to the space. (Why is it that civic-minded commercial institutions persist in exaggerating their institutional rather than their commercial character in such enterprises as this?) But the Chase Manhattan led to a substantial interest in the refurbishing of downtown Manhattan. Other nearby plazas, one at Skidmore, Owings & Merrill's Marine Midland Building (1961–67), with Noguchi's huge red cube spectacularly balanced on one of its corners, and those around Minoru Yamasaki's World Trade Center (1962–c. 1973),† initiated

* By Shreve, Lamb & Harmon; constructed 1929–31.
† In association with Emery Roth & Sons.

a chain of plazas in the financial district. The degree of their success as urban designs will depend on the preservation of some of the density of the earlier buildings around these plazas, in order to wall them in as outdoor rooms. It will depend as well on the preservation of much of the picturesque pomposity of the older skyscrapers, rising in a pinnacled huddle above the tangle of streets. On the other hand, should all new building follow the lead of Chase Manhattan and the World Trade Center, and eventuate as outsized, bluntly rectangular, monotonously gridded containers, then they will duplicate the effect of Lever House on Park Avenue. A fine building, it was imitated *ad nauseum* in mediocre variants, until the character of the place sank in its very "upgrading." The signs are ominous that such will also be the fate of the downtown financial district.

Whereas Times Square and Wall Street just happened upon fame, a third symbol of pedestrian congregation in Manhattan was magnificently planned. This is the Grand Central Concourse (1903–13), officially by Reed & Stem and Warren & Wetmore, although Reed & Stem together with Colonel William J. Wilgus, who set the program as chief engineer for the New York Central Railroad, deserve the principal credit. As this is written, much of its spatial grandeur has disappeared with the advent of three-dimensional advertising, business booths, and, above all, the gigantic Kodak saccharinities of landscape and family fun. The problem is not so much the invasion of this space by "dignified" advertising (as the agencies like to describe it), as the quantity and scale of the intrusion. What more telling sign of the times than a gaudy backyard barbecue outshouting the grandeur that was Rome!

In the early 1930's, up to the appearance of Rockefeller Center, these pedestrian gathering places were major symbols of the central city: Times Square, Wall Street, and the Grand Central Concourse. To them, two streets should be added: Park Avenue and Fifth Avenue. Of the two, Park Avenue had the greater visual distinction.‡ It was a landmark, and as such conjured up a definite image, whereas Fifth Avenue was a mere location. In fact, shocking as it may be in a metropolis of such magnitude, among familiar Manhattan streets only Park Avenue north of 46th Street boasts an elaborate esthetic treatment. As an environment for city living, it left as much to be desired as any Beaux-Arts boulevard. Characteristic of the buildings lining such boulevards, the façades to either side, perfunctorily decked in Neo-Renaissance trappings, masked rooms so ill-lighted and ill-ventilated, however spacious, that Lewis Mumford repeatedly denounced the quarter

‡ On Park Avenue, see Vincent Scully, Jr., "Death of the Street," *Perspecta,* 8 (1963), pp. 91-96.

FIGURE 3. *Park Avenue, New York, looking toward Grand Central Terminal, as it appeared immediately after World War II.*

as an elegant slum. But as a visual entity, the Avenue was impressive, particularly from the 1920's until the years immediately following World War II (Fig. 3). The green strip forming its axis ran between Neo-Renaissance apartment palazzi of fairly regular aspect. From the upper East Side this walled perspective dipped in a long slope to its semi-closure with the Grand Central Terminal, from the roof of which the gilded pinnacle of its office tower *à la château* rose as the climatic bauble of the axis. If the silhouette of this tower bulked sufficiently to provide a picturesque focus for the corridor, it still did not wholly barricade the long vista (as does the Pan Am cliff at present) and thus prevent its extension by imagination into the infinity of sky.

The relative uniformity of this vast corridor, with its few shops inconspicuously opened into the bases of the apartment palaces, typified the Beaux-Arts dream of the elegant residential boulevard. So did its discreet procession of marquees, of doormen, of limousines, of poodles out for an airing. So, finally, did the relative quiet of the precinct. Like all such Beaux-Arts schemes, Park Avenue was insulated from the boisterous reality of its surroundings; here astonishingly so because of its thrust through the very heart of Manhattan. To be sure, an effect which depended on identity rather than on variety, and which lacked distinction of detail, tended to be more exhilarating when experienced at automobile rather than pedestrian speeds. Even the planting of the median strip worked (and still works) to the disadvantage of the pedestrian. However attractive the foliage may appear as a pattern from above, and however convenient as a traffic separator, it so bisects the street that the pedestrian loses contact with the opposite sidewalk, and thereby loses some sense of the street as a corridor-like entity, as well as the visual vitality of the activities and the shops across the way.* These deficiencies notwithstanding, Park Avenue during the twenties and thirties provided a splendid and unified corridor of urban scale, one destroyed with the coming of the metal-and-glass office buildings after the war.

These have the usual dismaying effect of metal-and-glass buildings

---

* A planting barrier in the center of a street can be immensely successful where, as is the case of Commonwealth Avenue in Boston, the central strip is a real park with a walkway rather than the formal planting of Park Avenue, and where the buildings to either side are relatively domestic in scale and highly irregular. Particularly where it is somewhat irregularly planted, the park then becomes the continuous, if variegated, foil for the architectural diversity, with bays, porches, towers, and roofs of the buildings opposite glimpsed as changing vignettes through the foliage. Incidentally, it was possible to walk in the central strip of Park Avenue until this was whittled away to enlarge the traffic lanes to either side, but the walkway was very exposed.

9

en masse. The thin grids become monotonous. Yet within the over-all mass, the discord of one type of grid against another is jarring, for the virtue of such grids is their ordered geometry, and random variation disorders it without thereby becoming picturesque. Then, too, the flash of metal and enamel amidst the underwater blur of the tinted glass must suffice for the more positive effects of light and shadow of masonry buildings. On Park Avenue, the ragged manner in which unrelated plazas have chewed the boundaries of the street has also eroded its unity. The château tower of the Grand Central office building, which once shone as the climax of the Avenue, now exists as a wraith, making a dim appearance against the ponderous Pan Am wall behind. As if to complete the roster of misfortunes, the avenue is now but little livelier in aspect than when a residential corridor. In *The Death and Life of Great American Cities,* Jane Jacobs has remarked that nothing so devitalizes a street as an excessive number of banks, of which Park Avenue has more than its share; to her assertion it might be added that an excessive number of buildings discreetly dedicated to maintaining a "corporate image" works to the same end. Hence Park Avenue, like Times Square, and the Grand Central Concourse, has deteriorated as a landmark of the city, despite the burgeoning value of its real estate.

Compared to Park Avenue in 1930, Fifth Avenue had but little specific identity. It did have distinction, but of an adventitious sort. The city had adorned it with lighting standards and traffic signals slightly fancier than those of most streets. More important, an association of merchants enforced bans on projecting signs and on the shrillest forms of outdoor advertising. The luxurious quiet of the store fronts (more so then than now) complemented the splendor of window displays and shoppers. Above 59th Street, where Fifth Avenue fronts Central Park, the rows of mansions still recalled past glories. Apartment houses had already appeared in the area by 1930, however, and even then the fate of earlier grandeur was clear. Insofar as the Avenue boasted landmarks, these were limited: the Public Library at 42nd Street; the Plaza Hotel behind its park at 59th Street; in between some fashionable churches, of which St. Patrick's Cathedral and St. Thomas' were the most conspicuous; for a few, perhaps, the University Club; but for most, the major department stores clustered at various points along the way. Rockefeller Center radically altered the situation. It provided an anchor and focus for the Avenue. More than this, it provided a cardinal image of the city—so much so that if a non-resident is asked to mention the major landmarks of the city, he invariably mentions the Center, and very likely it comes at the head of his list.

A commercial venture designed to supply public space within a major American metropolis, and having the scale of Rockefeller Center, had no precedent. Throughout the nineteenth and early twentieth centuries, significant urban spaces consciously planned by private (as opposed to public or institutional) enterprise as adjuncts to business in major American cities were rare. The downtown areas of a few cities contained arcades of shops.† A few buildings boasted tall entrance court-yards, the most renowned being that of the Palace Hotel in San Francisco. The floors of some department stores (Wanamaker's in Philadelphia and New York, for example) centered around spectacular interior light wells comparable to those in certain nineteenth-century libraries and office buildings,‡ and kindred, too, to the one in Wright's Larkin Building (Fig. 142). Less exceptional examples of private provision for grand public spaces were the palm bedecked lobbies of the most impressive hotels of the nineteenth and early twentieth centuries. These boasted such extravagant use of space and embellishment that foreign visitors repeatedly gasped at the palatial qualities of American hotels. Few such lobbies remain. In New York, the lobby of the Plaza gives at least some notion of their splendor.

With the turn of the century came the greatest railroad terminals, consciously planned as "gates" to their cities at a time when railroads provided the principal means of entrance and could afford such civic largesse. Now the proud waiting rooms and concourses are going the way of Grand Central Concourse. Some, like McKim's concourse for the Pennsylvania Station in New York, have gone completely. Built in 1904–10, it was callously scrapped in 1964–65, after a life of less than fifty years.

If these efforts typified the range of private endeavor in the creation of urban spaces, public programs previous to 1930, as we have already observed, characteristically made their most significant contributions in parks. The most important of these being large landscape parks, like New York's pioneer Central Park (designed by Frederick Law Olmsted and Calvert Vaux in 1858), were thoroughly committed to rural rather than urban values. Even boulevards of the nineteenth century were predominantly links with landscape parks; designed to create "park systems," they enabled persons of means to ride by carriage through splendid residential corridors into the parks' country environment. Shop-

† The most impressive one still surviving is the metal-and-glass passage by John Eisenmann and George H. Smith through the Arcade Building (1886–90) in Cleveland, Ohio. An earlier, Greek Revival example, beautifully restored, is that between Westminster and Weybosset Streets in Providence, R.I. (1827–29); the design of Russell Warren, it was built by James G. Bucklin.

‡ See *American Buildings and Their Architects: Progressive and Academic Ideals at the Turn of the Twentieth Century,* fig. 140. Also see fig. 77 below.

ping and civic boulevards comparable to those of the great European cities did not exist.* Although Baron Haussmann's boulevard planning for Paris from 1853 through the early seventies inspired visions of comparable effects in the United States by the end of the century, they mostly went unrealized. The example of the White City at the heart of the Chicago Columbian Exposition of 1893 did influence grand architectural complexes for institutional building. As the Exposition had been separated from the nastiness of the city, so the monumental complex of what came to be called the "city beautiful" movement of the first three decades of the twentieth century also tended to quarantine itself in a garden environment beyond commercial contamination— one example being Maybeck's Palace of Fine Arts†; another, Park Avenue. Even when these monumental complexes were relatively close to their city centers, as in St. Louis, Cleveland, San Francisco and Denver, they tended to be unpopulated precincts of greenery and marble —at once within the city yet out of it. Often, as in St. Louis and Cleveland, they were so lavishly planned for future development that they long existed as misplaced chunks of prairie, pitifully naked of the magnificence which architecture and gardens were to have brought, and in recent years they have been increasingly devoted to less grandiose purpose.‡

As a check on such arcadianism,[1] with its genteel concomitant of the "higher life in art," the concept of Rockefeller Center was of some effect. So was the almost contemporaneous appearance of the nearby Museum of Modern Art. Instead of being given a Parnassian setting in some park, it was placed in the heart of the city, as a cultural Macy's. Its revolving door at street level gave access to activities varying from tea on the penthouse roof to facilities for rigorous scholarship, and to exhibitions ranging from the hallowed "fine" arts to movies and mass-produced objects of good design.

Such, in brief, was the tradition of American urban planning and its modest impact on Manhattan when Rockefeller Center opened up new possibilities.

* An arcaded shopping plaza and boulevard was, however, suggested in L'Enfant's Plan of Washington, D.C. (1790).
† See *American Buildings and Their Architects: Progressive and Academic Ideals at the Turn of the Twentieth Century,* Chapter 6; the Court of Honor of the Columbian Exposition appears in fig. 32.
‡ Compare with the similar effect of McKim's original overplanning for the stacks of the Boston Public Library; see *American Buildings and Their Architects: Progressive and Academic Ideals at the Turn of the Twentieth Century,* Chapter 7.

CHANNEL AND PLAZA: MERITS AND DEMERITS

The core of Rockefeller Center is the tight T-shaped plaza, consisting of a corridor, the so-called Promenade or Channel, which slopes from Fifth Avenue to the Lower Plaza (Figs. 4, 5, and 6). For a brief time the architects spoke of a "forum" for the Center.[2] Although they did not go on to use this term for the existing plaza, this unofficial designation affords a convenient, and deliberately grandiose, standard for measuring the successes and deficiencies of the Center's pedestrian space, the more so since the Center has become something of a forum for New York. Extravagant though this assertion may be, the Center is in fact as much of a forum as the city now boasts. By recalling the ancient prototype, but adjusting its facilities and functions to present-day conditions, one may suggest what the ideal forum might provide in the modern metropolis.

Above all, the ideal forum requires a pedestrian space which collects masses of people and distributes them with particular reference to the prestige activities central to the life of the city. Shops may intensify the activity of the forum, but the ideal demands more grandeur than a mere shopping mall can furnish. As the lobby serves the building primarily as a corridor, so the forum serves the city. Lobbies and fora should also be rooms. They are places for meeting and waiting. Both corridors and rooms, they should be strongly identified architecturally. Moreover, as in the plan of a building, or in the accumulated fora of the Roman emperors, they are richest when one space opens into another of a different, but related, quality; and when a central space possesses peripheral spaces of consequence leading to or away from it.

As outdoor rooms for congregation, they should boast some embellishment and certain conveniences (at very least, shade for summer, protection for winter, and benches) which will make meeting and waiting pleasurable. And because the forum is embellished, because it does attract crowds, it also becomes a place to visit for itself—a point of gravitation for the traveler. As a reminder to the townsman and a spectacle to the tourist, it embodies the values of its culture. Finally, therefore, the expressive quality of the forum depends on the density of human consciousness to which it appeals. Above all, we must feel the living, everyday activity of the city in the forum. But, thereafter, the appeal to our sensibilities is enlarged, and the symbolic significance of the forum enhanced, by the clustering of governmental and cultural institutions, and by the incorporation of old landmarks with the new. Insofar as the forum gathers to itself trophies of culture and tradition,

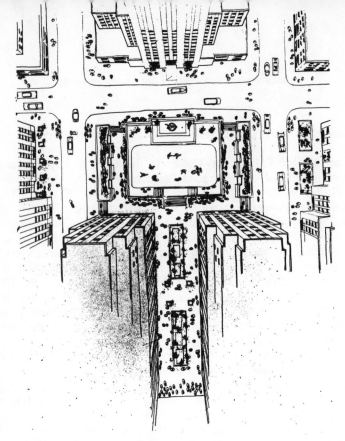

FIGURE 4. *Associated Architects for the Center: Corbett, Harrison & Mac-Murray; Hood & Fouilhoux; Reinhard & Hofmeister. Bird's-eye perspective of the Promenade (or Channel) and Lower Plaza, Rockefeller Center, New York, part of the initial building phase 1928–c. 1940.*

FIGURES 5, 6. *Rockefeller Center. Opposite, above: Promenade, below: Lower Plaza.*

as it also gathers people, it attains its ultimate significance as a place of civic ceremony.

In assessing the open space of Rockefeller Center, and in comparing it with some of its New York competition, one finds that the Center meets at least the primary criteria for a forum. It provides pedestrian space separated from wheeled traffic, and does so in relation to some of the prestige activities of its world. The embellishment of the outdoor space of the Center provides New York with one of its favorite show-pieces. Over-all control of shop fronts and signs unifies the space. Like the visual unity of Park Avenue during the thirties, the unification of shop fronts in the Center is achieved by sameness rather than by

14

variety, as classicistic Beaux-Arts theories of monumentality require; but here the regularity of the architectural frame ideally permits the display to predominate. A strip in the center of the Channel provides a series of stepped rectangular pools surrounded by seasonal planting, and sometimes with fabricated displays. The shape of the beds and, in summer, the water spilling from pool to pool the length of the incline encourages the leisurely movement down the corridor toward the climactic verticality of the RCA Building. As we advance down the slope of the Channel, the distant focus on the RCA Building, with the flutter of flags of the United Nations around the rim of the Lower Plaza, gives way to the near focus on Paul Manship's monstrous gilt figure of *Prometheus*—indifferent as sculpture (and unworthy of its sculptor), but superb as a visual magnet—until we finally overlook, with *Prometheus,* the fountain and diners in summer, the skaters in winter.*

For those who prefer to sit (and, on balmy days, can find a seat!) benches line both the Channel and the rim of the Lower Plaza. If the buildings to either side strongly contain the Channel, the Plaza by being sunken provides its own containment. The narrow, linear space opens to the broader, more static space at the climactic core of the Center. The space design is literal-minded, to be sure: there is nothing dynamic about it beyond the axis; no surprises of composition—only the surprise of gradually coming to a full view of the sunken section of the Plaza; no spectacular play of light and shadow; no interrelation between the interior space of the buildings and the outside; no extraordinary architectural or monumental effects, unless the thin edge of the RCA slab counts as such. But at least the rudiments of good planning for outdoor space are here. So far, so good. To this extent, the T-shaped space of the Center meets the criteria of a modern forum fairly well.

The space is less successful at collecting and distributing masses of people—a task at which Grand Central Concourse is unsurpassed in New York. The space of Rockefeller Center would undoubtedly have been more successful as a gatherer and distributor of people could it have been located on the east side of Fifth Avenue instead of the west, and somehow linked to Madison Avenue, although its importance as an urban renewal project would then have been less. A pedestrian plaza connecting these two fashionable shopping and office avenues would have created an even flow and scatter of people in all directions throughout the area, thus providing the same centripetal and centrifugal flow which makes Grand Central Concourse a hub of human movement.

* Sketches of this visual climax which unfolds as one walks down the Channel appear in *The Exploding Metropolis,* by the Editors of *Fortune:* Anchor edition, New York, 1958.

The Plaza at Rockefeller Center collects better than it distributes. It entices crowds from Fifth Avenue down the Channel toward the Lower Plaza; but at this point the Plaza does not afford a variety of destinations as attractive to most people as Fifth Avenue from which they came. The Center very definitely turns its back on what was once Sixth Avenue (now pompously rechristened the Avenue of the Americas, although New Yorkers customarily stay with the old name). [For a diagram of the entire complex in relation to its street pattern, see Fig. 22.] To be sure, two theatres originally fronted the Center's back door: the Radio City Music Hall for movies and variety shows, and the now demolished Center Theatre, which was eventually used for legitimate performances with an extravaganza flavor, such as ice shows. Oriented toward the Broadway theatrical district, these theatres were also consciously planned as magnets to draw people through the Center complex, but they were not physically linked to the Plaza.

The decided orientation of the Channel and Plaza toward Fifth Avenue is something of an accident. Although Sixth Avenue was a commercial backwater when the Center was begun, the architects were not unmindful of its potential for improvement. This was the more certain because the elevated which then existed over the street was to be replaced by a subway. (The *Sixth* Avenue Subway: no promotional folderol underground to match the "Avenue of the Americas" at street level.) The architects definitely meant to link the two avenues. At a very early stage in planning, in 1930, the architects had projected two department stores flanking what eventually became the RCA Building (Fig. 17). These would have been peripheral lures, drawing people into the central Plaza and beyond—toward Sixth Avenue if not actually to it.[3] With more such stores closing than opening in the early 1930's, the scheme was stillborn. Its demise probably worked to the ultimate advantage of the Center, since, up to then, the Plaza had been conceived as a mere island surrounded by streets (again Fig. 17). Now the architects were forced to consider the Plaza in more positive terms, since the management organization realized that the Center would have to generate its own shopping traffic exclusively from small stores, rather than depend on large outside organizations to solve most of the problem. It was decided, therefore, to make the Plaza a positive means of bringing customers into an underground shopping center. Conceived in 1931, this shopping center was to line the labyrinth of corridors which linked all buildings at basement level and provided access to subways. Hence, in 1931, the Plaza in the center of the street was pushed against the Channel and sunk to basement level, stairs leading down to it as the introduction to the underground shopping area (Fig. 7). A mall from the sunken plaza to the Sixth Avenue subway station under the

FIGURE 7. *Rockefeller Center, Variant schemes* (1932) *for the use of the Lower Plaza as an entrance vestibule to an underground shopping mall.*

dominating RCA slab was to provide the trunk for the branching of the underground shopping area beneath the whole building complex (Fig. 23).

Made for purely economic reasons, this decision was momentous in the planning of the Center.[4] The original scheme of a park in the center of the street would have provided little more than an ornamental safety island at a pedestrian crossing. Its linkage to the Channel converted this trinket to more extensive pedestrian use, and at no loss to its ornamental quality. Had the Lower Plaza retained its function as a grand vestibule to the basement shops, and to the Sixth Avenue subway, it would have created a flow of movement along the major axis of the Center. But at a cost. The outdoor space would have gained pedestrian flow with a loss of climax. Just where the climax should have occurred, the crowds would have been sucked underground.

Unfortunately at first, but again fortunately in the long run, construction of the subway was delayed. It did not open until 1940. Hence, as the core of the Center began to take shape by the mid-thirties, the underground shopping mall went nowhere. Obviously neither the flow of pedestrians nor the rentals from underground shops materialized. In desperation, an underground display center was tried at the Sixth Avenue end of the passageway.[5] Relatively few people, however, took the detour to visit this dead end. Some inexpensive restaurants strategically placed in the basement area proved somewhat more successful as lures, although most of the clientele were office workers in the buildings who made little use of the sunken Plaza to reach their destinations. There being no particular reason to descend to it, the sunken Plaza remained conspicuously deserted, and shop proprietors to either side grumbled ominously.

At this point, in 1936, the sunken space was sealed off to serve as an ice skating rink in winter, an unprecedented venture in such an intensely urban setting, which profitably enlivens an otherwise dreary space through the cold months. In summer, the rink converts to an outdoor dining area.† With this change of purpose, the emphatic connection between Fifth and Sixth Avenues through the Plaza disappeared. However, what had been merely a utilitarian corridor now became a genuine plaza. The gain was substantial. The Polish architect Jerzy W. Soltan, when visiting the United States in 1965, went so far as to pronounce the skaters the key to the Center's success. Douglas Haskell reported Soltan's remarks to the Harvard Urban Design Conference:

---

† Summer roller skating was tried briefly; but it was noisy and seemed to encourage rowdiness. In New York at least, and in the thirties, ice skating appears to have been the more aristocratic sport.

The Center's "emotional shock" waits at the very middle of it, in the "minute white square of the skating rink" dug in at the feet of the gray skyscrapers.

Here we find "Hanzel and Gretel skaters dancing in the skyscraper forest!" And after this fantastic juxtaposition in the programming—"a great decision, a surrealistic decision, a fairy-tale decision"—[Soltan] maintained that the architecture, "so very gray," and the sculpture, "so very gold," became "unimportant." Indeed, in a case like that, he went on, an architect might be excused from design, saying to himself, "The drabber the better. Let my main decision work for me."[6]

Of course Soltan erred in claiming that the "great decision" of the architects was ice skaters, since the skaters entered the scene in a belated effort to retrieve original miscalculations on the use of the Plaza. Nevertheless Soltan's observation has merit. For many, the recollection of the skaters in the "forest" of skyscrapers is doubtless the strongest after-image the Center invokes. (Prometheus himself seems to abandon his flying posture in winter—none too convincing in any event —and to don invisible skates in order to join the fun.) If events in the Lower Plaza are pleasant but less memorable in summer, there is then less need to "fill" it with colorful activity, for flowers and the fountain do much of the job, while the crowds, which willingly loiter, do the rest.

So, in addition to meeting an economic problem, the seasonal alternation of skating and outdoor dining nicely solved the problem of giving focus and (with the skaters especially) climax to the outdoor space. In the process, however, the central space did become something of a pocket. The aimless sightseer finds himself drawn down the Channel to the Plaza. He looks into the sunken section . . . and then? His momentary indecision suggests the greatest defect of the space. Without a specific destination in mind beyond the Plaza, our sightseer finds nothing in its design which opens to destinations beyond. Nothing in the design of the Plaza creates patterns of flow into, across, and out of it. To be sure, movement through the Plaza has steadily increased as the postwar building boom raised office buildings on the Avenue of the Americas in the vicinity of the Center. But the movement does not occur as part of an esthetic experience. The Plaza coagulates a static crowd, looking down at "something" (not necessarily taken in by those who pass through). The static crowd turns its back on the moving crowd. The moving crowd skirts rather than enters the Plaza. It zigzags into alignment with its chosen exits—streets or lobbies. And for those unfamiliar with the Center, once they are in the Plaza there is a sameness about all possible exits from it (except for the Channel) which makes it difficult to decide how to move. Thus, to the sightseer without a special destination in mind the "Where now?" which he asks himself as he stands in the Plaza is very often answered by "Back the way I came," and he returns through the Channel to Fifth Avenue.

Approached from Fifth Avenue, then, the space has a major defect: it dead-ends as a spatial entity right at the heart of the Center complex. Similarly, when the space is approached from what was once Sixth Avenue, the defect is one of lack of connection. Although the architects of the Center were aware of the problem from the start, and continually reminded themselves that Sixth Avenue would not always remain the shabby back door of the Center, they never quite solved the problem.

Reviewing the situation as it presently exists, we find that a minor alteration might have mitigated the dead-end aspect of the Plaza. A more direct linkage of the Plaza to the RCA Building—by the elimination of the private roadway between them, and by better provision for automobile approaches to the building's flanks, on 49th and 50th Streets— would have projected the Plaza toward the Avenue of the Americas. It would thereby have called attention, if not decisively at least forcefully, to the ground floor corridor of the RCA slab and the flanking streets as major axes.[7] The point is worth making simply because it indicates how abruptly the intervention of a street, even one as lightly traveled as this (officially, and confusingly, known as Rockefeller Plaza‡; Fig. 22), can terminate pedestrian space. Instead of participating in the space of the Plaza, as it might have done by rising out of it, the RCA Building merely overlooks the Plaza, being physically outside of the space it closes.

Of course the Plaza could have been opened up in a north-south direction, as well as along the principal east-west axis. This very nearly occurred to the north, where a spatial tentacle was projected from the Plaza to the Museum of Modern Art* on 53rd Street, two blocks beyond the uptown boundary of the Center complex (Fig. 22). The private

‡ Jane Jacobs, in *The Death and Life of Great American Cities*, pp. 181f., specifically praises this street for slicing the overlong blocks made by east-west streets in New York. It is a central theme of her book that short blocks make for a lively city—a good point, but the author's fondness for numerous streets would be easier to accept if her suggestions as to ways of discouraging vehicular traffic were more realistic. In this instance, it would seem that the extension of the plaza as pedestrian space is definitely preferable to a roadway, and also serves the purposes she had in mind.

* By Philip L. Goodwin, in association with Edward Durell Stone. This building for the Museum opened in 1939.

street (Rockefeller Plaza again) fronting the RCA Building runs for three blocks between 48th and 51st Streets. Extended two more blocks, it would have reached the Museum. The Center owned land in the middle of the block between 51st and 52nd Streets. Hence the acquisition of a similar strip of land between 52nd and 53rd Streets could have realized the goal. The site for the Museum (in which the Rockefeller family has been especially interested) was purchased in 1936, with the original entrance deliberately placed on axis with this street, which, it was thought, might eventually terminate at its front door. Influential in this decision, Wallace Harrison (and others) even envisioned a second plaza ringed with cultural institutions immediately north of the Center.[8] It was to have been closed at the uptown end by the Museum of Modern Art; at the downtown end, by the Associated Press Building within the Center. The contemplated plaza, it was hoped, would be flanked by the Columbia Broadcasting Company and by what is now the Solomon R. Guggenheim Museum on sites toward Fifth Avenue; by the Metropolitan Opera and the Philharmonic on interior sites toward Sixth Avenue. Had this scheme been realized, the present Lincoln Center for the Performing Arts would have substantially abutted the Center. It would thereby have been more vitally located within the city, although undoubtedly with some cramping of facilities. This clumping of cultural institutions might have had some of the undesirable effects of any such concentration. It is difficult, however, to imagine that it could have resulted in an impression as pompously sterile as that presented by Lincoln Center today, since this arts complex would have intermingled with the communications industry, shopping, and business.

The assemblage of the necessary real estate for a cultural precinct in the immediate vicinity of Rockefeller Center was begun. (The garden of the Museum of Modern Art is a legacy of this effort.) A prominent restaurateur in the area, however, refused to budge. Possibly more crucial to the failure of the scheme was a certain fatigue in the Rockefeller family at the prospect of another gigantic real estate venture while the first was substantially short of completion and burdened by expenses. Threatened with the loss of the Esso Company after World War II for want of space in existing buildings within the Center, Carson & Lundin's Esso Building (built 1946–47) went into the extension of the private street between 51st and 52nd Streets.† It was the end of the dream, although even before the war the Center had so raised the price of

---

† An attempt was made by the architects of the Esso Building to maintain an open quality through the ground floor from 51st to 52nd Street, but the corridor here leads to no destination of distinction.

FIGURE 8. *Rockefeller Center. View along the Fifth Avenue front from 51st to 49th Street. The tall building (right foreground) is the International Building, with the globe of Lee Lawrie's Atlas barely visible in its entrance court. St. Patrick's Cathedral is opposite. The low buildings flanking the Promenade in the next block are the British Empire Building and La Maison Française. Behind them, and in the center background (left to right), are two towers occupied respectively by Sinclair Petroleum and General Dynamics and a low block occupied by Eastern Airlines.*

neighboring property as to make another such large accumulation of real estate improbable. After the war it was unthinkable.

Had this cultural adjunct materialized, circulation within the Plaza at the core of the Center would have vastly increased. More important, the Plaza would have participated in the cultural and monumental life of the city and, through this denser appeal to the human consciousness, have approached the ultimate ideal for a forum.

Having lost the cultural plaza, the Center has St. Patrick's Cathedral as its single point of architectural reference outside the commercial world. St. Patrick's does for the Fifth Avenue elevation of the Center what Trinity accomplishes as the terminus for one end of Wall Street. It is important that St. Patrick's not only happens to be across the street from the Center, but also is visually related to the Center in a meaningful manner (Fig. 8). Fortunately, Saks Fifth Avenue, between 49th and 50th Streets, happens to be opposite the spatial climax of the Center. Save for the appropriate dazzle of its show windows, its reticence of flat surface and regular fenestration nicely complements the corridor of the Channel with its garden display across the street. One block farther north, it is the irregular "Gothic" mass of St. Patrick's,‡ raised on a stepped pedestal above street level, which provides the focus of visual interest. The shallow plaza opposite, opening into the International Building of Rockefeller Center, with its familiar *Atlas* by Lee Lawrie, is now the subordinate element in this second cross-street axis. The modest heights of the Center buildings on Fifth Avenue and of Saks Fifth Avenue opposite (will it last?) scale the buildings to the width of the street. They do not overpower the Cathedral, and they permit the major blocks of the Center to rise clear of adjacent buildings, at various distances from Fifth Avenue. The two blocks provide a beautiful example of architectural urbanity, where visual reciprocity enhances all the buildings.

The Fifth Avenue blocks between 49th and 51st Streets are also worthy of study because of the way in which the Center comes to the sidewalk as four identical six-storied masses, so as to enframe the plazas. The boundary of the street is firmly maintained by the rhythmic discipline of the building masses; moreover, there is the delightful surprise of coming upon the strongly contained open spaces. By way of contrast, consider the situation on the Avenue of the Americas, where the relation of the Center buildings to the street is nondescript, and where the relation of buildings to street and to one another in the blocks near by is even more appalling than that now seen on Park Avenue.[9] Each designer has

‡ By James Renwick, who began the design in 1858. The Cathedral was substantially completed in 1879 except for the spires. These were finished in 1888. Various architects are responsible for the apsidal chapels, on which work extended into the first decade of twentieth century.

gone his own way, creating a plaza for his building which asserts its independence of the work next door (Fig. 9).* Another block; another

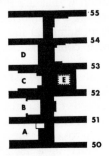

FIGURE 9. *Site plan of buildings and plazas in the vicinity of Rockefeller Center on the Avenue of the Americas: Time-Life (A); Equitable Life Assurance (B); J. C. Penney (C); Hilton (D); Columbia Broadcasting (E).*

treatment! The result is particularly damning to the architectural profession because all of the buildings went up within a few years of one another. Without minimizing the problems involved, it would seem that some cooperative endeavor should have been possible. Subway renovation going on at the same time might even have permitted an underground concourse with more than perfunctory linkages to the buildings in the area. But this opportunity for urban planning of consequence was also frittered away. At very least a few stores at ground level could have relieved this parade of dreary corporate pretension which manages to all but negate Eero Saarinen's fine, if somewhat overpraised, Columbia Broadcasting Building (completed 1965).

Surely no aspect of the Center is more instructive than its Fifth Avenue front and the visual reciprocity that it maintains with the buildings across the street. Fifth Avenue at the Center possesses that variety

* Consider, for example, the four skyscrapers, each occupying a full block of street frontage, which rose side by side between 50th and 54th Streets during the late fifties and early sixties. The first, completed in 1960, was the Time-Life Building by Harrison, Abramovitz & Harris. Asymmetrically placed on its site between 50th and 51st Streets, it has a plaza open to its downtown corner, which spills so amorphously into the street as to seem less a space contained within the site than a bite taken out of it. The plaza is fountained, and gaudily paved with an undulating pattern (apparently derived from similar pavements in Rio de Janeiro), and in utter discord with the reticulated elevations of the building. One block to the north, Skidmore, Owings & Merrill have produced an economy version of the Seagram Plaza for the Equitable Life Assurance Building (completed 1961), which appears rigidly axial, formal, and austere in respect to the fiesta flavor of the plaza next door. Another block, and Shreve, Lamb & Harmon has treated the J. C. Penney Building (1965) to a sunken court from which a black metal sculpture rises like some monster. Next to this, the Uris Brothers, with William B. Tabler, have tucked the entrance of the New York Hilton (1963) with its driveway loop beneath the squat stilting of the building. And so on.

and vitality with harmony and dignity which mark it as a superb urban achievement.

Four Outdoor Spaces in Midtown Manhattan

So much for the forum ideal as a means of measuring the qualities of Rockefeller Center's outdoor space. Admittedly, a private venture designed for profit in a period of dim civic consciousness is unfairly pitted against ancient fora accomplished in quite opposite conditions. In such comparison, the defects of the outdoor space of the Center are to be expected, while its substantial success comes as a surprise. There is, however, another remarkably revealing way in which to appraise the qualities of outdoor space at Rockefeller Center. Three other spaces of merit happen to be located near by. As if planned for the purpose, these are spaces of contrasting function and esthetics strung along Fifth Avenue from 42nd to 59th Street. Taken together, the four spaces provide as remarkable a demonstration of the civilizing effect of small parks and plazas in downtown areas, of the diverse functions which they can perform, and of the experiences which they can provide, as any American city boasts within the compass of an easy walk (Fig. 10).

At 42nd Street, immediately behind Carrère & Hastings' Public Library (1897–1909), Bryant Park (Fig. 11) is an example of the small Beaux-Arts axial park, with a central green and peripheral walks. Raised above the surrounding streets on a balustraded podium, the block-wide Bryant Park permits a breadth of sunlight and sky above the unbroken rectangle of lawn. The park is stiffly bordered by ornamental planting, with four rows of plane trees bringing shade to either side. Beneath the shadow and shelter of the interlocked branches, a geometry of walks, beds of ivy, and benches provide respite from the openness—although, sad to say, the area is somewhat unkempt; as in most American parks, less from negligent maintenance than from thoughtless use. The axis through the center of the Park is marked toward the Avenue of the Americas by a fountain, and is terminated toward Fifth Avenue by the rhythmic verticals of the Library stacks severely rising behind terracing and clumps of bushes. There New York has its outdoor reading room in summer, even as Boston librarygoers move into McKim's courtyard.†

Bryant Park is a place not only for browsing but for walking and loitering. It serves partly as a corridor because (like City Hall Park

† See *American Buildings and Their Architects: Progressive and Academic Ideals at the Turn of the Twentieth Century*, Chapter 7.

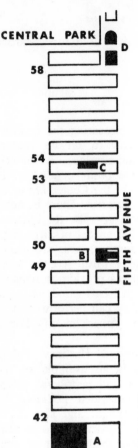

FIGURE 10. *Four small parks along Fifth Avenue, New York: Bryant Park (A); Promenade and Plaza at Rockefeller Center (B); Sculpture Garden of the Museum of Modern Art (C); Grand Army Plaza (D).*

and, with the aforementioned reservations, like the Channel at Rocke-feller Center) one can walk through it. Since Bryant Park is elevated above the street, however, it requires an effort to use its paths. Its walks, moreover, do not crisscross it, as in City Hall Park, leading to destinations beyond itself, but define its perimeter. Bryant Park there-fore encourages the purposeful walk less than the leisurely stroll. Shade and benches entice along the way, and entice the more strongly be-cause of glimpses of the sunlit expanse of lawn seen through the trees. The island-like openness of the lawn lends itself to occasional special exhibitions, like those of monumental sculpture held there in recent years. Hence Bryant Park becomes primarily an outdoor room, a little apart

FIGURE 11. *Bryant Park, New York, looking toward the rear elevation of Carrère & Hastings' Public Library, 1897–1911. The present arrangement of the Park dates from 1934.*

from the bustle of the city that so permeates the outdoor space of the Center. (And of course this bustle at the Center is year-round, whereas Bryant Park rather hibernates through winter, a time when few even cross it.) Specifically, only the perimeter of the Park is a "room" and, a little like an outdoor version of the Boston Public Library, the "room" looks inward on a central grassed "court." Sitting is far more important in Bryant Park than in the Center, which exists more as a corridor where sitting is something of a nuisance. Especially is this so along the Channel. Seating there should be off to the side, not at the focus of activity. In the Center, however, benches could not be placed in front of the store windows. Before they were introduced in the Channel some years after its

29

FIGURE 12. *Carrère & Hastings. Grand Army Plaza (usually known as The Plaza), New York, looking toward the entrance of the Plaza Hotel, with the Pulitzer Fountain.*

opening, the public was already sitting on the tan-colored marble frames of the planting boxes.

At the opposite end of the fashionable shopping strip from Bryant Park, a nick in the block at 59th Street provides another Beaux-Arts delight: this is the fountain square (Figs. 12, 13) which fronts Henry Hardenburgh's Plaza Hotel (opened in 1907). Providing a backdrop of pseudo-château sumptuousness to the square, the Hotel is as Edwardian as the carriages waiting for fares near by before making their leisurely circuit of Central Park. Mostly of stone, and with little planting, the square, as laid out by Carrère & Hastings, is counterpointed by the formal bedding around one of Augustus Saint-Gaudens' most important works across the way—Victory leading the mounted General Sherman. The forward movement of this bronze group visually links the two contrasting squares across the street. Hence the double square (officially Grand Army Plaza, but known simply as The Plaza) is organized by two axes: the one from the statue to the fountain, and parallel to Fifth Avenue; the other, at right angles to this, from the fountain to the Hotel. The Plaza serves primarily

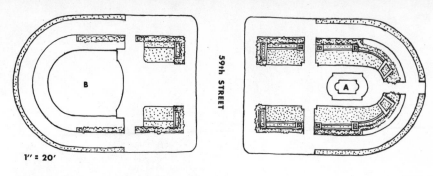

1" = 20'

FIGURE 13. *Grand Army Plaza*. Plan: (A) *Augustus Saint-Gaudens'* Victory Leading General Sherman; (B) *Pulitzer Fountain.*

as a landmark seen in passing. As if to emphasize the function of the park as a place to be experienced more in passing than in pausing, there are but few benches around either statue or fountain, although those who insist on sitting can use the ample moldings and parapeting around the fountain with which Beaux-Arts designers characteristically brought such features to the ground. Eastward across Fifth Avenue, Edward Stone's plaza fronts the General Motors Building (built 1965–68), in a double-tiered approach with sunken shops which seems to recall his early work on the design of the Center (Fig. 7). The plaza-base for the building is handsome at first sight, but in the posh, pseudo-discreetness of Cadillac styling—which is to say alluring, glossy, pretentious, and thin. Moreover, the double-decked plaza again exhibits the knack for the misplaced plaza that bedevils New York. It breaks the wall of buildings along the east side of Fifth Avenue at the point where the Savoy-Plaza formerly closed Carrère & Hastings' square across Fifth Avenue. Had the General Motors plaza been placed on the Madison Avenue side of the building with the Fifth Avenue elevation up tight against the sidewalk, the arrangement would have made more urban sense, but doubtless to the architects and their clients it would have provided a less swanky approach to the building. At least there are shops on this plaza, a welcome respite from the too frequent corporate resolve to be bleakly non-commercial in such places in order to give an aura of institutional monumentality, but without the monument to complete the gesture.

Whereas Carrère & Hastings' square is primarily a landmark plaza, Rockefeller Center a corridor plaza, and Bryant Park an outdoor room, the most complete approach to an ideal outdoor urban room in the area is Philip Johnson's walled sculpture garden for the Museum of Modern Art (completed in 1954, revised and enlarged 1960–64) [Figs. 14, 15, and 16]. A raised L-shaped area on two sides of the lower terrace provides places for sitting and dining, as well as a kind of elevated threshold from which we can survey the court when stepping out of the Museum. This plane overlooks a sunken plane of white marble slabs dotted with

31

FIGURE 14. *Philip Johnson. Sculpture Garden, Museum of Modern Art, New York, first version completed 1953.*

sculpture and with irregular islands of greenery. Pools arranged as a staggered canal are bridged by stone slabs and punctuated by fountains. The sculpture is so placed that it appears now against foliage, now against pavement, wall, or water. Stairs at the end opposite that of the shaded dining terrace rise to an elevated terrace; here there is more sculpture, and a view of the entire space. The topology of the garden enforces irregular diagonals and circles of movement. Space is experienced as broad plane, as intimate pocket, as directional corridor, as rise and

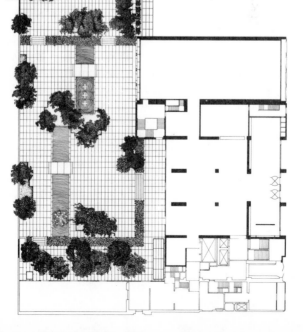

FIGURE 15. *Sculpture Garden,*
Museum of Modern Art,
New York,
enlarged and revised version
1960–64.

FIGURE 16. *Sculpture Garden,*
Museum of Modern Art,
New York.
Plan of the revised version.

descent. It is, moreover, variously experienced: at one moment the visitor is a participant in the movement; at another, its onlooker—or better, its overlooker.

Yet Johnson has disciplined the diversity of the spatial experience and the casualness of the activity within his outdoor room by the gravity of the Neoclassical bias of his design, here reinforced by an awareness of the austerity which underlies the surface picturesqueness of the greatest Japanese landscape gardens. He himself has testified to the impact which the Ryoanji Garden made on him. Its rectangle of raked sand, its three islands of moss-covered rock asymmetrically scattered in this simulated ocean, its viewing platform slightly raised and running the length of the walled precinct: all have their counterparts in the Museum garden; so transformed, however, that it is by no means certain that Johnson particularly recalled the Ryoanji Garden when he created his own.[10] No public outdoor space designed in the United States in the quarter of a century following World War II surpasses this one as a lively, yet dignified, urban space, organized for a variety of activities. And of course none is as fortunate in the high quality of its sculptural adornment.

Diverse as these four spaces are functionally and visually, they share in common the quality which accounts in part for the distinction of the space of the Center. All are substantially bounded from their surroundings, and hence visually contained as spaces. The containment is variously achieved: by wall, by distinctive pavement, by enframement with planting, by elevation above the street (Bryant Park), or by depression below it (the Lower Plaza of the Center). For subtlety of conception, the asymmetrical dynamics of Johnson's space, dependent on modern spatial ideas,‡ is superior to the outdoor space of the Center; but (quite apart from Johnson's ability as a designer) subtlety was both more possible and more appropriate in his commission. Bryant Park and the plaza at 59th Street are, like the Center, Beaux-Arts inspired, axially symmetrical spaces, and quite conventionally so. If they are in any respect superior to the outdoor space at the Center, it is in their architectural detail, retrospective though it is. Unlike the outdoor space of the Center, they depend on the permanent ingredients of architecture and the traditional use of plant materials for their expressive qualities. The Center plaza does not. Much more than the others it depends on display. Stripped of its display and the crowds around it, the Center space is nakedly box-like, its quasi-modern stylisms of slab-like surfaces accentuating the boxiness. Like the shop windows of Saks Fifth Avenue

‡ See Chapters 2 and 3 below.

across the street, the Channel and Plaza come to life in the changing display—gardens, flags, fountains, skaters—and the moving crowds. If the display is apt to be somewhat overlavish and artificial by standards normal to plaza design, suggesting the profusion of a flower show rather than a flower bed (and outdoing the shop windows in the decorative splash at the Christmas season), it appropriately celebrates the ephemera of the shoppers' world which it crowns. Here, in short, is the popular plaza, with enough carnival to make the experience festive, enough monumentality to give it civic dimension.

THE EVOLUTION OF THE CENTER: FROM OPERA COMPLEX TO "RADIO CITY"

Although only St. Patrick's in the immediate environs of the Center makes a profounder appeal to human consciousness than business and popular entertainment can provide, the entire project originally focused on a cultural institution. The Metropolitan Opera was once to have stood where the RCA slab now rises. Since Winston Weisman has recounted the history of the Center in detail, and David Loth in a popular account, its complex development need only be sketched here. In 1926, the supporters of the Metropolitan Opera Company opened a drive for a new building, hardly imagining that they would wait forty years for it to materialize in the Lincoln Center complex. Trustees for the Opera commissioned Benjamin Wistar Morris as architect early in the following year. Morris made designs for three prospective sites in 1927, all presenting problems. In one case, an inexpensive site on 57th Street was deemed too remote from the theatre and shopping district. In the other cases, more expensive sites on 63rd Street and at Columbus Circle would each have required such substantial office towers for revenue as to have swamped the Opera base. Then, in January 1928, agents for a real estate firm pointed out that Columbia University owned most of the area from 49th to 51st Street between Fifth and Sixth Avenues. Could the Metropolitan obtain a piece of property in the southernmost block on a long-term lease from the University, with perhaps some space for an approach in front of it? Once this possibility was called to his attention, Morris conceived of a much larger project. Why not utilize the whole of the University's holdings? The new Opera House

35

would be a low structure toward the center of the plot fronted by the plaza. He would surround this cultural and monumental core with a wall of revenue-producing office buildings. Morris prepared several versions of his scheme in 1928 and 1929, comprised of rather heavy buildings in the stepped-back silhouette customary for the period. As Weisman makes clear, to Morris should go credit for the initial conception of the unified treatment of the area with a plaza at its core. On the basis of Morris' scheme the Metropolitan interested John D. Rockefeller, Jr. in the project by the summer of 1928.

Originally, Rockefeller offered to give two million dollars for the plaza, and to provide the organization that would acquire the site for the Opera plus surrounding real estate. There were lots within the contemplated area which the University did not own, as well as leases to be adjusted on lots it did own. Once the entire parcel had been accumulated, the land would be leased to the Opera. Rockefeller was then to bow out of the operation, leaving his two million dollar gift of the plaza behind. As it turned out, his generosity did not solve the Opera's financial problems, and he was gradually drawn further into the scheme. As circumstances compelled him to assume the central role in the project, he turned to his own business advisors. He placed management and engineering companies of his choice in charge of operations, both dominated by John R. Todd. In September 1928, the Todd interests, in turn, employed L. Andrew Reinhard and Henry Hofmeister, young architects with experience in the design of office buildings, to lay out the site.* When these arrangements were made, it was presumed that Morris would design the monumental core, while Reinhard & Hofmeister worked on the commercial perimeter; but, coming in as they did on the Rockefeller side of the venture, the latter firm rapidly gained the whip hand. Although various firms were asked for suggestions at this time, the sifting process finally resulted in the definitive appointment of Reinhard & Hofmeister as architects on October 28, 1929. Morris was at this time demoted from architect to consultant. Two other architects joined him as consultants: Harvey Wiley Corbett and Raymond M. Hood.

In choosing Corbett and Hood, the predominantly practical firm of Reinhard & Hofmeister affiliated itself with two of the most progressive designers of business buildings in New York, each a partner in a leading architectural firm. Both were Beaux-Arts trained and conditioned, but hospitable to the ideas of the modern movement just then beginning to penetrate the United States from Europe. Both had designed what were at the time regarded as exceptionally handsome skyscrapers.

* Prior to their work on the Center, Reinhard & Hofmeister had principally engaged in office planning for the Todd-managed Graybar Building.

As costs for assembling the huge site mounted, the Metropolitan began to have qualms about its participation, for it was not altogether clear how the cost of building a monumental opera house and plaza at the center of the site could be balanced by leases on the land or rents from the offices surrounding it. In November, the stock market crash brought the trustees' fears to a head, and early in December the Opera bowed out. Morris also withdrew from the project. Rockefeller interests were left with a large site accumulated at great cost, and with a sizable rental to pay to Columbia University under a long-term lease. All this in the teeth of a depression! That John D. Rockefeller, Jr. had to do something with his holdings is certain. That, given the circumstances, he should have chosen to go through with the project on such a scale, and to make it of civic as well as of financial consequence, demanded courage. It also required his intense love of building.[11] In their scope and variety, Rockefeller's building interests were unmatched in the late twenties and early thirties. He simultaneously backed not only the Center, but a "Gothic cathedral" of extraordinary sumptuousness—Riverside Church in New York near Grant's Tomb (completed as the Center project got underway)—and, for good measure, the restoration of Colonial Williamsburg!

From the start the Center had been viewed as a self-supporting venture (the gift of the Plaza excepted). With the departure of the Opera, the business character of the enterprise became insistent; in fact, John R. Todd flatly informed the architects that henceforth "all planning for this Square would be based upon a commercial center as beautiful as possible consistent with the maximum income that could be developed [from it]."[12] Whereas the low block of the Opera and its plaza at the center of the property had dominated the early schemes, a tall office building now rose in the architects' projects. Fortunately for the investment, Todd & Brown managed to sign a client for much of the space in the projected central skyscraper on June 5, 1930. This was the Radio Corporation of America, then seeking to consolidate the offices of its manufacturing, broadcasting (National Broadcasting Company), and theatre (Radio-Keith-Orpheum) subsidiaries, a combination that was subsequently dismembered in part by anti-trust action. So class entertainment gave way to mass entertainment. "Radio City" was born.

While Todd & Brown were bringing RCA into the project, Reinhold & Hofmeister were fully associating themselves with the two firms from which they had drawn consultants. The agreement among them was dated May 30, 1930. Thereafter all drawings bear the names of the three firms in strict alphabetical order, which, in itself, underscores the group nature of the design: Corbett, Harrison & MacMurray; Hood,

37

[Godley, until 1931] & Fouilhoux; Reinhard & Hofmeister. The team designated itself as the Associated Architects. With respect to buildings erected toward the end of the decade, the roster varied (except for Reinhard & Hofmeister); but these later buildings merely filled in—with certain modest innovations—a compositional scheme and an architectural design which had been essentially determined by about 1932. Reinhard wrote long after the event that the reason for the affiliation was the managers' desire to have the designing services specifically of Harvey Wiley Corbett, Raymond Hood, and Wallace Harrison.[13] Corbett was more active in the very early stages of the design than later on, when Harrison and Hood (until the latter's premature death, at age fifty-three, in 1934) became the dominant participants for their respective firms.[14]

Less than a month after the withdrawal of the Opera, and a few months prior to their full association with the other architectural firms, Reinhard & Hofmeister and the management company settled on one of a number of block schemes which the architects drew up for the Center. Dated January 8, 1930, the scheme was labeled "G-3" (Fig. 17). G-3 was presented to the Center's Board of Directors early in February and was generally approved at the time. It is important because it arranged the building blocks much as they eventuated. G-3 was signed by Reinhard & Hofmeister only, and it may well be, as Weisman asserts, that the over-all composition of the Center primarily derived from this firm. Notice should be taken, however, that both Corbett and Hood were consultants at the time, even though their firms had not yet officially joined the team. Moreover, much of this, and every other, block scheme was substantially dictated by management.

Often a scheme early hit upon is lost to further ideas, sometimes for esthetic, sometimes for economic reasons, and then is resurrected. This was the case of G-3, and Weisman has reported its tortuous development in some detail. Here it suffices to say that the G-3 scheme with the Channel and central Plaza was temporarily shelved for a project which the managers believed would bring in more revenue. Its most striking feature was an oval-shaped building (to have housed a bank), looking not unlike a hatbox, placed on Fifth Avenue where the Channel now exists. This design was released to the public in 1931.[15] It was received so hostilely that the management firm returned in haste to the G-3 conception.

The G-3 scheme of January 1930 showed the site extensively covered by low nine-story buildings. This base was cut by the street pattern; the old plaza planned to front the Opera remained. But in what was its most important site-planning innovation, the G-3 scheme called for a pedestrian corridor to link this plaza with Fifth Avenue. The plaza

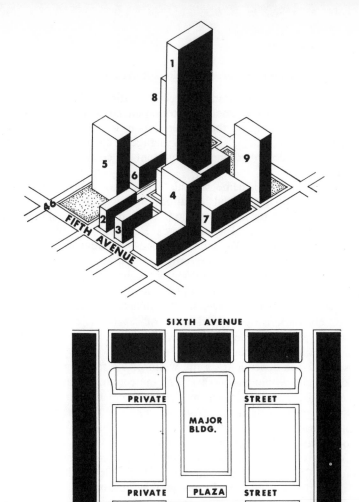

FIGURE 17. *Reinhard & Hofmeister. Plan of scheme G-3 for Rockefeller Center, 1930. In this scheme the four symmetrically disposed towers (buildings 4, 5, 8, 9) around the "major building" (1) were to have been 30 stories. The lowest portions of the complex were to have been 9 stories, with buildings 6 and 7 designated as department stores. Black areas on the plan (dotted in the block diagram) were not originally controlled by the Center, although the frontage along what was then Sixth Avenue was acquired just prior to the start of building. The Promenade appears in this scheme. Instead of the Lower Plaza, however, an island park occupies the center of the street at the heart of the project. Relative to what was realized, this scheme was much more concerned with automobile than with pedestrian traffic. Arrows on the original plan emphasized the one-way circuits designed for vehicular movement. Note also the widening of the crosstown streets through the project.*

was not yet sunken, nor was it coupled directly to the corridor—changes occurring later in 1930.† From the nine-story plateau, five towers rose; one of them, tall and thin, in the center (soon to be the climactic RCA Building); the four others, smaller skyscrapers, each in one corner of the property. Hood described the arrangement as comparable to that of a "five-spot card."[16]

The symmetry of the scheme at this stage was characteristically Beaux-Arts. Its over-all pyramidal organization suggested the typical stepped skyscraper silhouette of the period, even though the silhouette here spread over almost three of New York's elongated city blocks and had space between the towers. By 1930, stepped-pyramidal massing was all but inevitable for the New York skyscraper, the shape stemming from a historic zoning ordinance passed in New York in 1916, and in principle superseded only in 1961.[17] The 1916 law effected minimum control with respect to overbuilding, which in commercial areas threatened to make all streets dark canyons and most offices black cubicles. The law controlled the profile of the building bulk in three ways (Fig. 18): (1) a building could rise sheer from the pavement so many feet (the height of this initial rise dependent on the width of the fronting street and the location of the site within the block); (2) thereupon, the building had to be "set back" (the manner selected by the architect) so that the profile remained within a given angle drawn from the center of the street; (3) finally, once the setbacks had withdrawn the wall of the building back from the street so as to open it to a vital minimum of light and air, a sheer tower could rise as high as the owner chose on a certain percentage (roughly 25%) of the total area of the lot. Although the architects of Rockefeller Center had considerable freedom in their massing because of the large amount of land at their disposal, they essentially limited themselves in their tower emplacement to symmetry, pyramidization, and alignment of the buildings with the rectangular street pattern. These aspects of the design were doubtless more habitual than premeditated. Had the designers been tempted to stray from a conventional massing scheme, the management firm would have interfered

† Other changes subsequently made in G-3 included the elimination of the streets fronting buildings 8 and 9, new uses for buildings earlier planned as department stores, some adjustment of building heights, and the turning of the axis of the tower of building 4 (the International Building eventually) at right angles to that previously indicated, and a small plaza carved into the building bulk on Fifth Avenue. This breaking of the symmetry of G-3, which is congenial to the asymmetrical dynamics of modern composition (for example, see Chapters 2 and 3 below), occurred because the bulk permitted to the International Building under the symmetrical arrangement provided insufficient revenue. Concerning this change, see W. Weisman, *Architectural Review*, December 1950, p. 403.

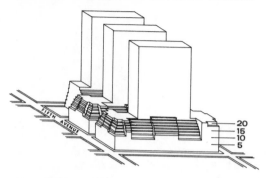

FIGURE 18. *Rockefeller Center. Theoretical diagram of the maximum allowable building bulk for Rockefeller Center under the New York "setback" law.*

because of the problems which the unfamiliar might have brought with respect to zoning variances, construction costs, and, possibly, client antagonism.[18] A bolder, though admittedly riskier, scheme might, for example, have angled the towers for their best orientation to sunlight, as modern practice was then recommending. Such angling might have mitigated the considerable swathes of shadow which the RCA Building eventually cast to the north, a defect which a hostile critic like Lewis Mumford was quick to notice on the building's completion.[19] Whatever the functional benefits of a less stereotyped alignment of the towers, the subsequent angling of a few hotel slabs built in the area after World War II tends to discourage any belief that the Center would have gained esthetically had its buildings been placed out-of-kilter with the insistent gridiron street pattern. On the whole, granting its fairly conservative arrangement, and considering both the skyscraping densities normal to midtown Manhattan and the expected return from investment, one can say that the five-spot tower composition was sufficiently enlightened as almost to appear visionary. Bulk use—largely by department stores, specialty shops, and theatres in the G-3 project, with the department stores omitted and broadcasting studios added in the completed Center—was as much as possible assigned to the plateau base so that the office towers might enjoy a maximum of air, light, and view.

The wide spacing of the towers permitted terrace roof gardens, apparently the particular enthusiasm of Raymond Hood.[20] In an initial series of schemes, which persisted through 1935, these gardens were conceived on a far more ambitious scale than was finally realized (Fig. 19), and in some projects included such roof-top attractions as a marionette theatre (like that on the Roman Pincio), a sculpture court,

FIGURE 19. *Rockefeller Center. Roof garden schemes with bridging over streets, 1932. Hopes for such extensive gardens persisted until 1935. The more detailed view (above) shows the roof of building 7 (modified from the G-3*

scheme), *looking west toward building 9 from a vantage point in building 4.
The general view looks northeast, with Sixth Avenue at the lower left, St.
Patrick's Cathedral at the upper right.*

and a greenhouse, in addition to a series of formal gardens. In the most grandiose schemes, bridges in mid-air were to have linked most of the verdant roofs. In fact, aerial bridges appear in a number of early projects for the Center. They were very much a part of the "metropolis of the future," where it seems, one never touched ground but lived aloft in a kind of Hanging Garden of Babylon, comprised of a set-back cubism of penthouses, cobwebbed by pedestrian bridges and elevated roadways. In the Center schemes, the gardens took on particular significance because of their scale. Not mere penthouse terraces, the roofs, linked by their bridging, provided a sizable area for strolling. Once management had eliminated the bridges, partly because their use would have required municipal hearings, but principally because of their cost, the roof-top garden was seriously compromised.

Had they been realized, roof-top gardens as lavish as these would have had considerable urban significance, but from our present vantage point their architectural interest would be severely limited. Just as the Channel and Plaza at street level do not penetrate the building mass, rather are bounded by it, so these projected roof-top gardens do not extend interior space—not in the sense in which interaction between interior and exterior characterizes modern architecture. Moreover, such designs were incongruous with a clerical environment. It was as though the stockbroker's formal gardens were to be flown into Manhattan from Greenwich or Oyster Bay. The illusory quality of the arcadian setting preferred for Beaux-Arts monuments seems the more emphatic when we think of the Center having an elephantine garden in a state of aerial suspension. During the period of design, however, the estate garden of the most grandiose schemes dwindled to a series of modest roof terraces physically separated one from another (Fig. 8). They are further disconnected in that they have been designed in the spirit of a flower show, with a "gardens of many nations" theme.[21] As such they serve primarily as attractions for the guided tour. Tulips on one roof for Holland, boxwood on another for England: the arrangement parallels the Beaux-Arts fervor for "period rooms."

Plazas on the ground, gardens on roofs, widely separated towers: all of these elements significantly, if not definitively, proclaim the spatial luxury of Rockefeller Center. Taken together, they mark the Center as a herald of modern ideals for American urban planning—an example of what modern European architects of the twenties envisioned in the skyscraper metropolis. For this reason, Sigfried Giedion celebrated the Center in his immensely influential *Space, Time and Architecture* (first published in 1941), even though the Beaux-Arts background of the Associated Architects combined with the caution of their clients to temper commitment to the modern point of view.

44

Another aspect of the Center identified with European modernism of the 1920's, and similarly diluted by Beaux-Arts predilections, was the shaping of the major towers in the five-spot composition as long, thin rectangular masses—or "slabs" as they came to be called.[22] This shape made possible the arrangement of shallow office space, having maximum contact with window areas, around a central utility core of elevators, conduits, and corridors. The basic idea for the slabs of Rockefeller Center was old—dating back to the plan for the Monadnock,‡ for example, and doubtless to much older structures since the arrangement would be a commonsense solution in other instances. But what was somewhat accidental and imperfect in the Monadnock became for the architects of the Center a consciously maintained standard, particularly in the two tallest buildings of the project—the 70-story RCA Building (1931–33) and its 41-story echo in the International Building (1933–35) at the northeast corner of the project (Fig. 22).* Indeed, the tower setbacks of both buildings were basically determined, not by esthetic criteria, but by the fundamental desire to insure that no office space was more than approximately 27 feet from a window.† Since elevators for tall buildings are grouped into banks, with each of the five passenger banks in the RCA tower serving between twelve and seventeen floors, the elevator core is obviously thickest in the lowest tier of stories (Fig. 20). It becomes progressively thinner as the building rises and elevators serving the lower tiers are eliminated, the 42 passenger elevators on the ground floor ultimately decreasing to 10 at the 53rd floor, which marks the start of the topmost bank.‡ As the elevator core shrinks, more and more floor space in a sheer rectangular slab without setbacks—like the United Nations Secretariat, to use Weisman's comparison—would have receded beyond the approximate 27-foot standard

‡ See *American Buildings and Their Architects: Progressive and Academic Ideals at the turn of the Twentieth Century,* Chapter 1.
* The same standard was used for the Americas Building over the Music Hall, the first Center building to be completed (31 stories; built 1931–32), and for the relatively modest RCA Building West (16 stories; 1931–33), just across 50th Street from the Americas Building and behind the RCA slab.
† The depth of the office space from the window wall was determined not only by a reasonable level of natural illumination for the whole of the rented area, but also by a feasible interval both technologically and functionally between the exterior wall and the rows of interior columns located a few feet outside the central core for elevators and utilities. Partitions hitched to rows of columns 27 feet from the window wall provided a public corridor toward the interior core, and a workable office depth toward the outer wall minimally interrupted by columnar supports.
‡ Two elevators included in the top tier are express from the ground floor to the observation roof and Rainbow Room. Four freight elevators running the full height of RCA complete the elevatoring.

45

set for the maximum depth of office space from windows. Hence the building perimeter had to contract to maintain the ideal conditions for office space around the utility core. Whereas the setbacks of the flanking walls precisely record the stages where this contraction of the elevator core occurs, the setbacks of the east and west fronts depend on esthetic decisions. So marked is the whittling of the end toward Fifth Avenue especially that, as one observer put it, the shape of the tower is more like a wedge than a slab. In any case, the setbacks carry the rationale for the narrowness of the tower to its ultimate conclusion (Fig. 21). "Cut out all bad space and let the building stand on its own," Hood repeatedly admonished.[23] And this was done.

The contrast between the solutions for the RCA tower and the United Nations Secretariat (Fig. 100) strikingly illustrates the perpetual paradox of function and form. Both buildings are slabs in the centers of such large sites that their architects had considerable freedom in molding the masses as they wished. By the early thirties, the New York building law of 1916, which necessitated setbacks in virtually all tall buildings, had to a considerable extent become an *esthetic* datum, probably because the designer spent a major part of his time in making his building an agreeable shape within the legally permitted envelope of space. Many came to believe that stepped buildings were so much more handsome than sheer towers that this legal requirement toward functional ends was, by the thirties, widely regarded as an esthetic

FIGURE 20. *Rockefeller Center. Two plans to left of the ground floor and a typical office floor (36th to 40th) in the RCA Building. Comparison of these plans indicates that as an elevator bank was dropped from the service core, a corresponding setback occurred in the building mass. This progressive reduction of floor area insured maximum conditions of light, ventilation, and view for all rental space.*

FIGURE 21. *Diagram at far right indicating the adverse effects of an uncompromising slab mass with respect to the proximity of all office space to windows. The area of the ground floor of the RCA Building (minus the peripheral stores) is here carried up as an unstepped rectangular slab, with an outline plan of the typical upper floor (36th to 40th) and its utility areas contained inside. The lightly shaded area roughly indicates floor space more than 27 feet from a window in the slab building; the darkly shaded area gives the same data for the typical upper floor in the RCA Building. Of course a floor area as large as that in the theoretical slab would require a somewhat larger core for elevators (E), corridors (C), and such services (S) as utility ducts, mechanical closets, toilets, and fire stairs.*

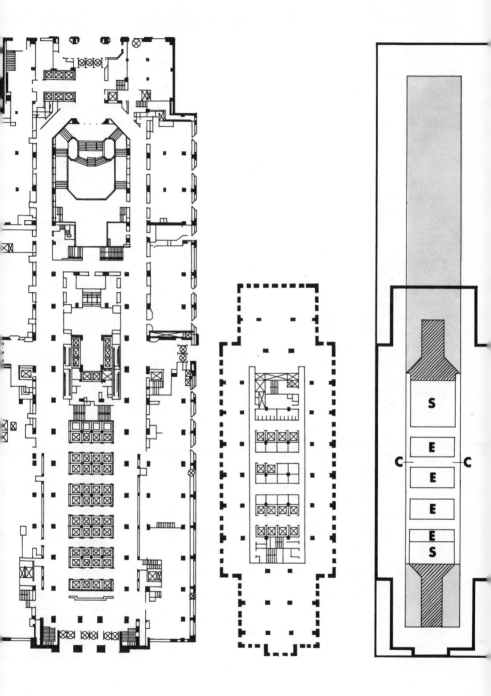

blessing in disguise. Setbacks gave variety to the alleged monotony of the office building wall and to its silhouette against the sky. They increased the visual stability of the building by decreasing its mass at the top. They terminated the vertical rise of the tower, but in a series of visual brakings rather than by the full stops of cornices—like those of Sullivan's Wainwright and Guaranty Buildings (Figs. 25, 145), or, alternatively, by a dramatic telescoping of the building mass as a tower or spire—as in the pinnacle of the Woolworth Building (Fig. 2). Incidentally, setbacks also provided terraces, although these were less spectacular in actuality than in fanciful schemes. Hence it appears that the Associated Architects of the RCA Building were too predisposed to the esthetic of a set-back tower to have seriously considered a sheer slab.* They seemingly started with an *esthetic* preference for a stepped building which they determined to make *functionally* ideal. The architects of the United Nations Secretariat essentially reversed the process. The slab form developed by modern architects during the twenties as a *functional* ideal for buildings of moderate height (particularly apartments) had become an *esthetic* preference by the fifties, and one of considerable symbolic impact.

The set-back slab (or wedge) of the early Center buildings, which put all space within something close to 27 feet from a window, was less used in later buildings. By the mid-thirties, it had gradually given way to the pure slab (Fig. 22; also applicable to the following observations). The trend toward sheerness began with the old Time-Life, now General Dynamics, Building (36 stories; built 1936–37) in the southeast corner of the site. This building has but a single setback, appearing near the crown. The absolutely pure slab appeared with the relatively modest Eastern Airlines Building (16 stories; 1938–39) placed on top of a spreading base in the middle of the southern block. Immediately thereafter, a smaller version of the General Dynamics Building housed United States Rubber, subsequently rechristened Uniroyal (20 stories; 1939–40) on the southwest corner of the site fronting the Avenue of the Americas. In short, slab massing in the Center initially realizes the early modern ideal of all office space relatively close to the window wall

* Harrison has told me that he did wish to eliminate all setbacks from the wall of the RCA Building fronting the Channel, and simply to retain the broad stepping at the sides of the building; thus the central part of the block would have emerged like a kernel breaking from its pod and have been very comparable in massing to Hood's Daily News Building a few blocks away (Fig. 24). It is too bad that Harrison did not win his point since a sheer slab as the climax to the Channel would have been preferable to the present eroded wall. But Hood preferred the complication of setbacks and, moreover, could reinforce his esthetic preference with the functional didactics of maximum light for offices.

by the use of setbacks; later, as this ideal becomes more abstract, a little less doctrinairely functional, but paradoxically more overtly "modern," it eventuates in the preference for pure slabs.

Since World War II the building bulk of the Center has increased in two ways. New office space has encroached on the roofs, once contemplated for gardens. In part, the normal desire for high returns from investment dictated the additions. In part, the additional office space met the demands of certain tenants for expansion, without which they threatened to leave the Center. But the increased building bulk of the Center also results from a widespread trend away from the slab-shaped tower and toward a somewhat fatter massing. The Associated Press Building (15 stories; 1938) prophesied this development within the Center. The client had exceptional needs, requiring deep loft space for its operations, since large unified areas are convenient both for editorial desks and for attendant banks of teletype machines. This necessity for floor space for machines anticipated a requirement of other businesses, since office procedures are becoming increasingly mechanized. In many instances, such office machines as computers are conveniently placed toward the center of large floors. Meanwhile, the increasingly mechanized control of environment has also tended to favor bigger building bulk. Improved illumination and air conditioning have made the proximity of office space to windows less axiomatic from a strictly functional standpoint than progressive theory around 1930 would have had it, even though vista remains psychologically (and hence financially) desirable for office space. Fluorescent fixtures and other kinds of elaborate ceiling lighting systems capable of providing what is popularly referred to as "daylight" illumination have more than tripled the foot candles typical in American office space between 1930 and 1960. As for air conditioning, the first fully air-conditioned office building in the United States, the Milam Building in San Antonio, had only been completed in 1928. In the early thirties, it existed as something of an experimental curiosity. Not surprisingly, therefore, air conditioning in the original Center buildings was limited to theatres and broadcasting studios, except for a portion of the office space occupied by the Radio Corporation of America.[24]† The cumulative effect of mechanical innovations of various sorts since 1930 has permitted a relaxation of the axiom that all office space should be within roughly 27 feet of a window. The Esso Building (33 stories; 1954–55) represents the first office tower in the Center (save for the Associated Press Building) to break decisively with the slab massing of the earlier buildings. The most

---

† Subsequent renovation has brought air conditioning to the entire Center, and has altered the lighting arrangements of the earliest buildings.

FIGURE 22. *Rockefeller Center. Aerial view taken around 1960 showing the original Center buildings, plus the additions of the Esso and the new Time-Life Buildings made after World War II. The block diagram indicates building designations as of 1970 and the order of their construction: (A) American Metal Climax (formerly Americas) Building, 1931–32; (B) Radio City Music Hall, 1931–32; (C) RCA Building, 1931–33; (D) RCA Building West, 1931–33; (E) British Empire Building, 1932–33; (F) La Maison Française, 1932–33; (G) Palazzo d'Italia, 1933–35; (H) International Building North, 1933–35; (I) International Building, 1933–35; (J) General Dynamics (formerly Time-Life) Building, 1936–37; (K) Associated Press Building, 1938; (L) Eastern Airlines Building, 1938–39; (M) Uniroyal Building, 1939–40, with an addition to the rear of the tower on the Avenue of the Americas, 1954–55; (N) Esso Building, 1946–47, by Carson & Lundin. The aerial photograph also shows, upper right corner, the new Time-Life Building, 1957–59, by Harrison & Abramovitz.*

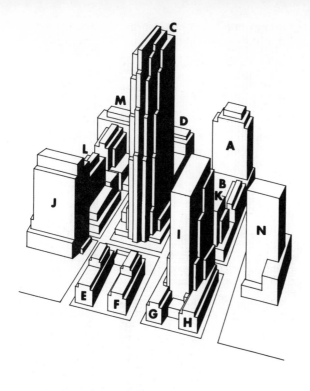

recent building within the area of the original complex, an addition for Uniroyal (19 stories; 1954–55) made to the rear of its original building, continued the trend toward bulky massing.‡ The combination of fatter massing and greater density of building within the Center has seriously compromised the spatial luxury envisioned in the original G-3 project, however spacious the Center remains in comparison with average commercial ventures.

The underground facilities at the Center are another distinctly urban feature (Fig. 23). The labyrinth of building and subway connections facilitates pedestrian circulation. A five-story garage, three of the stories

‡ The big exception to this trend is the new Time-Life Building (48 stories; 1957–59) by Harrison & Abramovitz. With this building the Center jumped the Avenue of the Americas between 50th and 51st Streets. This tower returns to slab massing, except for an interlocked mass at its base which provides for bulk floors (and therefore recalls the original ideal for the Center in a double sense). Most office space is no more than 31 feet from the window wall, although some, as in any pure slab, is deeper. Time-Life represents the first divergence from the standard Center style. Of course it is not seen as a visual part of the Center. Harrison tends to discount the limestone-clad verticals of the structural columns as a deliberate means of translating the old style into metal-and-glass wall construction, but the old style would seem to have been an influence. The two projecting verticals between each pair of columns are exposed air-conditioning and ventilating ducts. See *Architectural Forum*, 113 (August 1960), pp. 74–81.

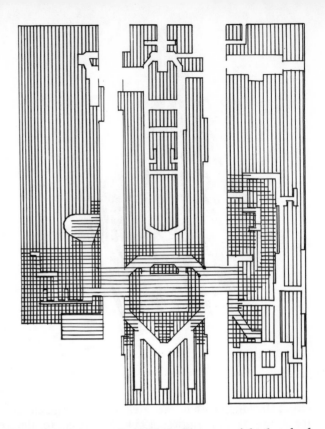

underground, in the middle of the south block holds over eight hundred cars. Grossly insufficient for the population it serves, it nevertheless makes better provision for parking than do most office buildings, and this is especially remarkable when we consider the time it was built. More important, the garage is supplemented by underground unloading and warehousing facilities for trucks.*

Such are the civic dimensions of the Center, as envisioned and as realized. Some disparity between vision and reality is to be expected. The substantial achievement nevertheless is impressive—at least in the construction up to World War II which completed the original scheme. Building since the War is another matter. Along with making the additions within the original complex already mentioned,† the management

---

* Much of the warehouse is devoted to a duty-free depot for the temporary storage of foreign goods. Requiring a special act of Congress for its bonded, duty-free status, this warehouse was part of the management scheme for luring foreign trade and travel interests into the Center.

† In 1963 the Center also acquired by purchase the Sinclair Building, which had been completed in 1952 by an outside real estate organization. In architectural treatment, it closely imitates buildings of the Center, effort having been made to identify it with the complex to which it now belongs.

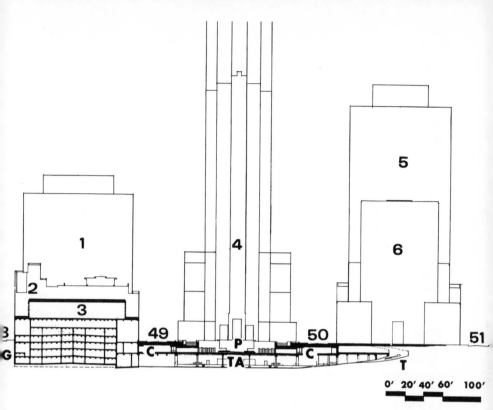

FIGURE 23. *Rockefeller Center. Underground pedestrian malls and truck delivery facilities. In the diagram opposite, vertical lines indicate the rectangular areas occupied by the buildings of the original Center. White areas through these rectangles are walkways, linked beneath the streets. Horizontal lines indicate vehicular ramps, garage, and loading area which cross the walkways at different levels. Fifth Avenue is at the bottom of the diagram. In the cross section above, looking west:* (G) *garage for 825 cars, three of the floors below street level and two above;* (TA) *trucking area with parking spaces for 40 trucks;* (T) *tunnel from 50th Street to the trucking area;* (P) *Plaza;* (C) *underground pedestrian concourse connecting all buildings and the subway. The buildings (shown in the profile of the late 1930's, but named as of 1970):* (1) *Uniroyal;* (2) *Center Theatre (demolished);* (3) *Eastern Airlines;* (4) RCA; (5) *American Metals Climax;* (6) *Associated Press.*

for the Center has participated extensively in building operations within its immediate vicinity up and down the Avenue of the Americas, often in concert with other real estate organizations. Whatever the economic justification for these buildings, and however admirably they may function as office space, they have neither extended nor enhanced the civic qualities of the Center. On the contrary, these new buildings, like most others in the area, have merely leeched onto the amenities and prestige of what had been accomplished, their scatter of misguided plazas and the extension of the underground pedestrian maze notwithstanding. No preplanning for integrated design of the area around the Center was attempted, even as a guide for voluntary use.

Although it is doubtful that the Center management could have effectively guided planning in its immediate vicinity, it was easier to ignore the possibility because the Center was so self-contained around its central Plaza, without substantial thrusts of space opening from and beyond it. In any event, if the management of the Center continues to accept applause for the civic virtue of its holdings, it might do well to observe the degree to which it basks in past glory. The thought is the more disquieting because the inactivity of the Center management with respect to planning during the decades immediately following World War II characterized a widespread dearth of imaginative planning at the time, even a callousness about the civic dimensions of architecture and planning, which has resulted in the substantial deterioration of the mid-town area.

Although the Center influenced (not always advantageously) many downtown redevelopment schemes in other cities after the war, its example was not immediately emulated in New York. Much publicized as an index to what the modern metropolis might become, the Center, in respect to New York itself, is rather more properly seen as marking the end of the Beaux-Arts tradition of grand planning, a phase which had also produced Grand Central as a magnificent interchange for the handling of trains, cars, and pedestrians. The underground tentacles of Grand Central spread in all directions to adjacent office buildings and hotels, while the steel bridging that buried the railroad tracks beneath the gardened corridor of Park Avenue also provided platforms for new buildings, originally for a number of apartment houses, that walled the street. In New York, postwar projects with the grand civic ambitions of Grand Central and Rockefeller Center barely reached the conceptual (let alone the building) stage by the end of the sixties. There were, of course, Paul Rudolph's megastructure scheme for the Graphic Arts Center, and schemes for the development of Welfare Island, and for a sub-city in the downtown financial district on made-land and platforms in the Hudson River. They somewhat recalled the earlier large-minded approach to the city, but were based on design and organizational principles that marked the beginning of a new tradition more than the continuation of the old.[25]

THE CENTER AS BUREAUCRATIC DESIGN

Commercial and functional premises conditioned the design of the individual buildings in the Center quite as much as they guided the scheme for the complex as a whole. The design progressed from committee analysis of cost and technology to committee decisions on appearance. As Reinhard stated, "The basis of the design of Radio City can be summed up as a constant study of finance and form [meaning the analysis of the building mass as determined by clay models on the basis of floor plans] with ornament [the exterior sheathing and interior decoration] a last consideration."[26]‡

Once the bulk models had been given agreeable shapes consonant with such practical considerations as economics, building ordinances, and the evolving layout of the entire project, certain special factors conditioned the specific form eventually given the buildings. These were advantageous in some respects, but not in all, to design of high quality. Of decided advantage was the client's determination to give his complex "prestige." In economic terms it is "prestige" which the designer confers on the building beyond that which is inherent in its location and accrued by its clientele. Hence he has most latitude, and for that reason most responsibility, where his client forgoes maximum immediate return in favor of that mixture of esthetics, promotion, and civic value which gives prestige, and the long-term rewards (financial and/or otherwise) which prestige brings. In this instance, prestige in the realm of design depended, like everything else, on group rather than on individual decisions. As Raymond Hood put it, "the cobwebs of whimsy, taste, fashion and vanity are brushed aside" in large group decisions.[27] So, of course, is the fire of individual genius, along with the possibility of genius going astray. It was relatively risk-free decisions that the team of designers from the Associated Architects sought. In Henry-Russell Hitchcock's words, they achieved an "architecture of bureaucracy" rather than an "architecture of genius."[28]

Both Reinhard and Harrison have left accounts of the office organization.[29] The over-all organization chart shows the Rockefeller interests

---

‡ Note that this approach is very similar to William LeBaron Jenney's definition of his aims with respect to his approach to commercial buildings in Chicago in the 1890's except that he significantly substituted "structure" for "form" but it is diametrically opposed to Louis Sullivan's ideas on the design of tall office buildings. See *American Buildings and Their Architects: Progressive and Academic Ideals at the Turn of the Twentieth Century,* Chapters 1 and 2.

at the top, the management company in over-all charge, and the Associated Architects in a lower tier of boxes beside finance, promotion, and construction operations. The theatrical equivalents of this hierarchy would be angel, producer, and specialties. Within the architectural organization, there was the usual round of regular conferences among the principals from management, engineering, and design; below these, the sub-conferences, the supervision of particular phases of the project by "job captains," each with his subordinates; the crew of modelers ready to translate the latest economic or design decisions into clay or plaster; the draftsmen; on down to the office boys rushing out the drawings for noontime or overnight duplication. But all this tells little about the development of the design itself within the organization. Who, for example, were especially active in the design of the Center? The principals have been mentioned: Reinhard, Hofmeister, Harrison, and Hood. Harrison also mentions Edward Stone, Earl Landefeld, George Pawley, and John Walquist.[30] There may have been others; but one is glad to fish from anonymity whomever one can, and thus to locate within the impersonal organization the cluster of individuals primarily responsible for bringing the design into being.

It is even more important with corporate practice of this size, to inquire how one idea wins out over all other ideas when the design is as consequential as that of the Center. Only a series of detailed case studies on the manner in which committees of designers have in fact realized projects of such magnitude can be ultimately informative about corporate consensus. Yet even from the outside it is possible to say something about the kinds of committees which have produced outstanding corporate design, and thus to appraise the design of the Center within a range of corporate possibilities. This effort is the more worthwhile because the esthetic of the Center has worn well, much more so than that of most of its prominent contemporaries. Compare it, for example, to William Van Alen's Chrysler Building (1926–30), designed in what would now be termed Art Deco (from its resemblance to the kind of decorative *moderne* featured at the Paris Exposition des Art Décoratifs of 1925), but which was perhaps at the time intended as an "automobile style," with the curved pleating of its tower, and winged radiator caps at the corners of its setbacks. Also completed in the early thirties, the Empire State Building boasted the absurdity of a dirigible mooring mast as a pinnacle for its splendidly isolated tower. Even Hood's McGraw-Hill Building is topped in a grotesquely ponderous cubist manner out of harmony with the treatment of the floors below (Fig. 29). To be sure the fantasy elements of the decorative *moderne* of the Chrysler Building especially have returned to favor along with the nostalgic revival of other aspects of the period. Against the monotonous grids that infested midtown and downtown Manhattan office buildings after World War II, the Chrysler affords relief. The very oscillation of taste for the Chrysler Building, however, illustrates the considerable success of the Center team in avoiding whimsies *à la mode*. The Center has never really lost favor with its public. The exterior design of the buildings has worn so well that not only have the postwar buildings within the original confines of the Center blandly appeared in the familiar wrapping, but several postwar skyscrapers nearby have mimicked the look of the Center in the hope of garnering some of its prestige. (The Sinclair Building, as mentioned earlier, eventually came into the Center complex.) Regarding the esthetic decisions of the Center team, therefore, we are less concerned with scouring the buildings for faults (which are many) than with discovering how the committee managed so well.

Starting with the assumptions that corporate design of distinction requires designers of some ability, and that these designers must be informed by a community of ideas capable of giving significant direction to committee decisions, what kinds of committees achieve works of merit? Specifically, what kind of team accounted for the success of the Center? At the risk of seeming categorical, it might be said that the unity of viewpoint which facilitates corporate success of this magnitude customarily is achieved in one of three situations. First of all, it may occur in team design which is severely determined by practical considerations, of economics, structure, and function. Most building of this sort has little to do with architecture, except as a business, beyond the often depressing but always necessary function of establishing hard-headed minima, and of standardizing short-cuts for design. Yet stringently practical decisions can provide a basis sufficiently impersonal and, at the same time, sufficiently integrating to result in corporate architecture of distinction. The vigor of some of the most minimally designed office buildings of the Chicago School testifies to the fact. So do many factories, or certain prefabricated schools erected in England after World War II. In fact more corporate design of high quality might result if practical considerations, when mandatory, were more strongly asserted and not tinseled with surface gaud, thus turning handsome necessity into mediocre "architecture." As for the Associated Architects, to be sure they worked with economic and technical considerations very much to the fore, yet they were never compelled to make them the sole determinants of their design. Quite the contrary: starting from the practical, they were positively encouraged to provide grandeur beyond the minima of their starting point.

The second situation unifying corporate design occurs when the members of the team all adhere to some style that is fashionable at the time. For instance, by the late twenties, progressive architects in Europe could work together on what was by then a clearly defined "modern" style. For that matter, previous to the nineteenth century, when styles were relatively stable over long periods of time, the communal mode of vision was more likely to provide the means of integrating group endeavor than in the present. Of course, some adaptation of a favored style might be imposed on the group by the force of one of its designers who appropriates a certain point of view toward design and certain form preferences among those which are current. The partiality of McKim and his partners for Renaissance forms is a case in point. So is Gordon Bunshaft's reconstitution of Mies van der Rohe's esthetic as a corporate style in the metal-and-glass office buildings of the 1950's which brought the firm of Skidmore, Owings & Merrill to international prominence.* Quite obviously, however, the committee design of Rockefeller Center was not disciplined by a favorite, established style.

All of which brings us to a third circumstance for successful team design, the one accounting for the design of the Center. In this case, the designers bring an eclectic background to the job at hand. The amorphous nature of this kind of committee means that fortunate circumstances, even sheer luck, is likely to play a larger role in determining the quality of the eventual result than is the case when committee efforts are preconditioned by practical stringencies or by stylistic preference. Except under the most favorable circumstances, a design committee with eclectic tastes is constantly in danger of losing sight of the building as an entity, especially if the project is to be an eye-catching commercial venture. Without care, the design may hitch forward as a mishmash of those "bright ideas" that seem good in the drafting room but appear as inconsistencies, or as dated clichés, in the finished building. Although the Center has its share of "bright ideas" grown dim, the coherence of the project as a whole stems from the successful interplay of the various ideas and backgrounds that the collaborators brought to the project.

Some of the conditions that influence the quality of the design of any such team have been mentioned: the talents of the principal team members; the balance maintained among the design, financial, technical, and promotional specialties (essential in a project as complex as Rockefeller Center); the civic consciousness of the client. Other factors, too, accounted for the success of the Center's design. The first was the progressive bent of the Associated Architects. Brought up in the Beaux-Arts tradition, all of the principal designers were nevertheless attracted to modern ideas, if not wholly committed to them. The management group selected its design team because of this outlook. It aimed—and properly

---

* On McKim, see *American Buildings and Their Architects: Progressive and Academic Ideals at the Turn of the Twentieth Century,* Chapter 7. On Bunshaft, see Chapter 4 below.

so for a project intended for immediate popularity as well as for long-range investment—at projection more than at innovation. The Associated Architects were to provide an efficient monumentality with a cautiously "forward look." That the team understood its management's wishes is made clear by the over-all design of the buildings, if not by much of the detailing. Whether the design continues to wear as well up to 2069, when the ground lease with renewal options expires,[31] is moot; but its chances seem good—and if the buildings become antiquated before this date, the whole project could be demolished and a fresh start made, as is the custom in New York.

Finally, the members of the Center team brought a substantial homogeneity of previous experience to the Center commission. In contrast, the architects on the international team responsible for the preliminary design of the United Nations complex brought such divergent experiences and philosophies to their task as to make effective cooperation all but impossible. Eventually the committee resigned itself to a diluted version of a scheme by Le Corbusier, its most forceful consultant, which he promptly repudiated with accusations that his colleagues had both appropriated and misused his ideas. The Center team, however, was not only well disciplined in the financial and functional demands of the skyscraper, but also was familiar with the esthetic which had developed as a norm for progressive skyscraper design during the twenties. Hence the Center design must be seen as an example in a sequence of designs.

With respect to the final design of the Center, Raymond Hood was the key member of the team in the sense that his newly completed Daily News Building (1930) haunted the Associated Architects throughout their deliberations (Fig. 24). This was so not only because of the striking merits of the Daily News Building but because it climaxed a development from Beaux-Arts "Gothic" toward a gothicized modern esthetic for the skyscraper, a development in which all the principal members of the team had shared.

Of the two expressive compositions for skyscrapers which overlapped in Sullivan's work and rhetoric: namely the organization of the building as an elevational composition with "beginning, middle, and end" or as a structural composition made "tall" by emphasizing the projecting vertical piers from base to cornice†—it was the latter which was most used during the 1920's (Fig. 25). The evolution of Hood's design from the Beaux-Arts Gothic of the Chicago Tribune Building (1922–24) [Fig. 26] to the gothicized modern of his Daily News Building has served

† See *American Buildings and Their Architects: Progressive and Academic Ideals at the Turn of the Twentieth Century,* Chapter 2.

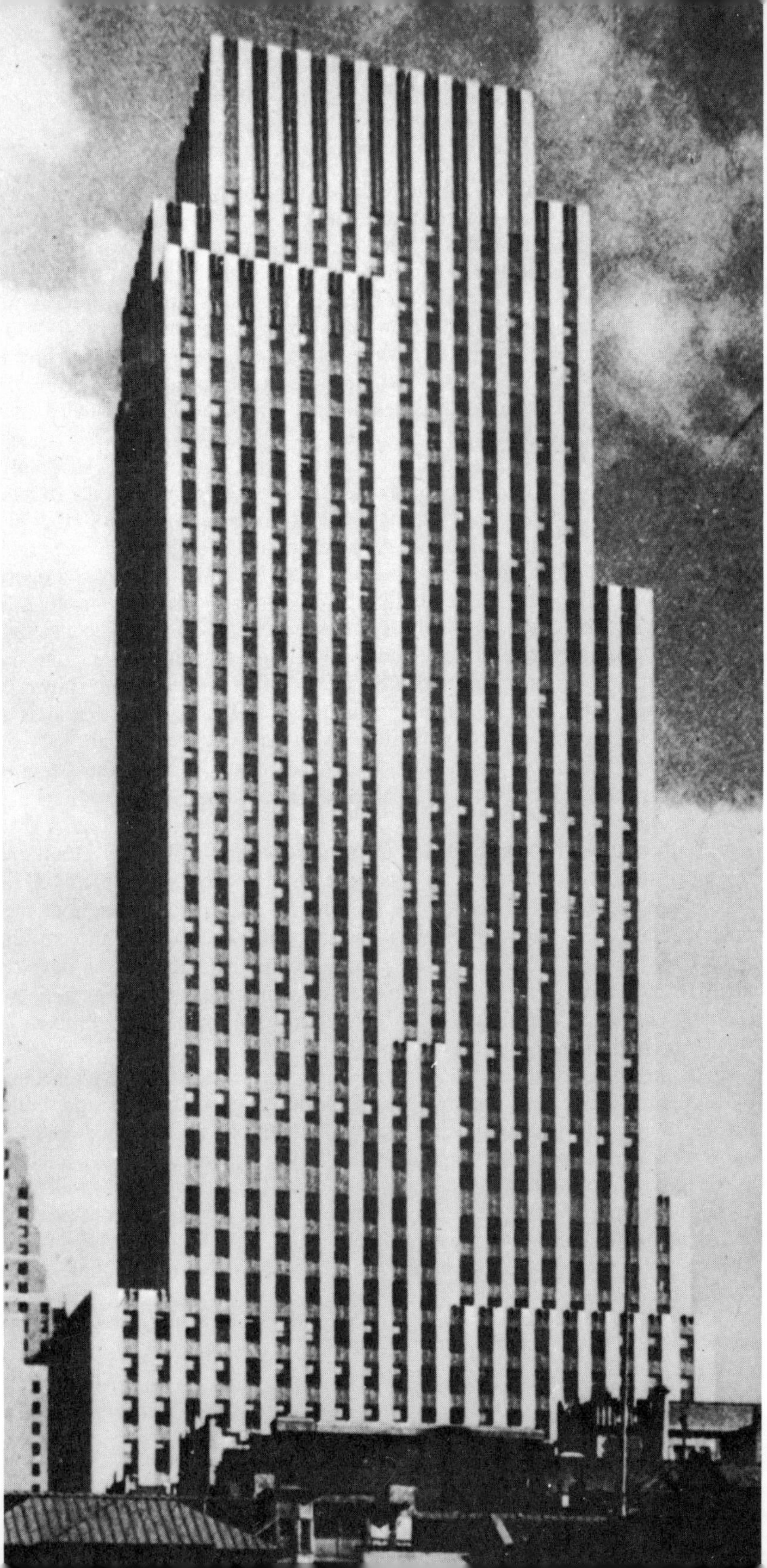

FIGURE 25. *Louis Sullivan. Guaranty Building, Buffalo, N.Y., 1894–95.*

FIGURE 24. *Raymond Hood. Opposite: Daily News Building, New York,* completed 1930.

FIGURE 27. *Eliel Saarinen. Design which took second place in the 1922 competition for the Chicago Tribune Building.*

historians as a demonstration of the growing awareness of modern European architecture in the United States.[32] Hood, together with John Mead Howells, won the Chicago commission in the famous international competition of 1922. Eliel Saarinen's entry, which took second place, was another Gothic design but a less literal one, and it has traditionally been regarded as an intermediary between Hood's two skyscrapers (Fig. 27). (Sullivan helped to foster this view in one of his last articles, where he praised Saarinen's design over that of the winner—and with an extravagance which has its pathetic aspect since his own Guaranty Building was superior to both.[33]) Even Howells & Hood's winning design, however, disclosed the rudiments of the compositional scheme typical of what, by the end of the decade, had become the semi-modern skyscraper in the United States. This is the sheer rise of the vertically striated wall through a series of setbacks, each of which is relatively open at the

FIGURE 26. *Howells & Hood. Chicago Tribune Building, Chicago, 1922–24.*

top (without cornice or similarly emphatic closure), so that the verticals of an upper stage seem to grow out of those immediately below. In the Chicago Tribune Building the composition is virtually closed at the skyline in the telescoping of the mass to a Neo-Gothic crown. Later examples, less specifically Gothic in intent, and tentatively modern, like the Daily News Building, replace the crown with a more open effect at the summit, where the verticals terminate at roof top in the same bluntly ragged edge of the setback stages below. Vaguely reminiscent of medieval crenelation, the visual effect is more that of a fluted edge.‡ The effect of openness at the summit is a timid Beaux-Arts venture toward the unbounded quality of the knife-edge terminations of the sheer planarity of modern elevations.

Around 1930, the broadside view of the Daily News Building was perhaps the favorite image of the skyscraper among progress-oriented architects. Among other things in its favor, it was not then, as now, screened by mediocre metal-and-glass neighbors, but rose in splendid isolation a few blocks east of Grand Central on 42nd Street from a ruck of low buildings—as though a shining new world had popped from the crust of the old. Its immediate impact rather conceals the superficiality of what is almost a two-dimensional effect. Sheer verticals in cream-colored brick alternate with russet stripes (the tan of the spandrel panels under each window eked out by tan blinds in the windows), and as crisply as though a ruled drawing in ink had been blown up to full size. Much more a graphic than an architectural effect, the thinness of this design (literally thin and conceptually thin) appears immediately when compared with Sullivan's elevations. The Daily News shows none of the traditional moldings of Sullivan's work; none of the sculptural quality of a wall conceived as a series of planes receding in depth from the face of the pier to the spandrel, thence to the inset plane of the window; none of the dynamics of the vertical elements interlocked with the horizontals; barely any of the play of light and shadow over the vibrant ornamentation. In effect, the alternate stripes, cream and tan, make a patterned slip cover for the skeletal innards. Yet Hood's effect is spectacularly achieved, with unprecedented audacity and lightness of effect, in a setback massing which (to repeat, especially in side view) has few peers. It was this image of the Daily News that haunted the Center team as a "modern" projection of the norm for Beaux-Arts Gothic.

The thrust of the Daily News elevations toward modernity seems to have been a bit too extreme for the forward-looking monumentality sought for the Center. The stripes were too strident; the sense of weightlessness

‡ The more adventurous designer of that time might have used a quasi-Mayan or quasi-cubist ornamentation for the setbacks of the Gothic fluting.

was at odds with monumentality. In effect the Associated Architects redid the elevations of the Daily News in a more conservative manner. This retrograde redesign suggested the work of Hugh Ferriss, an architectural delineator, whose soft pencil and charcoal renderings of skyscrapers were then much admired (Fig. 28). Lewis Mumford observed the connection in an unfavorable critique of the Center published at the time of the completion of the first buildings. Recommending that the Center be viewed at night, he wrote, "Under artificial lighting, in a slight haze, the group of buildings looks like one of Hugh Ferriss' visions of the City of the Future." After adding that an ash heap, properly illuminated, could also be impressive at night, Mumford went on, "Again life has imitated art, for these drawings of Ferriss, with their emphasis on mass, combining bulk and power with the soft romantic edge one can achieve only in charcoal, were the pinnacle which the Big Boys steadily sought to reach."[34] Mumford referred to Ferriss' *The Metropolis of Tomorrow*, which was published in 1929. Renderings of some of the most prominent American skyscrapers of the decade—all but one of them in the gothicized modern manner—provided a starting point for his visionary city. All seem heavier than the Daily News, and for the reasons which Mumford gave. They were "buildings like mountains," as the caption for the frontispiece put it, where "sheer planes" rose as serrated cliffs that successively eroded into "great set-backs."[35]

In extending the contemporary Gothic esthetic toward the Metropolis of Tomorrow, Ferriss depended on a composite of contrary influences: on Le Corbusier's "radiant cities" of widely spaced skyscrapers, but as modified by New York density and Beaux-Arts composition and symbolism. The entire population of this imaginary metropolis seems to have lived a glamorously decadent penthouse existence replete with martinis and costume balls, as though the milieu of *The Great Gatsby* had been transported from East and West Egg to Manhattan. Social considerations, except as they affected the limousine set, were nil.

Aside from its esthetic for mass and elevations, Ferriss' ideal metropolis may also have influenced the Center because of its widely separated skyscrapers, its intervening plateau of roof tops, and its suggestions for the separation of wheeled from pedestrian traffic. Where Ferriss' vision of the ideal metropolis differed from the Center scheme, the latter appears as the more progressive of the two. The brutality and gloom of Ferriss' skyscraper "mountains" revealed little of the Associated Architects concern for light, air, and view. Ferriss never considered any such garden platform spreading on low roof tops as the Center team briefly projected. Finally, pedestrian plazas had less importance in Ferriss' scheme than a more sensational, but cramped bridging of pedestrian arcades which crossed over streets and cut through buildings at various levels above the

65

FIGURE 28. *Hugh Ferriss. Two views (above) of a visionary skyscraper city from* The Metropolis of Tomorrow, *1929. Ferriss was not alone in such visions. Harvey Wiley Corbett, one of the principal designers of the Center, especially in the early stages, had been a champion during the twenties of a more enlightened, if less grandiose, scheme for a multi-level city. His rendering (opposite) shows a double-decked New York street with bridges and arcaded walkways which unite street and buildings with a pedestrian mezzanine.*

ground. So the Center, in effect, provided a partial critique of Ferriss' megalomania even as it incorporated something of his design and his urban thinking.

Not that the Associated Architects specifically cribbed from Ferriss. There was no need to do so, since Ferriss' vision was less the imaginative creation of an environment for a new social order than a rhapsodically uncritical projection of trends in skyscraper design current during the late twenties among the more progressive of the Beaux-Arts trained architects. Hence *The Metropolis of Tomorrow,* like Hood's Daily News Building, appealed to the design team of the Center in as much as it, too, suggested that modernity could be grasped merely by advancing along lines already established, and without a drastic shift of outlook. Both, in short, could stand as indices of the experience shared in common by the Associated Architects, and of its conservatism with liberal persuasions—qualities which accounted for the effectiveness of the team.

Had the Center been built earlier in the twenties, before the team had become aware of European architecture, would the urban planning ideals of the modern movement have been available to it?[36] Could it possibly have realized the buildings with the anonymity of elevation and quiet silhouette which have protected the Center against visual obsolescence? As Ferriss remarked of the progressive trend in skyscraper composition, "To many designers [the composition considered merely as a rudimentary stepped-back mass and its fenestration] . . . will still seem far from any final results: they seek some far greater refinement and delicacy than is here evident. To them, this form may be offered simply as a building in the rough."[37] And, as though to verify Ferriss' assertion, there was the criticism of the Center by Ralph Adams Cram, the leading Goth of an earlier Beaux-Arts milieu, who echoed the protests of much of the old guard. He assailed the utilitarian countenance of the Center buildings, and especially regretted the absence of the elaborate modeling at roof top which had previously characterized the skyscraper summit.[38] "Yet," as Ferriss observed, "there are designers to whom the very simplicity of such forms, the very absence of adornment is itself a recommendation. From them we may expect buildings exhibiting a certain starkness, and even nakedness—these qualities which are, indeed, the norm for all newly arisen forms." Designers of this description dominated the Center team.

If less awareness of the modern movement would have hurt the esthetic of the Center by compromising the negative virtues of its "nakedness," let alone some of its most creative aspects as urban planning, would a little more awareness have enhanced it? Even as he came to the Center project, Hood was immersed in his design for the McGraw-Hill Building (1929–30) [Fig. 29], which seemed at the time a more "modern" image than that of the Daily News. Because the Associated Architects could hardly have been expected to have adopted a more modern design than that represented by the quasi-modern McGraw-Hill, it is worth inquiring as to whether the Center might have been improved with its inspiration. In a fundamental sense, the McGraw-Hill is no more modern than the Daily News. The slip cover of vertical stripes for the Daily News is simply changed to one with a horizontal pattern for McGraw-Hill, the russet and cream striations of the former becoming turquoise and cream for the latter.* In another sense, however, to dismiss Hood's change of pattern as mere surface effect is unfair. He did have reason to consider his McGraw-Hill Building as being more committed to "modern" than was the Daily News. As we shall see, it did represent a development beyond the earlier building. Long horizontal bands of windows ("ribbon windows," as they came to be termed) were among the hallmarks of modern architecture during the twenties. Since the steel frame, employing thin columns widely spaced, sufficed as the total support for the building, the wall could exist as a non-structural membrane stretched around the frame merely to provide weather protection for the interior. Under these circumstances windows did not need to be isolated units. The wall could be lavishly opened, especially where the columns were set back from the edge of the floor slabs, as they tended to be in modern buildings of the 1920's. Then window bands might run continuously across the wall from edge to edge, or, for that matter, completely around the building. (Indeed, the cantilevering of the floor slabs outward from the exterior columns permitted the entire wall to be glazed, and the "window wall" ultimately became as much a cachet of modern architecture as the "ribbon window" —compare Fig. 29, for example, with Figs. 53 and 54.) The seeming thinness of the walls and the excessive amount of glass emphasized the volume of interior space rather than the exterior mass of the building. The window treatment, moreover, suggested even from the outside that the interior space was continuous, open, light, and airy.

---

* Again a comparison with a Sullivan work is possible: this time the Carson, Pirie, Scott Store (illustrated in *American Buildings and Their Architects: Progressive and Academic Ideals at the Turn of the Twentieth Century,* fig. 61), and with the same result as that of the Wainwright or the Guaranty with the Daily News.

FIGURE 29. *Raymond Hood. McGraw-Hill Building, New York, 1929–30.*

By recessing the supporting columns and emphasizing the window voids, the canonical modern approach of the twenties to architecture placed a premium on the expression of architecture as interior space at the expense of architecture as structure.† Although progressive theory at the time urged frankness in the revelation of structure, the supporting columns tended to appear (when not concealed by partitioning) only inside the building, engulfed by the space they sustained. Hood came to this modern preference for a predominantly horizontal treatment for windows directly from the earlier verticalism of his Daily News Building; thus in the McGraw-Hill design, he seems to have been somewhat timid about fully asserting the windows as ribbons projecting in front of the recessed structural columns. Accordingly, in McGraw-Hill the columns come to the surface of the wall. To prevent their interference with the "look" of unbroken horizontals, Hood cosmetically sheathed the columns in turquoise-colored brick where they abutted the windows, and then hung the windows with turquoise-colored blinds. The result is superficial as architecture, however dazzling it may have appeared at the time as a "modern" performance. But, to repeat, Hood had some reason to believe that McGraw-Hill was a more advanced expression of modern architecture than his Daily News Building. In the earlier building, the intent of his design had been the expressionistic, even romantic, dramatization of the height of the structure. To the devout modernist of the twenties the effect was doubly suspect in that Hood (like Sullivan, and like architects working in the Neo-Gothic tradition of skyscraper design) intensified the vertical effect by arbitrarily multiplying the pier-like stripes so that they disguised the wide spacing of the columns natural to skeletal framing. Finally, the modernist might also complain that pier-like elements rising from the ground belied the "floating" effect of the tiers of cantilevered balconies possible with skeletal construction. In short, whereas Hood eventually came to view his Daily News as a modernized version of traditional skyscraper design in the Neo-Gothic mode (as we, too, have come to see it) the McGraw-Hill seemed to him a new departure, more frankly avowing modern conditions. So Hood could justify the change of direction in the striping in the two designs as something more than the arbitrary substitution of one pattern for another.

Had the Center architects dared to venture farther into "modern"—had they gone as far toward "modern" as their milieu permitted—they might well have followed Hood's lead. But they did not. Fortunately, they stayed with the Daily News Building, and with Hugh Ferriss. The weight of structural and functional logic may be on the side of the fenestration of the McGraw-Hill, as opposed to that of the Daily News, but the earlier

† For further discussion, see pp. 119f. below.

building seems the more satisfactory design today. Again we confront a frequent paradox in functional design. Although the ribbon window is visually satisfactory in relatively low buildings (where European architects had developed the motif) and where the breadth of a building stabilizes the seemingly unsupported spandrel walls, the piling of cantilevers to skyscraper altitudes eliminates the plane of the earth as a stabilizing point of reference. Piled too high, the horizontals take on the appearance of a monstrous layer cake. We long to prop the layers. Around 1930, however, the excitement of experimenting with the new esthetic of the ribbon windows often outweighed any thought as to its esthetic deficiencies for skyscrapers.

Of course the possibility of horizontal fenestration for the Center was explored.‡ However much ribbon windows may have tempted the architects, office planning specialists opposed them. Ultimately the Associated Architects chose the pier-and-spandrel window motif. As a general rule, office planners prefer an elevation that permits a piece of wall between every window or two; for this, the pier-and-window treatment is ideal.[39] The pier affords a recurrent interval of wall against which office partitioning can butt, and behind which it can be flexibly adjusted. Where space rents by the square foot, these are important considerations. By contrast, ribbon windows or (after World War II) metal-and-glass grids virtually establish an inflexible module since they require the hooking of all partitions to the vertical mullions between each of the window units, while the kinds of partitioning which may be used are often limited. In the Center, where the pier is nearly as wide as the window—the average being 46 inches for the one, 49 inches for the other—the margin of adjustment for office planning is especially generous (Fig. 20).

Benefits to office planning notwithstanding, had the architects been more ardent modernists, they might just possibly have convinced management that horizontal fenestration should be adopted for expressive reasons. They might have argued that the Center would soon appear "dated" unless the more "modern" window treatment was substituted for the more traditional approach. (After all, the benefits of pier-and-window wall did not prevent the widespread use of the "all-glass" wall during the fifties.) But the Associated Architects were sufficiently attuned to the semi-modern, gothicized skyscraper esthetic to have willingly followed the directives of the office planners. Had they wished a more modern

‡ At least four different patterns were considered for the window wall: vertical striping; horizontal striping; the regular punch of windows into a flat wall plane; and the third pattern again but with rectangular surface designs of a dark material set into the wall somewhat in the manner of the Viennese modernist, Josef Hoffmann. Henry H. Dean, "A New Idea in City Rebuilding," *American Architecture,* April 1931, pp. 114f., illustrates these possibilities.

FIGURE 30. *Rockefeller Center. Profile view, from the north looking down-town, of the original Center complex, a view now substantially blocked by additional building in the area. The major buildings visible are (left to right) the International Building; then, in an overlapped cluster, those for Esso, the Associated Press (the low building) and RCA, with the tower of the Empire State Building in the distance behind; finally, the American Metal Climax (once RKO) Building.*

veneer, moreover, they would have gone counter to Mr. Rockefeller's mildly expressed preference for a "Gothic" effect for the buildings. As a layman, he was bound to be somewhat traditional in his esthetic prefer-ences, while he certainly appreciated his office planners arguments as to the functional and financial advantages of vertical fenestration. As a lay-man, too, he undoubtedly preferred an esthetic based on expressionistic rather than on technological reasons. Hence he must have felt that the primary characteristic of the skyscraper is not its skeleton or its spaces, but its height—desiring, in Sullivan's words, "every inch of it tall."[40] Whereas one way of arguing is architect's logic; the other is everyman's experience.*

* See also pp. 106f. below.

For a combination of practical and expressive reasons, therefore, the architects fortunately stayed with the image they understood, whereas they might have attempted a reckless gesture toward a future which they only partially comprehended. On the whole, the timing of the Center for this particular team seems to have been ideal. In conjunction with the progressive orientation of the team, and its homogeneity of experience, the timing of the commission encouraged the well-established esthetic ideal, infused with as much influence from the modern movement as the team could assimilate.

So the sawn limestone verticals alternating with dull, slate-gray, cast-aluminum spandrel panels sufficiently blur and blunt the building surfaces, together with weather and grime, that they assume a neutral, cliff-like quality around the colorful plaza and its activity. Viewed from the north and looking downtown, the flank of the Center was once especially effective and, as Mumford suggested, especially at twilight. Unfortunately, like the familiar broadside view of the Daily News (which may have recommended a comparable effect for the Center), this, too, has been muffled by postwar building (Fig. 30). Originally, however, the Center itself provided a skyline, a little apart from, but athwart, the ragged backdrop of towers farther downtown. Then especially, its breadth of surface and sawed-off severity of silhouette gave it a dam-like countenance. As such, the broadside view of the Center anticipated the sort of silhouette which the popularity of slab massing brought to Manhattan after World War II. Although this silhouette achieved special prominence in the United Nations Secretariat, it appeared with more consequence to the New York skyline in the lumbering breadth of the Chase-Manhattan skyscraper, so disruptive to the towered prickle of the financial district, and an augury of more such disruption to come.

ART, ELEVATORS, AND THE MUSIC HALL

To return to Hood's boast, "the cobwebs of whimsey, fancy, taste, fashion and vanity" were indeed substantially "brushed aside" by the Associated Architects in roughing out the over-all esthetic effect of the Center complex. It is less *en masse* than in detail that flaws appear. This is to be expected. A design team which works as an eclectic group with only the homogeneity of experience and point of view to unify its work is bound to do better by the project as a whole than in detail. On such a team it is in matters of detail especially where "whimsey, fancy, taste, fashion and vanity" are likely to obtrude. The "inspiration" of one conferee collides with the "inspiration" of another. *Ad hoc* compromise is necessary; worse, a melange of individual hunches goes into the project. Consistent detailing in bureaucratic design, on the other hand, tends to result from the discipline of a corporate style, whether (as we have already observed) this be dependent on specific historical precedent, or on the rigorous rationale of technological process and functional purpose, or possibly on styles which minimize ornamentation for elemental forms, as did modern European architecture during the twenties with its combined emphasis on a functional esthetic and purified geometry of shape. Thus—merely to glance at the most prominent building of the complex—the east front of the RCA slab would be better without the erosion of the setbacks; still better (although less immediately startling and less functionally pure) were it somewhat broader.[41] The entrance could have been incorporated within a rugged block. The verticals would then have risen from a firmer, more austere base; not from the existing complication of a stepped composition gouged with openings of various sizes. A more commanding entrance into the RCA slab, and one better integrated with the fountain below, would have provided a stronger climax to the Channel axis (something which only the mammoth annual Christmas tree now accomplishes), as well as some sense of an extension of the Channel axis through to the Avenue of the Americas.[42] The monumental severity of its entrance makes the International Building on Fifth Avenue far the better of the two.

As for the occasional stone grilles on the elevations—the trivial patterns cast into the spandrel panels, and the pie-crust fluting toward the tops of some of the buildings (doubtless a concession to Rockefeller's "Gothic" predilections)—such details may be gratefully ignored. The architects themselves apparently had second thoughts on these matters, for superficial decorations largely disappeared from the later buildings as it became more conventional to be "modern." Most of the embellishment of entrances and focal wall surfaces was left to painters and sculptors. We forget how significant the collaboration then seemed, all the more because the artists experimented extensively with materials and processes, making use of polychromy on metal and stone, of glass and aluminum, and of photomurals.[43] The results are now primarily of interest as a demonstration—and as revealing as any available—of the death throes, both formally and symbolically, of an idyllic, Neoclassical allegory in the grippe of the cubist virus. Some future iconographer, taking the pulse of the 1930's, will find the themes and their treatment revealing; but they need not detain us for long. The sculpture, most of it plaques and reliefs adorning portals and walls, blends innocuously into the architecture. Of more than routine interest is an early relief by Isamu Noguchi over the portal of the Associated Press Building, which shows a cubist laocoon of reporters and pressmen ensnarled in a ribbon of paper from a teletype machine; in the lobby of the General Dynamics Building, Carl Milles' wooden horseman listens to a songbird, with taped trills on the hour; on the west façade of the RCA Building, above mosaics by Barry Faulkner, four allegorical reliefs on modern invention by Gaston Lachaise; and, best of all, the bronze doors for the Palazzo d'Italia on Fifth Avenue by Giacomo Manzu, which were not part of the original program. These at least provide a sampling of the most significant sculpture at the Center. Lee Lawrie had the lion's share of the commissions, including *Atlas* at the entrance to the International Building on Fifth Avenue. As sculpture, *Atlas* is mediocre; but its silhouette is splendidly decorative within the severely contained court—demonstrating that, even where quality is limited, sculpture can be a considerable asset if it complements its architectural setting in a positive way. Like Paul Manship's tawdry *Prometheus* in the Lower Plaza, *Atlas* has become something of a trademark, not only for the Center but for Manhattan as well.

The Center's equally elaborate mural program is principally remembered for the nasty controversy which resulted in the expunging of Diego Rivera's *Man at the Crossroads Looking towards His Future,* the artist having refused to delete Lenin from a prominent place in its cast of characters. The other major murals, by José Maria Sert and Frank Brangwyn in the RCA Building, and by Dean Cornwell in the Eastern Air Lines Building, are iconographically as pompous as Rivera's, and formally weaker. On the whole, those few works which essayed less on man's destiny, and modestly stayed within the purview of the commercial program of the Center, fared best; such as the photomural by Margaret Bourke-White of radio apparatus, in the lobby of the National Broadcasting Corporation; another by Edward Steichen on the history of aviation, in the Center Theatre; and Stuart Davis' witty painting *Men Without Women,* in the "smoking room" of the Music Hall. The photomurals have disappeared, but men can still enjoy Davis' semi-abstraction in his brash billboard style.

The program for extensive collaboration among the artists was admirable in principle. Its chief failure lay in the choice of most of the artists. Harrison, for one, had hoped for murals by Matisse and Picasso. Again full commitment to the modern movement was impossible in America around 1930. Although Harrison and certain other enlightened members of the group knew something of modern painting and sculpture, the team as a whole knew little of either. Harrison remarked in retrospect, "One of the greatest differences between the development of modern architecture in the United States and Europe is that the European architects knew modern painting and sculpture, whereas we didn't." In fact the cardinal principles of modern European architecture in the twenties

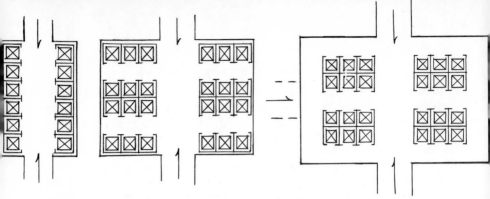

FIGURE 31. *Typical elevator layouts. Left to right: in-line, alcove, central room, and enfilade arrangements. The enfiladed scheme adopted for the Center not only provides convenient locations for the building directory (D), but, with wide corridors, is also well adapted to shopping arcades (although shops are minimized opposite elevator areas in the Center to avoid congestion). In all back-to-back arrangements of the elevators rows, structural columns concealed within each of the blocks (at C) can be conveniently cross-braced to stabilize the frame.*

had very largely derived from a visual revolution initially occurring in the other arts.† "In the beginning," he went on, "we knew only the architecture, as we saw it, a few of us, first in the foreign architectural magazines, like *L'Architecture Vivante,* and then in our own. Most of us learned of the painting and sculpture afterward."⁴⁴ Too late, it should be added, to make collaboration among the arts at the Center the triumph which generosity and good intentions should have made it.

Then, too, the times were unpropitious for a collaborative venture in the arts simply because of the anomalous position of painting and sculpture in the United States in the thirties, befuddled as they were with the competing claims of a dying academicism, a rampant regionalism, and an unassimilated modernism. When the new Time-Life Building came to be adorned in the early sixties, the situation had changed. An abstract mural by Fritz Glarner extending the length of a corridor across the front of the lobby is a work of real merit, although its potential as architectural adornment all but disappears in its situation.‡

There remain only the interiors to discuss. Omitting the roof top Rainbow Room, and considering only the more accessible interiors of the Center, four especially merit attention: two elevator lobbies, those for the RCA slab and the International Building, the foyer of the Music

---

† See Chapters 2 and 3 below.

‡ With the narrowness of the corridor in mind, Glarner designed his unified mural panel as a concealed triptych for viewing by pieces as well as a whole. Even so, it is still impossible to view it properly. Moreover, the garish architectural surrounding fights with the painting, which cries for a setting with austerity as well as spaciousness.

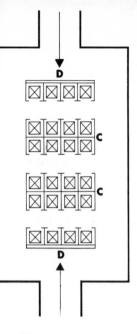

Hall, and, of course—what is next to the Plaza the most familiar image of the Center—the Music Hall itself.

Of the lobbies, the first observation is the practical matter of the elevators. The RCA and International Buildings seem to be the first important instances of the placement of the elevator banks as parallel slabs, open at either end, in the center of a broad lobby, and at right angles to its axis (Fig. 31; also Fig. 20).[45] Prior to the Center, elevators tended to be arranged side by side along the corridor (as, for example, in PSFS, Fig. 37, where Howe & Lescaze retained a traditional arrangement), or in a series of alcoves off the corridor (like the alcoves off the central reading area typical of Richardson's libraries). In still another scheme, one popular during the twenties, the cabs were arranged back to back in open-ended, double rows, and set as freestanding slab-like units in an interior room usually located at the center of the ground floor. Corridors from two, more usually from four, directions led into the elevator room. Obviously in buildings requiring many elevators, this last scheme handled traffic flow better than in-line and alcoved plans. Just as obviously there was a problem of orientation in the mixture of cross and circular patterns of movement around the elevator blocks. The arrangement at Rockefeller Center, however, permits continuous traffic flow and quick identification of the desired elevator, advantages comparable to those of an efficient library stack. Directories at either end of the row of elevator banks face the incoming visitor. Once he spots the desired bank, he leaves the through corridor to wait for his cab, thus permitting the main flow of traffic to move unimpeded through the lobby. Since the lobbies of most Center buildings are, like the elevator aisles, open at both ends, movement through the base of the buildings is exceptionally efficient. Each bank is limited to four cabs on either side of its feeder cross aisle because a greater number would delay loading and consequently slow the staggered timing of the runs. Placed back to back, the rows of elevators conceal the cross-bracing for the skeletal frame at regular intervals of roughly 28 feet.

Once this elevator arrangement had been perfected in the Center, it became a virtual standard for all office structures wherever the plan permitted. The slab-like treatment of elevator banks is of more than technological interest, however, because elevators provide a major expressive element in office building lobbies. The slab treatment of the banks gives them a more positive architectural quality than does arrangement along a wall—a potential more consciously employed in the pylon treatment of the elevators in the lobby of the Seagram Building.*

With respect to interior decoration the lobby of the International Building and the foyer of the Music Hall are worth viewing as period pieces of Art Deco: design in which, in this instance, Beaux-Arts monumentality is wedded to jazz cubism and the Hollywood stage set as this was imagined for films of sophisticated life lived among skyscrapers. Miraculously intact, may these interiors continue to escape renovation. Stairways in tall spaces dominate both interiors. Within a narrow, columned hall which is markedly axial, the stair in the International Building is an escalator on axis and rising to a mezzanine as though it were a grand staircase (Fig. 32). This use of an escalator to a mezzanine floor, as Wallace Harrison has admitted, came to the Associated Architects from the contemporaneous Philadelphia Saving Fund Society Building.† Despite the rigidity and austerity of the treatment, and despite its compression into its tall corridor space, the treatment suggests the basic mock-up for the stage set for a Hollywood musical of the thirties before the decorative "finishing touches" had been applied.

In the foyer of the Music Hall these finishing touches are decidedly complete. A lofty room of generous width, its colors are the muted tans, bronzes, browns, and reds by which much modern of the thirties was given a "high club" flavor, and dotted with easy chairs and floor "ash receivers" to complete the allusion. With a magnificent sweep of stair at one end curving up to balconied overlooks, and another sweep down to lounges, the generous space as easily absorbs the movement of people at many levels as the carpeting and acoustical materials absorb sound. Almost as dominant as the stairs, cylindrical chandeliers, like upended pinnacles from the Empire State Building, hang as confections of frosted

* See pp. 92f. below.
† See pp. 261f. below.

FIGURE 32. *Rockefeller Center. View from the second-floor balcony of the four-story-high lobby of the International Building.*

glass, crystal beads, and bronze, from coved, gold-leafed ceilings. A paradisic garden mural in stylized flower shapes climbs the curved wall of the staircase. The setting—frivolous, but decorous too—calls for Packards, tuxedos, and evening gowns. Yet it manages to convey the message —frivolity with decorum—to the motley crowd waiting, patient and impressed, under the watchful eyes of a generous corps of ushers, for the "next show."

Aside from the nostalgic interest that Art Deco began to occasion toward the late sixties after an interval of neglect, the movement is historically interesting as a search for design capable of relating to the modern world, not with the technological purity of more earnest expressions of modernity, but with an abandon calculated to stimulate popular fantasy. Its formal and symbolic interest centers in the means by which the elitism of "abstract art" was transformed into a popular

79

FIGURE 33. *Rockefeller Center. Music Hall. Compare with Hans Poelzig's Grosses Schauspielhaus (opposite), Berlin, remodeled in 1919.*

imagery of modernism affecting the gamut of design from flashy consumer goods to architectural monumentality. Technically, Art Deco fascinates because of the evidence it gives of the delight in working new materials (like aluminum or stainless steel), or in creating new effects from old ones (like glass). Even the painters and sculptors working at Rockefeller Center eagerly sought to exploit materials in fresh ways. More than this, what was sought were surprising effects from an extravagant *palette* of materials: all kinds of metals (polished, matte, plated) mixed with glass (frosted, etched, even carved), not to mention the burgeoning availability of new kinds of plastics, and all of this in combination with exotic uses of traditional materials like stones and wood veneers. Finally, for students of architecture, there is a decidedly architectural quality about much Art Deco because its stylization is never far from the straight edge and compass.

Surely the architectural possibilities of Art Deco are conspicuous in the Music Hall itself. Its telescoped sequence of gilded acoustical plaster arches, dramatically focused on the proscenium of the great stage, is suspended from huge trusses which span the auditorium.[46] Among American theatres it is in the vanguard of those fully committed to modern

design. By way of preparation, Reinhard and Harrison accompanied the
then impresario for the Center, Samuel L. Rothafel ("Roxy" as he
was popularly known),‡ to Europe to inspect modern theatres.[47] What
they saw during their tour may have had less effect on the final design
than two remarks Roxy made during the boat trip over. Harrison has
recalled that, insofar as it was feasible in a theatre of such size, Roxy
wanted to emphasize the union of performance and audience within the
big space. To this end he wished to locate most of the seating on one
floor, with minimal balconies. Harrison also reports that a spectacular
sunset at sea inspired Roxy's wish for a "sunburst" around the audience,
a device which would both focus the eye of the audience on the stage
and radiate the activity of the stage to the audience, thereby intensifying
the sense of unity. If any modern European theatre influenced the Music
Hall, Harrison maintains that it was Hans Poelzig's Grosses Schauspielhaus in Berlin (remodeled in 1919) [Fig. 33]. The magical effect of the
sunset notwithstanding, Poelzig's theatre may have made a greater contribution to the Music Hall than Harrison's recollection assigned to it.
Poelzig designed his theatre in collaboration with Max Reinhardt, and

‡ Rothafel was the impresario for two theatres in the Center, the Music Hall and
RKO Roxy. He shortly disagreed with the management, however, whereupon RKO
Roxy became the Center Theatre. This was eventually demolished to make way for
the United States Rubber (now Uniroyal) Building.

for his use. The renowned director believed that architectural stage sets should replace painted scenery, that the stage should extend into the seating area, and that the audience should be given an architectural setting unifying play and playgoer. Surely at least the last part of Max Reinhardt's program was comparable to Roxy's notion about the design of the Music Hall. As eventually executed, a tier of three shallow mezzanines replaced the customary deep balcony. At either side of the stage, a stepped ramp climbing up the walls of the seating area to the first mezzanine makes it literally possible when desired to surround the audience by the performance. But the principal means of providing a sense of surround was of course the ceiling "sunburst."

It radiates the splash of the spectacle that Roxy bequeathed to the theatre.* An impression of one of tne first shows could be an impression of the most recent. "Orchestras began to come out of the floor playing Tchaikowsky's '1812 Overture,' and hordes of young girls in pretty ballet skirts began to tiptoe out of red silken hearts, only to tiptoe back into them again, while colored lights ran riot and monstrous organs played giddily."[48] Slightly exaggerated, what with the multiple orchestras and organs, the account is true in essence. If the thin, slotted pleating of the sunburst overhead is of a piece with the spectacle, it nevertheless represents a welcome change from the gilt chandeliers, scarlet velveteen, and gold tassels which had hitherto generally characterized theatre décor, while preserving the festive sumptuousness traditional in theatre interiors. The architects decorated the Music Hall with the techniques of architecture rather than with those of interior decoration. They designed curved surfaces with acoustical properties. They enlivened the gilding with concealed lights in changing patterns and colors, thus converting the sunburst into an aurora borealis. Although without apparent influence on the Music Hall, the classic American prototype is Adler & Sullivan's Auditorium in Chicago (Fig. 34). Here, too, curved shapes appropriate for ideal acoustical conditions telescope toward the stage, and even incorporate ventilating grilles, while Sullivan sprinkled the foliated surface ornament with light bulbs in a primitive example of festive integration of electric light with architecture. To compare the vigor of Adler's arches and the lyricism of Sullivan's ornament with the mechanical sleekness of the Music Hall ceiling is to discover again the difference between the architecture of genius and that of bureaucracy. Most people will prefer

* More serious entertainment was originally contemplated for at least one of the theatres, and Robert Edmond Jones was engaged as art director to supervise its presentation. Both theatres proved to be too large for anything but movies, vaudeville, and spectacles. Roxy and Jones were poles apart in their ideas on entertainment, and Jones left his job almost before he had begun it.

FIGURE 34. *Adler & Sullivan. Auditorium, Chicago, 1886–89.*

the mechanistic over the personal design, which is precisely what good bureaucratic design is supposed to insure by virtue of its group nature. To experience the two over a period of time, however, is to feel the powerful, and even poignant, image of the one over the thin appropriateness of the other.

Although there was nothing unprecedented about the Music Hall's ceiling, no previous theatre canopy boasted a more complex technological apparatus of lights, air-conditioning equipment, and amplifiers on such a scale. In thus wrapping the audience in a complex visual, auditory, thermal, and (on occasion) olfactory environment, the ceiling of the Music Hall demonstrates as spectacularly as any other single work of the period the vastly extended range of interior controls which modern technology gives to the architect.

83

THE CHALLENGE OF THE CENTER

The picture of thousands slumped in upholstered ecstasy beneath this mechanical heaven is possibly more disturbing than enthralling. So at least it seemed to virtually all of the thoughtful critics who evaluated the Center as it began to emerge—and precisely because they were thoughtful. Their disillusionment owed much to the fact that the high cultural ideal which had inaugurated the Center scheme had become dissipated in variety, broadcasting, and commerce. Those interested in modern architecture and planning attacked the partial modernism of the Center for its distortion of modern ideals. In both respects, the Center, which has been among the most adroitly promoted ventures in commercial real estate,[49] was partially victimized by its promotional promises. Thus Lewis Mumford could fairly condemn the Center in the early thirties for its cultural, esthetic, and urban deficiencies as "mediocrity—seen through a magnifying glass."[50]

There is some profit in criticizing the Center by the highest standards; as much can be learned from its shortcomings as from its virtues. But after all of its limitations have been tallied—the drawbacks of group design, the priority of finance and technology over art and culture—Rockefeller Center still emerges as a considerable triumph.

It provided the most complete embodiment of the modern ideal of the skyscraper metropolis of the period. The ideal had its deficiencies, since European theory had exaggerated the functional, humanistic, and symbolic benefits of skyscrapers—their remoteness in fact making them the more irresistible in theory. Defective as imagined, this ideal metropolis was even more so when translated into the Center complex: no accommodations for living; no broad green spaces; inadequate provision for parking and traffic; a compromise esthetic, and so on. But that a team dominated by a practical point of view should have designed a complex embracing many of the cardinal ideas of modern urbanism in the very center of Manhattan was in itself as remarkable as that a similar group of men, forty years earlier, had made a reality of Beaux-Arts competition projects in the Court of Honor at the Columbian Exposition.[51]† In both instances, large-scale, quasi-visionary urban schemes, essentially formulated in Europe, and grandiosely characteristic of the ideals of their respective periods, were injected in an abrupt and spectacular manner into the American environment. Both American

† Illustrated in *American Buildings and Their Architects: Progressive and Academic Ideals at the Turn of the Twentieth Century,* fig. 32.

84

complexes were realized in an atmosphere of practicality, system, and promotion, which transformed them from their European prototypes into something cruder socially, esthetically, and symbolically. Even so—or, perhaps, by virtue of this transformation—they acquired their own kind of vitality in combining commercial functions with civic concern.

Only the example of some large-scale complex like the Center could have inspired the redevelopment of downtown areas prevalent since World War II, even though imperious emphasis on the colossal commercial skyscraper has encouraged too much of it away from more balanced, more humanly scaled, urban renewal. Moreover, the mass destruction of blocks of old structures in order to build a completely new fabric, however warranted for the Center, has proved a disastrous precedent for other renewal situations.

Nevertheless, a measure of the quality of the Center appears in comparisons with subsequent large-scale projects inspired at least in part by it: Pittsburgh's Golden Triangle and Philadelphia's Penn Center, to cite merely the first major projects to have been realized since World War II. Both are more spectacularly sited than the Center, even if a little less at the heart of activity; both have had the advantage of some government funds, which the Center did not; both have had the experience of the Center on which to draw. Yet Rockefeller Center surpasses both of them visually, urbanistically, and even theoretically. Far more than these and other successors, it gives a sense of "place," and this in a city notorious for forces continuously at work to create placelessness. Here is *the* city square; *the* city Christmas tree; *the* city Easter display. Lesser aspects of the Center, too, as we have observed, have reinforced this sense of place; the skaters, *Prometheus, Atlas,* even the Rockettes. Through the mid-sixties—more than three decades after its inception, Rockefeller Center had yet to be matched.

CHAPTER II

The American Acceptance of the International Style: George Howe & William Lescaze's Philadelphia Saving Fund Society Building

Engineering may change completely from year to year, but the aesthetic of the New Pioneers has already shown a definite continuity of values separate from, and even on occasion in opposition to, those derived from the practical and the structural. . . . no name may be more than denotative for the work of the New Pioneers. Yet, for all their vagueness of over-statement Oud's claim that the new manner is "pure" architecture, or Lönberg-Holm's that it is a "time-space" architecture, even Van Doesburg's that it is "elementarist," have some slight meaning. To add another similar term profits little, but perhaps "technical" might be suggested. For the architecture of the New Pioneers in its establishment represented to a large extent—although not quite completely—the triumph of the technical point of view in the same way as the architecture of Romanticism represented in general the triumph of the anti-technical point of view. . . .

When the work is known, however, it is enough to call the architecture of the New Pioneers the international style of Le Corbusier, Oud and Gropius, of Lurçat, Rietveld and Miës van der Rohe, which is enrolling more and more the younger architects in Europe and many as well in America about to begin their building careers.

HENRY-RUSSELL HITCHCOCK,
Modern Architecture: Romanticism and Reintegration, 1929,
the first American attempt at a comprehensive treatment
of international developments in the modern movement
through the nineteenth century and the early twentieth.

CONSERVATIVE CLIENT; RADICAL BUILDING

Whereas Rockefeller Center exemplifies Beaux-Arts ideals becoming modern, Howe & Lescaze's contemporary skyscraper for The Philadelphia Saving Fund Society (1929–32) is fully committed to European modernism as this developed in the twenties. In fact, any list of the most

,can buildings embodying what has come to be popularly
ictional" phase of modern architecture, which began to
ery end of the 1920's in the United States, would surely
robably at the top—PSFS (thus neon letters announce it
to downtown Philadelphia), and along with it Richard Neutra's Lovell
House (1927–29) in Los Angeles (Fig. 71). Judged in terms of quality
and theoretical commitment, they are the pre-eminent American exemplars
of this kind of modernism. Of the two, PSFS is of course the more
conspicuous, and available to the public. In the development of the
bare-bones esthetic of modern skyscraper design, PSFS is the most important tall building erected between the Chicago School of the eighteen
eighties and nineties and the metal-and-glass revival beginning around
1950.

Today, the thirty-two-story skyscraper—still Philadelphia's tallest
building aside from the tower of the Victorian City Hall—may not at
first sight seem worth thoughtful scrutiny. The kind of design that
seemed daring around 1930 has become familiar by now and, what is
more, familiar in the devastating sense of having become *passé*. Writing
in 1949, in the first reappraisal of the building since the flurry of publicity
on its completion, Frederick Gutheim placed it in "an awkward age"
of modern architecture. "Not new enough to be contemporary," it was
then "not old enough to have become a readily placed historical monument."[1] As this is written in the sixties, PSFS still exists in the limbo
between past and present, although it begins to acquire the patina of
history.

It has been the more neglected because it does not seem at first
sight to be of much interest as an innovative building. Although it does
epitomize the coming of the European functionalist style of the twenties
to the United States, this event occurred so late as to make the building
seem more a synthesis of previous developments than a herald of new
departures. Yet it is precisely here, first as a synthesis, then as an
American synthesis, that PSFS is particularly worth scrutiny today. Close
observation, furthermore, reveals that PSFS is rather more innovative than
its appearance, date, and provincial position suggest. Finally—and Robert Stern[2] has developed this idea—PSFS is not quite the unadulterated
exemplar of the International Style that it seems to be. Far more deeply
committed to the modern movement though it may be than Rockefeller
Center, a residue of Beaux-Arts theory and design nevertheless permeates it. This too distinguishes it from its European prototypes.

A glance suffices to show how much more complexly the building
is massed than the average office skyscraper (Fig. 35). Although one is
immediately tempted to consider the complexity as a cubist tour de force
which has been arbitrarily determined by visual preferences, such is not

FIGURE 35. Howe & Lescaze. *Philadelphia Saving Fund Society Building, Philadelphia, 1929–32. Angled view showing the north (Market Street) and west (12th Street) elevations.*

the case. The massing discloses functional considerations. Since the building owes its very existence to these considerations, this is the proper place at which to begin its examination. In fact, journalistic reports indicate that at some point in the preliminary discussions of the design in 1930 a member of the Building Committee interrupted the architects' presentation with, "Gentlemen, this building will never be built."[3] Yet it was built, substantially as presented, with James M. Willcox, the President of the Society, leading his committee toward its eventual acceptance. He did so, as he later assured the press (and reassured his Board and the general public), not because the building was "ultra-Modern"— a quality he distrusted—but because he believed it to be "ultra-Practical."[4]

As the chairman and most forceful member of the Building Committee of the conservative institution which sponsored such a radical building, and without whose approval and support the building would surely have gone unrealized, Willcox is worthy of analysis. Unfortunately, he is an enigmatic client. He was outwardly aloof (so much so that George Howe always referred to him as "Mr. Willcox" whereas he addressed the other executives of the bank familiarly), and he was autocratic. Typically, he rarely consulted his committee, but himself made most of the decisions about the building in private discussion with Howe, the partner with whom Willcox exclusively consulted. The mystery is deepened in that Willcox had given no previous evidence of being interested in modern architecture. Quite the contrary, he was a respecter of tradition, although apparently not a connoisseur of the visual arts to any marked degree. He was, however, much traveled, and so well-educated that he must have been among the few American bank presidents of the twentieth century who were fluent in Latin. His portrait in the Board Room reveals something of his complex nature. Thin, elegant, with the long tapered fingers of an esthete, he sits with a certain indolence of posture strange to corporate portraiture; yet his steel-blue eyes look implacably penetrating. On second glance, what seems like indolence may actually be the act of settling back for keener observation. Though his physical powers were waning when the new building was being designed, he had lost none of the keenness of his mental faculties, and he doubtless viewed the skyscraper as something of a capstone to his service with the Society. He retired as President in 1934, and served as Chairman of the Board, a post newly created for him, until his death in 1935.

Proud of the institution over which he presided, he sought a monument worthy of it; yet he was equally concerned that it be a sound investment. In that he sought to guarantee a future for his building, he was an ideal client. This meant the anticipation of future office needs, possibly even of a "new look," so that PSFS would remain competitive with office buildings for decades—as indeed it has. But Willcox was an exacting client too, constantly testing Howe with respect to both his practical and his esthetic ideas.[5] As in all such novel ventures, only personal confidence could have brought the project to fruition. Strong in his personal trusts and distrusts, Willcox trusted Howe. After all, Howe was no wildly revolutionary modernist; but, like Willcox, saturated in the great tradition. In a series of commissions for branch banks for PSFS during the twenties, Howe had step by step reached beyond his Beaux-Arts training to grasp the future. Moreover, Howe's background and urbane intelligence attracted Willcox. As a final means in his testing process, it is reliably reported, Willcox frankly asked Howe whether he would pledge his word "as a gentleman" that he was providing the Society with a respectable building and not simply seeking novelty that would bring publicity to himself. "As a gentleman" Howe gave his word. Even if the report of this episode is not quite literally true, it essentially characterizes the milieu of client-architect consultation in which the design of PSFS matured, remote indeed from the "brave new world" élan of contemporary European modernism. That a man of Willcox's years in this conservative milieu could have ventured so boldly and astutely into an enterprise new to his experience is extraordinary. When Philadelphians praised PSFS to Howe, he frequently waved aside the compliments with, "It's Mr. Willcox's building."

THE "ULTRA-PRACTICAL" CONSIDERATIONS

The "ultra-Practical" features of the architects' scheme account for the unique massing of the building, which most clearly appears in aerial perspective (Fig. 36).[6] There was, first, the unusual suggestion that the bank move upstairs to the second floor so as to leave the ground level for revenue-producing shops, although there were some precedents in Philadelphia for this kind of arrangement. However, there was a subtler argument in favor of the elevated banking room. This building was (and is) in a high-volume, middle-class, rather than a luxury, shopping area, almost opposite the Reading Terminal. Its location was specifically chosen to attract the frugal middle-class depositor on whom savings banks thrive. Whatever encouraged shoppers in the vicinity of the bank would therefore work to its advantage. A ground-floor banking room would not generate shopping traffic, and would probably decrease it, much as strings of banks along certain downtown streets in New York make

FIGURE 36. *PSFS. Aerial perspective view.*

walking so dull as to drive pedestrians to other streets.* Whether it
was the bankers or the architects who first broached the possibility of
the second-floor banking room—and there is some uncertainty on the
point—the architects early were enthusiastic about its design possibilities
and fought for its adoption, while the bankers remained understandably
hesitant. As late as the end of April 1930 a final decision had yet to be
made.

Once approved, this elevated banking room determined the base of
the building: on the ground level is a band of shop windows forced
very low; above, the broad sweep of the curved glass wall (30 ft. high,
on a cantilever projecting 6 ft. 5 in.) to advertise the banking room.
The escalated entrance to the bank occurs at one corner of the building
on Market Street; the entrance to the elevator lobby of the office tower at
the other on 12th Street (Fig. 37). This idea of escalating the bank's

* See p. 10 above.

clientele at a corner of the building to the banking room, with entry to it at the center of one of the sides, would perhaps have appealed only to architects imbued with the modern philosophy of a dynamic approach to planning through the three-dimensional manipulation of space asymmetrically arranged. It is, for example, vaguely reminiscent of the manner in which the ramp brings one up beside the living room and terrace of Le Corbusier's famous Villa Savoye, although the partners, at best, could barely have heard of this, almost precisely contemporaneous, design when they planned the PSFS elevated banking room.[7]

The dynamism and asymmetry of the stores and banking room characterize the entire composition of the base of the building. Above the billboard scale of the curved glass window wrapped around the banking room, the sheer granite sheathing masks the trusses which span the banking chamber (Fig. 39). Above this, the base is topped by three more floors, which are devoted to bank operations—a compositional transition from banking chamber to office tower which may for convenience be designated as the "notch" of the building. Above these the cantilevering of the floors over Market Street signals the start of the rental office tower.

The tower reveals that the "ultra-Practical" rationale applies to the total composition as much as to the base, and results in the same dynamic asymmetry (Fig. 38). It is so shaped, and is so positioned on its base as permanently to ensure light and air for the interior. To be specific, the slab shape of the tower assures that no office space is more than 28 to 29 feet from a window. As a constituent shape of early modern massing, the slab was at this very time more spectacularly emerging as the dominant focus of Rockefeller Center.† The off-center positioning of the tower on its podium further ensures well-lighted offices for there is a roughly 45-foot setback against future building to the west on Market Street, as well as a 20-foot setback plus the width of 12th Street to the east. Market Street protects the front (north) elevation, while the spine—encasing elevators, fire stairs, and vertical utilities—barricades the rear (south) elevation against future building. This narrow spine at the rear of the building and at right angles to the slab of the office tower gives a T-shaped configuration to the tower as a whole. For roof-top glamour, the architects added the complex packaging of an executive suite and terrace; an observation platform (now a TV relay station), topping the spine as the highest element in the building; and, finally, the billboard shield of the cooling towers for air conditioning. Hence the massing: complex, but utterly logical. As Howe wrote in one of his letters to Willcox, "an organic asymmetry has been

† See pp. 45ff. above.

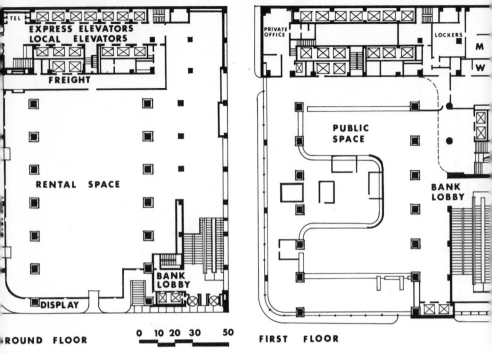

FIGURE 37. *PSFS. Plans of the ground floor (for stores) and of the elevated banking room (here labeled "first floor"). The entrance to the banking room is by stairs and escalator from Market Street (lower right corner of the plans). The entrance to the office tower is on the ground level, behind the stores, from 12th Street (upper left corner of the plans).*

produced far more interesting than the usual scholastic and unthinking axial symmetry." "The soundest precedent for such asymmetries," he went on, doubtless thinking of Le Corbusier's *Vers une architecture,* which makes the same comparison, "are to be found in the grouping of numerous buildings in Greek architecture, as on the Acropolis, for a modern building is really a group of many smaller buildings. While thinking always in terms of utility and economic soundness we have constantly kept architectural effect in view and by a logical and reasoned use of the elements natural to a business building have produced an irregular and organic mass of impressive effect."[8]

The evolution of the mass from the utility and economics of its interior space is further demonstrated in a cross section of the building (Fig. 39). This shows the structural columns for the office tower rising, four abreast, from a deep truss (16½ ft. deep) which bridges the banking chamber in a 63-foot span, and thus permits the broad open space below. Compartmented office spaces toward the top of the building;

94

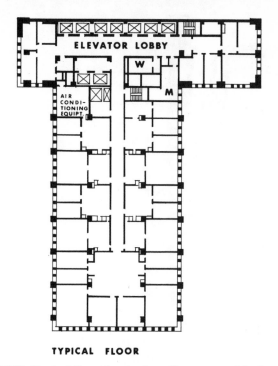

TYPICAL FLOOR

FIGURE 38. *PSFS. Typical floor plan in the office tower, with the elevator spine to the rear. The tower slab is asymmetrically placed with respect to the base of the building for maximum light and air.*

open space at its base: this concept had been one of the starting points of the architects' thinking. Later, in a general article on modern architecture written after PSFS had been completed, Howe expressed the seeming defiance of gravity natural to modern skeletal construction in a metaphor which vividly describes this cross section: "the true sculptural quality of an organic design arises from the moulding of internal space and the shaping of the skeleton to contain it. The functional architect delights in [the] huge torso [of the building] swaying on tendoned ankles. He would no more attach false stone pedestals on them than he would put lead shoes on Pegasus."[9] The supports at either end of the trussing provide flanking rows of columns for the interior of the banking chamber, quite as monumental as their classicistic veneered equivalents in Beaux-Arts banking rooms, but here sheerly clad in marble with a severity and breadth of surface which suggests the most rudimentary of Egyptian piers (Figs. 44, 45).

The more-than-one-story-deep trusses not only bridged the space below but provided partial support for the vaults. An air-borne vault is somehow the ultimate in the early modern quest for antigravitational effects. The webbing of the trusses was also interwoven with air-condi-

95

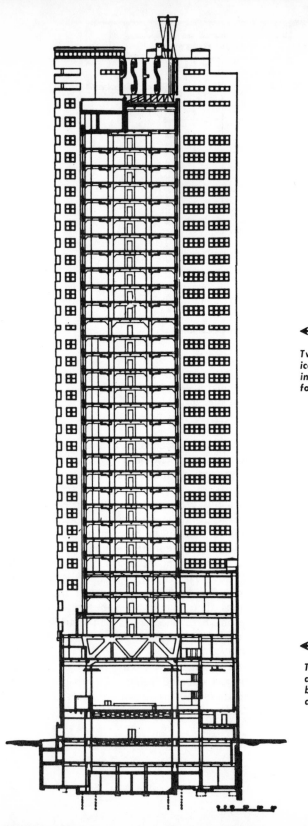

Twentieth floor: mechan-
ical equipment, includ-
ing air-conditioning
for offices.

Third floor truss space:
air-conditioners for
bank. Store conditioners
are in basement.

tioning and other mechanical equipment for the bank. The twentieth floor contains similar equipment for the office tower, a change in function that is indicated by the reduced width of the ribbon window. This subtle, but frank, revelation of the special character of the service floor further testifies to the scrupulosity of the architects in making the different internal functions of the building explicit on the exterior. Although such frankness with respect to service floors in skyscrapers continued to be rare right through the sixties, examples do occur and multiply from the fifties on. But, as Banham has written, the concern to give some architectural articulation to the mechanical system, instead of burying it, is one of the more progressive aspects of PSFS.[10]

Air conditioning is, in fact, another radical aspect of PSFS. It was the second skyscraper in the United States to be completely air-conditioned, preceded only by the twenty-one-story Milam Building in San Antonio, which was completed in 1928, four years prior to PSFS. The architects had recommended it from the beginning; but the Building Committee had originally decided to air-condition only the first four floors (stores, banking room, and executive offices), plus the roof-top executive suite. Desiring to make PSFS as attractive as possible to prospective tenants—and especially mindful of the competition of the Fidelity-Philadelphia Trust and the Girard Trust Buildings then rising, neither of which boasted air conditioning—the Committee gave serious thought to extending the system throughout the building. A particularly stifling summer in 1930, as building operations got under way, is supposed to have accelerated this change of thinking, but only after the steel had been erected to the twentieth floor. Finally, in its own space within the building, PSFS installed another pioneering feature: acoustical ceiling tiles, clipped onto a metal framework in a manner which has become standard practice.

Such, in brief, were the "ultra-Practical" considerations that characterized this innovative design. As in other modern buildings, its unornamented quality could also be regarded as a practical feature. At least Howe & Lescaze emulated other modern architects in justifying an esthetic preference for laconic precision as an economy measure. The economy of this austere esthetic here, as in other modern buildings, however, was counterbalanced by the meticulous craftsmanship which such austerity demands, and by the frequent complexity concealed behind apparent simplicity, as in the complicated bracketing required to suspend the cantilevered granite curve of the banking chamber over the shops. In PSFS the very expensive materials employed, both inside and out, further increased initial costs. The exterior of the building appears metallic in photographs, and the architects doubtless approved of this crisp, sheer, homogeneous effect as the outward semblance of the (much cruder)

FIGURE 39. *PSFS. Cross section through the office tower slab.*

metal skeleton. In fact, had the Philadelphia building code then permitted, they would have used metal spandrel panels, instead of brick, beneath the windows.[11] PSFS is, however, largely a masonry-sheathed building. Polished charcoal-colored granite clothes the base, up to the top of the trusses over the bank space. Sand-colored limestone covers the three floors in the notch, as well as the columns of the office tower. The spandrels of the office tower are a dun-gray, mat brick, with black brick partly glazed, partly unglazed, for the spine. The prominence of the aluminum windows is of course primarily responsible for the metallic aspect of the elevations. These windows were among the earliest to make large-scale use of this material.

As the onset of the Depression drove down the cost of materials, the clients wisely refused the timid course of cutting corners, as they wisely declined to halt building operations altogether. Instead they made the best of the bargain and somewhat increased their expenditures for quality materials. As a result, PSFS not only presents the ageless solidity of fine masonry with metals on the exterior, but in the stair hall and banking room offers an even more sumptuous display of contrasting marbles set off against glass and satin-finished stainless steel. This last marked yet another innovation, since PSFS was even more venturesome in its extravagant use of stainless steel than of aluminum. The clients salved their consciences with respect to this extravagance, not only because they bought at bargain rates, but because they expected that such quality would reduce the cost of upkeep. This has proved to be the case. Beautifully maintained, solidly built and equipped, functionally planned with careful thought for its future, PSFS has proved a handsome investment. Well might Willcox have praised its "ultra-Practicality."

The "Ultra-Modern" Design

If "ultra-Practical" considerations provided the starting point for Howe & Lescaze's design, what resulted was an "ultra-Modern" image, as judged by visual standards prevailing in the early thirties. The architects were fully conscious of their radicalism. Late in life, George Howe liked to quote the philosopher Edgar Singer: "Only the art whose purpose is to change the purposes of the beings to whom it is addressed is a fine, freeing art. The artist must be a messenger of discontent."[12]

Howe approached his radical position gradually. Born in Worcester, Massachusetts, in 1886, progressing through Groton to Harvard, then to the École des Beaux-Arts, along the way he had married into a family prominent in Philadelphia, and had settled in that city in 1913. There he soon joined the firm of Mellor & Meigs. He speedily achieved a partnership; so speedily, that as early as 1916 the firm became Mellor, Meigs & Howe, when its youngest partner had barely turned thirty. The firm enjoyed a national reputation for suburban houses, particularly for adaptations of the local colonial masonry tradition, and increasingly during the twenties for variants on French manorial buildings. In later life, Howe dismissed the suave eclecticism of this period as "Wall Street Pastorale." Yet even during his eclectic period, Howe was interested in simplification. To this end he and Meigs went abroad in the early twenties to study the peasant farm houses and the more vernacular manors of Normandy and Brittany, bringing the results of their studies to suburban Philadelphia. Howe's fascination with the elemental forms of vernacular building was part of his growing interest in the modern movement generally. Even as a student he had been remotely interested in modern developments, especially in Jugendstil (the German equivalent of Art Nouveau), and as a practitioner he continued to read widely about them. "In 1928," he later said, "I delivered my last Jumbo, Anti-economy Romantic Country House package." At the age of forty-two he courageously abandoned one of the most profitable practices in Philadelphia to strike out in a new direction.

He practiced alone for the better part of a year. It was during this period, when he had left his old partners Mellor and Meigs, and prior to inviting Lescaze into partnership, that the design of PSFS as it exists today began to emerge. The commission for the building at 12th and Market Streets had come to Mellor, Meigs & Howe as early as 1926, when Howe designed a conservative set-backed tower veneered in a semi-modern manner, and topped by a huge illuminated globe.[13] Fortunately, the PSFS design was delayed while the bank tested the site with a temporary structure, leaving in abeyance all decisions—whether to build a skyscraper or a small building, even whether to build at all—until the results of the test were in. By the time the trial period was over, the 1926 design was unthinkable to Howe, and he prepared new schemes in March 1929, one of which anticipates many of the principal features of the completed building, as well as its modern appearance (Fig. 40). The office tower already appeared as a narrow slab. The elevator spine was clearly revealed at the back of the structure, with its lobby off 12th Street. The columns for the office slab came down, as in the final building, four abreast on the girder which spanned the three-story banking room and permitted the open space flanked by the rows of pier-like columns. Lastly, the tower slab was asymmetrically placed on the total available site so that light and air would be permanently assured to the offices; this meant using the width of 12th Street plus a narrow setback to protect the east elevation, and

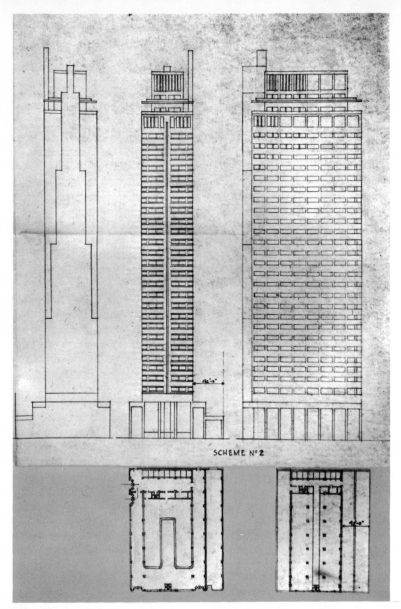

SCHEME N° 2

FIGURE 40. *PSFS. Projected scheme number 2 for the skyscraper, dated March 20, 1929, by George Howe. Left to right: rear elevation showing stepped projection for elevators; front (Market Street) elevation with vertical strip window rising the height of the building and the depressed roofline of the store to the right to emphasize the symmetry of the design; side (12th Street) elevation. Below: plans of the ground-floor banking room and of a typical floor in the office tower.*

a setback twice as wide to protect the west elevation against the possibility of a future skyscraper on the adjacent site.

In the March 1929 projection, the asymmetry of the tower placement is concealed by the depressed store at ground level, which Howe appended to the basic composition as though it were not part of the skyscraper. This Beaux-Arts partiality for symmetrical composition harassed the scheme throughout. It is notably evident in the vertical window running the full height of the front façade, a device to light a fire stair (the enclosure of which plunges through the center of the banking room and immediately behind the plate-glass window, in a particularly awkward manner). It is evident as well in the arbitrary symmetry of the stepped elevator tower, tacked as a kind of bustle to the rear of the slab and creating awkward wall surfaces behind.‡ The façade of the ground-floor banking hall recalls the traditionally becolumned Beaux-Arts image, although the planar sheerness of its suggested treatment and the extensive use of plate glass derive from modern design. The same dilution of modern ideas with the classicistic remnants of academic composition appears in the roof-top pavilion, which houses the executive suite and building machinery. A little thin on the Market Street elevation, the pavilion is especially elegant in the broadside view. There the proportions of the window openings create a handsome counterpoint of large and small, of horizontal and vertical, and the wall is visually braked to a halt rather than physically capped by a cornice or by a stepped pyramidal composition.

In sum, the scheme of March 1929 displays a compromise between Beaux-Arts and modern, its deficiencies stemming especially from the rigidities imposed by Beaux-Arts symmetry. But many of the most creative features of the final building appear in this scheme. Compared to the contemporaneous protomodernism of the Daily News, McGraw-Hill, or Rockefeller Center, Howe's scheme was far more advanced.

About a month later, on May 1, 1929, William Lescaze signed a partnership agreement with Howe. Howe had made the overtures. The partnership promised to be mutually advantageous. According to the terms of the agreement, Howe was to manage the business and client side of the firm; Lescaze would manage the drafting room and supervise construction. The partnership provided a base of operations in New

‡ The symmetrical arrangement, which reflects the progressive fall-away of the elevator banks (see p. 45) is, moreover, thoroughly impractical. Practical considerations would dictate that the low-bank elevators be placed side by side, the elevators in the next higher bank be adjacent to one another, and so on. Such arrangement is not only practical for the elevator machinery but convenient for the passenger. It would be very confusing to enter a lobby and find elevators to the lower floors at either end of the range of cabs.

York where Lescaze was practicing, as well as in Philadelphia. Howe had the more discriminating taste, and by far the more experience in practical building. Lescaze was the better draftsman and, most important for Howe, he was committed to the modern movement. To venture into modern architecture in the United States in 1929 was not only risky, but lonely as well. One needed information. One needed companionship too; this for personal support, but also in order to feel oneself as part of a group engaged in a movement which *must* triumph simply because it was right. Here was the peculiar challenge of European modernism of the twenties: the excitement of doing something differently, but with the conviction that what was different must eventually become the norm. In Europe the modernists had come to their convictions as students and young men. In the United States at this time, save for émigrés like Neutra and Schindler, it was a few successful practitioners saturated in Beaux-Arts training who groped, more or less wholeheartedly, toward modern ideas; and some, like Howe, perhaps, must have felt a passionate yearning to recover lost youth.

It has been customarily assumed that the design of PSFS owed more to Lescaze than Howe: that Lescaze almost wholly originated the design for PSFS (as seems to have been the case for most of the work done during the brief partnership), with Howe serving merely as critic. The design of March 1929, however, indicates that prior to the partnership Howe had substantially blocked out what came to be the final design of the skyscraper. Although Lescaze does not recall ever having seen Howe's early scheme, it is too close to the building as realized not to have been influential. It may well have been so quickly absorbed and settled upon as to have become an assumption for the design when serious work on it resumed at the end of the year—so much "given" that it did not need to be "designed." Of the always ticklish decision as to who is responsible for what in any collaboration, where the collaborators themselves may be hazy, we need say little more here.*

Once the partnership was consummated and design on PSFS resumed, Lescaze's more unequivocal commitment to modern architecture speedily eliminated the stultifying symmetry of the initial scheme. The junior member of the new firm,[14] born in Geneva, Switzerland, in 1896, and therefore ten years younger than Howe, had studied at the Zürich Technische Hochschule, an institute offering an architectural curriculum comparable to that of American universities. Lescaze specifically chose the school because Karl Moser was on its faculty. From him, Lescaze

---

* See the more detailed discussion in articles by Jordy, pp. 61–71, and by Stern, pp. 90–92 cited in the introduction to the Notes for this chapter, at the back of the book.

imbibed a predilection for modern architecture. He worked in the war-devastated areas of France in 1919 and 1920, and came to the United States in the latter year. He left Europe, as he recalls, for no better reason than that his interest in the "monumental" led to Moser's suggestion that "maybe America" might offer more promise for an ambitious young architect than postwar Europe. He worked in Cleveland for three years as a draftsman before returning to New York in 1923 to open his own office. During the none too prosperous years immediately following his eastern move he realized a few modern interiors and some minor buildings. He also designed two projects: a scheme entered in the international competition for the League of Nations and a deluxe version of "The Future American Country House," as the editors of the *Architectural Record* called it on its publication.[15] These were the adventurous days of modernism, and the country house flaunted an airplane runway and hangar. A washroom off the family hangar included, in addition to the usual facilities, a faucet for gasoline to remove the grime of flying!

Lescaze's Philadelphia connections began with the renovation of the offices of a young Philadelphia investment broker, who introduced Howe to Lescaze. At about the same time, and shortly before the formation of the partnership, Lescaze received a commission from the Leopold Stokowskis for a new nursery school for the Oak Lane Country Day School. This well-known structure, designed in 1929 by Lescaze, and allegedly the first school building in the International Style to have been realized in the United States,[16] was the initial fruit of the partnership. Negotiations on the PSFS skyscraper and, in the fall, assessment of the advisability of proceeding with the commission following the stock market crash seem to account for a hiatus in its design from the spring of 1929 until the end of the year.

Between December 1929 and July 1930 Howe & Lescaze produced a near final design for the building—this phase clearly dominated by Lescaze. Then a model was made and presented to the Building Committee late in July 1930 (Fig. 41).[17] At the very beginning of this period of intensive design, Lescaze conceived the distinctive base of the building, which was essentially like the one that now exists. His familiarity with cubist vision and the asymmetry typical of modern vision eliminated the Beaux-Arts compromise of Howe's early scheme. As it appears in the model, the base logically embraces a complicated plan, one especially so because of the second-floor banking room. For the monumental earlier base with but a single floor of usable space, the newer design substitutes an eight-story podium for the rental office tower, containing space both for stores and for the bank. The bustle-like appendage for the elevators in Howe's early scheme is here expanded into a forceful block, converting the slab to a T. Finally, the classicized pavilion of Howe's scheme gives way to a less elegant roof-top structure, which was more "modern" (in the sense of the "modern" of the time) in that it was mechanistic rather than architectural in concept, appearing like the superstructure of an ocean liner. It recalled Le Corbusier's famous exhortation to architects in his *Vers une architecture* of 1923 that they look to the functional, yet abstract, forms of contemporary machinery if they would capture *l'esprit nouveau* in their buildings.

Despite these advantages, the model reveals deficiencies too. Barely discernible in the photograph are the gaucheries of *moderne* detail, exciting then but faded now. The zigzag shop windows and the projecting slab folded like a piece of cardboard over the Market Street entrance to the bank are examples. So is the overly complex vertical treatment of the windows at the corner of the spine, depending, like the McGraw-Hill Building (Fig. 29), on a two-dimensional color pattern rather than on more basic architectonic definition. The bracketed sign in the "notch" is unfortunate. So, above all, is the pointless canopy hung around the floor immediately above the trussing for the banking room. The architects justified this projection as a ceremonial parasol shading important executive offices,† or alternatively as a distinguishing feature for an upstairs "merchandise mart." Their halfhearted rationalization underscored its principal purpose as a visual fillip to massing which threatened to become stodgy. For the same reason the top of the base is interlocked with the bottom of the office slab in a kind of cubist knot, again more appropriate to painting than to architecture. Both the canopy and the interlocked masses are awkward gropings toward the forceful cantilevering which eventuated over Market Street (Fig. 35).

If the critical juncture of the major masses at the "notch" is unresolved in the model, so is the composition of the roof-top complex. Despite its boldness in concept, the rigid symmetry of the composition jars with the asymmetry of the rest of the massing. The large scale of the window fronting the aggressive thrust of the executive suite‡ is a notable defect in a composition which underwent much juggling before its final determination.

So the model was both brave and clumsy. The Building Committee hesitated over such "ultra-Modernity." It must have been at this time that one of its members promised the architects that it "would never be

---

† The offices for the chief executives of the bank are actually located at the bottom of the spine on a series of floors immediately over the entrance to the office tower on 12th Street. Their placement was probably undecided in July 1930.
‡ Today this window would uncomfortably recall a television screen. This is no fault of the design of 1930, but it indicates how architecture is visually devalued when too readily identified with product design; see also p. 344 below.

FIGURE 41. PSFS. *Two views of the model of the building as presented July 1930.*

built." By what miracle of persuasion on Howe's part and understanding on Willcox's the design weathered the initial shock at its presentation we cannot tell, since written records of meetings between clients and architects do not exist, except for a series of masterly memoranda in which the architects accounted for all of their major design decisions in "ultra-Practical" terms. As late as November and December of 1930 the architects were still preparing variants of their design with a more traditional look in response to suggestions from members of the Committee disquieted by its revolutionary nature.[18] Once they had partially acquiesced to the architects' point of view, however, it seems to have been relatively easy for the architects to demonstrate that all the suggested compromises with tradition were hopeless.

On one point, however, the architects could not budge the Committee. Or rather they could not budge Willcox.[19] Howe's early scheme (Fig. 40) shows the columns of the office slab at the wall surface, but in the model these are set behind the wall, with the floors cantilevered from them to a parapet running under the ribbon windows. The cantilevered floor slab with the ribbon window had become protocol in modern architecture because, as Howe argued with Willcox, the window bands celebrated the ultimate reality of skeletal framing. Howe's reasoning for favoring ribbon windows was identical to that which had inspired Hood to a similar, even if somewhat faked, window treatment for the McGraw-Hill Building.* The skeletal-framed skyscraper is a stack of horizontal spaces supported by widely separated supports of minimal bulk, where volume not mass, void not wall, is the essence of the building. Cantilevered balconies best express this structural logic. Willcox did not dispute Howe's rationale in favor of the cantilevered window ribbons; he deplored its result. Ribbon windows suggested factories or warehouses to him—and, indeed, the American factory building, with its reinforced concrete skeleton filled in with glass areas even more markedly horizontal than the Chicago window, was a primary source of inspiration to the modern architect. True to his conditioning by modern European architecture, Howe found factories and warehouses to be more handsome than most so-called "architecture." But he further assured Willcox that fine proportions, handsome materials, and careful detailing would provide the architectural distinction required in an office building.

---

* That Howe & Lescaze were more profoundly sensitive to the skyscraper as volume rather than mass appears in the very nature of this model when it is compared with the clay and plaster models made for Rockefeller Center (and presumably for the McGraw-Hill Building). This model, hollow and of light construction, is typical of the kind favored by modern architects, just as clay and plaster models emphasize the compositional bulk and external patterning prized in Beaux-Arts design; see p. 56 above.

That most prospective tenants would in the early thirties be sufficiently discriminating to associate Howe & Lescaze's ribbon windows with anything other than an industrial structure Willcox doubted. As for Howe's first argument, that the piling of a series of horizontal spaces was the essence of a skyscraper, Willcox counterattacked with the argument that it was quite as logical to consider the height of the building—the *pile* rather than the *spaces*—as its essence. "In discussing the subject a few days ago with a man of decided artistic cultivation and accomplishments," Willcox wrote to Howe—

> he said your sketch with its explanation is very interesting, but he added, why not follow out the idea to its logical conclusion. If the walls of the building are only a curtain why not get away from anything that suggests masonry and substitute large units of flat material that would look more like a curtain and not a wall, heavy glass if you will that will keep out the weather and could be made to produce decidedly attractive color effects. Of course, he went too far [the Hallidie Building was forgotten,† and the metal-and-glass walls of the fifties were yet to come], but it seems to me he grasped your idea.[20]

In short, just as Rockefeller wanted "Gothic" verticality for his Center, whereas Hood wanted modern horizontality, so Willcox fought the same battle with his architects. Once more, should the design emphasize the expressive height of the skyscraper or the functional realities of its structure and space? The opinion of real estate experts seems to have been decisive on this issue for the Center; the nuisance of columns freestanding in the space close to the windows appears to have been the deciding factor here. As in the case of the Center, the management group argued that columns in the wall, rather than inside it, provided convenient anchors for office partitioning. The architects pleaded in vain for their modern point of view. Willcox was adamant. The outermost columns of the office slab would be moved to the walls. Verticals would be introduced into the window wall. "For my part," Willcox had concluded in his earlier letter to Howe, "I don't see why vertical could not be combined with horizontal lines as decoration, if they would relieve the monotony and be decorative. That, not structure, would be their justification."

With these demands the client, by sheer chance, saved the design! What was a mediocre design in the model, however exceptional for its

† Illustrated in *American Buildings and Their Architects: Progressive and Academic Ideals at the Turn of the Twentieth Century,* fig. 31.

day, became a distinguished design with the addition of the verticals. But only because of the way in which the architects handled them. Had the architects literally followed Willcox's suggestion, they need only have created a "decorative" slip cover of vertical stripes up the sides of the office slab, as Hood had substantially done for the Daily News Building or as the Associated Architects, following suit, would soon do at the Center. Architecturally, Howe & Lescaze chose a more profound alternative. They pulled the structural columns partially through the side walls of the office slab—and, in the process, incidentally, demonstrated how sincerely they argued from structural principles in originally recommending the alternate scheme of the continuous cantilevers. In so doing, they visibly opposed the structure (or rather the most dramatic aspect of it) to the spread of the space inside (Fig. 42).‡

If the projecting columns facilitated office planning, it also resolved a number of esthetic problems which had plagued the model. Willcox got the expressive lift he sought in the tower; but the architects retained to a considerable degree the sense of the horizontal spread of the floors which they had sought. In short, the opposed verticals and horizontals dramatized both aspects of the tower. The monotonous banding of the continuously cantilevered office floors is visibly propped and visually enlivened by the projecting columns, which also provide rhythm, as well as light and shadow. These qualities heighten the contrast between the slab of the office tower on the one hand, and the smooth enclosure of the base and spine on the other. The contrast is effected naturally, without the tortured two-dimensional design by which the fenestration of the spine had been differentiated from that of the slab in the model. The awkward interlocked juncture of the office slab and its base is rectified. The cantilevering, now limited to the narrow face of the slab over Market Street, is the more effective for there being less of it. The

‡ This gave one final twist to an age-old architectural paradox—one with particular relevance, however, for modern architecture, which has, in theory, if not always in practice, made a fetish of revealed structure, thereby indicating the technological bias of its esthetic principles. To make structure more apparent (a matter of design) is not always to utilize it with the utmost efficiency (a matter of technology). In fact, the most efficient frame for PSFS would have been that originally recommended by the architects, with inset columns and cantilevered slabs. By moving the vertical columns outside the wall so that they abutted the ends of the horizontal beams, the connections between columns and beams became inherently less stable, just as table legs set at the very corners of the top are inherently less stable than those slightly recessed from the corners. The weakened connections required special triangular bracketing for the frame (apparent in the cross section, Fig. 39). This bracketing made the frame a stack of rigid, arch-like units, technically termed "portal frames"; see discussion in *Engineering News-Record*, November 10, 1932, pp. 549–52.

FIGURE 42. *PSFS. General view from the west showing the 12th Street elevation. The tower of John McArthur, Jr.'s Victorian City Hall, 1871–94, appears in the right background.*

visible column, moreover, provides an anchor which intensifies the act of projection as the essential drama of the cantilever. This cantilever of the floor slabs beyond the containing rhythm of the protruded columns also energizes the forward thrust of the entire tower. The verticality of the tower is set against the horizontality of the base. Horizontality here is appropriate because it *is* a base, and appropriate, too, for the bulk space which it contains. Finally, the columnar treatment of the exterior is homogeneous with the columnar emphasis within the banking room (Figs. 37, 44).

All in all, the projecting columns of the office slab may be regarded as the third major design decision in the determination of the mass. The first was Howe's initial separation of the major units of the massing, his conception of the office tower as a narrow slab asymmetrically placed on a base, his determination of the basic nature of the structural skeleton, and his treatment of the windows substantially as horizontal bands. The second was Lescaze's transformation of this semimodern, semi-classicistic image (which, to repeat, he insists that he did not actually see, but of which he must have been aware) into a more specifically modern image. Thus Lescaze would seem primarily responsible for the asymmetry of the base, the cubist forcing of the spine into a strong opposition with (and support of) the other compositional elements, the intensification of the window banding, the accentuation of the contrast among the major compositional elements by means of color contrasts and other surface effects, and, finally, the redesign of the penthouse complex as it appeared in the model which prepared the way for the eventual solution. Although neither partner can be considered especially responsible for the projecting verticals when they both fought so persistently for the circumferential cantilevers, the effect of this decision is something of a return to the rhythmic structural sense of Howe's Neoclassic project. Certainly, the projecting columns provided the final key to the puzzle of the massing. Once in place, all the pieces locked together as a visual and logical entity. With the decision to project the columns, the basic composition of the exterior mass was fixed up to the roof top. Working drawings were filed in January 1931, and excavation began in February.

The last vestige of symmetry disappeared with the rethinking of the roof-top complex. Redesign became urgent when air conditioning required cooling towers, which were eventually screened within the triangular space of the hinged billboard. The accommodation of this dominating mass on the roof top would have been difficult within any of the symmetrical schemes. The further desire to angle the signs for maximum visibility militated against a symmetrical treatment. If such empiricism encouraged asymmetry, reasons of esthetic congruity doubtless encouraged the irregular arrangement too (Fig. 36). The perch of the erstwhile observation platform is asymmetrically counterweighted by the immense sign. The depressed wedge of the corner solarium splits the walls of the office tower rising above it, permitting the board room to fit on one side (over Market Street) and the executive dining room on the other (over 12th Street). Finally, with the abandonment of the observation platform for the more lucrative television facilities, Louis McAllister added a particularly graceful antenna (1949–50) to complete the composition as it now exists. The uniqueness of this roof top among American skyscrapers is surprising. One wonders why this kind of asymmetrical Acropolis to modern functionalism has not inspired others. Blunt it may be; but it is much sounder and potentially much more expressive than the skyscraper crown that is spire or cornice, or in which there is simply sheer termination of the geometrical mass.

Surveying this exterior massing as a whole, Gutheim has well expressed the contrasting qualities apparent in the building, and attributed these to the contrasting sensitivities of the partners. "Most of all, the building has that unique combination of boldness, of rugged strength approaching ugliness that was Lescaze's polytechnic contribution, and of richness, luxury and refinement approaching over-refinement that was Howe's."[21] The statement seems fair enough from what one knows of the work of the two architects apart from their collaboration—always providing that Howe's contribution to PSFS is not limited to the mere refinement of his partner's broad design.

The same paradoxical qualities of form appear in the interior (Figs. 43, 44 and 45). Here the precious qualities of the expensive materials, and, despite the planar boldness of the design, their more complex relationships tend to emphasize the "refinement approaching over-refinement." Both architects, however, were actively engaged on the interiors. Perhaps the single vantage point from which best to seize the sumptuous elegance of these interiors is a position in the banking room looking across the space toward the two mezzanine balconies, although the photographs do not do the actual experience justice. The yellow sienna marble fronts of these balconies flow in an S-curve behind the columns, the alternate faces of which are surfaced in Belgian-black and oyster-white marble. The columns support a dull maroon-colored shelf, which serves as a baffle to lighting troughs projected just under the off-white acoustical ceiling. Originally (before alterations) the concealed lighting made a luminous plane of the ceiling. Vents for the air conditioning are also concealed with the lights by means of the dropped shelf. Hence the ceiling design integrating lighting, air conditioning, and acoustical properties, is, as Banham points out, a primitive, but significant, unification of environmental elements—one eventuating in the om-

FIGURE 43. *PSFS. Escalated entrance to the banking room.*

nipresent mechanical ceilings that only became perfected and prevalent in the 1950's.

Where not of metal and glass, the walls are sheathed in two shades of gray marble. The floors are dark gray granite, the counter fronts are Belgian black. Chrome furniture upholstered in blue leather (all of it originally designed or specified by the architects) completes the basic design of the interior. The asymmetrical oppositions are forceful, but subdued in color and sumptuousness. The room was even more subdued originally, when the only artificial light was that gently spread across the ceiling and that from chrome-plated counter lights.[22] Not even the big curved window wall dispelled the shadowy quality of the interior; although it must be admitted that this window wall highlights the marble sheen in patches of reflection and glare, thereby making the organization of the interior less sharply defined than would have been

FIGURE 44. PSFS. Perspective drawing of the banking room.

FIGURE 45. PSFS. View showing the entrance and curved mezzanine balconies of the central banking space prior to the opening of the building. This interior was subsequently altered in minor ways.

FIGURE 46. *PSFS. Typical office space with furnishings selected or designed by the architects, taken at the time of the opening of the building in the mid-thirties. Note especially the ceiling and fixture treatment.*

the case with more even lighting, duller surfaces, and stronger color contrasts. Opposed to intense colors, Howe especially sought the muted splendor of this interior. To his clients he summarized the over-all effect of the building: "The design is 'modern' in the sense that it is based on economic and structural logic. It is, however, subdued and dignified in ornament and coloring."[23] On its completion, the London *Architectural Review* heralded the room for its "simple and impressive grandeur which is unique in modern architecture."[24]

The same subdued effect appeared in the office corridors. In these, Belgian-black wainscoting, regularly interrupted by flush doors in blue with stainless steel hardware, is topped by plaster walls painted a dull yellow, with some in Pompeian red.[25] The walls of the roof-top executive suite furnish a veritable catalogue of rare woods set off one against the other in broad planes, like the marbles in the banking room. Since the architects designed not only these interiors as spaces, but also much of the furniture in the areas occupied by the bank, plus much of the equipment throughout the building, PSFS provides one of the most comprehensive demonstrations (perhaps literally the most lavish demonstration) of the integration of industrial interior design with the so-called functional style of modern architecture. Unfortunately, we cannot examine here the

FIGURE 47. *Skidmore, Owings & Merrill. Branch office of the Manufacturers Hanover Trust Company at Fifth Avenue and 43rd Street, New York, built 1953–54.*

quality of this design, ranging from the tradition-inspired modern of the roof-top executive suite (which seems closer to Howe's sensibility than to his partner's) to check-writing tables asymmetrically supported on a single sinuous bent of chrome tubing in the banking room (closer to Lescaze's). In this interior design, the influence of Walter Baermann, a German émigré engaged by Howe & Lescaze about 1931, seems to have been particularly important.[26] Nor is it possible to detail the extent of this design: not only a full schedule of furniture, but office doors, hardware, plumbing fixtures, equipment design, clocks, typography—most of it still in use, some of it faintly dated, much of it meriting inclusion in the history of modern design.

It required a quarter of a century before a few of the best modern rental office buildings began to approach the ideal of comprehensive design embodied in PSFS. Since then the design of rental office space itself has surpassed the standards of the early thirties (Figs. 46 and 47), thanks largely to the integration of lighting and air-conditioning equipment in gridded constructions either hung as a screen below the real ceiling or built into coffered ceiling slabs. The ceiling thereby becomes neatly planar, like the windows and office partitions, while its grid may be exploited visually so as to provide rhythmic integration overhead with modular window and wall units. Hence office spaces can be more homogeneous architecturally than was then possible, when individually suspended lighting fixtures and projecting structural beams disrupted the ceiling plane and visually oppressed the space.[27] In other respects, however, the extensiveness of the design program in PSFS matches or excels that in any subsequent skyscraper. As for quality, this design surpasses the exquisite formulary design of office buildings in the fifties and sixties by Skidmore, Owings & Merrill, owing to the intensity with which Howe & Lescaze considered their building as a "custom" commission. Despite its implications for standardization, the PSFS design strikes us as having been designed for a specific building, whereas it is both a strength and a weakness of comparable design by Skidmore, Owings & Merrill that it gives the sense of having been created as a prototype for general application (as is often the case). Among modern American office structures designed prior to the sixties which are especially famous for their interiors, one would compare this aspect of PSFS with Wright's interiors for the Larkin and Johnson Wax companies and, among rental buildings, with the Seagram by Mies van der Rohe and Philip Johnson.* And not even the Seagram boasts the complexity of the interior program for PSFS.[28] The classicistic suavity of the Seagram interior design gives it an authority beyond the almost too rambunctious modernism which (rather touchingly from this vantage point in history) comes so close to intruding on the monumental dignity of the PSFS banking room.

With the completion of the furniture design some time after the tenants had begun to occupy their offices on August 1, 1932, PSFS was complete. On the whole, Howe might well have made the statement of architectural principle by which he at one point justified the design to Willcox into the epigraph for the building.

Sound architecture must be able to bear the closest analytical examination, externally, internally, structurally and mechanically, and the solution of each problem which presents itself in the development of a design must be not only possible, but possible in a concise and orderly form as a consequence of the organic foundation of the original conception. . . .

Finally it may be asked whether beauty has not been slighted in a multiplicity of technical considerations. . . . Modern architecture originated not in a search for a purely practical solution of modern problems but in a dissatisfaction with the superficial inorganic beauty of superimposed traditional architectural elements and ornament. As would naturally be the case the search for an organic

* See pp. 269f. below.

beauty led back to the very conception of design and it was found that the beauty sought could be found . . . only in an expression of the human, structural and mechanical functions of architecture. Our purpose as artists, as opposed to mere builders, in moulding these functions to your purposes has been to achieve beauty, and it is our opinion that we have.[29]

Comparable statements of intent abound in the modern movement, but few of its buildings so well meet Howe's exacting criteria.

PSFS as a Manifestation of the International Style

Such is the functional rationale of the building, and some of the design decisions which stem from this rationale. The structure is not merely a pastiche of modernisms imported from abroad and arranged in an arbitrary manner such as to affect a modernity that would set the crowd agog for a season or two, not merely the tired conjunctive "and so European modernism of the twenties finally reached the United States" by which history acknowledged and simultaneously dismissed it at the time and for three decades thereafter. The glib convenience which represents PSFS as an example, however excellent, of what had occurred abroad has tended to disguise the seriousness and uniqueness of the building. Even in its esthetic, moreover, where it appears most derivative, PSFS is rather more exceptional than a casual glance suggests.

At first sight, to be sure, it appears as a composite image of a mechanomorphology inherited from those European architects who for more than a decade had sought both a theoretical rationale and a vocabulary of forms expressive of the technological, social, and psychic realities of the modern world. George Howe admitted as much. To Willcox he praised the "new system . . . without personal bias since it is not my own discovery but that of many other men seeking a technically and expressively satisfactory solution of modern architectural problems."[30] There was doubtless an element of strategy in Howe's statement. By thus presenting the firm's design within the context of a group endeavor, he hoped to convince Willcox that the radical venture was no mere novelty, but a shrewd investment in a movement well under way, one which would inevitably prevail in the architecture of the future. Strategy aside, however, Howe's statement was essentially a matter of conviction.

As to what to term this "new system," Howe and Lescaze remained empirically inexact—and their imprecision has persisted. They often referred to their kind of architecture simply as "new," "modern," or "organic." As for the last term, while not inappropriate to Howe & Lescaze's philosophy of design and often employed by architects working in the modern style predominating in the twenties, its overtones are naturalistic rather than mechanical. "Organic" has, moreover, become so much the property of Frank Lloyd Wright as to make it an impossible label for the kind of modern advocated by Howe & Lescaze—especially impossible in any book devoted to twentieth-century American architecture. As for "new" and "modern," these can obviously serve at any time in history to designate whatever is current. Yet it might be argued that the movement in which Howe & Lescaze participated deserved these overworked adjectives more than most. No architectural movement reveals more impatience with the past,† nor a more self-conscious pursuit of a specifically "modern" expression. But labels which might have been barely acceptable in the early thirties have become less so, because the "modern" which then predominated has been succeeded by other kinds of "modern," partly continuing, but also partly opposing, the tradition of the twenties. "New" and "modern" were stop-gap tags for the movement. Alternatively, both Howe and Lescaze, like others at the time, spoke of "functional" architecture. And they might even have opted for some such terse concoction as the "machine style,"‡ by way of celebrating another fetish of the movement. These labels, while more specific, are also unsatisfactory, a matter to which we shall return.‡‡ Moreover, Howe invariably hedged on "functionalism," even as he used the term in writing to Willcox.

For the moment, then, as a matter more of convenience than of conviction, let the movement be designated by yet another label which came into currency as PSFS neared completion. Henry-Russell Hitchcock and Philip Johnson captioned the pioneer exhibition of the movement, presented at the Museum of Modern Art in New York in 1932, as the "International Style." Again the label is uninformative, beyond its obvious assumptions.[31] By the thirties, a group "style" existed. "International" in its origins during the early twenties, it became even more so as it gained wide acceptance among progressive architects and clients. Many movements in the history of art have similarly expanded. "International Style" has the further disadvantage of being the historian's term. Neither architects who worked in the Style during the twenties nor critics who evaluated the work at the time used the label. It happened to have been coined when the major work in the Style in its purest form had already

† True, even though there were more links with tradition, implicitly and even explicitly, than may have seemed clear at the time, as Reyner Banham especially points out in his *Theory and Design in the First Machine Age*, New York, Praeger, 1960.
‡ Not, however, the "mechanical" or "mechanistic" style—terms so pejorative that only academic antagonists of the progressive movement used them.
‡‡ See Chapter 3 below.

been realized, even though Hitchcock and Johnson could not have known in 1932 the degree to which this would be true.[32] But the neutrality of the label has worked to its advantage. The magisterial manner in which these authors surveyed the achievement of the decade and announced its distinguishing principles have given the label authority. At this point, then, let us blandly follow their lead.

In their catalogue of the exhibition, Hitchcock and Johnson defined the International Style as having three overlapping principles. First, it is an architecture of volume rather than mass. Secondly, composition depends on the rhythmic organization of regular units, with asymmetrical arrangements predominating over the symmetries of academic architecture. Finally, ornament is outlawed.

To elaborate: the reticular skeleton of columns and floor slabs constructed of reinforced concrete or steel completely supports the building. Since the enclosing walls perform no supporting function, they can be stretched like a membrane around the open box of space within. The membranous quality of the wall (more apparent than real) testifies to the importance of this volume of space as the essence of the architecture, much as our experience of a circus tent, even from the outside, is less of the canvas walls than of the big volume of peaked space lightly defined by the stretched fabric. This apparent dematerialization of the wall is achieved in several ways. Most importantly, as we have already observed, it is accomplished by setting the supporting columns back from the outermost edges of the floor slabs; since the walls are non-bearing, they may be opened as extravagantly as the architect chooses to extensive windows, whether in bands or even as entire walls. The textureless continuity of the wall surface typical of buildings in the International Style increases its intangibility, since the eye has no roughness or pattern to hold onto, while the smoothness suggests a skin-like (or to return to our comparison, a canvas-like) material pulled tautly around the total volume of interior space. Elimination of moldings and ornament from the wall and from door and window openings further minimizes the sense of depth and weight. Placement of windows at the outer plane of the wall, so that they are not inset but at the surface, also disguises its depth. Flat roofs, in addition to providing usable decks, replace the cap of the traditional building. Roof decks also accentuate the sense of the building box as a hollow container. And of course, nothing dramatizes the apparent weightlessness of the walls, or the volume of space which they lightly define, more than the stilting of the building on its slender, widely spaced supports. The openness of the interiors proclaims the spatial emphasis of the building. Inside, the columnar supports are frequently exposed, the better to display the partitioning walls as mere diaphragms in the total volume of enclosed space, thereby modulating its continuity

119

(1) *skeletal frame, giving point supports instead of walls;*

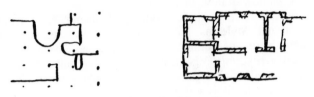

(2) *open plan, instead of boxed rooms;*

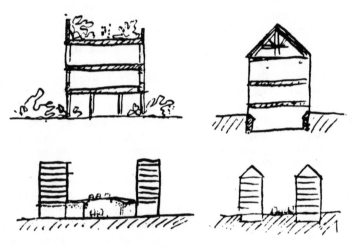

(3) *roof terrace, instead of pitched roof;*

FIGURE 48. *Le Corbusier's "five elements" inaugurating "a new era (cycle) in architecture".*

rather than walling it into "rooms." Since standardized units are essential elements in the design—most conspicuously, the repeats of the structural column and those of the factory-produced window unit—it is their arrangement in regular or contrapuntal rhythms which principally articulates the volumetric composition. Moreover, since these depend on functional

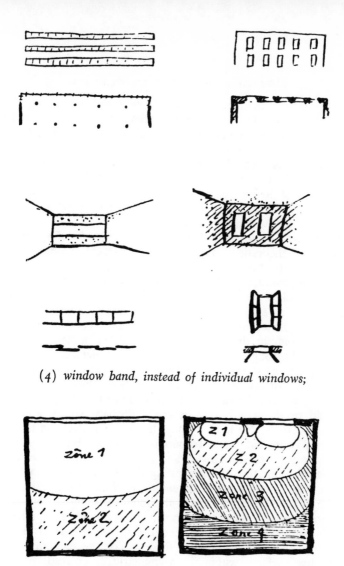

(4) *window band, instead of individual windows;*

(5) *hence an asymmetrical composition for façades consonant with the functional demands of the interior.*

rather than on formal considerations, they tend to occur in asymmetrical arrangements. Such are the ingredients of the style that Hitchcock and Johnson termed "International."

Before leaving the subject, it may be well to glance at Le Corbusier's slightly variant primer of the Style.[33] His staccato enumeration of what

121

he found to be the five elements of the "new architecture," together with the terseness of his sketches, makes particularly vivid the prototypical building within the movement (Fig. 48). First: widely spaced, regularly ordered supports in a continuous space, instead of the bearing walls of traditionally compartmented plans. Second: the free and open plan instead of rooms. Third: the roof terrace instead of the roof. Fourth: the window band instead of holes in the wall. Fifth: the freely organized façade, unfettered either by dogmas of symmetry or by the traditional alternation of window-wall, window-wall.

Le Corbusier's prototype is basic to the esthetic of PSFS, which Howe also justified on theoretical, as well as on practical, grounds. In 1936, four years after the first tenants had moved into PSFS, and five years prior to the appearance of Sigfried Giedion's historical exegesis of the concept in his phenomenally successful *Space, Time and Architecture,* Howe undertook to explain the mysteries of this relativistic esthetic at a gathering of art historians.[34] He might well have been describing PSFS to his learned, but, at this late date, still puzzled audience. The "functionalist," he said, sought "to reduce the material elements of architecture to their simplest, most serviceable form and smallest compass in order to lay bare the abstract space-time idea in all its clarity." The reduction of the walls to planes, the skeleton to lines, and the columns (in plan) to points would result in a purely geometrical space which would be essentially "non-visual." No longer would the eye glut itself on the extravagant textures, ornament, or bulk permitted by the Bacchic materialism of Beaux-Arts esthetics. To Howe (and here he designated the movement by yet another term, this one suggesting its affinities with contemporary developments in painting and sculpture), "abstract architecture addresses itself directly to the imagination. and the intellect, using the eye only as a recording instrument." As a stylus only, vision would trace relationships made as impalpable as architects could manage. In the banking room of PSFS especially, the inability of the eye (or the camera) to fix the sheer, reflective surfaces within the asymmetrically entered space can be disconcerting. This very impalpability of the material substance of the building "threw the mind back" to the experience of "pure space" defined and conditioned by the barest geometrical cues, the transparent relationship of dots, lines, and planes changing with the movement which the unfocused spaciousness encouraged.

To ensure the space-time dynamics of their diagrammatic architecture, Howe & Lescaze utilized the full range of architectural devices associated with European modernism of the twenties. There is, first, the asymmetical composition designed to keep us visually, kinesthetically, and psychically off-balance. There is the extravagant transparency of sheets of glass extending inside out, or outside in. There are other continuities where we might expect breaks, like the windows bent and folded around corners. There are open forms, especially evident on the exterior in the thrust of the cantilevers beyond the enframement of the structural columns, or in the abrupt termination of the projecting columns of the office tower, which stop short of the parapet at roof top and are left uncapped. There are interpenetrations and interlockings of shapes. There are violent juxtapositions which wrench the eye from one shape to another, particularly where an older style would have called for transitional elements from form to form. Finally, there is an intrinsic lack of interest in the unembellished parts, which encourages the eye to move on—to abandon the part for the ensemble. The textureless sheen, particularly at the base of the building on the exterior and in the banking room inside, quite literally enhances this visual slipperiness. That Howe & Lescaze could create so much space-time movement within the spatial and functional restrictions of a skyscraper, that they could remain so faithful to the theoretical commitments of their esthetic position without sacrificing practical considerations, is a measure of their achievement.

PSFS WITHIN THE SPECTRUM OF THE INTERNATIONAL STYLE

Hitchcock and Johnson included PSFS in their exhibition of the International Style. Thus Howe was right in reassuring Willcox that the validity of the design was not merely attested by the word of its two architects, but also by comparable design within a widespread movement. Even so, every movement as extensive as the International Style exhibits a range of expressive possibilities. Within this spectrum where is PSFS?

In this connection we do not speak of fundamental principles, but of different qualities of experience possible within the Style. These in turn depend on different modes of conceptualization, as they are conditioned by the architect's temperament, and by varying emphases which he gives to the Style, formally in his composition or expressionally in his understanding of the relationship of his design to its world. At the risk of seeming categorical, where differences are subtle matters of emphasis only, five different modes of conceptualization are discernible within the International Style. All are in accord with the principles of the Style as Hitchcock and Johnson described them. All allude in varied ways to the machine as the totem of modernity. If this agreement with respect to fundamentals were not the case, if our categories did not blur and overlap, the group Style would not exist. In this as in every style, however, diverse modes of conceptualization not only define the expressive range of the Style, but act as thrusts within it which simultaneously enlarge its possibilities and threaten its stability.

FIGURE 49. *Le Corbusier. Villa Stein, Garches (near Paris), 1927. Front elevation.*

The first of these conceptual emphases within the International Style is virtually unique to the work of Le Corbusier, and hence something of an aside in a discussion of PSFS. As the foremost propagandist for the Style, however, and its most imaginative visionary as well, Le Corbusier epitomized the *élan* of high adventure which inspired both Howe and Lescaze in their embrace of the "modern." Hence Le Corbusier's polemical stance influenced the two American architects more than his work, except insofar as this partook of the Style of the movement. Le Corbusier's work reveals a peculiarly witty and poetic sensitivity for unexpected juxtaposition. Within his larger composition of primary shapes (*prismes purs,* in his phrase), he incorporates bits and pieces from the machine world. These are sometimes ready-made objects lifted in their entirety from their mundane context; sometimes fragments of this environment; sometimes invented shapes merely haunted with allusion to things of the modern world around architecture. Le Corbusier's use of this machine imagery differs from that of other architects working in the Style in the degree to which he introduces into his compositions incidents which resist total absorption within the whole. They are deliberately disruptive, partly because of shape, partly because of allusion. The front elevation of the Villa Stein at Garches near Paris (1927) suffices as an illustration (Fig. 49). The abrupt pop of the small balconies recalls similar look-outs in the superstructure of the ocean liners which Le Corbusier called to architects' attention in his enormously influential *Vers une architecture* (first published in 1923, and republished in English with the title *Towards a New Architecture* in 1927) [Fig. 50]. Especially is this true of the topmost balcony. The broad plane of the wall suddenly erupts into three dimensions, forward and back. Here, as is frequently the case in his work, Le Corbusier contrasts the rectangularity of the resulting cubicle of space with the curved forms of the back wall. These suggest the shapes of ventilators and other such structures aboard ship. (This particular shape actually takes its contour from a bathtub inside. Hence it refers to modern transportation machines not only metaphorically, but literally as well, where odd-shaped pockets of space are often molded around equipment.) Other nautical reminiscences are the openings in the roof of the cubicle, making free-form cutouts of sky. As for the aston-ishing shelter over the main entrance, a gangplank comes to mind, or more likely, the strutted wing structure of the primitive aircraft, which also appear in Le Corbusier's book as talismans of modernity.

He does not always use the flotsam of technology so directly. Rhyth-mic patterns bring modern machines to mind more obliquely. Although horizontal window bands are among the hallmarks of the International Style, in the Stein elevation the composition and kinds of rhythmic pat-terns they establish suggest equivalents in the liners pictured in *Vers une architecture:* the window band at the second-floor level jostled by the tumult of shapes below; the band for the third floor serenely uninter-rupted; and both forced low with respect to the bold rise of the "super-structure" with its lookout above. Or, consider, finally, such an incon-spicuous detail as the positioning of the secondary entrance beside the garage door. It is off-center with respect both to the balcony and spotlight above, and to its own flanking windows. The resulting composition is analogous to frequent skewed arrangements of components in machines, where functional requirements may disrupt symmetries. Because the door is subtly freed from the compositional schema implied in the elevation, it takes on a degree of independence of the building, a certain willfulness. In other words, although Le Corbusier did place the door so skillfully as to energize the ambient composition tremendously, its skewed position simultaneously suggests that it has all but escaped the architect's design. Since the door also appears to be a prefabricated item from a manufac-

turer's catalogue, it seems the more independent of the architect's design*
—like the stack of a liner, the wheel of an automobile, the propeller of
a plane. For that matter, like the entrance door of the Stein façade or
the spotlight immediately above it, the door is, by virtue of both its un-
settling placement and its prefabricated quality, bluntly experienced as a
"part," a "thing," a "component," an "object," which comes to architecture from the world outside of art.[35] Although within "art," the door
simultaneously exists in the other realm (if the pun may be forgiven) of
the "non-arti-fact." As such, it tautly mediates between our consciousness
of what belongs to "architecture" and what to the everyday technology
from which "modern architecture" derives its laconic exhilaration.

Le Corbusier's particular sensitivity to this ironic collision of form and
metaphor recalls the contemporaneous attitudes of Dadaists and Surre-
alists,[36] although the positivistic and logical side of his temperament
limited their influence on him to a partial similarity of spirit, not to similarity of aim. For this reason the *jeu d'esprit* of disruptive incident does
not confuse the lithe serenity of the *prismes purs*. Le Corbusier's fervor
for the ideals of classical architecture further disciplines the allusive incident within his compositions. In *Vers une architecture* photographs of
modern machines are juxtaposed with others of sculptural details from
Greek and Roman buildings. Both show clarity of primary shapes, tense-
ness of rhythmic harmonies, and precision in the articulation of parts. Like
the sculptural ornament in classical architecture, too, sculptural fillips such
as the roof-top balcony in the front elevation of the Stein Villa are meaningful as pure geometrical forms and as representational allusions. They
relieve his early designs of bland anonymity (a monotonous factor in too
much of the International Style) even as they anticipate, in a piecemeal
manner, the vigorous sculptural quality of his late buildings. So the inspiration of the machine revivifies classical ideals, making them relevant to
modern experience.

To the lyric spirituality (humanistic rather than religious) of Le Corbusier's commitment, PSFS is alien. Howe and Lescaze, like most innovators at the time, were, however, caught up in the euphoria of his vocif-

---

* In fact, Le Corbusier may have designed the door, but he designed it *as if*
it had been prefabricated. Since manufacturers then provided but few items appropriate to the International Style, architects were often forced to custom-design
building components in accord with *standards* which, in their opinion, were ideally
suited for factory production, as the design of PSFS demonstrates. (In this connection, note also the experience of Irving Gill, described in *American Buildings and
Their Architects: Progressive and Academic Ideals at the Turn of the Twentieth
Century,* Chapter 5). Persuaded by the rationale of the designers, and equally by
the market generated by the increasing popularity of modern architecture, manufacturers gradually made available the kinds of products sought by the progressive
architects of the twenties.

FIGURE 50. *Examples from among the analogies suggested for modern architecture in Le Corbusier's* Vers une architecture, *first published in 1923.*

FIGURE 51. *J. J. P. Oud. Housing, The Hook of Holland, 1925.*

erous propaganda. The brave new world of modern design never seemed fuller of promise than in Le Corbusier's staccato exhortations in *Vers une architecture* in behalf of *l'esprit nouveau,* with their legerdemain of machine-into-house-into-Parthenon-into-house-into-machine.

A second kind of conceptual emphasis within the International Style centers in the purification of primary forms. All architects who worked in the movement shared in this concern, but again, Le Corbusier deserves particular notice. None of the leading architects working in the International Style were as obsessed as he with proportional schemes and with formulae of rhythmic organization which promised to guarantee harmonic relationships. This emphasis on the purification of form, however, appears more exclusively in the work of J. J. P. Oud (Fig. 51) and in that of Ludwig Mies van der Rohe (Fig. 52). Lacking Le Corbusier's metaphorical surprise of incident, an imagery that goes beyond the geometrics of architecture, the compositional styles of Oud and Mies are more narrowly visual—even though Mies especially endows the formal properties of his work with symbolic content. Their work, too, reveals inspiration from the classical past; but it depends less on the classical image experienced as a sculptural entity than on the classicizing process—on refining, adjusting, simplifying, perfecting primary shapes and their relationships. Howe's refinement of the forms of PSFS may at first sight seem to relate to this kind of expression within the International Style. The resemblance, however, is superficial. There is a vast difference between perfecting a design so that it will accord with an esthetic of ideal form and the chastening of a design so that it will carry out a technological, functional, and expressionistic concept with maximum elegance. The difference is clear despite the fact that Howe at least, in his more theoretical moments, would so minimize the physicality of form as to transport it to the space-time nirvana of plane, line, and point. Hence it is to the less

FIGURE 52. *Ludwig Mies van der Rohe. Wolf House, Guben (Germany),* 1926.

abstract, less metaphoric, and less idealized aspects of the International Style that PSFS is especially related.

For our purpose the technological and functional emphases within the International Style must be considered together, however awkward the coupling may be. Unfortunately, the rationale of the International Style was confused in this matter, implying that technological advance automatically brings functional improvement. This notion was curiously old-fashioned for a movement so determinedly "modern," recalling as it does nineteenth-century links between the idea of adaptive evolution and that of inevitable progress. Nevertheless a mixture of technological and functional idealism comprised the very heart of the ideology of the International Style, including its disaffection with what it considered to be the excessive formalism, monumentality, and eclectic historicism of Beaux-Arts design. Hence all architects working in the International Style were centrally concerned about expressing technology and function, at least insofar as these were understood at the time. Obviously, however, some architects gave these two aspects particular attention, and in this group surely were Howe & Lescaze. Not only could Howe write to Willcox that, "Sound architecture must be able to bear the closest analytical examination, externally, internally, structurally and mechanically, and the solution of each problem which presents itself in the development of a design must be not only possible, but possible in a concise and orderly form as a consequence of the organic foundation of the original conception."[37] But also PSFS does in fact substantially meet Howe's demands for preciseness of functional arrangement, revelation of structure, use of new materials, and incorporation of mechanical equipment. In the completeness with which PSFS actually met the functional standards merely promised for most modern buildings of the period, it probably outclassed the other buildings in Hitchcock and Johnson's book.

Any discussion of the technological and functional qualities of the International Style leads to paradox because polemics so far outran practice, as Banham makes clear in his *Theory and Design in the First Machine Age*. Had the International Style really been abreast of advanced technology in structures, for example, its characteristic shapes would more likely have been curved rather than rectangular. After all, a lesson in curvature might have been learned from the machines persistently invoked in the propaganda. Even though the curved surfaces of the machine housings of the period tended to be mounted over linear frameworks, these curvatures were often so shaped and related to one another that they did more than enclose functioning parts—they possessed structural or at least stiffening properties as well. Developing theory in aerodynamics, although hardly as relevant for stationary objects as the somewhat later popularity for bogus "streamlining" might have indicated, should nevertheless have suggested, even in the twenties, that skeletal framing was not exactly *avant garde* structurally.

At the very least architects might have taken cognizance of the radical civil engineering of their day. They did have a casual acquaintance with such examples of curved reinforced-concrete engineering as Robert Maillart's bridges or Eugène Freyssinet's vaults for industrial structures. But these do not appear in the International Style (although, in fairness, it might be added that, if they had, the architects would have beaten all but a very few engineers at their own game). Exterior walls in these modern buildings typically went up as traditional masonry construction of blocks or tiles, which was then plastered with a skin of painted cement to give the pseudo-membranous aspect that the Style required. Even the relatively conservative notion of modular panel units for the flexible partitioning of continuous interior space made but little headway within the International Style. Most architects working in this style were not particularly alert to new materials or interested in pushing old ones to new possibilities, glass excepted. Metals appeared in some new uses (chrome tubing, for example), generally minor ones: for trim, appliances, and furniture. Nor did the architects give more than perfunctory heed to innovations in mechanical equipment, beyond some redesign of appliances and lighting fixtures. For temperature and light control, it would be truer to say that conditions of intolerable climate and glare within the glass box encouraged mechanical remedy, than that mechanical invention inspired architectural advance—an example of function following form in a clear inversion of Sullivan's axiom. It only reinforces observations already made to note that Howe & Lescaze did design a system of modular paneling for office partitioning in PSFS; they did make relatively extensive use of aluminum and stainless steel, which were then new materials (and they wanted to use

FIGURE 53. *J. A. Brinckman & L. C. van der Vlugt. Van Nelle Tobacco Factory, Rotterdam, 1927–30.*

metal for the spandrel panels); they did completely air condition the building; they did create a skeletal frame of greater technological interest than those typical of contemporary modern work abroad.

Whatever the technological and functional commitment of the International Style in fact, the "look" of it surpassed the actuality. For those architects whose design especially depended on the technological and functional bias of the International Style the "look" was that of the factory. Its epitome may well be the finest factory of the decade: the Van Nelle tobacco and coffee processing plant (1927–30) in Rotterdam, officially by Brinckman & Van der Vlugt, but apparently largely designed by Mart Stam, who was then working for the firm (Fig. 53). An even more familiar example of the factory image, because it served as the leading school for the dissemination of the program of the International Style, is the workshop block of Walter Gropius' Bauhaus (completed 1926) at Dessau, Germany (Figs. 54, 55).† Of the leading

---

† See also his City Employment Office in Dessau (1928). Unbuilt projects by Gropius for two other academic complexes, an Academy of Philosophy at Erlangen (1924) and an Engineering School at Hagan, Westphalia (1929), invoke the factory image even more directly than the Bauhaus. All are conveniently illustrated in James Marston Fitch, *Walter Gropius*, New York, Braziller, 1960, figs. 14–16, 44–47, and 87.

FIGURE 54. *Walter Gropius. Bauhaus, Dessau (Germany), 1925–26. View from the southwest showing the workshop block and the bridge to the classroom block.*

FIGURE 55. *Bauhaus. View from the northwest showing the workshop block, left, linked by the low block for dining and other community facilities to the dormitory block, right.*

protagonists of the movement, Gropius was the most completely committed to a technological point of view in both practice and theory, even to his insistence on "teamwork" in design.

Whereas the emphasis on pure form favored abstract composition, the organization of the major elements in the composition of the Van Nelle factory derives, like that of PSFS, from functional cues; as does the looser, if somewhat more arbitrary, pin-wheel scheme of the Bauhaus. A comparable distinction between formalists and functionalists within the International Style tends to appear in the different ways in which they compose doors and windows. The formalist is preeminently concerned with the size and placement of an opening in its relation both to the total plane of the wall and to other openings. He therefore characteristically views the window as a shape among other shapes, more specifically as a rectangular plane among other rectangular planes, in a composition which we grasp as form before we consider whether or not the form accords with use. (For example, the elevations by Oud and Mies which we have illustrated are noncommittal about the plan they enclose.) The functionalist, on the other hand, may use openings with diversity of size, arrangement, and even detailing, and let interior organization condition their arrangement. Surely the Van Nelle factory, the Bauhaus, and PSFS all reveal this kind of window treatment. By comparison with formalist compositions within the Style, they also show less interest on the part of the architect in creating intensity of shape for its own sake. Clarity of detail may even blur because of the architect's concern to accommodate his detailing of openings and appurtenances appropriate for the variety of uses embodied in the program. The Van Nelle factory demonstrates the effect. It is perceived, not as a composition of decisively formed shapes, but as a vivacious ensemble of varied door and window shapes, mullion patterns, railings, penthouses, and inclined conveyor enclosures, its multitudinous panes and linear elements catching light in adventitious ways. At the opposite extreme, if a large area is wholly given over to a single activity as in a factory, the ardent functionalist will not hesitate to fill his elevation with identical window elements. Or, by way of another example, he may follow Sullivan's advice to the designer of the office skyscraper: above the second story "we take our cue from the individual cell, which requires a window with its separating pier, its sill and lintel, and . . . make them look all alike because they are all like."[38] Relatively speaking, therefore, the functionalist tends to organize his openings as a *pattern of use* (whether comprised of varied or of identical components), whereas the formalist tends to make *intensity of shape, size, position and the visual rightness of relationships* his principal concern.

Two other tendencies may differentiate formalists within the International Style from their functionalist counterparts. The functionalist is more willing than the formalist to settle for the standardized product, to leave bolting exposed, to let utility elements occur where they will. Not always, to be sure, since Howe & Lescaze smoothed over the factory-like frankness that appears, for instance, in the workshop block of the Bauhaus and in the Van Nelle factory. The frank use of factory elements was especially not to Howe's liking, conditioned as he had been by Beaux-Arts preference for sumptuous effects. Moreover, Howe & Lescaze worked for a client who very much feared that his building might be mistaken for a warehouse, which must have redoubled the architect's determination to produce something else.

Finally, because the functionalist is usually eager to express whatever complexities his commission may provide, he is more likely than the formalist to skim the Style for the range of its effects; in other words, he tends to be inclusive. The formalist, however, is exclusive, for he characteristically pursues the austere course of simplifying and purifying all form toward some common denominator, so that all detailing within the building is homogeneous. All three of our functionalist examples reveal the encyclopedic approach to the Style—the Bauhaus doing so in a particularly didactic manner. In fact, of all the major exemplars of the International Style, the Bauhaus perhaps most clearly reveals the gamut of its characteristic motifs: on this elevation one way to compose a wall in the International Style; on that elevation, another. It is as though the visual effects of the Style had appeared in a compendium of architectural elements—such as *Sweet's Catalog* (the formidable compilation of architectural components which is found in all American architectural offices)—and then been used by Gropius for selecting the ingredients of his design. The all-glass wall of the Bauhaus workshops opposes starkly plain walls. Ribbon windows and single windows exist together. The single window appears both in rhythmic repetition and as an occasional exclamatory punch in extensive stretches of blank wall. Windowed-and-cantilevered-balcony units occur in an all-over textile-like repeat on one wall. Here, too, are the floating volume, the bridge of space, and the use of severely plain typography peripherally positioned within the composition as a stridently vertical opposition to horizontals. Gropius organized this anthology of the Style in a tensely knit, asymmetrical composition of contrasting patterns reminiscent of the texture problems assigned in the introductory workshop courses at the school (Fig. 56). Had Herr Professor prepared a demonstration of the full range of the visual possibilities of the Style for his students, he could hardly have done better. To his credit, Gropius achieved his design without pedantry, in part no doubt because he was working on it at a time when it had just become possible to find out exactly what

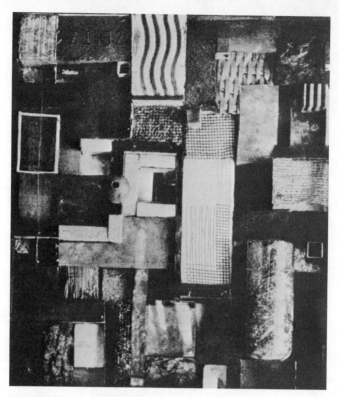

FIGURE 56. *Texture collage utilizing various materials, done for a foundation design course at the Bauhaus.*

the full range of the Style's effects was and thus to achieve authoritative synthesis. In the Bauhaus design, his act of compilation was simultaneously an act of discovery.

This is not quite the case with PSFS, where the esthetic is also compendious (and appears even more so when we trace the course of the design, taking stock of what was tried and what discarded). But the compendium occurred a trifle late for the moment of revelation. Hence there is more the sense of the formula manipulation of motifs already familiar to the *avant garde*. If the manipulation of a pre-fabricated vocabulary of form seems stiffer in PSFS than in the Bauhaus, the program of a skyscraper provided for less freedom of action than did that of a spreading school in an open field; moreover, Howe & Lescaze elected to pursue a program which was more rigidly rationalized both functionally and technologically than Gropius'. For example, in the Bauhaus design, Gropius confronted nothing like the regularity of the fenestration of an office tower.[39] He barely revealed vertical com-munication, nor did he package functions as precisely as did Howe &

FIGURES 57, 58, 59. *Alvar Aalto. Sanitarium, Paimio (Finland), 1929–33. Above: view toward the entrance, with projecting bedroom wing. Opposite, above: bedroom wing. Below: schematic plan of the upper ground floor.*

Lescaze. In these respects PSFS is closer to the Van Nelle factory. Although the detailing of PSFS possesses little of the vivacity of intricate incident seen in the Van Nelle factory (and in this respect partakes of the relative sobriety of Bauhaus detailing), the eye nevertheless finds almost as much difficulty in concentrating on the particulars of shape and detail in the one as in the other.

If PSFS exhibits the functional and technological bias of certain

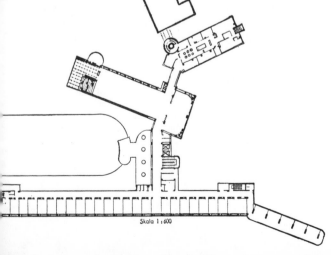

Skala 1:600

buildings within the International Style, it also possesses what have been loosely termed expressionist qualities. Difficult as it may be to define any of the nuances of the Style thus far encountered, the expressionist emphasis is most resistant in this respect. In the first place, "expressionist" should not be confused with "expressive," since all the approaches under discussion are expressive of aspects of "modern architecture" as it was viewed in the twenties. For present purposes let the label refer to the manipulation of the vocabulary of the Style for its most spectacular, most theatrical, effects.‡ Spectacular effects obviously depend on the extraordinary: on astonishing performance, abnormal scale, violent contrast, intense energy, exceptional insistence . . . the list could be slightly extended,* but this much is relevant to the expressionistic aspects of the International Style. Obviously, then, what is or is not expressionist is very much a matter of degree. Doubly so because we must feel this forcing of effect *as a cardinal purpose;* in other words, we must feel that the design originates in a theatrical conception of the Style. In the twenties, the very starkness of an occasional building in the International Style set down amidst traditionally eclectic neighbors had its dramatic aspect. And, significantly, both the architects and the client for PSFS considered the "advertising value" of its modernity as among the assets of the design. Thus, even while Willcox still questioned the merits of his architects' proposal in other respects, he admitted its virtue as publicity "at least in Philadelphia."[40] But the sensationalism of novelty *per se* inevitably dulls as the infrequent comes to prevail. Inherently, the International Style was not expressionistic. Its focus on the communal and normative left little room for the idiosyncratic and flamboyant in which expressionism flourishes. Its slight of monumentality and strictures against ornament discouraged grandeur of scale or opulence of treatment, other areas of expressionist exploitation.

Certain elements within the International Style might have been expected to whet the appetite for expressionism more than they actually did. An obsessive rationalism seems to have subdued the sensational effects that an exaggerated use of stilting, cantilevers, and roof decks could have brought. At the time, however, any comparison of modern buildings with their traditional counterparts must have made these elements seem sufficiently extraordinary in themselves as to have dis-

---

‡ It seems unnecessary to complicate the definition by including mention of the larger German Expressionist movement of the teens and twenties, even though there are some peripheral manifestations of it in the expressionism of the International Style. Expressionistic architecture outside the Style does not concern us here.
* For example, stupendous mass, with its resulting sense of colossal force, provides another possibility for an expressionistic architecture; but the lightness and openness of the International Style precluded it.

couraged their unusual emphasis beyond an occasional fillip, like the bristle of cantilevered balconies from the dormitory wall of the Bauhaus.† In Alvar Aalto's famous tuberculosis sanitarium (1929–33) at Paimio, Finland (Figs. 57, 58 and 59), which makes more serious use of cantilevered balconies, they project at intervals from narrow slabs containing the bedroom cubicles. Aalto thereby combined attenuated mass with hovering projection in what then seemed sufficiently dramatic to border on expressionism, even if the subsequent proliferation of comparable effects in tropical hotels has dulled the initial impact of the combination. The cantilevering of PSFS (more of a compositional fillip than that of the sanitarium, yet more functional than that of the Bauhaus) possesses the same qualities, but in a subdued sense.

When expressionism did get more than a toehold in the International Style, it occurred in four of its clichés: in slab massing, in the glass wall, in the window band, and in the staccato asymmetries of assertively opposed wall planes and openings. PSFS shows all of them. As for the first of these, the slab mass, which appears in the PSFS tower, and which accounts even more than the balconies for the drama of Aalto's sanitarium, we have already discussed the expressionist overtones of lithe energy in this functional form.‡ Glass walls, too, as they appear in the Van Nelle factory and in the workshop block of the Bauhaus (to use as examples merely what has already been mentioned) provide the climactic aspects of these buildings. Justifiable on functional grounds, floor-to-ceiling glazing, especially without compensation for the extremes of temperature and glare which it brings, has often proved less practical than expected. Whether used for practical reasons or not, however, fully glazed elevations are sufficiently extravagant that super-logic in this instance spills over into super-spectacle; especially was this the

---

† It is worth recalling that despite the enthusiasm of the architects of the International Style for cantilevered balconies, not they, but Frank Lloyd Wright made the most spectacular use of them, and especially from the late twenties onward. Although he had used cantilevers with remarkable originality in earlier designs (for example, in the Gale House and in the Sugar Loaf project, figs. 131, 134), his bold use of them begins with the cross stacking of barge-shaped cantilevers in the Elizabeth Noble apartment project for Los Angeles and the pin-wheel configurated cantilevers of St. Mark's Tower for New York, both designed in 1929 (see Hitchcock, *In the Nature of Materials,* figs. 303–7). Extravagant cantilevering of the sort that Wright favored tends toward bulky construction, which the penchant for membranous lightness forbade to the International Style. Among the important works in the Style, one finds that the only cantilevers approaching the forcefulness of Wright's are those in Mies van der Rohe's project for an office building in 1922 (illustrated in Johnson, *Mies van der Rohe,* p. 31). This project was, however, without immediate issue either in the Style, or in Mies' subsequent work.

‡ See pp. 45f. above; also *American Buildings and Their Architects: Progressive and Academic Ideals at the Turn of the Twentieth Century,* Chapter 1.

case in the twenties when the spectacle was new. Window walls vividly expose on a grand scale the interior volume of space and the activity within as the cardinal reality of the building, through a medium which is itself scintillant with the activity of light.* It was primarily for its dramatic potential that Howe & Lescaze wrapped the banking room of PSFS in the curve of an outsized window. If they also argued that the big windows illuminated the interior, the glare from the glass, compounded by its reflection in the marble and by the uneven distribution of the light within the room, has created as many problems as it solved.

As for the other kind of fenestration which especially lends itself to expressionist effects in the Style, long window bands not only dramatize the continuity of the interior space, but provide surface patterns of marked directional quality. On both scores they intensify the visual dynamics of the building (like their counterparts in transportation machines, to which a building so banded was often compared) and especially where the banding follows long curves or folds around corners. For these, as well as for functional reasons, Howe & Lescaze would have banded the towers in horizontal stripes except for Willcox's fortunate objections. By the time PSFS was completed, window bands had become one of the vulgar "streamlined" effects popular in the thirties.

In the designs of Howe & Lescaze, along with other architects of an expressionist persuasion within the International Style, however, the dynamic banding often appears in combination with contrasting window patterns and shapes, or with contrasting textural and color oppositions of wall treatment, so that the over-all effect is visually disruptive in its stridency; deliberately "jazzy," to use the term then applied to its most extreme and ephemeral manifestations. Although such compositions may be dictated by functional considerations, they may be quite arbitrary, and are usually less satisfactory when the latter is the case. Even the functional composition, however, may be forced to the brink of dramatic statement, as, for example, in the Van Nelle factory, where the long banded curve of the office wing collides with the complicated cubistic stair and shaft area, and this, in turn, with the expanse of the glass wall in the processing section. Although subordinated to the essentially rationalistic image of the whole, this tincture of expressionism accounts for the exceptional liveliness of the factory. The fact that the Van Nelle factory was consciously designed to become a self-advertisement of its enterprise when illuminated at night gives further proof of expressionist concerns. More relevant to this study of PSFS is the commercial ex-

---

* This is not always the case, since glass walls go dead in certain lights; but, in their enthusiasm for glass, progressively inclined architects in the twenties paid little heed to its deficits.

FIGURE 60. *Erich Mendelsohn. Schocken Department Store, Stuttgart (Germany), 1926–28.*

pressionism of a work like Erich Mendelsohn's Schocken Department Store (completed in 1928) in Stuttgart (Fig. 60). The arbitrariness of this composition is decidedly expressionist in intent, which the booming typography underscores. Although the varied compositional effects of the façade to a degree reflect different uses for the space inside, they are so extravagantly asserted, with such obvious aim at publicity, as to subsume the functional starting point in the expressionist aim. Yet in respect to stridency, the Stuttgart store was no match for some of the early versions of PSFS (Fig. 61). These, under Lescaze's influence, were so afflicted by ribbons, zigzags, and cubist elements in headlong collision that it never will be entirely clear how, even with Howe's sense of propriety, the design was eventually purged of these excesses.

As realized, PSFS owes a more specific debt to a later, and finer Schocken Store (completed in 1930), this one in Chemnitz (Fig. 62).

FIGURE 61. PSFS. *Preliminary design for the base of the building by William Lescaze, dated December 25, 1929.*

FIGURE 62. *Erich Mendelsohn. Schocken Department Store, Chemnitz (Germany), 1928–30.*

Here, too, Mendelsohn used expressionist elements, but disciplined them with more functional and formal ends in mind. The base of PSFS is, in fact, virtually a compressed version of the Chemnitz store, and necessarily loses much of the drama in the compression (Fig. 35). Not that Howe & Lescaze specifically intended a version of Mendelsohn's store; but the image of the recently completed German building was familiar at the time and became something of a paradigm for expressionist buildings in the Style. In PSFS the shop windows are comparably handled beneath the cantilevered masonry band, projecting to the building line and having their transoms recessed. The bold corner curve of the bank window is similarly halted, by an extravagant band of vertical glazing over the entrance at the edge of the building. The notch in PSFS and its window treatment seem dependent on the rooftop setbacks of the Chemnitz store.[41] Surely the obsessive banding of the onetime scheme for the office tower and its fenestration are generally related to Mendelsohn's kind of expressionism.

Finally, PSFS, like Mendelsohn's store fronts, was given the expressionist appeal of a gigantic billboard, for this was a time when the billboard-as-architecture was central to the quality of modernity sought in the typographical wake of abstract and near-abstract painting. Even without lettering, the elevations of many buildings in the International Style suggest an advertising layout. Howe doubtless simplified matters when he informed Willcox that his conversion to modern architecture had begun in the mid-twenties when he tried to integrate a sign with the Renaissance trappings of the two branch banks with which his association with PSFS began; but, exaggeration or not, the statement itself indicates the importance of advertising layout in the formation of the Style. In this instance, both architects and clients were particularly pleased that the billboard aspects of the skyscraper were of a piece with the "PSFS" sign in scarlet neon against its blue background at the summit. At last a cardinal function of the skyscraper, corporate advertising, became explicit in the architectural integration of the building and its sign.† In this matter, the architects even performed the role of publicity agent for the bank. They argued that the full name of the bank, which appears in early schemes for the building, would be illegible from the ground. Why not "PSFS"? The frequent fragmentation of words into nonsense combinations of letters in cubist paintings may have encouraged the architects' suggestion. The New Deal's use of abbreviations for governmental agencies, which popularized this shortcut to identifica-

---

† By way of measuring Howe & Lescaze's accomplishment, compare their finesse in handling the roof-top sign with the clumsiness of Hood's solution for the McGraw-Hill Building, Fig. 29.

, had yet to get under way, and the bankers at first questioned this breezy idea. (They may have done so again when it became a Depression joke among Philadelphians that the bank had raised a coded distress signal to Washington warning that Philadelphia Slowly Faces Starvation.) Today, however, PSFS is, for all practical purposes, *the* name of the bank.[42]

In short, as we review four, overlapping expressive possibilities within the International Style (we have yet to discuss a fifth)—the machine analogized in architectural form as surrealist image, as purified form, as rationalized technology and function, or as expressionist dynamics—we find that PSFS appears predominantly as a technological and functional image, but one dramatically heightened and given publicity value through expressionist devices. In thus eschewing the more abstract and metaphoric versions of the International Style, PSFS generally characterizes the advent of the style in the United States. Significantly, the most prominent modern and near-modern American skyscrapers of the period, the Daily News and McGraw-Hill Buildings, as well as Rockefeller Center (Figs. 22, 24 and 29), share the technological and expressionistic bias of PSFS. And so does Neutra's "Health House," built in Los Angeles for Dr. Richard Lovell (Fig. 71). To the technological aspect of the Lovell House we shall return; but here it must be stated that if the building is not as overtly expressionist in its banding as is PSFS,[43] the ribboned surfaces are there nonetheless, although disguised by interruptions. Moreover, the Lovell House exists in something of the same milieu of publicity as PSFS. Would Le Corbusier have advertised his famous Villa Savoye as a "Health House"? He certainly believed that his clients' health would be benefited by life on its open decks (and repeatedly said as much). Yet "Health House" is too literally associated with swimming pools, trapezes, sunny California, and the real estate publicity agent to have accorded with the Calvinist aspect of *l'esprit nouveau*.

Although PSFS characterizes American use of the most technological and expressionistic manifestations of the European International Style, it has certain qualities that distinguish it from European examples generally, even from those to which it seems closest. In comparison with the Bauhaus, the Schocken Store at Chemnitz, and the Van Nelle factory (miscellaneous examples of the fully developed International Style selected from those already mentioned), PSFS reveals a weightier sleekness in appearance, being less nervously lithe and therefore, perhaps, more reassuringly efficient. The comparative weightiness of PSFS depends partly on the Beaux-Arts background from which American modernism so abruptly arose. For the rest, its peculiar qualities may partly reflect a tradition of heavier, blunter visual standards for American building components at the time—the difference, if one can say so without insult to the building, being comparable to that between the American and the European car.[44] Above all they may depend on the comfortable acceptance of a more fully developed mass production, so that, by contrast with PSFS, the European buildings seem substantially handtooled. Thus, despite its custom design, PSFS appears as a more impersonal building than the three European examples. More an object within the realm of mass-production techniques and rationalization than the polemical herald of a brave new world, PSFS pays for its assurance by presenting a somewhat less compelling image than they. From our retrospective point of view, the promise of "modernity" in the European buildings gives way to its certainty in PSFS, even if its bravado in the face of Beaux-Arts hegemony by no means suggested any such settled outcome in 1932.

THE UNIQUENESS OF PSFS WITHIN THE INTERNATIONAL STYLE

So PSFS belongs to the International Style. More specifically, it emphasizes some aspects of the Style over others, and these indicate peculiarly American aspects of the building. But all that we have thus far said does not touch upon two aspects of PSFS which somewhat set it apart from European examples in the Style, and are thereby suggestive with respect to possible "American" qualities in a building that the architects themselves were content to identify with the European movement.

The first of these distinguishing aspects is the projecting columns of the office tower. With minor exceptions at best, European buildings in the International Style boast no such bold revelation of structural support on the exterior.[45] Nevertheless the exposed columns do suggest a fifth, and final, possibility within the compositional gamut of the International Style. It might be termed the structural approach, or better (for reasons which will shortly appear) the constructivist approach. If the enclosed volumes of the base, spine, and roof top of PSFS are cubist inspired‡— and we here use "cubist" and "constructivist" in a general sense, as we have already used "expressionist"; that is, as contrasting manners of work-

‡ One might say "purist inspired," since the purists (see pp. 193f. below) tended to transform the complex planar faceting of earlier cubism into larger, textureless shapes with a volumetric quality. I have preferred, however, to use the more general term, to indicate that the architecture was generally influenced by developments in cubism, rather than specifically influenced by purism, although it is of course a "volumetric cubism" of simple geometrical shapes which characterizes the cubism of the International Style.

ing with and of feeling about form possible within the International Style, without more than allusive reference to *the* Cubist and *the* Constructivist movements of the twenties—then, PSFS presents a boldly dichotomous image. Whereas the cubist portion of the building adheres to the canonical nature of the International Style, the projecting columns represent a fundamentally different view of architecture. On the one hand, the *container* which envelops; on the other, the *component* which builds. Container, component; cubist, constructivist: translated into the metaphor of the machine, it is the encasement as opposed to the assemblage of working parts.

Although not predominant as a compositional mode in the International Style of the twenties, the constructivist approach, emphasizing the component parts of a building, nevertheless manifests itself in various ways. All are to some degree evident in PSFS. Constructivist composition within the International Style may appear as *revealed structure,* or as *prefabricated parts,* or, finally, as a *configuration of primal visual elements.* Only some such omnibus description as "constructivist" embraces the three possibilities.

To elaborate: in the International Style, revealed structure typically occurs as exposed columns inside the boxed volumes of interior space, as in the banking room of PSFS (Fig. 45), or, with less architectural pretension, as the unadorned cylindrical columns of Le Corbusier's interiors (Fig. 48). To be sure the columns in the banking room are, for the International Style, unusually conspicuous, and Howe & Lescaze fully intended that they appear as major elements within the space. Even so, the box of space as a whole counts for more here than the columns; all the more because the alternate facing of their four sides as planes in black and oyster white marble diminishes our sense of the columns as solid entities.

Prefabricated parts may also be used to emphasize the building as an assemblage of components. In the PSFS interior, as in the International Style generally, however, prefabrication is not conspicuous in an esthetic sense, except in incidental items attached to the box or inside it (like fixtures, doors, and window units) as opposed to major items used in the construction of the box itself (modular panels, for example). Thus the granite slabs which comprise the wall of the banking room or the base of the building outside are not individually emphasized as they come together to make the whole. Instead they are smoothed into as nearly seamless an effect as possible. Such reticence in the expression of structure and prefabrication in a style so conspicuously technological in its premises is another of its paradoxes. Not until the thirties did panel construction begin to bulk large within the modern movement (a number of experiments toward this end in the twenties notwithstanding), and not until the fifties—with the coming of metal-and-glass panelized wall systems and their complementary systems of panelized ceilings, with the proliferation of panelized plywood systems, with the use of precast concrete elements that are derricked into position—did the constructivism of the prefabricated part have important esthetic use in modern architecture.

Insofar as the constructivist approach does appear in the International Style, it predominantly employs primal linear and planar elements, which combine in space to make the building in an almost abstract manner— one derived more from principles of painting than from concerns with structure or prefabrication. In short, the constructivist aspects of the Style were more visual than technological. The banking room exhibits this kind of constructivism; to what extent will be more evident if we first examine two wholly consistent examples, which were done by one of the leading designers in the Style. A look at Mies van der Rohe's project in 1923 for a brick country house, and then at the actual building for which it was the prototype, the famous German Pavilion at the Barcelona Exposition of 1929, is the more appropriate because Howe made some particularly revealing remarks about the latter shortly after the completion of PSFS.

As a metaphor in architecture evoking (not deliberately perhaps) the atomic nature of matter—an aspect of reality which the modern world was just then coming to know—Mies' project of 1923 (Figs. 63, 64) is unsurpassed in its purity, in part because it remained at a theoretical level. The drawings show a building wholly comprised of planes, almost all either straight or L-shaped, so as to maintain an open relationship one with another, which U-shapes would tend to close. Seen in plan, solid planes of brick alternate in an asymmetrical pin-wheel configuration with transparent planes of glass for windows and doors. Quite obviously the threefold aspect of constructivist composition appears here in an integral manner: structure (masonry walls of brick, technically conservative, but laconically proclaiming the building method); prefabrication (glass panels as window-wall elements); and, above all, the assemblage of primal visual elements as the essence of the design (walls, windows, floor, roof as opaque or transparent planes coming together in space as discrete entities to make a "house"). Mies magnifies the planar quality of the wall elements by extending both solids and transparencies as unbroken entities between the horizontal planes of floor and roof. Neither floor nor roof is fitted to the configuration of the walls. Hence they also exist as independent planes. In fact, the walls boldly extend beyond floor and roof planes, out over the countryside (literally, off the sheet of drawing paper in various directions). In their spread they extend the plane of the floor out across the plane of the landscape, gathering it in, but simultaneously suggesting its infinite extension as a spatial continuum,

FIGURE 63. *Ludwig Mies van der Rohe. Project for a brick country house,* 1923. *Elevation.*

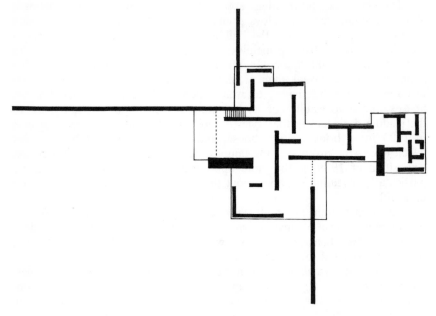

FIGURE 64. *Project for a brick country house. Plan.*

and one so homogeneous in its consistency as to disregard (in Mies' drawing at least) all landscape incident. Where the planes as primal building elements—solid and transparent, vertical and horizontal—create a relatively dense configuration a "house" results—as a field of forces disturbing, but not disrupting, the larger continuum. The planes reaching out from one "house" could well attract other planes, and thus configurate —like stars in a constellation—other "houses" just off the page.

When Mies later returned to the project of 1923 in an actual building—the Barcelona Pavilion—he inevitably reduced somewhat its theoretical purity, and especially its expansiveness. Unlike the earlier project, the Pavilion is confined to a near rectangle which the U-shape of a major segment of its walls semi-enclosed (Figs. 65, 66, and 67). The basic rectangularity of the organization of the Pavilion substantially stabilizes the pin-wheel dynamics of the 1923 scheme, and the raised platform further bounds the composition, much as the stylobate base delimits the classical temple. Amidst the planes, a rectangular roof slab supported on eight free-standing columns evokes the specter of a classical temple, giving a focus, however tenuous, to the composition. To this "temple" focus the planar wall elements are freely, but rigidly, related. (These wall elements are non-structural, even though some of them may appear to assist the columns in supporting the roof plane.) In this conversion of the early scheme, Mies magnified, as he doubtless intended, the architectural image of support and supported, or structure and enclosure; but at some cost to the cosmic reach (whether consciously intended or not) of the project. It was precisely this skeletal image of the rectangular *prisme pur* embedded in the open composition of the Barcelona Pavilion, and the docility with which the independent wall planes tended to echo this rectangle, that enabled Hitchcock and Johnson to overcome certain reservations and include it within the canon of *The International Style*.

The Barcelona Pavilion can be seen in two ways: as a construction of discrete elements, or as light planes modulating a continuous space. Seen in the first way, the Pavilion anticipates Mies' late work in the United States, where structure assumes visual dominance in his building. Seen in the second way, the Pavilion is secured to the International Style. So Howe viewed it. Indeed, it would be difficult to push the spatial theme further than he did in his talk, "Abstract Design in Modern Architecture," to a group of art historians during the mid-thirties. In Mies' Pavilion, he asserted, "the space-time idea is most clearly expressed." Having reminded his audience that the Pavilion had existed only for the duration of the Exposition, Howe continued:

> Its disappearance is perhaps prophetic of a period when we shall have reduced the time element in our lives to a complete abstraction and nothing will remain to architecture but pure conceptual space. . . . mere planes and axes of reference by which space and time relations may be registered. In architecture . . . the movement of human beings through space corresponds roughly to time in matter, and physical space delimited by one or more axes or planes to theoretical space. In this building the contemporary space-time idea as flowing, continuous and relative is carried to the furthest limits of architectural expression . . . the visible elements are an obligatory development of the space idea, not a mere whim of personal taste.[46]

Nothing will remain to architecture but pure conceptual space: How in the light of this statement does the banking room of PSFS appear?

FIGURE 65. Ludwig Mies van der Rohe. German Pavilion at the International Exposition, Barcelona (Spain), 1929. Views into the Pavilion looking across the large pool.

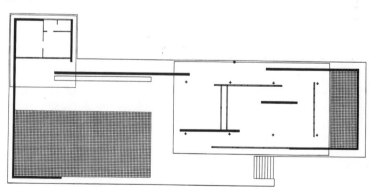

FIGURES 66, 67. *German Pavilion at the Barcelona Exposition. Above: view of court with small pool and sculpture. Below: plan. Shaded areas are pools.*

Our experience there is somewhat surprising. The banking room is rather more constructivist in aspect than most interiors in the International Style, what with the prominence given the columns, as well as the out-sized wall planes, window walls, S-curved balconies, and ceiling planes, all in contrasting colors and materials so that they appear to come together as separate entities to make the big box of space. Awareness of the constructivist aspects of the banking room tends, however, to be subordinated to that of the space of the room as a volume, so that the space seems rather to contain the constructivist elements than to be built of them. The varied textures and colors that distinguish the separate elements of the interior blur kaleidoscopically in the sheen and reflection of surfaces. The ribboned sinuosities of counters and balconies, as well as the change of the marble for alternate sides of the columns, somewhat confuse the space, as though streamers were dropped in it. The off-balance dynamics of approach and entrance to the room confound immediate comprehension of the logic of its organization. So consciousness of the deliberate "build" of the interior, which the constructivist esthetic might have emphasized, gives way to the more heady experience of the "space-time continuum" that Howe attributed to Mies' constructivist pavilion.

But the boldly projecting columns on the exterior of the PSFS office tower are another matter. These anticipate Mies' late work, in what has come to be called by some the Second (or American) Phase of the International Style.* Indeed, the dichotomy in PSFS between the cubist and the constructivist modes makes it of special interest. As no other building in the International Style, it mediates between its European and its so-called American phases. Synthesizing one, it prophesies the other.

If the projecting columns of PSFS anticipate future developments in American architecture, they are also projections of past American experience with the skyscraper. There is no need here to study the history behind Sullivan's pier-and-spandrel buildings, especially as Weisman has done so already, pointing out the probable influence on Sullivan of his awareness of earlier pier-and-spandrel commercial buildings in Philadelphia.[47] It is useful, however, to mention Wright's early pier-and-spandrel project of 1912 for the *San Francisco Call,* which followed Sullivan's lead,† or, more to the point for PSFS, of the side elevations of the Larkin Building (Fig. 144), where the density of Sullivan's projecting piers is replaced by widely separated piers with horizontal windows stretched between. And there is the long tradition of Gothic for sky-

---

* See Chapter 4 below, pp. 228f., for a discussion of the limited extent to which Mies used exposed structure before coming to the United States.
† Conveniently illustrated in Hitchcock, *In the Nature of Materials,* New York, Duell, Sloan & Pearce, 1942, figs. 187 and 188; and in Drexler, *Drawings of Frank Lloyd Wright,* New York, Horizon, 1962, fig. 45.

scrapers, which had presumably conditioned Willcox's prejudices. already observed it in the Woolworth and Chicago Tribune buildings (Figs. 2, 26), and have watched the Gothic becoming quasi-modern in Eliel Saarinen's project for the *Tribune* Competition, in the Daily News Building, and in Rockefeller Center (Figs. 27, 24 and 22). As part of this process of pier-and-spandrel Gothicism becoming "modern," the projecting piers with their structural implications tended to recede into the wall as vertical stripes, the better to assert the wall as a skin lightly enclosing a big volume of space.‡

What precedents, then, can be found within the architecture associated with the International Style which defy the trend toward the wall as a membranous envelopment of space, and assert the projecting columns on the scale and in the manner of PSFS? They are few. Among the few, however, two designs with projecting structural columns are especially plausible as influences on PSFS: one by Max Taut, the other by Richard Neutra. Taut's scheme, together with that by Walter Gropius and Adolf Meyer (this without projecting columns, however), were most frankly expressive of skeletal construction among the entries in the Tribune Competition (Figs. 68, 69).[48] Far cries from either Howells & Hood's winning design or Eliel Saarinen's quasi-modern second-prize winner, had one of these German designs been built it would most appropriately have returned the esthetic of unadorned skeletal construction for commercial buildings to that city which, more than any other, had fostered, then forgotten, it. The Gropius-Meyer design literally fills out the frame (one of barest essentials) with equivalents of the so-called Chicago window. To be sure, there are arbitrary elements about the design, none more so than the spotty, right-angled pattern of balconies in a misplaced effort to relieve its monotony. On the other hand, Taut's scheme, except for its entrance and some decorative variation of the window motif in the tower, is very consistent. Compared to PSFS it is particularly interesting because Taut countered the directional neutrality of the Gropius-Meyer grid with projecting columns, thereby emphasizing the height of the building. Like Howe & Lescaze (and like Mies after World War II), he abruptly clipped these columns at the top, leaving them without a cornice. Because of the prominence of the Tribune Competition, Howe & Lescaze may well have been at least vaguely aware of Taut's project, which had an exceptionally structural approach to the wall when measured by the standards of the European International Style of the twenties.

The second scheme with projecting structural columns, this one American, resembles PSFS more remarkably: namely, Richard Neutra's

‡ See Chapter 1; also *American Buildings and Their Architects: Progressive and Academic Ideals at the Turn of the Twentieth Century,* Chapter 2.

FIGURES 68, 69. *Left: Walter Gropius and Adolf Meyer. Project submitted for the Chicago Tribune Competition of 1922. Right: project by Max Taut.*

project of 1926 for a store and office building in his ideal Rush City Reformed (Fig. 70). According to Lescaze, Neutra's project exerted no direct influence on PSFS,[49] which the development of the design seems to substantiate. Indirectly, however, it would seem to have been influential, since Neutra's visionary commercial building and PSFS are strikingly comparable. The partners may have generally recalled it when finally forced to a vertical treatment of the tower, and perhaps this vague recall reconciled them to their fate. In any event, to such literate modernists it was readily available in Neutra's *Wie Baut Amerika?* published in 1927 or (a more likely source) as the final plate in Henry-Russell

154

FIGURE 70. *Richard Neutra. Project for a skyscraper for his "Rush City Reformed," 1927.*

FIGURE 71. *Richard Neutra. Lovell "Health" House, Los Angeles, 1927–29.*

Hitchcock's *Modern Architecture: Romantic Disintegration and Reintegration,* 1929. Like Howe & Lescaze, Neutra also designed an International Style jack-in-the-box, where the constructivist office tower pops from the cubist base. Like Howe & Lescaze he too cantilevered his floors from the narrow face of his tower. Like them he abruptly cut off the projecting columns at the top of the building to eliminate the cornice, except for a vestigial outrigging. This happens to be a luminous plane designed to wash the building with a graduated light after dark so that it would glow against the sky, much as Lescaze depicted PSFS in his early drawing done on Christmas Day 1929 (Fig. 61).

   Whatever the relationship between the two designs, it is of particular consequence that, once he had come to the United States, Neutra immediately began to oppose the volumetrics of the European International Style with the structural implications of skeletal construction, much as Mies followed a similar course on his arrival toward the end of the thirties—and in the same Chicago environment which had led to Neutra's *Wie Baut Amerika?* a decade earlier. Neutra's Lovell House (1927–29) likewise reveals an interest in the skeleton (Fig. 71). Here the volume is not enclosed in the European manner with the surface continuity of a stretched skin; instead, the metal skeleton is very evident at the plane of the wall and provides the framework for hanging and fitting the wall planes and windows which close the space. The volumetric nature of this skeletal construction makes it a less bold statement of the complementary

opposition of container and component than either his own
Rush City or PSFS. Significantly, however, the first two Amer___ buildings to receive world renown as exemplars of the International Style
already prophesy the most significant manner in which the new environment will extend the style. Both PSFS and the Lovell House already look
forward to the American works of Mies.[50]

In one major respect PSFS is unlike Neutra's project for Rush City.
This is in the provision which Howe & Lescaze made for packaging
elevators and vertical utility stacks behind the constructivist tower, and
for separately packaging specific functions both on the roof and within
the base. Of course the discrete revelation of different functions radically
distinguishes PSFS from other American skyscrapers. Moreover, if we
search the European International Style for buildings approximating PSFS
in this respect, we find them to be in a definite minority; these few are
freely composed on a functional basis with stair towers boldly evident,
as the Van Nelle factory or the sanitarium at Paimio (Figs. 53, 58).
Even these towers, however, tend to be handled as complicated cubist
fillips to façades of window bands or window walls. The European buildings do not quite possess the didactic separation of elements which PSFS
reveals; all the more startling in the typical skyscraper in the International Style, where the favored image was the glass tower rising sheer
from base to cornice as column or slab, or, more rarely, as some type
of prism. The principal exceptions in the International Style to the skyscraper as crystalline tower are a few schemes by Russian Constructivists
like the newspaper building projected by the Vesnin brothers, which may
have influenced PSFS directly, or El Lissitzky's "Skyhook" office building,
which may have had an indirect influence. Surely Constructivist technological fantasies were peripherally significant.

To be sure there *is* a tall building in the International Style that
seems to have influenced the exceptional massing of PSFS. This, as H.
Allen Brooks has pointed out,[51] is E. Otto Osswald's design for Tagblatt-Turm (1927–28) in Stuttgart (Fig. 72)—or rather a sketch of it.
Francis Keally, a traveling American architect, made a quick sketch of
the building which appeared in the *Architectural Record* for February
1929, immediately across the page from a design by Mellor, Meigs &
Howe, and just as Howe was working on the first designs of the PSFS
skyscraper. Howe could hardly have missed it. Resemblances between
Keally's sketch and the final massing of PSFS are indeed striking, although
the design that Howe produced in March of 1929 (Fig. 40) indicates
that the influence of the Tagblatt-Turm only came at a later stage of the
design after Lescaze had joined the enterprise. In any event, the irregular massing, the projecting bustle to the back with horizontal window
bands, the narrow slab-like mass to the front, and especially the window

FIGURE 72. E. Otto Osswald. Tagblatt-Turm, Stuttgart (Germany), 1927–28. Drawing published in the Architectural Record, February 1929.

bands cantilevered over the street with the boldly opened storefronts below and the executive lounge at the roof—all these aspects of the sketch make it consequential for the design of PSFS. But there are cardinal differences too, differences which indicate that, influential as Keally's sketch may have been, its influence was quite literally skin-deep. First, the structural image of the projecting piers for the tower slab is missing. Second, there is no indication from the sketch that disparate functions within the building were as decisively parceled in the Tagblatt-Turm as in the PSFS design. (In the Tagblatt-Turm, for example, elevators seem to have been placed in the tower slab, and roof-top accommodations are symmetrically distributed.) In short, the most distinctive aspects of PSFS, making it the thoughtful design within the modern movement that it is, are either ambiguous in the sketch of Tagblatt-Turm or missing from it.[52]

Parallels to the rigorously functional massing of the skyscraper as it appears in PSFS are again especially to be found in the American future. The work of Louis Kahn is a case in point, to which we shall return.* More directly comparable to PSFS, however, is Skidmore, Owings & Merrill's Inland Steel Building (1956–58) in Chicago (Figs. 73, 74). Its vertical package of utilities rises behind and above the office tower. Structural fins along the broad faces of the tower completely support the floors within. The floors therefore slide past the inner edge of these supports, and at both of the narrow ends extend beyond them as cantilevers. All floors are therefore completely free of interior columns.† To be sure, Inland Steel perfects the functional packaging and revealed skeletal structure which PSFS brings to the skyscraper. Consonant with the cubist interlocking of forms in its massing, in PSFS a few of the utilities spill out of their container and into the office tower, although it is worth noting that Howe's original scheme of March 1929 (Fig. 40) shows a somewhat neater bundling of the separate functions. The imperfect packaging in PSFS further appears in the inclusion of office space within the extremities of the spine. The structural columns project only half their depth from the floor slabs instead of full depth as at Inland Steel, while the column-free floors of the later building represent an improvement of the PSFS design. Moreover, the columns in PSFS are lost to view in the package for bank and stores at the base of the building. Such are the ways in which Inland Steel exceeds PSFS in achieving didactic clarity in the revelation of function and structure. But PSFS is clearly prophetic of future developments in the American tall building, and its more elaborate functional packaging (especially on the roof) is even bolder than they. Furthermore, the visual decisiveness of the components of PSFS is superior to, if less spectacular than, the wavy surfaces and blinding sheen of Inland Steel's sheet-metal sheathing.

* See Chapter 6 below.
† Despite its chance, but significant, parallel to the PSFS office tower, the office block of Inland Steel has its apparent source in Mies van der Rohe's house for Dr. Edith Farnsworth (1945–50) in nearby Plano, Ill.—or rather a stacked multiple of this house. The over-all massing represents a variation and rationalization of Mies' massing for the Seagram Building; see Chapter 4 below.

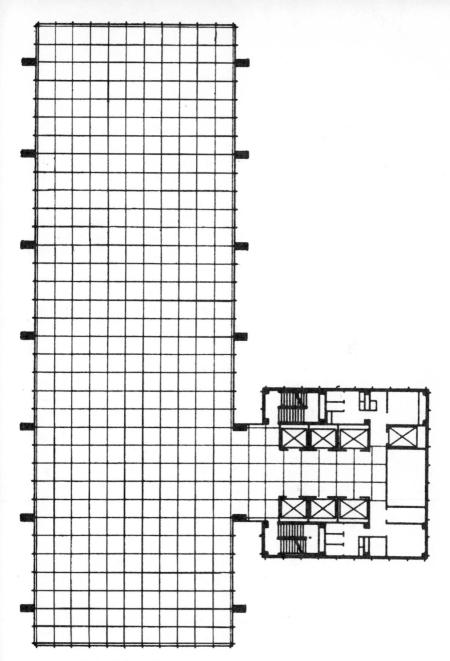

FIGURE 74. *Inland Steel Building. Plan.*

FIGURE 73. *Opposite: Skidmore, Owings & Merrill. Inland Steel Building, Chicago, 1956–58.*

PSFS AND BEAUX-ARTS DESIGN

It is the final paradox of a building customarily ticketed as a principal exemplar of European modernism at the moment of its arrival in the United States that it looks beyond the International Style by going behind it. Robert Stern has pointed out that the complex articulation of the plan and also the massing of PSFS distinguish it from the omnibus spatial container characteristic of the International Style. These are qualities found in the most creative Beaux-Arts design.[53] On the one hand, the *cloisonné* of compartments, as Bernard Maybeck termed it,‡ may make the Beaux-Arts plan ornamental—sometimes purely ornamental in that the geometrical shapes arranged like the pattern for an intricate jewel on paper have little to do with functional concerns. On the other hand, a functionally articulated plan revealed in its mass is the rationalistic counterpart of the ornamental plan in Beaux-Arts design. Like a thin thread, this rationalism runs throughout Beaux-Arts theory, grounding its flights toward pomposity in common sense. By the twentieth century, this rationalism owed as much (or more) to an infiltration of ideas from the diffuse tradition of nineteenth-century picturesque rationalism.[54] As Stern has emphasized, this constellation of ideas initially came to Howe in his classes at Harvard with Charles Herbert Moore, who had based his philosophy of architecture on a rationalistic view of Gothic. If Moore emphasized the importance of the visible articulation of plan and mass, his *Development and Character of Gothic Architecture* (1890) also presented the medieval cathedral as the resultant of its structure in one of the more rationalistic accounts of the development of the cathedral. Howe carried Moore's ideals into his Beaux-Arts design, not systematically, but as fundamental conditioning. Various aspects of PSFS, like the sumptuous use of elegant materials, and the rows of column-piers flanking the banking room, possess overtones of monumentality and permanence which proclaim the more elegant side of Beaux-Arts training. In Howe's early work these overlay, but never dislodged, his rationalistic bent. In fact, his groping rationalism led him to modern architecture. He brought a traditional rationalism to the new rationalism in PSFS.

The more narrowly modern point of view of Lescaze, apparent at its worst in the *moderne* ephemera of the model, at its best in the courageous forcing of the building as a fully committed modern statement,

‡ See *American Buildings and Their Architects: Progressive and Academic Ideals at the Turn of the Twentieth Century,* Chapter 6.

was always checked by the traditional aspects of Howe's taste, and by his brand of rationalism. If Lescaze seemed to be *the* designer of PSFS as long as it was viewed as merely another episode in the International Style, the contributions of Howe to the design have loomed in importance as the revolutionary moment of modernism recedes and modern architecture increasingly looks to the "great tradition," at one time scorned by shallow modernists as a Beaux-Arts preserve. Whereas the early thirties favored angled photographs of the building showing it as a dynamic tumble of cubist planes and volumes (Fig. 35), untilted views revealing the particularate definition of space, mass, and structure, together with its over-all solidity of aspect, are more likely to be favored today (Fig. 42).

Indeed, the present limitation in our view of PSFS is likely to be the reverse of that of the thirties. We may fail to appreciate fully how far adherence to the principles of the International Style brought PSFS beyond the pseudo-modernism of the Daily News and McGraw-Hill Buildings, and that of Rockefeller Center; how impossible it would have been without the example of modern principles for Beaux-Arts rationalism to have produced more than some substantial compromise with traditional design for PSFS. In the thirties, Beaux-Arts principles were "given," and the degree of modernity measured the revolution. Today, inevitably, the modern principles of the International Style are "given," and the degree to which traditional precepts have enlarged the polemical point of view seem more important, or at least more interesting, than may its modernity.

In fact, the uniqueness of PSFS, both as a building and as an historical event, appears in its extraordinary ambiguity, as reconciliation, synthesis, and prophecy. It reconciles the rationalism of the academic tradition with that of the modern movement. It synthesizes both brands of rationalism within a comprehensive view of the International Style, the functional, expressionist, and constructivist modes of which are especially evident in a startlingly dichotomous union of container and component. It prophesies developments of special consequence in modern American architecture in its bold revelation of the projecting structural columns and its discreet compartmentalization of functions.

For these reasons and for its intrinsic quality, it stands as the most important American skyscraper between Sullivan's work of the nineties (the masonry construction of the Monadnock makes it something of a freak) and the Seagram Building at the end of the fifties, all rooted in rationalistic philosophies of architecture. As an esthetic achievement, PSFS is somewhat less than the best of the work of Sullivan and Mies. Their rationalism is that of the penetrant vision, creating from reality metaphor that opens to imaginative realms of order well beyond, yet integral with, their prosaic starting points. On the other hand, PSFS has its own superiority. For the analytical precision with which it meets a complex architectural program, for elegance and comprehensiveness of design without sacrifice of this analysis, and for creative expression of what was relevant at a moment of momentous esthetic and philosophical change in modern architecture, PSFS has at least as much to teach.

CHAPTER III

The Domestication of Modern: Marcel Breuer's Ferry Cooperative Dormitory at Vassar College

Ironically, here was a style [the International Style] which, more consciously than any other in history, was directed towards the improvement of the comfort and convenience, health and happiness of society as a whole, yet there has probably never been an architectural movement more deeply distrusted by the public.

Some process of humanization was necessary . . . Americans looked again at the stone and wood barns of Pennsylvania, the white clapboard walls of New England, the low, rambling ranch houses of the West, and found them good. . . .

MUSEUM OF MODERN ART, Built in U.S.A.: 1932–1944, the catalogue edited by Elizabeth Mock for an exhibition at the Museum in 1944

The real impact of any work is the extent to which it unifies contrasting notions, opposing points of view. The easy method of meeting contrasting problems is the feeble compromise. The solution for the contrasts between black and white is gray—that is the easy way. Sun and shadow does not mean a cloudy day. The need for black and the need for white still exist. . . .

MARCEL BREUER, Sun and Shadow, 1954

GENTLING THE AVANT GARDE

If PSFS is easily passed over because it exists in the limbo of the all-too-familiar and the not-quite-historical, the same could be said of the Dexter M. Ferry Cooperative House (1948–51), a dormitory at Vassar College in Poughkeepsie, New York (Fig. 75). Ferry House hides behind a corner of the Victorian-mansarded Main Hall (1860–61) by Renwick,

FIGURE 75. *Marcel Breuer. Dexter M. Ferry Cooperative House, Vassar College, Poughkeepsie, N.Y., 1948–51. The natural cypress which originally appeared in the paneling of the window areas has been painted black; compare with Figure 83.*

Auchmuty & Sands.[1]* The stiff effulgence of this immense reddish-violet brick block gives no forewarning of the taut precision and low spread of the dormitory it conceals. Originally designed for a more isolated site, and in fieldstone which proved to be too expensive,[2] Ferry House seems startlingly out of place on first encounter. It appears somewhat like the House of Tomorrow set down on those exposition grounds where a gargantuan Victorian relic has long housed the major exhibits.

Once the initial impact of the incongruity wears away, however, the contrast has its own appeal. Moreover, spankingly trim as it at first appears, surrounded by the bulk and autumnal colors of Main Hall and its other architectural neighbors, Ferry House is nevertheless so unpretentious that it readily wins acceptance. Its unpretentiousness is due partly to its domestic scale, partly to the integrity of the design, which scorns theatricality, partly to our familiarity with this kind of modern building. Even when it had just been built, and was causing some stir among alumnae as Vassar's first (and belated) venture into modern architecture, Ferry House was really less a House of Tomorrow than a House of the Recent Past. It was, in effect, a public summation of a modern type which Walter Gropius and Marcel Breuer had developed in a number of private houses from around 1938 onward. With the abandonment of their collaboration, the type came to be more especially associated with Breuer, whose American buildings proved to be more inventive than Gropius' work in this country. Ferry House is no masterpiece. It makes no pretense of being a "major work." Breuer would surely prefer to be judged by more ambitious undertakings, no matter how justified his probable satisfaction that Ferry House serves Vassar so well.

* Historically, James Renwick (1818–95) is the important member of this firm.

For our purposes, however, this building available to the public can serve as an index to Breuer's domestic style. Not a complete index, because the budget for an expensive private house gives leeway in the elaboration of its design, while even a minimally budgeted house may possess an individuality all but impossible for dormitories. Thus we begin, admitting that Ferry House is a modest building, and a somewhat bland one owing to the nature of the commission, yet a building of merit. Criticism customarily overlooks unassuming buildings of quality. But in this instance, the relative modesty and blandness of Ferry House make it particularly appropriate for comment. These very qualities characterize a widespread tendency during the late thirties and forties for modern architects to gentle the *avant garde* insistence of the International Style of the twenties.

To be sure, what was *avant garde* in the twenties was bound to be more acceptable in succeeding decades. Growing familiarity with the Style was, however, merely one factor in its acceptance. Other circumstances hastened its spread during the thirties and forties. Specifically, during these decades, the International Style characteristic of the twenties became more domesticated, vernacularized, diversified, and adapted to popular taste (where it was not vulgarized). Ferry House conveniently illuminates all four of these interrelated developments.

PROCESSES OF DIFFUSION

To speak first of the domestication of the International Style during the thirties and forties is to speak somewhat elliptically, since houses were predominant among the buildings executed in the Style during the twenties. But whereas the concern of the twenties had been with the modernity of the house, the concern of the mid-thirties—by which time the ideology had become fairly well established and its adherents could relax a bit—was to reconcile the *avant garde* esthetic to images and values traditionally adhering to "house" and "home." The English *Architectural Review* aptly, if somewhat pretentiously, summarized this phase of the International Style as the "new empiricism."[3] Although the attitude characterized in the *Review* had international repercussions (the article, for example, centered on Danish house design), the domestication of the International Style in the United States assumed qualities that were only partially duplicated abroad.

The construction of large buildings had come to a near halt with the Depression. Rockefeller Center and PSFS, both commissioned before the crash and built during the depth of the Depression, were among the exceptions. Not until the fifties could modern commercial and institutional buildings be realized in any quantity, and then they, rather than houses, provided the most creative American commissions for at least a decade and a half. Not even a depression quite halts house building. There are always some, lucky enough to have gone unscathed or adventurous enough to be willing to scrape, who insist on a house. Possibly the emphasis of the propaganda for modern architecture on economy and function (both somewhat exaggerated), as well as on informality appealed to imaginative clients during the Depression, as they have ever since. In any event, these prospective homeowners were fortunate to find talented designers, some just then venturing into professional life, but also some of middle age and even beyond, who had time and incentive to give relatively small houses the careful study which they rarely receive in prosperous times, when talent is lured to larger commissions.

In the creation of new house types, no previous decade and a half in American architectural history can compare in inventiveness with that from roughly 1935–50. These house types were immediately and extensively influential in current building, and of major import for future developments. In this respect, the American situation somewhat differed from that abroad. There was the Gropius-Breuer version of the European International Style, as modified by the architects' experience with the New England wooden vernacular. There was Wright's development of his early "prairie" style into what he termed "Usonian" houses, doubtless attracted not only by the utopian ring of the word as it appeared in Samuel Butler's *Erewhon,* but as well by the American flavor of the "US."[4] At the opposite extreme, there was Mies van der Rohe's severely classicistic Farnsworth House in metal and glass, and the related, yet unique, "Glass House" which his disciple, Philip Johnson, built for himself. Finally, there was the West Coast redwood translation of the International Style. Originally centered in the San Francisco area (and sometimes termed the "Bay Region Style"[5]), it also appeared farther south in California, and in pockets of the Northwest, particularly around Portland and Seattle. Houses in this style revived the indigenous and largely anonymous tradition of nineteenth-century carpentry, and at the same time they substantially accounted for the rediscovery of the wooden houses of Greene & Greene and Maybeck. They also depended, more heavily than the most ardent local enthusiasts liked to believe, on eastern work in the Gropius-Breuer manner. (Reciprocally, the West Coast development may, in minor respects, have influenced Breuer.) The eclectic West Coast tradition comprehended other ways as well. Some of its architects translated the structural precision of Mies' metal frames into wood. Most borrowed at times from Wright and the Japanese tradition. Especially in California, there were those who tended to link house and garden more positively than was practical elsewhere. California's warm, relatively bug-free environment encouraged extravagant openness in design, while semi-aridity and the vaunted informality and athleticism of life in the region abetted propensities in modern architecture for "gardens" that featured patios, terraces, and swimming pools as much as foliage.

This ferment of origination in modern domestic architecture in the late thirties and forties subsided in the fifties. House design during the fifties largely coasted on its immediate heritage, as the most creative architects grasped at the larger commissions with which business, institutions, and, at last, even government began to favor modern architecture. For Breuer, as an example, Ferry House was something of a turning point. This was his first commission for other than houses that Breuer saw to completion†; yet he was nearing the age of fifty. Appropriate as a first step toward larger non-domestic commissions just then about to come his way, this institutional building was, in fact, a large house for twenty-seven girls who would self-help their way through college by doing their own housekeeping. Doubtless a number of its former residents have already graduated to smaller Ferry Houses of their own.

Nothing furthered the domestication of the movement—the shift in its central concern from the *modern* house to the modern *house*—more than the modification of the mechanistic appearance of early modern by an overlay of vernacular, folkish, and regional features in the late thirties and forties. In their propaganda of the twenties, the modernists among European architects frequently drew analogies between primitive or folk-ish forms and those of the machine. These comparisons emphasized the simple shapes common to both (the more so since the complicated aspects possible to both were conveniently ignored). Simple shapes were praised as having more or less inevitably emerged from material, structure, and use. Moreover, they were seen as the result of anonymous communal standards expressive of time, place, and technology, which architects working in the International Style believed the techniques of mass production must find for the modern world.

Despite this coupling of folk arts and the machine during the twenties (more in theory than in practice, however), the machine image decidedly dominated during the decade. Between 1930 and 1935, however, Le Corbusier built three vacation houses (two on the Riviera, one of which appears in Figs. 87, 88, 89, and one in Chile⁶) in which he subordinated the machine image to regional traditions of building in masonry and

† Previously, he had designed a number of projects for non-residential buildings, but had never realized them. He has continued to do houses subsequent to Ferry House, but larger buildings have been the more important commissions for this latter part of his career.

wood without compromising his own architectural ideals.‡ These houses, as we shall see,[7] would strongly influence Breuer's career. The widespread interest in the vernacular during the early thirties is also revealed in the work of Alvar Aalto, which was much publicized at the time. He had begun to make use of brick and wood, traditional to building in his native Finland. With these materials, Aalto, like Le Corbusier, demonstrated that modern architecture need not possess the textureless walls given it in the twenties, machine-thin in appearance like the bodies of automobiles, and as precisely edged. For interior use, he designed chairs of bent plywood, an alternative to chrome tubing, and one no less committed to modern form and technology. The same decade saw the re-emergence of Frank Lloyd Wright from fifteen years of professional obscurity, a limbo to which both Beaux-Arts and modern esthetics had relegated him. The arch opponent of what he denigrated as the "cardboard" style of early European modernism, Wright, in the thirties and forties, more than regained the professional acclaim that he had briefly been given from some modern European designers after the German publications of his work in 1910 and 1911.[8] Now he also basked in popular renown, especially in the United States, as an "American" and "mid-western" architect, even though his significance was world-wide and clearly transcended any such limiting labels.

In the United States, the thirties were a time especially congenial to the rediscovery of regional traditions, and not in architecture alone. Domestic problems forced the country to turn inward on itself, where it remained focused until foreign events broke the isolationist trance. There was the publicity on the South as an economic problem area, and the positive achievements that resulted from it: the Tennessee Valley Authority; the emergence of a southern literary tradition; the regional "agrarianism" of certain southern critics; the popularity of regional studies in sociology under the leadership of Harold Odum at the University of North Carolina. Other sectional problems forced themselves on public consciousness too: the Dust Bowl and the migrant workers in California particularly. There was the parochial vitality of regional realism in painting, and much the same emphasis in all the arts sponsored by the Works Progress Administration. Underlying these and other overt manifestations of regional consciousness, there was the cult of local self-sufficiency—the consequence of a time when few could travel and most were skimping.

‡ With the curved masonry wall and sculptural stilts of his Swiss Dormitory for the Cité Universitaire in Paris (1930–32), which owes much to his explorations of regional masonry traditions, Le Corbusier more conspicuously inaugurated a development which forecast the rough sculptural massiveness of his late work. Illustrated in Le Corbusier, *Oeuvre complète, 1929–1934*, p. 74–89.

Regionalism, in short, was "in the air." The regional component has often been too glibly invoked to account for the diversity of expression in modern architecture in the United States after 1935. Yet its influence should not be underestimated. Lewis Mumford's praise of the redwood modern of California as an indigenous "Bay Area Style" is testimony; so is Wright's allegiance to the midwest. Even Mies van der Rohe's esthetic, ostensibly free of locale in its austere dependence on skeletal minima, is so kindred to the most skeletal of the Chicago commercial buildings of the 1890's as to seem inconceivable without their proximity.* For Gropius and Breuer the national mood coincided with their own need to adjust to their new environment. Not since McKim, Mead & White and other academic architects had more literally investigated a riper colonial and early national tradition[9] did the exploration of the New England past prove as consequential for current design.

Regional differences were especially obvious in the United States because the centers of modern architecture were widely separated, existing as pockets of activity in the suburbs of certain cities: principally New York, Boston, Chicago, Los Angeles, and San Francisco. In the beginning, not even these suburban areas as a whole were affected; rather only such enclaves as New Canaan, Connecticut, or Lincoln and Lexington, Massachusetts. Like psychiatrists of the period, modern architects tended to cluster; they often stayed close to the architectural schools from which they had graduated. They enjoyed one another's company in what was then a rather lonely point of view. They shared with potential clients the liberal attitudes toward culture that filtered into the environs of the biggest cities. They also sought the advantage of the client preconditioning for modern architecture which their professional predecessors and colleagues had brought about.

Of course the diversity apparent in modern American architecture in the late thirties and the forties was not attributable to regional factors alone. Nor was this diversity a strictly American phenomenon. In Europe, the architecture wrought in the International Style was relatively homogeneous between 1926 and 1932, but after this climactic period which saw completion of the major buildings in the Style,[10] the quest for diversity of expression began. Only the concerted attack by architects who worked in such a group Style, with its pretensions to universality could have challenged the hegemony of Beaux-Arts academicism. (Witness the disarray by 1915 of progressively inclined American architects from the middle and far west who individually had challenged Beaux-Arts dominance.) By the mid-thirties, the battle for modern architecture was sufficiently won that the monolithic thrust of the crusade could slacken.

* Although see p. 223 below.

In characterizing the architectural trend immediately after World War II as the "new empiricism," the *Architectural Review* maintained that the tough didacticism of *the* "modern style" had dissipated everywhere toward more comfortable, more particularate, more varied versions of "modern." Yet this tendency seems to have been especially marked in the United States. The reasons are not altogether clear. Surely the social upheaval preceding and following World War II disrupted European achievement. The repression of modern architecture by totalitarian regimes in some countries was abetted by that of highly centralized and deeply entrenched academies in others (especially in France). The anarchic situation in American architectural schools, however, ensured that teachers with a modern point of view would infiltrate some of them. Moreover, since Americans had no emotional investment in the theoretical formulation of the Style, it may have been easier for them to accept the finished product as the starting point for individual expression. Then, too, the emigration of leading professionals, especially from Germany, and the consequent disruption of the group quality of the by-then well-established International Style in an unfamiliar and vaster setting doubtless encouraged each man to find his own way. Diversity of expression within the modern movement may also have been intensified in the United States by the shift from urban conditioning of the Style in Europe during the twenties (even though the actual building may have occurred in the country) to suburban conditioning in the United States, with the concomitant client demand for distinctive rather than conforming design. Certainly the social commitment of European modernism of the twenties, which had aspired to provide standardized housing for all classes consonant with the highest standards of technology, was seriously (and tragically) eroded in America, New Deal social reforms notwithstanding. Finally, Europe possessed no modern master whose antipathy to the International Style commanded the respect and influence (even among those committed to the Style) that were Wright's. The "American" qualities of his work, evident in his buildings and conspicuous in his writings, together with the prestige both enjoyed from the mid-thirties onward, made modern design in the United States difficult without at least oblique reference to his accomplishment. There were exceptions, most notably the work of Mies van der Rohe†; but they were few.

In any event, there was in Europe nothing at the time akin to the

---

† On the other hand, early in his career Mies had been inspired by German publications of Wright's work in 1910 and 1911; see his own statement on the influence of Wright, quoted in Johnson, *Mies van der Rohe* (1953, 2nd ed.), pp. 200f. Echoes of this influence appear in Mies' project of 1923 for a brick country house and in his Barcelona Pavilion (figs. 63–67).

confrontation of Mies and Wright, not merely as individual practitioners, but as rallying points for progressive designers in the profession as a whole. Nor did regional developments abroad become as sharply defined (even if somewhat fraudulently so) as the New England modern and the Bay Area Style. In short, nothing at the time in Europe matched either the widespread influence of competing modes of expression in America, or the lively interaction among them—so lively, indeed, that not a few architects worked in all four manners, whether simultaneously, successively, or in various combinations—and with Japanese and Corbusian touches thrown in for good measure!

The increasing diversity of the International Style in America from the mid-thirties to the fifties resulted in large part from the sheer activity in modern architecture which occurred during these years, and to the pedagogic nature of much of this activity. Major designers, Wright included, did not lock themselves in their offices, but taught. They thereby diffused their own ideas as they speedily revolutionized architectural training. Especially for emigrés, like Breuer, teaching provided the wherewithal for getting a foothold in their new environment, and for experiment. Although commissions to modern architects came slowly during the late thirties (and were interrupted by the war, though by no means so severely as in Europe), they increased steadily during the forties. The wonder is how during the thirties Mies van der Rohe, Gropius, Breuer and others, with so few commissions in hand, could sustain their careers at all—yet suddenly they were building again. And soon they were building in a volume unknown at any previous time in their careers.

At the beginning of the thirties the leading American professional architectural magazines published only occasional articles on "far out" developments abroad. These were much too occasional to substantially challenge the influence of the weight of editorial commitment to design in Neo-Colonial, Neo-Renaissance, Neo-Gothic and other modes of eclectic historicism, including some mildly cubist treatments of Beaux-Arts massing. Before the end of the decade, however, these same magazines had blossomed with modern architecture. The sheer momentum of "catching up" by both architects and editors at a time when the modern movement tended toward diversification inevitably boosted current American contributions to modern architecture to international importance, and especially so after World War II. To be sure, American buildings and designers had attracted the attention of progressive European architects during the twenties. As we have seen, the work of Frank Lloyd Wright, for example, had been admired by some European architects and influenced in piecemeal fashion the International Style.[11] (To those infused with *l'esprit nouveau,* however, his work as a whole appeared as that of a "nineteenth-century romantic.") In addition, there was the inspiration of American technology, with European enthusiasm for the myth and reality of the assembly line being at least as important as that for American building techniques. There was also some influence from American factories and grain elevators. Above all, there was the obsession abroad with the skyscraper, and with the throb of modernity emanating from the American city of skyscrapers. Yet the promise of American building for the creation of a genuinely modern architecture had largely been unrealized. Most of the modern European architects would have agreed with Le Corbusier's verdict in a typically staccato account of a visit to the United States in the mid-thirties: audacious possibilities—but a "land of timid people."[12] At the beginning of the thirties most progress-minded American architects did not argue the European judgment. Witness George Howe's modest avowal to Willcox that the quality of the design of PSFS was derivative, dependent on the virtues of the movement which it exemplified. He spoke as though good work in a good cause were sufficient achievement in itself. (And in fact it would have been in 1930, even had PSFS been no more than this.) By the end of the decade, however, American architects, including emigrés like Breuer who became Americans, could already legitimately claim to have made contributions to the mainstream of the modern movement. During the fifties—despite superb work in other countries by a few major designers like Le Corbusier and Aalto, and radical developments in reinforced concrete construction by such engineers as Nervi, Torroja, Candela, and Morandi—modern American architecture, taken as a national lump, had become more influential than that of any other nation. By the fifties, the very diversity of the American contribution had become a factor in the degree of this influence.

The years from about 1935 to 1950 also saw the popularization of modern architecture. In this case, too, the trend was international, but it was especially evident in the United States by the late thirties, and became even more conspicuous there after World War II. Just as variety inevitably occurs with the development of any style as circumscribed as the International Style of the twenties, so does popularization, once the style of an *avant garde* becomes established. Indeed, the very variety of the possibilities within the Style by the late thirties hastened its popularization, making it easier for modern architecture to appeal to "every taste." Such popularization never centers in the philosophical reach of a style, but in its consumable features. Thus the open plan, outdoor living, the interior court, the emphasis on convenience and informality—in short, the "modern look"—entered the consumer magazines; especially publicized were the cozier variants which the "new regionalism" provided. Redwood, the barbecue patio, the "family room," the "picture window," the kitchen "pass-through," the "carport," the "deck," the "storage wall," the "ranch house," the "split level," and so on: these eventually became the bywords (rather the *buy*-words) of the house builder. His more or less "modern" product spread rapidly and widely after World War II.

In their presentation of modern architecture, the consumer magazines accomplished much that was useful, more that was superficial, and at least as much that was atrocious. The regional aspects of modernism, unfortunately, led to flag-waving, as the vulgarization of any kind of regional idealism always does. Thus an "American" modern was suddenly proclaimed in the pages of the consumer magazines. And its "humanism" and "individuality" were implicitly, and sometimes overtly, contrasted with the "mechanistic" and "communal" (even "communistic") qualities of early European modernism.[13] The comparison was the more contemptible because European modernists had for two decades sponsored a sizable portion of the "new ideas" presented by these "home-making" magazines, the publishers and editors of which had been profitably plumping for Colonial, Cape Cod, Provençal, and the like. If the coarser forms of patriotism in the wake of regional consciousness were simply irresponsible, the comfortable "humanism" encouraged by popularization represented a genuine threat to the integrity of the modern movement. To appropriate William James' famous dichotomy, but using it in a more superficial sense than he intended: the tender-minded humanism of convenience, relaxation, and escape threatened the tough-minded humanism of the early modern quest for the reconciliation and enhancement of modern life with what was technologically, psychologically, and symbolically at the heart of modern existence.[14] Whereas the invitation to flop and forget in the surfeit of gimmickry and neo-tradition is the core of a pseudo-humanism, it is no part at all of genuine humanism. True humanism makes man more alive, not more inert—fiercely and thoughtfully alive in terms of the central meaning of his situation, and in his capacity both to cope with it and to create in it.

It was against this background, with regional influences enlarging the possibilities of the International Style while also sentimentalizing the movement for popular consumption, that Marcel Breuer addressed a symposium at the Museum of Modern Art in 1948 on "What is happening to modern architecture?" The same year he received his commission from Vassar. His comments therefore reflect the architectural balance for which he strove in Ferry House. Their pungency makes them worth quoting at length.

I don't feel too much impulse to set "human" (in the best sense of the word) against "formal." If "human" is considered identical with redwood all over the place, or if it is considered identical with imperfection and imprecision, I am against it; also, if it is considered identical with camouflaging architecture with planting, with nature, with romantic subsidies.

If International Style is considered identical with mechanical and impersonal rigorism, down with International Style! Anyway, the word is an unhappy one, just as unhappy as "functionalism."

However, all this controversy was in order, I am afraid, about twenty-five years ago. Since then, many things have happened. For instance, just as Sullivan did not eat his functionalism as hot as he cooked it, Le Corbusier did not build his machine for living! His houses are much less machines for living than, for instance, the three thousand family housing developments of the West Coast, the same pseudo-prefabricated houses, hill up, hill down, in rigid rows or in rigid curves—though quite redwoody. . . .

God knows, I am all for informal living and for architecture in support of and as background for this, but we won't sidestep the instinct towards achievement—a human instinct indeed. The most contrasting elements of our nature should be brought to happiness at the same time, in the same work, and in the most definite way. The drive toward experiment is there, together with and in contrast to the warm joy of security at the fireplace. The crystallic quality of an unbroken white, flat slab is there, together with and in contrast to the rough, "texture-y" quality of natural wood or broken stone. The perfection of construction and detail is there, together with and in contrast to simplicity, broadmindedness of form and use. The courage of conception is there, together with and in contrast to humble responsibility towards the client. The sensation of man-made space, geometry and architecture is there, together with and in contrast to organic forms of nature and of man. *"Sol y sombra,"* as the Spanish say; sun *and* shadow, not sun *or* shadow.[15]

Sun *and* shadow: later, in 1955, Breuer entitled a book on his architectural philosophy with this Spanish axiom derived from the sunny and shady sides of the bull ring.

That Breuer avoided the flabby sentimentality of much professedly "modern" work of the late thirties and forties immediately appears in the uncompromising clarity and abstractness of form of Ferry House. Thus it conforms with the early modern conviction that, in his words, "A building is a man-made work, a crystallic, constructed thing. It should not imitate nature—it should be in contrast with nature."[16] Yet it is equally evident that Ferry House partakes of the developments which modified the International Style of the twenties, and which provided the theme for Breuer's half-approving, half-admonishing remarks at the Museum of Modern Art.

Thus Ferry House typifies the tendency of the relatively high, compact boxes generally characteristic of the massing of European modernism of the twenties to give way, in the American environment, and under the vernacular influence, to a horizontal building spreading to its site (Fig. 75). This feeling for the stretch of the building in relation to the plane of the earth surely owes something, too, to the "rediscovery" of Wright in the thirties; in fact, by the end of that decade, the great professional had become a great celebrity as well. One block of Ferry House, containing the community facilities of lounge and dining room, is placed directly on the ground, and opens generously to its surroundings. The dormitory segment, however, is raised above the ground on stilts, but these are so low and the block and its run of windows so extended, that even this portion of the building relates to the plane of the earth. The glazed entrance link between the two blocks (Fig. 85) interlocks indoors and out in an intimate association.‡ In the twenties, the roof terrace and the sky were emphasized; thus providing a panoramic view of nature like that seen from the decks of ships. A sun deck, inevitably, appears on the roof of the lower block of Ferry House. (Modern architecture has so thoroughly made its point in this respect that the sun deck has become *de rigueur* for dormitories, and for girls' dormitories especially.) In this spreading building, however, the ground terrace dominates the sky terrace. The flagstone paving of vestibule and common rooms extends outside (but in economical macadam, instead of the flagging which Breuer would have liked[17]) until checked by low parapets and hedges (Fig. 84). Strongly bounded, this terracing is never amorphously merged with nature, but delineated with the decisive rectangularity of the rooms inside. As the *Architectural Record* said of the building at the time of its initial publication, it is less that the inside is extended outward, than that the outside is brought in.[18] Rooms within "rooms" as it were.

The influence of traditional building on modern architecture in the late thirties and forties is evident in this feeling for the earth. It is equally evident in the walls and window enframement of Ferry House; here we

‡ Compare Ferry House with Gropius' own house in Lincoln, Massachusetts (1937), on which Breuer collaborated shortly after both men had arrived in the United States. Illustrations are conveniently available in James M. Fitch, *Walter Gropius* (New York, 1961), figs. 91–94. In the Gropius house the compact rectangular volume dominates, with a covered entrance to the front and a screened porch to the rear abruptly projecting, but both seeming retractable, like the head and tail of a turtle into a protective shell. Although outdoor spaces do penetrate the box elsewhere—at two corners and in the semi-inclosed roof-top terrace—they also appear boxed, as though rectangular packages of space had been packed within the larger box. But compared with Gropius' earlier houses for the Bauhaus faculty in Dessau, Germany (Fitch: figs. 35–43), his Lincoln house shows much more feeling for the interaction of building and site.

find substantial rematerialization of what early modernism had demateri-alized. At the time, however, when Ferry House was built, the trend toward greater interest in weightier architectural effects was no more than tentative (the work of a few designers like Aalto and, especially, Le Corbusier excepted). The brick-textured walls of Ferry House replace the seamless weightless-looking painted concrete surfaces typical of the International Style in the twenties—and had the budget permitted, Breuer would have specified fieldstone. The texture of the brick was originally complemented by the natural grain of the cypress panels between each of the windows in the dormitory. They weathered so badly, however, as to require painting, which was done with a dull black.*

The window treatment in Ferry House also indicates the initial phase of a trend away from the membrane-thin appearance of walls typical of the International Style of the twenties. Whereas in the twenties the plane of the windows had usually been brought to the plane of the wall, thereby minimizing its depth, Breuer recessed the windows of Ferry House. Those in the dormitory block are only slightly, but markedly, set back in a series of planes. Those in the communal block occur well under the edge of the projecting roof plane. Inspired by traditional carpentry, even the enframements for the plate-glass window walls of the lounge area possess a depth of membering when viewed at close range, which earlier modernism would have reduced to linear attenuation.

Subtle as these typical changes in modern design from the twenties to the forties may seem, transformations of consequence within any well-established style are likely to make their initial appearance in just such details. Hence small changes should not be ignored in Ferry House, even though the cumulative effect of them only minimally increases the visual palpability of the building over its predecessors of the twenties with

---

* The painting is unfortunate but instructive (compare figs. 75 and 83). It ad-versely affects the building in several respects. The textural play among brick walls, wood panels, and metal sunshades is considerably diminished. The vertical opposition of the boarding to the horizontal continuity of the window band has disappeared. Finally, and most disruptive to the intended effect, the paint alters the scale of the window band by making it appear narrower and, in the process, so decidedly subordinates the apparent size of the windows that they now seem smaller than the solids, whereas this relationship was originally reversed. Originally, too, the black enframement of the windows—really a series of screens in front of the cypress paneling—assertively opposed the wooden panels, and therefore gave windows and panels the same independent visual quality as the sunshade panels overhead. All in all, the painting of the cypress boarding, though restrained, has reduced the dynamic opposition of visually independent building elements which once provided an enlivening counterpart to the elemental rectangularity of the dormitory block. The alteration has, moreover, increased the abstractness of the building and, in a positive sense, given it greater elegance. In these respects, the changes have inadvertently returned it toward the esthetic of the twenties.

respect both to the weight and girth of its parts, and to the textural insistence of its materials. On the whole, Ferry House retains the planar, transparent, airborne qualities of modern architecture of the twenties. Its window details become linear at a distance. White paint subdues the texture of the brick—as paint now eliminates the grain of the cypress. Evidences of "new empiricism" notwithstanding, Ferry House remains within the International Style; on the edge of change, but only on the edge.

BREUER AND THE MODERN IDEAL OF "OBJECTIVITY"

In the background of Ferry House lies the Bauhaus. It was here that Marcel Breuer's professional career began.[19] He was formally admitted to the school in 1920, when he was nineteen—just half the age of Walter Gropius. Only the year before, Gropius had become director of the Bauhaus; in the years ahead he would become Breuer's partner. Breuer himself was a lucky individual—and a perceptive one, too. He came to the modern movement in architecture as a neophyte at the moment when it was about to be definitively realized. Moreover, he came to the right place to learn. As much as any other architect, he literally grew up within the movement.

Once graduated, Breuer headed the carpenter shop at the Bauhaus, concentrating his work on furniture design. In the course of his experiments there, he apparently made one of the momentous discoveries in modern furniture design. He purchased a new bicycle in 1925, and the handlebars suddenly suggested the possibility of furniture frames in continuous curves of tubular metal. When he first apprised the bicycle manufacturer of his design, the man refused to produce it, arguing, in effect, "Whoever heard of furniture made from metal tubing?" In a short time, however, Breuer's first design of 1925 for a chair with a frame of bent, chrome-plated metal tubing had attracted a number of modern designers and, by the late twenties, such tubular furniture had become a hallmark of modernity. Who today can escape the ubiquitous progeny of Breuer's invention? His much pirated tubular design for a cantilever chair (Fig. 76) only appeared in 1929, one slightly anticipated in comparable, but apparently independent, designs by Mart Stam† and Mies van der Rohe. All three designs utilized the flexibility of the tubing in a cantilever construction designed to give springiness without conventional springs. Breuer's design postdates his departure from the Bauhaus in 1926. In the

† Stam is credited by some with having slightly anticipated Breuer in the use of tubular steel for furniture as well.

FIGURE 76. *Marcel Breuer. Cantilever chair with bent metal, chrome-plated tubular frame,* 1929.

same year Gropius, too, had left the Bauhaus. Both set up independent practices in Berlin. The state of the German economy, and then the advent of Nazism, made it an ill-starred moment for such ventures. Breuer did, nevertheless, finally manage to build his first house in Wiesbaden in 1932. Thereafter Nazism made creative effort in Germany impossible. With little to do, he traveled extensively in Europe, especially around the Mediterranean. In 1934, in collaboration with the Swiss architects A. & E. Roth, he designed an important apartment house in Zurich for the eminent historian of modern architecture, Sigfried Giedion. By 1935, he was in England, which Gropius, also fleeing from Nazism, had reached the year before. From England, Gropius was called to the Graduate School of Design at Harvard in 1937. Once in Cambridge, he immediately asked Breuer to join him.

So the two men who had done much in the twenties to inaugurate modern principles of design at the Bauhaus were reunited in a similar teaching enterprise in the United States. Gropius' leadership, Harvard's tolerance of new ideas (for which Dean Joseph Hudnut of the Graduate School of Design specifically deserves recognition), the university's prestige, and the passage of time, which had steadily seen converts to modern principles: all these factors worked together to spread the Harvard revolution in architectural education. In little more than a decade, every architectural school of consequence was at least professedly "modern." Whereas the Bauhaus had been *avant garde,* the Graduate School of Design was a major force in the reorientation of the entire profession. And in this reorientation, the practice which Gropius and Breuer established together had almost as much impact as their teaching. They maintained their partnership until 1941, when Breuer left Harvard to set up his own office. It is not minimizing Breuer's personal achievement in a building done almost a decade after he had established independent practice to observe that Ferry House owes much to the ideals and experience which he held in common with his erstwhile mentor, colleague and partner. But there is also no denying that Breuer's American work has been the more creative, however important Gropius' European buildings, and his Harvard teaching.

As a direct descendant of the kind of modern architecture which predominated in Europe during the twenties, Ferry House inherits the predisposition of the movement toward objectivity. So pervasive, indeed, is this theme in modern European architecture of the twenties, that "objectivity" better characterizes developments during the decade than the customary designation of "Functional Style" (or "Machine Style"), or even that of "International Style" which we have thus far tolerated. After all, critics and historians must categorize, if only for convenient reference, and every label is to a degree libelous. In his talk at the Museum of Modern Art, Breuer complained with reason against the customary designations for the progressive European work of the twenties. Since any new label is likely to fare no better, and since custom is, in any event, against any shift of label at this late date, let us stay with custom. A matter of practical convenience, however, does not absolve the critical historian from the duty of attempting to penetrate to the fluid core of a widespread conviction, which once stirred the creative imagination and gave urgent meaning to a community of action. In so doing he may at least point toward an alternative label, and thereby do more than merely deplore the inadequacies of what has become accepted terminology. It is doubly important to ferret the essence of a complex movement where one seeks the core of the meaning of one phase of a movement which continues to subsequent phases. What we today call "modern architecture" has substantially developed as an extension (and in part, as a dilution) of the esthetic, sociological, psychic, and philosophical ideals of a group movement of the twenties. If designated as the Functional Style or the Machine Style, however, then the movement is defunct as a generative force for what is happening now—the trunk severed from its branches. Although functional and mechanistic concerns pervade current building, modern architecture is no longer centered in these concerns to the extent that it seemed to be in the twenties. Nor can modern architecture presently be defined in terms of the esthetic principles with which Hitchcock and Johnson categorized it in 1932. In short, "modern architecture" of *that* time, if characterized by *these* terms, is without profound connection with "modern architecture" of *this* time.

The customary labels for the modern movement of the twenties suggest surface aspects only of the initial manifestation of a new approach to architecture (and they continue to be useful for this purpose). They do not touch upon the fundamental motivation of the movement which relates what was "modern" then to what is "modern" now—and makes "modern" mean more than merely the latest thing. Although the point needs to be made for any understanding of the history of modern architecture in the twentieth century, it is the more essential in comprehending the career of an architect like Breuer, whose work has developed with (and contributed to) the movement—and the later phases of which do not repudiate his earlier convictions, but build upon them.

It would seem that *objectivity,* an objectivity comprehensive in scope and appropriate as an expression of modern experience—for convenience, let us term it *symbolic objectivity*—is at the core of the radical reorientation which occurred in what turned out to be the most influential architectural achievement of the twenties.[20] Consider the nexus of terms prevalent in the polemics of the decade and evident in the buildings. *Fact, type, standard, simplicity, object, pure form, Style* in the sense of *The Style, intrinsic form* (a phrase which Breuer has used), *inmost essence:* from *fact* to *inmost essence* which nevertheless holds onto its factual starting point. The goal of symbolic objectivity was to align architecture with the pervasive factuality of modern existence, with that "ineloquence" (to call up Bernard Berenson's tag[21]) which characterizes the modern imagination. The aims of simplification and purification at the core of the movement, providing it with a morality of Calvinist austerity, actually stemmed from a diffuse conviction on the part of many progressive designers and theorists during the nineteenth century to the effect that architecture should be "honest," "truthful," and "real," especially with respect to the revelation of functional program and of materials and structure. During the twenties this moralistic heritage acquired an antiseptic cleanliness, an irreducible bareness, which symbolically, if not quite literally, accords with the morality of objectivity appropriate to clinic and laboratory.[22] Through this tradition of objectivity Ferry House is best understood. At the risk of ludicrously inflating the importance of what even Breuer doubtless considers a building of modest pretension within his oeuvre, it is well to explore the nature of this symbolic objectivity a bit further. To bring the burden of momentous considerations to bear on so modest an exemplar may, in fact, be the more revealing just because the choice of illustration is randomly representative rather than exceptional in character.

To begin, it is worth noting that the history of architecture reveals no previous major movement of which the kind of objectivity to which we allude is so centrally and comprehensively both the principle and the ideal; at least not an objectivity which resides in a blunt factuality valued for itself, as well as for its potential to promote primal esthetic and symbolic meanings by virtue of its very bluntness. To be sure, there were those in the nineteenth century who appreciated works of engineering in their conviction that modern technology must inform a viable modern architecture. Theorists like Eugène Viollet-le-Duc, Gottfried Semper, and Horatio Greenough come immediately to mind—men whose ideas inspired the modern movement of the twenties. Yet praise for engineering in the nineteenth century was sporadic and exceptional; moreover, its most ardent proponents among those who hoped for more rationalistic architecture tended to view engineering ambivalently. Witness the kind of buildings that Viollet-le-Duc and Semper recommended, and even realized, when they turned from theory to actual design. As for Greenough, once he had attacked what he disliked, he was mute as to what he specifically recommended in its stead. Or witness the more familiar fate of the Chicago "commercial style." The quick retreat in the nineties from the blunt skeletal esthetic for Chicago commercial buildings exemplifies nineteenth-century hesitancy in defiling the "fine arts" with coarser stuff. The uncompromising directness of the design briefly filled Chicagoans with a degree of pride, while winning plaudits from liberal-minded visitors. Yet, as we have seen,‡ enthusiasm for the raw factuality of the buildings carried reservations. Thus even Montgomery Schuyler, whose appreciation of the significance of the Chicago commercial buildings is more evident than that of any other critic in the nineties, deplored the spindly minima of the Reliance Building. Even Sullivan and Wright viewed the

‡ See *American Buildings and Their Architects: Progressive and Academic Ideals at the Turn of the Twentieth Century,* Chapter 1.

structural and material essence of the skyscrapers as a starting point for design with greater decorative elaboration. Since practical considerations, more than esthetic conviction, motivated the stringency of the Chicago style, its pragmatic virtues were readily compromised with the beguiling argument that both function *and* art could be served simply by adding the art. Only the modernist concerns of the twenties brought the Chicago commercial buildings to eminence, even as these same concerns led to the re-evaluation of nineteenth-century engineering that brought some of it into the architectural fold as part of the larger history of the modern movement.

It is equally true that much folk and vernacular building, which is exceptionally abundant and varied in the nineteenth century, approaches the objectivity prized by modern European architects in the twenties. The same nineteenth-century theorists who praised engineering also inclined toward enthusiasm for the functional buildings and contraptions that originated in folk tradition or were of anonymous invention. Here, too, Viollet-le-Duc, Semper, and Greenough come to mind. And here, too, what they admired in theory is seldom what they recommended for practice. Modern architects of the twenties, on the other hand, could wholeheartedly embrace what even the most liberal nineteenth-century rationalists viewed with sympathetic circumspection. At least twentieth-century modernists could be enthusiastic about folk and vernacular design insofar as it tended toward laconic statement (and not toward the complex ornamentation which, as the enthusiastic too often forgot, is apt to characterize such design whenever it has artistic ambition). The "objective" emphasis of the modern movement responded directly to the objectivity, implicit in the accumulated "rightness," which stabilized decisions in such unself-conscious design showing direct use of materials, revealed structure and—of most importance for those who worked in the ambience of the International Style—elemental shapes.

Finally, in regard to nineteenth-century design and that of the opening decades of the twentieth, it would seem that the convictions of the International Style were anticipated by many professional theorists and practitioners who sought to purify and simplify architecture as it then existed, and to do so less by baring its structure than by stripping its forms (although, in fact, those interested in rationalizing design in one way were very likely to be at least somewhat interested in rationalizing it in others). Irving Gill is an example*; but the list is long, including some of the most consequential names in the history of nineteenth- and early twentieth-century architecture. Claude-Nicholas Ledoux, Karl Fried-

* See *American Buildings and Their Architects: Progressive and Academic Ideals at the Turn of the Twentieth Century,* Chapter 4.

rich Schinkel, Sir John Soane, Benjamin Latrobe and other Greek revivalists; Henri Labrouste and the Néo-Grecque group; William Butterfield and other Victorian "realists"; Otto Wagner, Peter Behrens, Hendrik Petrus Berlage, Charles F. Annesley Voysey, Charles Rennie Mackintosh, Josef Hoffman: the roster can be substantially augmented, until, with Adolf Loos, Tony Garnier, and Auguste Perret, we stand on the threshold of the International Style, their works and ideas impinging on the Style, although not fully belonging to it. However much the modern architecture of the twenties depended on this pervasive heritage of purification and simplication, earlier efforts toward these aims nevertheless differ in quality from that of the International Style. Throughout the nineteenth century, they mainly represented the rationalization both formally and functionally of traditional forms. Although these were often reconstituted with fresh vision and purpose, they nevertheless persisted as the recollected basis of the rationalizing process. Occasionally an isolated work or group of works so drastically challenged tradition as to seem radically at odds with it; yet the sum of these exceptions did not alter the essential historicism of nineteenth-century architecture. More rarely, and especially as the nineteenth century gives way to the twentieth, an entire career (Gill's, for example) centers in a process of simplification which pushes beyond eclecticism. Yet even this kind of simplification is more reform than reorientation. To be sure, Gill's reform (to follow up on our example) focuses on an objective analysis of empirical aspects of building; but without the larger commitment to objectivity as the psychic and cultural essence of what is piercingly "modern." Even those on our roster who came closest in spirit to the International Style, and who directly influenced it, like Loos, Tony Garnier, and Perret, did so tangentially, individualistically, and only in certain phases of their careers. These facts of their situation, quite apart from the specific nature of their design, suffice to indicate their limited commitment to the principle of objectivity in the comprehensive sense in which the architects of the International Style embraced it. It is axiomatic, after all, that if an objective point of view provided the leverage whereby architecture became fully modern, the proof would lie in a group demonstration. Thus the work of Loos, Tony Garnier, and Perret, no more than Gill's, can be included within the International Style.

Now it makes no difference whether the quality of objectivity as understood by the architects of the International Style is quite as much the essence of modernity as they believed it to be. The point is that they acted as though it were—as though authentic modern experience was essentially rooted in an omnipresent quality of objectivity. Hence the first step in gaining creative access to this quality was an unflinching acceptance of the modern world. Although certain developments preceding the

185

International Style may be termed "modern" in varying degrees and for varying purposes, there was no architecture committed so unequivocally to what was "modern," simply because no previous group of architects had so fully dedicated themselves to this aim. To *be modern;* to accept the modern world and modern experience as the central premise for design; to locate a significant theme for this purpose; to demonstrate their thesis so massively in theory and practice as to drag the entire profession willy-nilly to their point of view: this is the unique accomplishment of the exponents of the International Style. As for the scope of the demonstration, the implications of objectivity within the International Style are at once literal, visual, psychic, and cultural, hence ultimately symbolic.

The International Style acknowledged the objective realities of the modern world in four major ways. It adopted a technological approach to design. It emphasized mass housing. It attempted to visualize what the modern metropolis might be. Finally, it united these three concerns within a group style capable of creating a harmonious and homogeneous environment. Had the objectivity of the International Style gone no further than this credo of literal intent and its substantial (if partial) realization, it would already have been without parallel in any previous movement in the history of architecture.

As for the technological pretensions of the International Style, we have already observed how far polemics outdistanced performance.[23]† Not that the discrepancy discounts the effort, since the propaganda of intent, in this instance as in others, opened the way to subsequent accomplishment in fact. Even so, it may come as a surprise to observe how relatively conservative Ferry House is as a technological achievement twenty years after the innovative decade. In this respect it typifies most other modern buildings of its time. If not in every detail, the technology of Ferry House could have been essentially realized (mechanical equipment and some of the materials excepted) more than half a century earlier. Any thorough-going technologist would smile at such a timetable for progress. In fact, Breuer's early tubular chair is technologically more advanced as a piece of furniture in the late twenties than is Ferry House as architecture for the late forties. The Vassar building's allusions to advanced technology are limited to a progressive use of techniques and materials already well established in architecture and furniture design: for example, to the stilting of the building on its frame, the plate-glass walls, and the tubular-and-sheet-metal sunshade.

It was not technology in the sense of radical innovation and optimum performance that directly conditioned the International Style as much as the objectivity implicit in the method, aims, and moral implications of an

† See pp. 130f. above.

idealized view of the mass production of the period. Design should not be the product of individual whimsy. Within the technological purview available to him, the designer should be rigorously concerned with function, materials, construction techniques, and with economics. Style was inherent in the laconic embodiment of these concerns in an integrated design, not in the application of fashionable or traditional forms. Through just such technological analysis, the design lost its overtly personal, its excessively subjective, quality. It thereby approximated the objectivity of a *type, standard,* or *norm.* As the typical took precedence over the unique, the architect expected to move from the periphery of modern society to its center, from the studio to the factory, from his elitist role of custom designer for a few to the popular role of designer for mass production. Architecture would be reborn, so the modern architect hoped, not only with newfound appearance, but with newfound social responsibility as well.

To their credit, as part of their concern for types, standards, and norms, these designers gave attention to mass housing. This they regarded not as a problem to be solved by peripheral philanthropic gestures in which a few charitable-minded professionals might occasionally and condescendingly indulge, but as a central challenge for the profession as a whole. Nor did they conceive of mass housing merely as villages of cottages in the manner of the garden-city planners of the late nineteenth and early twentieth century. On the contrary, those architects who were most thoroughly committed to the International Style sought a solution for housing with buildings which technologically, formally, and symbolically acknowledged modern conditions; the housing, moreover, was to be part of a metropolitan order designed from the same point of view. Shortcomings notwithstanding—and they were legion—the ideals, even the considerable accomplishment, remain. Never before had such a sizable group of architects confronted with such candor and courage its professional responsibilites in the modern world. Surely, their concern with mass housing in an urban context marks the extent of their objectivity.

Since the integrity of the International Style depended on its objective adherence to the imperatives of modern technology, a cardinal paradox ensued, and it bedeviled the movement. The emphasis on the type, the norm, the standard to be found in current technology deflected attention from *innovation,* which customarily would have been the primary concern of the devout technologist. Whereas the quest for the typical depends on a relatively stable situation, the quest for the innovative implies constant change. In one respect, this inconsistency of viewpoint within the International Style deflates its pretensions to modernity; in another, the effectiveness of the movement was the greater precisely because it did fail to keep abreast of pell mell technological advance. Because the modern architects of the twenties cared primarily about the types that might result for an architecture alert to current technology, their propaganda was not futurist in quality. It could be the more persuasive in being the more immediate. Look around you, it said in effect, at those things which *are* modern. The future *is:* here, now! Embrace it. Or, put another way; to catch up to the present is to realize the future. By implication—but only by implication—the objective acceptance of current technology would open the way to the eventual acceptance of subsequent technology (as, in fact, the succeeding history of modern architecture has demonstrated).

In seeking standards expressive of a technological environment, the architects of the twenties looked, with the eyes of artists, not of technicians, at the anonymous and semi-anonymous products of the machine. They delighted in those which had been designed in a straightforward manner for ease of fabrication and appropriateness of use in well-proportioned, unadorned shapes. For the same reason they were also drawn to the functional aspects of the folk and vernacular arts, standardized by generations of selectivity within the anonymous tradition of craftsmanship. Indeed, it might be claimed that the architects of the International Style treated the culture of modern technology as though it possessed the abiding norms of a folk culture. In any event, nothing better indicates the technologically conservative nature of the revolutionary moment of the twenties than this tug toward the folkish.

Breuer was in the vanguard of those architects who took a serious interest in the primitive and vernacular after 1930. How much Le Corbusier's example may have stimulated this interest is uncertain, since Breuer's boyhood in a peasant village in Hungary had imbued him with a profound feeling for folk expression. Whatever the case, he did visit the De Mandrot House (Figs. 87, 88 and 89), the first of three vacation villas that Le Corbusier designed in the thirties. Breuer, according to his recollections, saw the house as it was being completed about 1931, shortly before Mme. De Mandrot moved in.[24] Immediately thereafter, from 1932 to 1935, he emulated Le Corbusier's example and made extensive travels around the Mediterranean, including visits to Spain, Morocco, and Greece. During this time, he studied indigenous and anonymous buildings and other functional structures with particular care. He always regarded these journeys as the completion of his education. A kind of post-graduate course, they terminated the European phase of his professional life, and prepared him for what he was to do in the United States. In the early thirties, none of the other architects important in the European movement (unless Aalto is an exception) studied folk craftsmanship more extensively than Breuer—more closely than Le Corbusier, who characteristically took brusque cognizance of the primal forms and experiences embodied in folk building, paying less attention to its craftsmanship. Indeed, impressed though he was with the form and philosophy of the De Mandrot

House, Breuer remembers his disappointment at its shoddy workmanship.

Breuer expressed his admiration for folk building in an important talk in Zurich in 1934. It merits extensive quotation, not only as a personal statement, but as an articulation of group concern in thought and practice with folkish prototypes for modern buildings during the thirties and forties, especially because of the connections made between folkish norms and mechanized standards.

If we ask ourselves what is the source of the solid, unselfconscious beauty, the convincing quality and reasonableness of peasant work, we find that the explanation lies in its unconsciously, and therefore genuinely, traditional nature. A given region has only a few traditional crafts and use[s] a few definite colors.

Roughly speaking, the same things, or variants of the same things, have always been made there. And even these variations are obedient to a regular and recurrent rhythm. It is their uninterrupted transmission through local and family associations which conditions their development and ultimately standardizes them as type-forms.

In one direction at least our modern efforts offer a parallel. We seek what is typical, the norm: not the accidental but the definitive *ad hoc* form. These norms are designed to meet the needs, not of a former age, but of our own age; therefore we naturally realize them, not with craftsmen's tools, but with modern industrial machinery.

If one examines industrial standardization, one cannot fail to perceive that it is representative of an "art," of a traditional development which is the result of exploring the same problem over and over again. What has changed is our method: instead of family traditions and force of habit we employ scientific principles and logical analysis.

· · ·

The ability to face a problem objectively brings us to the so-called "revolutionary" side of the modern movement.[25]

As is true in many other aspects of modern life, in modern architecture the primitive and the machine are the poles that meet. Their confrontation is manifold, from the realm of the psyche, where the machine is a god or demon alternatively extending and threatening human powers, to the realm of culture, where technology confronts, and is confronted by, "underdeveloped" societies.

In his Zurich talk, Breuer might have been speaking of Ferry House. It partakes of the objectivity of science and technology on the one hand, of vernacular building on the other. Both of these polar manifestations of objectivity invoke the primal, the basic, the impersonal, as does the design of Ferry House. In actuality, vernacular building could have been sifted for intricacy of form as well as for austerity. It could be further argued that complicated forms may symbolize science and technology as readily as simple ones. After all, the "go" of the machine might also have inspired modern architects, at very least as a subordinate interest to their fascination with its cowling; even as it had once captivated George Herbert Wyman in the fantasy of cables, pulleys, frames, cages, and pierced ornament that functionally bedeck the central light court of his Bradbury Building (completed in 1893) in Los Angeles (Fig. 77). So great was Wyman's enthusiasm for the dynamics of machinery that he even jutted balconies beside each of the elevator landings to reach glazed mail chutes. The pleasure of watching the rise and fall of the elevators is increased by the occasional zip, zip, zip of letters racing through the transparent channels, as well as by the activity of people moving around the light court, in and out of the offices opening onto it. Of the Bauhaus staff, only Paul Klee would have fully appreciated the potential for delight in such juxtaposition of mechanical and human movement, of which the nineteenth century made much (Fig. 78). Since the innards of most machines are visually complex, the early modern preference to indicate objectivity with simple shapes so comprehensive as to embrace technology on the one hand and the vernacular on the other was as much an esthetic predilection as an analogy from fact. The technological and folkish implications of this objectivity blur into its esthetic meaning.

Although the boast of objectivity may seem to have been anti-esthetic in its implications, what the International Style really attempted was a supra-esthetic. Such was the case at least if measured by the characteristic nineteenth-century celebration of the work of art as a unique entity created by individual genius. In this sense, the objectivity of early modernism required an esthetic beyond taste, one even beyond "art." Only through an objective esthetic, its adherents maintained, could modern architecture become integral with the modern world of machine fabrication, mass production, and urban concentration, and bring to this world a clarifying order. That simple shapes in simple relationships are the inherent and universal (hence objective) source of beauty is sanctioned by the long tradition of Platonic and Neo-Platonic esthetics. In the twenties, Socrates' familiar statement on this matter in the *Philebus* was frequently adduced, implicitly if not explicitly.

I do not mean by beauty of form such beauty as that of animals or pictures, which the many would suppose to be my meaning; but . . . understand me to mean straight lines and circles, and the plane or solid figures which are formed out of them by turning-lathes and rulers and measurers of angles; for these I affirm to be not only relatively beautiful, like other things, but they are eternally and

FIGURE 77. *George Herbert Wyman. Bradbury Building, Los Angeles, completed 1893. Interior light court showing elevator cages with exposed machinery. The vertical elements projecting off the ends of the elevator shafts are glazed letter chutes to boxes in the lobby.*

absolutely beautiful . . . And there are colors which are of the same character. . . .[26]

Simple shapes, strongly asserted, and easily apprehended as the objective basis of a universal beauty are so evident in Ferry House that those who know the Vassar campus might ask what other, among its buildings, gives as intense an after-image of the Platonic ideal? To this ideal, architecture as *the* geometrical art repeatedly recurs. Bared of the muffling effect of embellishment, architecture renews itself in the elemental geometry natural to it.

For Ferry House of course Neo-Platonism was less immediately at hand than the esthetic for austerely abstract shapes inculcated by the movements in abstract and near-abstract painting which emerged from cubism around 1920, and then somewhat reacted against it by depending less on visible nature than cubism had. As both student and professional, Breuer, like other progressive designers in the twenties, was caught up in this fervor for purification. Since he has never been a partisan for any one movement, but created his own synthesis of what he found useful around him, there is no need here to dwell on differences among the contesting variants of purified cubism. Suffice it merely to characterize, and this superficially, the heritage from modern painting which accounted for the esthetic of PSFS and which eventually, in a more knowing manner, came to Ferry House.

All of the purifying movements in modern abstract and near-abstract art depended directly or indirectly on cubist fragmentation of the object in nature into facets and planes, flat, folded, and curved (Fig. 79). These permitted not only great independence of verisimilitude, but independence of fixed vantage point as well, hence many views of the same object could be incorporated within a single image—front, back, and sides being simultaneously glimpsed. Mobility is implicit in the comprehension of any fragmented image. Broken objects call on us to "pick up the pieces," either physically or mentally. The induced mobility resulting from fragmentation is intensified in cubism (in much of early cubism especially) by the very complexity of its faceting, with its multiplicity of elements, ambiguously transparent and semi-transparent, and organized so as to maximize the shifting tugs among the bits. Wright's fragmentation of his building mass achieved a comparable effect,‡ as did the broader, simpler planes of PSFS.

Cubism as it specifically appeared before World War I could be simplified or "purified." This simplification was most directly effected by enlarging the elements of cubism, by suggesting ideal surfaces rather than specific textures and by treating folded and curved planes as the enclosures of sizable volumes with gently graded surfaces rounding from light to shadow. Influenced by a limited and short-lived movement in Paris around 1920 called Purism, Le Corbusier's *Still Life* (Fig. 80) replaces the mesh of tugs of early Cubism with ampler oppositions. In other Purist paintings, the studio subject matter of guitars, playing cards, fruit, and pipes, which typified earlier Cubism, is abandoned for motifs from objects more specifically "modern." Even in *Still Life,* Le Corbusier has treated the studio objects as though they were machine parts or mass-produced

‡ See *American Buildings and Their Architects: Progressive and Academic Ideals at the Turn of the Twentieth Century,* Chapter 3.

FIGURE 79. *Georges Braque.* Oval Still Life (Le Violon), *1914.*

containers for mass-produced products. The possibilities for the transformation of such forms into architectural enclosures are obvious.

Whereas Cubism and related movements continued to possess a lurking "subject matter" in the representational remnants from figures and landscapes, and especially from still lives, the "subject matter" of the Dutch *De Stijl* (one of the wholly abstract movements in painting which proliferated around 1920, but one of particular influence on architecture) is simply the equilibria of tensions, fluctuant yet stable, created by non-

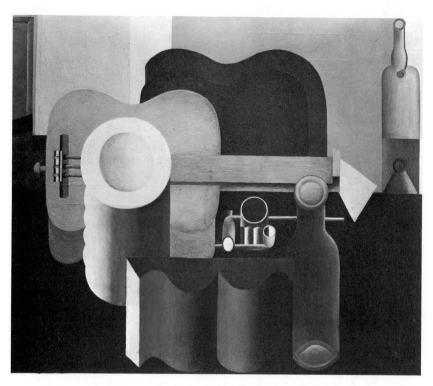

FIGURE 80. *Le Corbusier.* Still Life, *1920.*

representational forms (Fig. 81).* *De Stijl* thereby provides purely visual analogies to the action of natural forces in the universe. In short, the lingering particularity of Cubism and Purism is given universality by *De Stijl*. What it *depicts* about the world outside art, at once matter-of-fact and mysterious, coincides precisely with what it is, as a work of art—or, better perhaps, as an art *object*. The familiar name of this movement, "The Style," in itself indicates the universality of its intent. And, in fact, the eventual omnipresence of The Style in the design of modern architecture, furniture, appliances, typography, and advertising layout justified the austere grandiloquence of the designation. Beyond particularities, *De Stijl* half deceives us into believing that it occurred with an inevitability transcending its specific invention.

* Mondrian, whose work here illustrates *De Stijl* principles, broke with the group very early and came to refer to his painting as Neo-Plasticism. The distinction is, however, unessential for present purposes. In briefly emphasizing the influence of *De Stijl* on architecture, moreover, I have deliberately passed over the mystical aspects of Mondrian's quest.

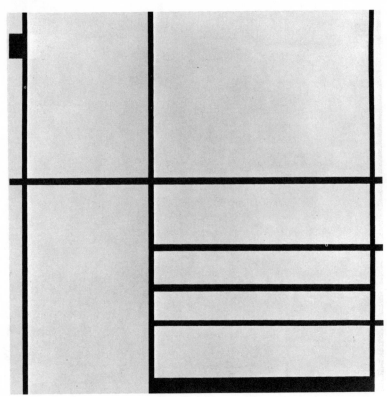

FIGURE 81. *Piet Mondrian.* Composition in White, Black, and Red, 1936. *The long thin rectangle at the bottom right and the near-square upper left are red.*

De Stijl when compared to Cubist space, from which it derives, shows an intensification of the qualities of planarity and continuity. Completely at variance with the Renaissance ideal of the picture plane as a transparent window through which the spectator looked into spatial depths simulating those visible in nature, the modern concept emphasized the picture plane as the positive referent for all spatial activity—from which forms break away into "depth," but to which they are simultaneously returned as "flat shapes." This concept reaches a climax in *De Stijl.* *Composition,* a typical Mondrian, strikes us first as an asymmetrical grid. Black lines bound the individual squares and rectangles, most of which are white or off-white.† Since, however, the lines bound several squares

† Occasionally, as in the example illustrated, the black lines do not wholly bound the color elements of the composition. Thus the red near-square in the upper left corner is unbounded by black lines top and bottom, as is the long red rectangle cut by the bottom edge of the canvas. This partial bounding gives these color

and rectangles in their course across the canvas, many of them running to the very edge of the canvas and suggesting their extension beyond it, the "grid" falls apart into "verticals" and "horizontals." (Mondrian may also emphasize the discreteness of these grid-making elements by slight differences of thickness among the lines.) It is then the *action* of verticals moving across a field in right-angled opposition to the horizontals that *makes* the squares and rectangles. At first sight the resulting scaffold of black lines usually appears to be slightly in front of the squares and rectangles. But since it is only in the act of their crossing that the verticals and horizontals make the squares and rectangles, both the linear boundaries and the areas bounded must occur on the same plane. Look again, and suddenly the rectangles pull away from the lines, which change into a "black background." In the process, "in front" becomes "behind"; "lines" become a background "plane"; the "flatness" of the canvas and of all the forms on it becomes "spatial." In some of Mondrian's paintings, a few of the squares and rectangles are painted in primary colors—red, yellow, blue; often all three appear in the same canvas, although our example uses red only. The colors of these areas, together with their size and placement relative to others, further complicates the sensation of movement back into depth and out again, of expansion and compression. Here space is the hairbreadth oscillation of the picture surface. Every relationship is unstable; paradoxically so, since the elemental components themselves possess the Neo-Platonic virtues of clarity and stability, which are aspects of their eternal appeal. Ancient absolutes are absorbed into the new relativity.

Theo van Doesburg, the chief propagandist for *De Stijl,* has succinctly described the visual experiences provided by it, and, in the process, has characterized a central preoccupation of certain competing movements as well.

At root, these experiences are founded on the clear knowledge of primary and universal experience in order to arrive at a method of organizing a new harmony. The basis of this harmony lies in the knowledge of contrasts, of a complex of contrasts, of dissonances, etc. which makes visible the multiplicity of contrasts [in the world], giving enormous tensions which create by their reciprocal suppression an equilibrium and repose. This equilibrium of tensions forms the quintessence of the new constructed unity.[27]

---

elements a positional ambiguity with respect to the plane of the grid, thus further complicating the oscillation of elements forward-and-back in space described immediately below. The incompleteness of the boundaries of the small red elements also suggests that they can slide up and down in the groove of space allotted to them.

The atomized solid of Cubism disappears. So does the Cubist organization of the painting as a clump of form, in itself suggestive of an object-like entity which recalls, however tenuously, the physical existence of the object in everyday experience whence it derives. *De Stijl* provides no sense of core whatsoever. The entire surface is a taut, planar continuity, in which ground and figure, or space and what is in space, fluctuate in a relational manner. *De Stijl* abandons the realm of material solids and ventures into the realm of pure (visual) forces as they operate in a continuum, to produce equilibria among themselves.

Both the forms and ideas of Cubism, Purism, and *De Stijl* appeared in three-dimensional structures, sometimes as abstract sculpture, sometimes as works enlarged to quasi-architectural scale. It was in this milieu, in which visual entities were built of elemental components, that the Constructivist movement appeared in Russia, and spread diffusely. For our purposes it may be illustrated by Frederick Kiesler's much illustrated display for the Austrian exhibit at the Paris Exposition of 1925 (Fig. 82), inspired quite as much it would seem by Constructivism as by *De Stijl,* even though Kiesler was never formally allied with either the Russian or the Dutch movement. For Mondrian's lines and planes, Kiesler substituted boards and panels. It may be easier to grasp the essence, if not fully the subtlety, of Mondrian's vision from what is, in effect, a three-dimensional approximation of his painting. Here again simple elements come together in an atomistic organization; as these components tend to fly apart in a visual sense, they engender opposing forces, and their "reciprocal suppression" establishes an equilibrium within the continuity of space. Kiesler's construction is obviously applicable to industrial design and architecture. Breuer's cantilever chair (Fig. 76) illustrates the constructivist influence in the former; Mies van der Rohe's project of 1923 for a country house, together with his Barcelona Pavilion, illustrates it in the latter (Figs. 63–67).

Hence the stimulating milieu in which Breuer received his training, at the apogée of a visual revolution. The formal aims of this revolution insofar as they had become axiomatic in modern architecture before World War II may be summarized as *purification* of shape, *dematerialization* of building substance, *asymmetrical but equilibrated tensions* in composition, *continuity* of space and surface, with some *fragmentation* of wholes into planar and linear parts (an aspect Mies van der Rohe's American work after World War II was to carry further‡). This list recapitulates in variant form what Hitchcock and Johnson had described in the *International Style,* with the possible exception of their emphasis on the rhythmic repetition of identical elements as an aspect of design which more centrally concerns architects than painters and sculptors.

‡ See Chapter 4.

FIGURE 82. *Frederick Kiesler. Display for the Austrian exhibit at the Paris Exposition of 1925.*

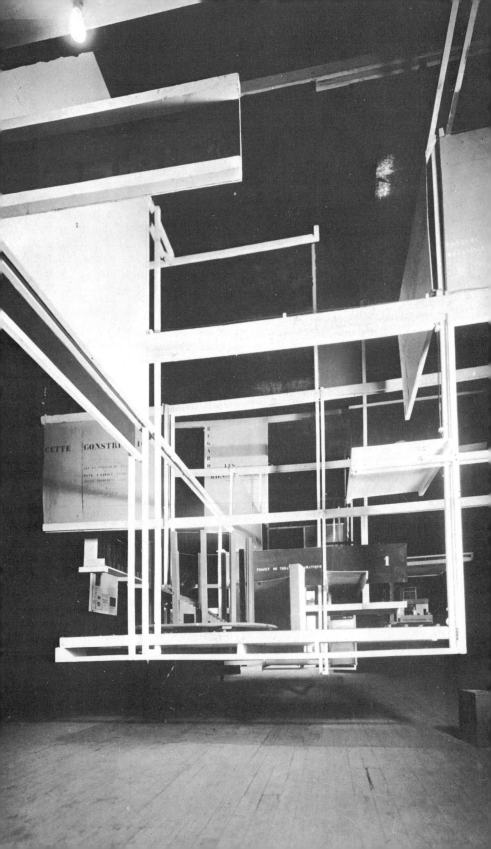

THE DESIGN OF FERRY HOUSE

These qualities all appear in Ferry House (Figs. 75, 83 and 84). The canonical approach of early modernism is most evident in the raised dormitory block. Although it may seem that the sharp demarcation of such a block amid its surroundings, both physically and visually, precludes even faint suggestion of spatial continuity, such, as we have already indicated, is not the case. Stilting and the flat roof permit the integration of inside and out in a particularly dramatic manner, as the traditional architecture of the period does not. The long window band, which Howe & Lescaze had sought in vain for PSFS, becomes the outward sign of spatial continuity within. Even though the interior space is intensively compartmented, as any dormitory must be, the ribbon repeat of window/wooden panel, window/wooden panel the length of the wall suggests that the compartments are molds which were dropped into the big block of space without destroying the sense of a homogeneous whole. Moreover, because of its levitation in space, because of the exaggeration of the hollowness within, and because the walls retain much of the sense of lightness which had characterized the International Style of the twenties, the entire dormitory block exists as a mold, or (to return to an earlier metaphor) as a *container,* immersed in the stuff it contains. Beaux-Arts boxes of space become space lightly boxed.

So the dormitory block primarily exhibits the container approach to spatial continuity classic in European modernism of the twenties. The community block at ground level, on the other hand, fragments the building into *components.* Such fragmentation permits the space to penetrate the interstices, making it appear that the parts have come together in space to create the building. Hence in Ferry House, as in PSFS, the two major modes of composition in the International Style occur in juxtaposition. In Ferry House, more decidedly than in PSFS, it is the component rather than the container which predominates. If the raised dormitory block appears as an elemental box across which the ribbon window is stretched, the ribbon itself is snipped into pieces.* The treatment of the sunshade above makes more evident this fragmentation of a functional whole into its constituent elements. Whereas typical Beaux-Arts design would have employed a projecting enframement or deep insetting to shade the windows, and whereas early modern buildings in Europe would have spurned all such projections, Breuer here treats the tubular bracketing as a dis-

* The painting of the cypress panels has of course diminished the impact of this fragmentation; see note, p. 178.

FIGURE 83. *Ferry House. Oblique view showing the lounge block to the left, the raised dormitory block to the right, with the connecting link of the glazed entrance. This view shows the original unpainted cypress siding for the window paneling of the dormitory.*

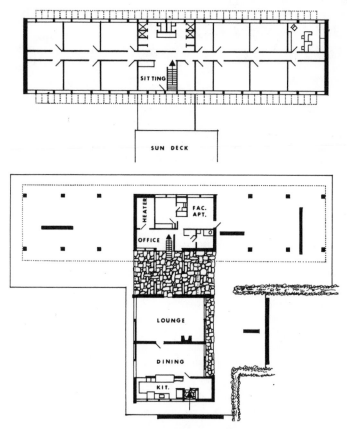

FIGURE 84. *Ferry House. Plans. The dotted line indicates the outer limits of the stilted dormitory block overhead. The solid line marking the perimeter of the first-floor plan indicates the edge of the macadamed terrace.*

FIGURE 85. *Ferry House. Entrance and sunshade detail.*

crete appendage to the wall (Fig. 85). He not only visually separates the corrugated sunshade from its support, but slices the sheeting into panels. The splinters of sky between the panels, the diagonal slashes of sunlight across the wall, and even the flicker of light on the corrugated edge intensify the vibrant separation of the elements in space. Like Breuer's own cantilevered chair, like Kiesler's exhibit, or Mondrian's painting, this sunshade separates plane and line. It objectifies the distinction between the functional provision for shading (or in the chair, for sitting) and the structural support necessary to maintain this function in space.

The same constructivist fragmentation appears more complexly with-

202

FIGURE 86. *Ferry House. Interior of the entrance hall.*

in the entrance lobby; here Breuer controls what would otherwise have been a flaccid flow of space by sharply opposing one building element to another so that the spatial continuity is not statically boxed, but dynamically modulated (Fig. 86). The perfectionist eye may discern some bluntness of juncture, some want of refinement, in places where a tight budget necessitated economies, and where detail is customarily glimpsed on the run; but scrutiny also reveals the care with which Breuer fashioned this lobby. Again the dynamic quality of the ensemble depends primarily on a spatial definition achieved by means of floor-to-ceiling planes, so positioned in space and distinguished by color, texture, or material that they visually separate one from the other. In fact, it comes as something of a surprise to find that every component in our view differs in one or more of these respects from every other. There is the flagstone floor, the rough plaster ceiling, a smooth plaster wall panel, another of brick painted white, and a third of plate glass.

The dull black door marks a spatial boundary to be sure, but as a buoy in the channel of space. The horizontal stair enclosure in bright red against the white ceiling gives further evidence of Breuer's preference for strong, unnatural color accents as another means of differentiating what is man-made.[28] A cylindrical steel (lally) column painted white and, finally, the stairway in a natural wood finish complete the atomized environment. Its treads visually independent of their support, like the sunshade outside, the stairway provides yet another instance of Breuer's easy reconciliation of modernity and tradition, for he transforms basic carpentry into a constructivist composition integral with the space-making esthetic around it. If this kind of reconciliation of old and new is by now commonplace, Breuer's example has been as responsible as any for making it so. To avoid restlessness and yet obtain a vibrant order from such diverse elements is a considerable triumph, the more so since only the effort of cataloguing reveals the extent of the diversity. In the lobby especially we perceive that Breuer's particular sensitivity to the tactile properties of materials goes well behind the regional and vernacular interests of the thirties and forties, and back to such basic Bauhaus problems as texture abstractions (Fig. 56). By studying these, the student designer obtained the visual "feel" of combinations of materials. That Breuer himself early developed a special sensitivity for tactile values is proved by the contrast of the chrome metal tubing, the highly polished lacquered wood, and the caning of his cantilever chair.

The fragmentation of Ferry House goes beyond such details as the dormitory window band, the sunshade, and the constructivism of the entrance vestibule to the larger elements of the composition. If the raised dormitory box exhibits the primal container, the grounded box which houses community functions is made of discrete ground-to-cornice planes of solid brick or wood alternating with transparent sheets of glass (Figs. 84, 85). Again separate functions—enclosure and view, the bearing wall and the non-bearing infilling between—are objectified in their coming together with the visually discrete plane of the roof and that of the flagstone floor to create the elemental box of shelter.

Just as the details and one of the principal blocks are *visually* fragmented, so the total composition is *functionally* split in regard to the community and the dormitory. The compact block provides for sociability. Rooted, it opens hospitably to terrace and lawn. The other, cellularly spreading, is appropriately aloft and, insofar as any college dormitory merits the description, aloof, with space beneath for bicycle storage, Ping-pong (as Breuer hoped[29]) and whatever other pleasures a sheltered place opening to the landscape affords. To glance once more at Breuer's early cantilever chair, its separation of seat and support anticipates what he termed the "bi-nuclear" plan of Ferry House. He popularized the plan-type in a series of houses beginning in 1943. The bi-nucleation generally locates the living and adult entertaining functions of the house in one block, the sleeping and the children's play area in the other, with the entrance coupling serving as both buffer and link between the two.† To a degree, this bi-nucleation recalls the revelation of the interior spaces in the exterior massing of PSFS; but not so elaborately, nor in the same extraordinary circumstances. After all, there are a number of early modern complexes, particularly of a non-residential nature, which parcel functions as crudely as the communal/dormitory division of Ferry House. Yet, if Ferry House is indeed to be considered a "house" in view of its domestic scale and the series of houses from which it derives, then the bi-nucleation does represent an alternative to the kind of enclosure typical of the early modern European house. Enclosure was normally (if not quite invariably) effected by a simple box-shaped container or a dense complex of cubes, highly abstract in character and revealing little of the plan. American spaciousness not only provided elbow room for such site-consuming compositions, but, ever since the last quarter of the nineteenth century had encouraged a particularly vital tradition of open house planning.[30] The bi-nucleation of Ferry House doubtless owed something to Breuer's feel for these conditions.

Finally, the fragmentation which Breuer applied in Ferry House to such constructivist details as the sunshade and the stairs, to the planar making of the communal box, to the functional division of the total composition, he also extended to the site. Parapet walls and hedges in a reticulated configuration (originally to have been much more extensive) act in the space in a nexus of visual tugs—conditioning the space without confining it. So the consistent fragmentation of Ferry House, from architectural detail to site, provides a tensional counterpoint to the simple volumes by which we initially perceive it.

Breuer's work in furniture design may have made him particularly alert to the constructivist undercurrent in the International Style of

---

† For sloping sites the bi-nuclear plan has the further advantage that the two blocks can be placed at different heights with the coupling ramped between the two. The big disadvantage of the plan is its extensive perimeter wall, making it more costly than compact schemes, although Breuer has also explored the principle of bi-nucleation in other kinds of plans. For example, certain of his houses popularized what has come to be called "split level" planning. These are of course old plan types, but they took on fresh vitality in the forties, and substantially as a result of Breuer's example.

FIGURES 87, 88, 89. *Le Corbusier. Madame De Mandrot House, Le Pradet (France), 1930–31. Above: entrance elevation. Opposite, above: terrace elevation. Below: plan of the principal living floor. The heavy black elements are masonry slabs which, together with three columns, provide the principal support for the roof. Entering the living room from the entrance ramp* (E), *Madame De Mandrot's quarters are to the left; the kitchen with toilet facilities, together with a bedroom for domestics, is to the right. The stair goes down to more rooms on a lower floor. The stone terrace, lifted well above the ground, extends from the living area.*

the twenties. Even his earliest houses in the International Style reveal Breuer's interest in constructivist details and features as accents within the neutral space. In visiting the De Mandrot House in 1931, at the time of its completion (Figs. 87, 88 and 89), he was quite literally on the spot at the moment when Le Corbusier decisively changed the mode of making the *prisme pur;* foregoing the stretched skin that would have effected *continuous enclosure* of the cubic container characteristic of his earlier work and substituting *independent wall planes* which come together to make the box of space; or, to use the illustration at hand, turning from the compositional mode which predominates in the dormitory segment of Ferry House to that which predominates in the lounge area. Just possibly Mies' fragmentation of the major building elements of the Barcelona Pavilion into planes and columns (Figs. 65, 66 and 67) may have prepared Le Corbusier for his compositional venture in the De Mandrot House. Here, too, Le Corbusier abandoned stilts to place his house on a masonry platform designed in a manner which suggests Mies' use in his Pavilion of the stylobate of the classical temple, although Le Corbusier characteristically elevated his house well above the ground-

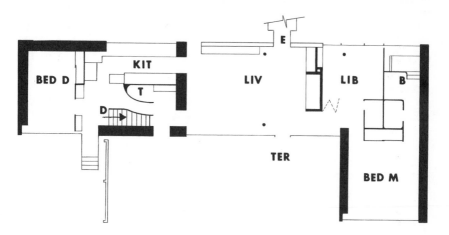

hugging horizontality of the Pavilion. Whatever the influence of Mies' constructivism may have been on the De Mandrot House, Le Corbusier remained essentially more faithful to the *prisme pur* than did Mies.

The De Mandrot House is essentially an L-shaped box on an artificial platform. Masonry-bearing walls, as simple slabs and L-shaped slabs, establish the perimeter of the house and provide most of the support for the roof. Wherever necessary, a free-standing column supplements the slabs. Like Mies in the Barcelona Pavilion, and earlier in his 1923 project for a country house (Figs. 63, 64), Le Corbusier extends these planes from ground level to roof line, thereby emphasizing their planar quality. Like Mies, too, Le Corbusier infills the intervals between the bearing-wall slabs with non-bearing elements, which also appear as planar entities, but are forcefully differentiated from the masonry segments in order to indicate their contrasting function within the structure.‡ Obviously Le Corbusier's treatment of the window infilling contrasts markedly with Mies' handling of the same detail as an invariable floor-to-ceiling repetitive rhythm. In the De Mandrot House, the window panels, with their asymmetrical wooden grids and random plaster panels in vivid colors, are more pictorially than structurally inspired by De Stijl. The playfulness of the window panels contrasts with the solidity of the masonry platform and walls.

The influence of the De Mandrot prototype on other modern architects during the thirties and forties was immense, probably because Le Corbusier managed to retain the primal volumetric shape of his prisme pur, while infusing this hallmark of the International Style of the twenties with constructivist tendencies. What was familiar in the movement opened to new possibilities. The greater freedom of manipulation of design elements permitted by this constructivist infusion countered some of the purist rigor of earlier cubistic composition in the International Style; its structural implications reduced some of the abstractness. Indeed, the De Mandrot prototype provided the ideal means by which the International Style would variously amalgamate constructivist elements in the work of Mies and Wright. No one showed the way more effectively or influentially than Breuer.

The impact of Le Corbusier's vacation houses does not appear in Breuer's work before he reached England in the mid-thirties; then initially it occurs in his Ganes Exhibition Pavilion (1936) in Bristol, on which he collaborated with F. R. S. Yorke (Figs. 90, 91). Here the placement of the masonry slabs on diagonals in conjunction with the curved wall makes the construction of the box superficially more dramatic, but actually blander and more arbitrary, than that of the De Mandrot House (although the composition surely derives from Le Corbusier's similar treatment of masonry walls at the rear of his dormitory for Swiss students at the Cité Universitaire in Paris of 1930–32). The contrast between the masonry slabs as the anchoring elements of the composition and the paneled infilling with its lively variety as they visibly build the box of space of the Ganes Pavilion, "circumscribing

‡ This comparison with Mies is literally true only in regard to his 1923 project. As previously noted, the marble wall slabs of the Barcelona Pavilion are not actually load-bearing, since the roof slab is completely supported by the columns. The slabs *appear* to assist in the support of the roof, however, and if, as is probable, Le Corbusier knew of the Barcelona Pavilion when he designed the De Mandrot House, he may well have mistakenly believed that they did perform some structural function.

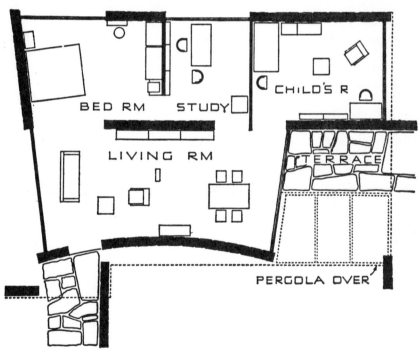

FIGURES 90, 91. *Marcel Breuer and F. R. S. Yorke. Ganes Exhibition Pavilion, Bristol (England), 1936. Above: general view. Below: plan.*

and defining space without destroying it,"[31] eventually became a cardinal aspect of Breuer's American work—eventually, not immediately.

In Breuer's first American works, most of them done with Gropius, the interior volume of space is bounded by the primal boxes familiar to the International Style, and is not the result of a cluster of freely disposed planes as in the Ganes Pavilion. Occasionally, however, even in his earliest American houses the container will be made in part by masonry slabs, while sometimes terrace parapets and retaining walls move out from the *prisme pur* of the house to condition the surrounding space.[32] Then, beginning around 1945, in a series of designs,[33] Breuer increasingly considered the ground plane as a field for a spreading arrangement of vertical planes, parapets, and screens in various materials asymmetrically related at right angles to one another across intervals of space. In some instances the box itself is partially made of, or penetrated by, walls that extend to the surrounding landscape. This stretch of the building as a rigidly ordered, but open, geometry of primal shapes departs from the De Mandrot example, where the compositional elements were distributed along the boundary of the box, marking it out and setting it apart from the surrounding landscape. If the kind of spreading, ground-hugging composition achieved by Breuer owes much to his feeling for the American suburban environment, and to Wright, it doubtless owes something to Mies' *De Stijl*-like, spreading compositions of slabs. Not until 1947 did the Museum of Modern Art present the first comprehensive exhibition of Mies' work ever held anywhere (just after his sixtieth birthday!),[34] and with it the first book, by Philip Johnson, devoted to his achievement. Even so, Mies' concern for a structural architecture had begun to be felt among knowing modernists by the mid-forties. Although Breuer's early awareness of *De Stijl*-inspired constructivism makes his debt to Mies less definite than that to Le Corbusier, his sudden interest at this particular time in the extension of the box of the house by expansive configurations of planes which are so specifically reminiscent of Mies would seem to be significant.* There is, moreover, in Ferry House, as in other buildings of the period, a delib-

---

* The compositional mode employed by Mies in the house scheme of 1923 and in the Barcelona Pavilion, continues through the early thirties in a series of houses in courts utilizing the same elements as those which comprise the Pavilion. In two respects, Breuer's compositions in this vein differ from Mies'. In the first place, Mies' development is rather away from the openness of the pin-wheel configuration of the 1923 project to more bounded compositions: initially to the platform restriction for the compositional elements comprising the Barcelona Pavilion; then to the rectangular walls enframing the houses in courts; finally to the glass boxes of the forties and fifties, where the "walls" are boundaries in plan even if ambiguously so in fact. Above all, Breuer's compositions differ from Mies' in the Corbusian boxes of space at their core.

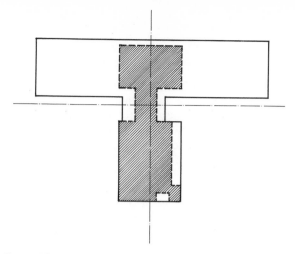

FIGURE 92. *Ferry House. Diagrammatic plan showing the slightly skewed, cross-axis. The solid line indicates the perimeter of the roof at both levels. The shaded area indicates the perimeter of the interior space of the ground floor.*

erateness of composition which seems to owe something to this quality in Mies' work. Breuer's earliest American work reveals a playful ingeniousness in its constructivist composition which is present here—in the metal sunshades especially, and perhaps in a detail like the stairway in the entrance hall.† On the whole, however, Breuer seems to seek a gravity and stability in equilibrating the discrete elements of Ferry House, and in relating the whole to the plane of the ground. He enhances these qualities by subjecting the asymmetrical tensions of the atomized parts of Ferry House to the discipline of a cross-axis (Fig. 92; and see Fig. 84). The evident axis, off-center through the transparent entrance link, dominates the composition and preserves the tensional quality of its asymmetry. But Breuer covertly counters the asymmetry with a subordinate cross-axis which bisects the nucleated mass. This counter is the stronger in that it seems to run through the building from what would normally be its "front" to its "back," whereas the major entrance axis penetrates the "sides" of the building. The composition is not unlike Wright's cross-axial organization of Unity Church (Fig. 149), even to the near cubic compactness of the unit on one side of the axis running through the entrance corridor link, and the long thin rectangular unit on the other. As in Unity

† Breuer's original paving plan, which called for the use of random fieldstone in the outdoor area around Ferry House, is another—and here a rather inappropriate—example of playfulness. Consisting of a path through the entrance link, plus random branchings leading to free-form "islands" of bluestone, this ground pattern would have been very arbitrary had the budget permitted it, and second thoughts not eliminated it. See the plan accompanying the original presentation of the building; *Architectural Record,* June 1952, p. 119.

Church, and in much other modern architecture, the dynamics of the composition are intensified by this elimination of the fixed points of reference implicit in "front," "back" and "sides."‡ The covert symmetry of Ferry House, pervasive but yielding to asymmetry, is comparable to what Mies was doing at the same time in a very different way, and more subtly, in the Edith Farnsworth House in Plano, Illinois (1945–50) and in the Lake Shore Apartments (1948–51). Both foretell the commanding axis of Mies' Seagram Building (completed in 1958), which bisects the rigidly frontal mass, and reasserts, with authority, an axial formality of composition akin to that favored in Beaux-Arts inspired works.* Thus the asymmetrical dynamics found in the composition of PSFS, and characteristic of the first phase of European modernism, is substantially stabilized in developments which get under way shortly after World War II.

In plan and massing, Ferry House anticipates axial symmetries to come. But overall the composition remains asymmetrical and tensional, objectified in primal entities, which interact to create a dynamic equilibrium within a spatial continuity.

Breuer and the Architectural Situation Around 1950

To describe in this breathless manner the formal content of the objectivity sought by the International Style is to anticipate the symbolic sense in which the movement relates to modern science and technology. Even the most technologically oriented of the arts, whatever its propaganda boasted, could not have been expected to keep abreast of burgeoning developments in science and technology—a sufficient challenge for scientists and engineers themselves. Under the circumstances, and especially considering the peripheral and precious position of the arts in a technology-oriented society, it would have been creditable had modern architects been merely wistful that somehow, some day, architecture would be relevant to technological realities. To have gone much further, however, and (together with modern painters and sculptors) to have realized the means whereby visual experience could in its own way participate in these central realities is among the substantial achievements of the modern imagination.

In its *own* way: this is not of course the way of the scientist, but that of the artist, wherein the "feel" for scientific reality is permeated

‡ Observe, for example, the play between the axial, symmetrical plan of the banking room of PSFS and its asymmetrical entrance, p. 94 above. For a discussion of Wright's Robie House in the same terms, see *American Buildings and Their Architects: Progressive and Academic Ideals at the Turn of the Twentieth Century,* Chapter 3.
* See Chapter 4.

FIGURE 93. *Ferry House. Interior of the lounge looking toward the dining room. The kitchen is barely visible behind the sliding panels.*

with the "feel" for relevant human experience. The symbolic objectivity at the core of the radical transformation of architecture in the twenties ultimately provides a visual analogy to what, in the twenties at least, had been regarded as the lucidity of the new technology—a technology confident and self-assertive, yet humanely ordered and scaled. Opposing nature, Ferry House nevertheless enhances and is enhanced by its natural environment. All of which brings to mind Le Corbusier's familiar metaphor[35]: the ocean liner is a self-contained, man-made object set against its environment, yet intensely of it too; a product of the machine, but providing the antithesis of a mechanized existence. Architecture should be patterned on the ship. Essentially, his is the classical, humanist ideal restated in terms relevant to the modern world. In contrast to Wright's naturalistic bias, it does not blur the distinction between the things of nature and those of man, rather sets them in a drama of confrontation and reciprocity, with the result that the qualities peculiar to each are actually intensified.

In a less grandiloquent, more prosaic, sense, Ferry House faces up to the unheroic aspect of modern life. It flaunts ease of maintenance and encourages the informality of blue jeans and Bermuda shorts (Fig. 93)—and this only a few steps from the Victorian "sitting rooms" of

Main Hall. The laconic, taut, dynamic qualities of the forms of Ferry House are equally expressive of the present situation. The mobility of modern life, implicit in the fondness of modern architects for metaphors of transportation, appears in the flexibility of the interiors of Ferry House, with its spindly furniture lightly poised on carpeted islands and readily rearranged. Symptomatic merely of restlessness? Perhaps, but to the architects of the twenties, this mobility symbolized the litheness of the modern intelligence. In accord with this sense, Le Corbusier brought the ship deck to modern architecture, with its stripped spaciousness ready for any activity and its portable equipage in flux with changing need. The ship deck encouraged fresh combinations, a kaleidoscopic camaraderie or, alternatively, solitude. Remarkably often, Le Corbusier created open spaces in which both extremes are possible. When considering the communal spaces of Ferry House, however, we find that the one-big-happy-family seems a little too omnipresent within the compact box of space provided as a lounge; the more so because of its plate-glass exposure. To escape constant "cooperating" there is always the dormitory (which may be but little improvement); but public spaces, too, should offer semi-public areas—places to be alone, or almost alone.

At the very least the dormitory should have had the more isolated, leafy surrounding for which it was originally intended. As it stands, Ferry House is over-exposed. This, too, may be an expression of modern life, with its admirable frankness, yet loss of privacy. Although a sort of youth-hostel heartiness may be considered appropriate for such a cooperative enterprise as Ferry House, it caters too exclusively to the extroverted, normative range of human experience. It is too uncongenial to ceremonial and other experiences of a more complex emotional nature. There are many exceptions; but the typical vice of modern architecture from the twenties through the forties is a candor approaching starkness on the one hand, and blandness on the other. The first predominated during the twenties with the chilliest extremes of "functionalism": the second in the late thirties and forties with the regional and vernacular gentling of mechanistic abstractness. If Breuer avoided the sentimentality common to most vernacularization of early modernism, he did not wholly avoid a certain blandness in Ferry House. This blandness occurs in part because he seems to have conceived it from the outside. Not in a formalistic sense, of course, since the zoning for use is perfect, and perfectly recorded in the massing. It is the emotional conception that is external. So much so that little remains to be experienced inside. Even the fireplace, of which Breuer usually makes much, often creating a free-standing, sculptural entity of it, is here routinely handled.[36] In fact, Ferry House has something of the quality of furniture in its emotional externality, as though the carefully crafted boxes with their sliding planes were enlarged cabinets providing neutral, if very pleasant, compartments for the storage of human activity.

If his background as a furniture designer accounts in large measure for Breuer's virtues as an architect, it has also had its drawbacks.[37] It has encouraged his thinking of buildings as objects meeting basic functions in a manner which is at once formally decisive and inventive, but at the same time emotionally unobtrusive. Forms like the sunshade and the stairs elaborate his architectural storage units as freely, but as soberly, as the legs and back of a well-designed chair exist as a semi-sculptural structure for their prosaic function. Such detailing, admired and appropriated by fellow professionals, is ingenious, vigorous, and economical, with a commonsense elegance that appears deceptively effortless. It includes less obtrusive details like the sliding windows and screening, which Breuer had perfected through a series of houses. But this very strength has also been a weakness. Thus the playfulness of the constructivist sunshade makes it seem a fixture rather than a wholly architectural element.† More seriously, Ferry House as a whole reveals the incomplete transformation of this inheritance from furniture design into architectural scale. It lacks that progression in scale, whether in size or modeling (of which Wright's Robie House is a consummate example), whereby the eye measures the whole in terms of a gradient of importance. No such gradient exists here, but rather abrupt jumps from one size to another. On the other hand, these are not decisive jumps, which occur when architectural scale is achieved by its deliberate forcing. Juxtaposing the very large to the relatively small—for example, the windows to corner towers in Wright's Larkin Building, or the studio laboratories to their utility towers in Kahn's Medical Research Building (Figs. 144, 177)—serves to increase the sense of magnitude. In Ferry House, however, the openings are roughly all of the same visual size and value, whatever the differences in their actual dimensions. Thus the contrast between the sizes of the transparent wall of the community block on the one hand and the ribbon strip of the dormitory on the other is insufficient to set them decisively against one another. The various openings seem to have been designed with more concern for the major units of the composition and less for the composition as a whole. In much the same manner, standard storage cabinets are habitually arranged in a room for convenience and pattern, but rarely with the further end of decisively conditioning the scale of their environment. Finally, neither the cabinets nor the detailing within the openings is

† The same fault, on a larger scale, occurs in the sunshades of Breuer's UNESCO Building in Paris.

resonant beyond the range of a close view. Taken together, these subtle deficiencies of scale contribute to the blandness of our experience of the building.

Vitality of scale—that is, of parts to the whole and to human size—gives a building grandeur, and especially if the scale does not merely relate to the physical size of the human being, but is appropriate to the impact of the building on the human emotions as well. It is the common deficiency of the superb craftsman as architect that his sensitivity to form and its proportioning tends to be lavished on details (objects) rather than on the larger-than-life-size environment of mass and space which are especially the province of architecture. Exceptional as their buildings are, Greene & Greene did not entirely escape this common weakness of the craftsman-architect; neither did Gill or Maybeck. Nor has Breuer. This deficiency is the more remarkable in Breuer's case since his craftsmanship has none of the sentimental overtones of theirs, but depends on an intensely conceptual approach to architecture.

The Italian critic Paolo Portoghesi has spoken of Breuer's "neatness, naturalness, and facility"[38] as being both the badge of his integrity and a possible limitation to his ultimate achievement. With Breuer increasingly concerned with larger commissions requiring a more complex emotional approach than his houses, the crucial question is that which Baudelaire posed about Manet in the 1860's: Will he overcome the gaps in his temperament?[39] The very normative quality of Breuer's career—providing the historian with what is possibly the neatest case-study of the central development of modern architecture from the twenties through the middle decades of the century[40]—has depended as much on the relative mildness and sobriety of his creative temperament as upon his technical mastery and formal inventiveness. By way of recapitulation, he came to the revolution at the start of its decisive phase. His earliest furniture epitomizes the gawky stage of casting about for a basic vocabulary appropriate for modern expression. He embraced the mechanistic emphasis of the twenties. He gradually integrated regional and vernacular elements with machine-like forms during the thirties and forties. In the fifties, finally, he has turned to larger commissions, among them those for monumental buildings. These have compelled him to express the profounder reaches of human experience, as, for example, in his influential Abbey Church of St. John the Baptist (1953–61) for the Benedictine College at Collegeville, Minnesota (Fig. 94).[41] Always a little behind the greatest innovators, but well in the lead of the pack, he has been receptive to the forms and ideas characteristic of every stage of the modern movement as it developed from the group style of the twenties. He has steadily synthesized both forms and ideas with an originality, practicality, and lucidity which have made

FIGURE 94. *Marcel Breuer, Hamilton Smith associated. St. John's Abbey Church, Collegeville, Minn., 1953–61.*

his work influential—doubly so, because he has consolidated each phase of his career with an almost methodical integrity before moving on to the next.

To venture into Breuer's latest phase is to go beyond Ferry House. Suffice it merely to say that if the Abbey Church in Collegeville goes *well* beyond Ferry House both in formal inventiveness and in emotional profundity, certain virtues and defects seem to persist, especially on the exterior where banner and church possess a furniture-like quality, as of entities that could be pushed about. (At this writing, however, I would not press the point, since I have not visited the building. Moreover, in photographs, St. John's appears to contain the outstanding sacred interior to have been built in the United States in the decade and a half following World War II.) As the Abbey Church develops from Ferry House, it represents a further stage in the unfolding of the sym-

217

bolic objectivity which has been at the heart of the modern movement since the twenties. It is the most telling criticism of the usual labels for European modernism of the twenties, whether "Functional Style" or "Machine Style" or "International Style," that all describe what no longer exists and therefore tend to obliterate the element of continuity which unifies modern architecture of the twenties with subsequent achievement. In effect, all of these labels reduce radical innovation to a passing phase, and thereby deny that radical innovation occurred at all. But the spirit of objectivity continually developed in Breuer's work and the authority which his architecture derives from it—an authority even more evident in the work of Mies and Le Corbusier—make it apparent that the mechanistic emphasis of what is termed the Functional Style or the Machine Style, and the particular "look" of what is termed the International Style, were but superficial manifestations of a more essential impetus. We must return to this matter.‡

At this point a brief look at the Abbey Church of St. John the Baptist will suggest the way in which the symbolic objectivity at the heart of the most influential developments in modern European architecture of the twenties opened to subsequent possibilities. The symbolic aspects of the Abbey Church occur in forms which are so elemental that they also have the aspects of blunt objects. Like the sunshade on Ferry House, the bell tower ("bell banner," as Breuer prefers to call it) in front of St. John's is a functional utensil which achieves an intensely modern expression because it is so designed that paradoxically we comprehend it as "art" and as a primal appliance-like entity outside of art. From *fact* to *inmost essence* which nevertheless holds onto its factual starting point: the blunt out-there of non-art, the realm of mere things, exists in a tense ambiguity with the in-here of the human impress by means of which modern man makes an affirmative, even if equivocal, sign of his existence within a universe of other kinds of existence. The very tensional quality of the symbolism, in which the fact is symbolic and the symbol factual, accords with the tensional dynamics favored in modern composition. Whereas modern composition is collisive (A *against* B) rather than elisive (A *into* B), the symbolic implications of its forms also depend on a mode of expression which keeps the object and its meanings equally (or at least fluxuantly) vivid at all times, so that the esthetic experience exists in the gap between the two.

Ferry House exemplifies a position somewhere between the mechanistic polemics of the twenties and the more profound appeals to human consciousness which modern architecture from the fifties onward essayed. It demonstrates, as does Breuer's entire career, that modern

‡ See pp. 376f. below.

architecture since the twenties has, on the whole, been most creative where the premises of the decade were enlarged, and not repudiated for the cheap success of applied ornament, sentimental historicism, acrobatic structure, or cozy gimmickry. To be sure, Ferry House loses some of the fierce conviction of the polemical austerity of the twenties, and to this extent represents an easing of tautness after the crusading moment. At the same time that it agreeably consolidates what had been done, however, it modestly, yet decisively, records the augmented potential of the International Style as this appeared in the thirties and forties.

CHAPTER IV

The Laconic Splendor of the Metal Frame: Ludwig Mies van der Rohe's 860 Lake Shore Apartments and His Seagram Building

> We refuse to recognize problems of form, but only problems of building.
>
> LUDWIG MIES VAN DER ROHE,
> from the journal G, 1923

> . . . architecture should be related to only the most significant forces in the civilization. Only a relationship which touches the essence of the time can be real. This relation I like to call a truth relation. Truth in the sense of Thomas Aquinas, as the Adaequatio intellectus est rei. Or as a modern philosopher expresses it in the language of today: Truth is the significance of facts. Only such a relation is able to embrace the complex nature of civilization. Only so will architecture be involved in the evolution of civilization. And only so, will it express the slow unfolding of its form.
>
> MIES VAN DER ROHE, Address in San Francisco, 1960, on the occasion of his receiving the Gold Medal of the American Institute of Architects

"ALMOST NOTHING"

When one thinks about it, few cultural phenomena of the postwar years are more astonishing than the contribution of Ludwig Mies van der Rohe to the United States, or America's contribution to his genius.

In 1937, when he arrived in the United States from Germany, who would have expected that a deliberate and austere perfectionist would so spectacularly succeed in the bustling pragmatism of this new environment? Yet when Mies reached the United States at the age of fifty, he had in a sense only begun his career.

His preceding practice of over thirty years in Europe had resulted in far more projects than realized buildings. During these decades he had completed just six houses that he cared to remember, plus two small apartment buildings, a memorial monument, half a dozen exhibition structures, and some furniture design—statistically about one realized building every two years! Moreover, they were for the most part small commissions and would hardly have been important were it not for their quality and their significance as embodiments of Mies' philosophy of architecture. Only a select group of architects, critics, and discriminating clients knew of his European work and, as we have already observed, the first book on his work, by Philip Johnson, appeared only after Mies had been ten years in the United States, by which time he was nearly sixty.

In his adopted country Mies not only built many times the number of buildings which he had realized in Europe, but his commissions were far larger and more prominent. The work of a perfectionist who had appealed to a very restricted audience suddenly became so influential that the Miesian reticulated skeletal building, infilled with glass and panels of various sorts, transformed American cities during the fifties. Overnight, it seemed, the skyscraper silhouette of brick and stone at the heart of large American cities gave way to highly polished reticulated metal-and-glass walls reflecting other highly polished reticulated metal-and-glass walls nearby. In the suburbs and countryside, a comparable style appeared in low, spreading shopping centers, schools, and industrial complexes. From the United States, the style spread throughout the world. In this spread, some buildings were good; inevitably, most were mediocre or atrocious. Few approached the quality of Mies' design. None surpassed the best of it.

Shortly after Mies had arrived in the States he went to Chicago. There he soon headed the architectural school at the Illinois Institute of Technology, just as his compatriot Walter Gropius had gone to Harvard a few months earlier. In downtown Chicago, Mies saw for himself the skeletal buildings in metal, glass, and terra cotta built during the eighties and nineties of the nineteenth century.* They inevitably appealed to Mies, who once characterized his architectural ideal as "almost

* Although the use of reinforced concrete construction developed rapidly in the United States during and after World War II, and though Mies increasingly worked in this material (invariably assigning his IIT students the problem of alternate designs for the same skeletal building in steel and concrete), it was his use of the steel frame that initially accounted for his American influence. In fact, his first completed tall building in Chicago, the Promontory Apartments (1946–49), originally designed in steel, had to be redesigned in reinforced concrete because of restrictions imposed on the use of metal following the outbreak of the Korean War.

nothing." In coming to Chicago, he happened upon the one city in the world which offered so thorough a demonstration of his philosophy of "almost nothing" in buildings so explicitly modern.

It is not that the Miesian skeletal building might have gone unrealized had he happened to settle in another American city. Mies himself scotched the easy equation of his work with that of the Chicago commercial buildings of the late nineteenth century. Asked by the critic Katharine Kuh whether his living in Chicago had affected his work, he replied in the negative.

> I really don't know the Chicago School. You see I never walk. I always take taxis back and forth to work. I rarely see the city. In 1912 when I was working in the Hague I first saw a drawing by Louis Sullivan of one of his buildings. It interested me. Before I came to Chicago I also knew about Frank Lloyd Wright and particularly about the Robie House. If you remember, I wrote about Wright in the Museum of Modern Art catalogue for my 1947 exhibition.

> As to your question, no: living in Chicago has had no effect on me. When I first arrived, I immediately went to the campus of the then Armour Institute (now the Illinois Institute of Technology). I felt I ought to turn around and go home.[1]

The picture of Mies burying himself in taxicabs, oblivious to the very "influences" with which historians have customarily coupled his work, has its ludicrous aspect—or at least it does once the historian recovers from its humbling warning against glib generalization. Whether in fact the shell of his taxicab as thoroughly protected Mies from the bombardment of his surroundings as he suggests is, however, doubtful. Of course he may have peeked! Of more importance, so perceptive an observer of technological norms as Mies hardly needed a tour of the Loop to come to his late style. He had absorbed the "rightness" of this barebones technology for its time and place from the preconditioning of all the years before.

It was, so to speak, the Chicago within that made him aware of the possibilities in the situation in which he found himself, possibilities that might nevertheless have been subtly altered in some other situation. Dependent on vision rather than visit, Mies' feel for the Chicago tradition of skeletal building as an epitome of the American norm in non-domestic building might as well have come from other sources. For example, one of his first American students, Myron Goldsmith, recalls that Mies was much interested in a publication in 1939 of the factories of the Detroit architect-engineer Albert Kahn. A photograph of the interior of the Glenn

FIGURE 95. *Albert Kahn, Inc. Glenn L. Martin Bomber Plant, addition to the assembly building, Middle River, Md., completed 1939. Interior view published in* Industrial Architecture of Albert Kahn, Inc., *1939. The Glenn Martin plant was unprecedented in enclosing an area 300 by 450 feet without interior columns beneath the longest flat-span trusses used up to this time. The entire project, from the date of commission to the start of manufacturing, required a mere 81 days.*

Martin bomber plant from this volume provided the background on which Mies pasted planes (geometrical rather than aeronautical in this instance) to create a project for a concert hall (Figs. 95, 96), which is among his early American designs.[2] This project, made in 1942, can well symbolize the collision of two worlds: on the one hand, that of the abstract form of floating planes, which goes back to the Barcelona Pavilion (Fig. 66), and then, behind the Pavilion, to the diffuse influence of purified cubism; on the other, that of the prosaic grandeur of the girdered factory space. Abstract form and prosaic fact, these two concerns of Mies' structural esthetic here come together, not so much amalgamated as co-existent. They had already been joined in Mies' designs of 1940 for the first building for the campus of the Illinois Institute of Technology, where a structural esthetic of lines and planes is integral with the minima of actual structure. In his initial buildings for IIT, Mies declares both his allegiance to the factual side of the American situation (he would put it more grandly—to the factual side of the "epoch") in which he found himself, and his readiness to set aside everything adventitious to the facts. By whatever interior route, by whatever freak of good fortune, Mies had arrived at the place of all places that possessed the tradition most sympathetic to his structural esthetic. But it was he who revitalized the all-but-forgotten tradition, and made even more relevant than it had been in the nineties the half-boastful, half-rueful assertion of the Chicago

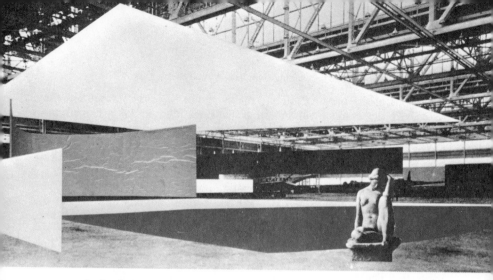

FIGURE 96. *Ludwig Mies van der Rohe. Project for a concert hall, 1942. The freely disposed planes that make the performance area are superimposed on the interior view of Albert Kahn's Glenn L. Martin bomber assembly building.*

architect to the critic Montgomery Schuyler, "I get from my engineer a statement of the minimum thickness of the steel post and its enclosure of terra cotta. Then I establish the minimum depth of floor beam and the minimum height of the sill from the floor to accommodate what must go between them. These are the minima of my design."[3]

Almost nothing: by this motto Mies means that sound architecture emerges so intimately from its structure as to seem its inevitable consequence. But Mies' "almost nothing" is a trap for the simple-minded. His deprecating phrase conceals the number and intensity of the esthetic decisions that his spare architecture calls forth.

Looking closely at the early Chicago skyscrapers we readily observe the crudity of most of them. Frames and windows are often ill-proportioned. The masonry and terra-cotta sheathing is often clumsy in both its profile and its surface ornamentation. The juncture of one member or one material with another is often awkward. There are, to be sure, fine buildings among these early Chicago skyscrapers. The majority, however, are boldly, vitally, courageously gawky. The gawkiness might be forgiven had the boldness been maintained. To the architects of the Chicago commercial buildings of the 1880's and 1890's, however, "almost nothing" was too largely a practical program and too little an esthetic ideal. Only Louis Sullivan realized the esthetic possibilities that the technology might provide, and even he, as Mies remarked, obscured its lessons in the personal quality of his genius. The rest eventually came to regard the commercial buildings as something to be ashamed of—provincial production. Before 1900, the directness of treatment had begun to disappear behind masonry and terra-cotta wrappings embossed with historical detail. Witness the "Gothic" veneer of even so daring a building as the Reliance.†

With Mies, however, the pragmatic "almost nothing" was at the core of profound awareness. He extended his "almost nothing" by his equally famous aphorism "less is more." In reducing the building to its essence, he believed, the designer can concentrate on perfecting this essence, until naked construction becomes architecture. Less becomes more in that the building is objectively experienced as an ascetically beautiful "thing in itself." The essence of what it *is* also exists in the truth of its world, which justifies the esthetic both in fact and in metaphor. Like *The* Style, *The* Building. "I don't want to be interesting," Mies said, "I want to be good." Or again, "I've simply tried to make my direction clearer and clearer. . . . I don't think every building I put up needs to be different, since I always apply the same principles. For me novelty has no interest, none whatsoever." More than his great contemporaries, Mies specifically set out to create an architectural language that would transcend mere personal brilliance. Wright and Le Corbusier gloried in individual expression: Wright proclaiming his individualistic intent from the beginning; Le Corbusier, in the twenties at least, propagandizing for a universal style, but having an impetuous vision which conspicuously overran it even within the decade. Mies, on the other hand, focused intently on technological minima, on the joining of piece to piece, and on proportions. His characterization of his own architecture as "almost nothing" conceals in an elliptical manner his piece-by-piece approach to the building. The architecture *happened* from his contemplation of the building process. The neutral rectangular containment of his buildings, throughout most of his American work, was to serve him much as blank canvases in various proportions serve the painter. Given the rectangular container as the most universal of architectural shapes, he could better concentrate on making vivid what had come to seem more important to him than a startling mass. Similarly, if he emphasized the building as structure in his American work, he did not look for the exceptional structure, but to normative skeletal framing, occasionally extended in span by girders and space frames. Any exceptional aspect, whether of mass or of structure, would compromise the universality of The Building. "But we are

† See *American Buildings and Their Architects: Progressive and Academic Ideals at the Turn of the Twentieth Century,* fig. 23.

not decorating," Mies said. "This is structure. We put up what has to be built, and then we accept it."[4]

In this connection, the disparate ways in which the Greek temple haunted Mies and Le Corbusier is particularly revealing of the opposed natures of their genius. Le Corbusier's comprehension of the temple is closer to the Greek approach, even where his evocative image is, of the two, the more remote from its prototype. In a profoundly Mediterranean manner, Le Corbusier leaps to the sculptural totality of a building like the chapel at Ronchamp (Fig. 167). Then (and here the parallel with the ancient situation breaks down), in effect, he asks himself how he will build it (a problem which the Greek architect eventually did not have to face, since construction was standardized). As if to prove the hierarchy of his interests, Le Corbusier usually builds his radical visual conception in a very conservative manner.‡ Mies, on the other hand, is profoundly Germanic in his technological, almost pedantic, dissection of the temple. The age-old Germanic nostalgia for the classical ideal becomes, not a quick perception, but the dogged pursuit of the purified part and its assemblage to an idealized whole. It is not so much the emotional embrace of a totality, as the initial control of emotion as it focuses on the fabric piece by piece, scraping, simplifying, adjusting, combining. Eventually the piece catches fire from the suppressed passion expended on it and, in the terms of Mies' aphorism, less does indeed become more.

This self-effacing concern with the elemental vocabulary of building and its combination for clear and elegant expression—this abnegation of genius—has made Mies the supreme grammarian of modern architecture. Grammarians inevitably appeal to professionals more than to the general public. Mies is thus an architect's architect. The public tends to measure his achievement through his disciples, who in turn comprehend his meaning with varying degrees of profundity. In any area of human endeavor, quests, like Mies', for ultimate simplification commonly appeal to the extremes of professional intelligence and sensitivity. The luminous philosophy for a few becomes an easy formula for most. Such disparity of comprehension is, after all, the fate of a universal language.

Because Mies concentrated not so much on buildings as on The Building embodied in its structural process, he was not vitally interested in expressing the various uses which it might serve. If his Building works in many ways, it does so because almost any activity may be fitted to the noncommittal spaciousness of his rectangular envelopes. Mies specifically said as much in reference to Sullivan's famous slogan, although he too narrowly restricted the meaning of "form follows function" to the

‡ See p. 343 below.

manner in which the building records the use within: "We reverse this [concept], and make a practical shape, and fit the function into it."[5] His ascetic boxes have, in project or in actuality, variously encased a house, a chapel, a theatre, a drive-in restaurant, a museum, classrooms, apartments, and offices. Thus almost all of his American buildings are the same Building. More specifically they belong to one of two general types: either a skeletal rectangular block, or a rectangular pavilion composed of platform base, columns, and roof slab (and derived from his Barcelona prototype, Figs. 65, 66 and 67). In like manner all Greek temples are the same temple. Le Corbusier made this argument in his *Vers une architecture*. Equating the Greek temple to the kind of mass-produced product from the assembly line which he hoped for in modern architecture, he described it as "a product of selection applied to an established standard." In his American work especially, Mies took this verdict more to heart than Le Corbusier himself. "If you have something good," Mies argued, "why change it?" But the rugged power of the Poseidon Temple at Paestum could become the lithe elasticity of the Parthenon,[6] just as, for example, something of the same contrast could develop in two of Mies' best known skyscrapers. His apartment complex at 860–880 Lake Shore Drive in Chicago (Fig. 102) is really a version of his Seagram Building in New York (Fig. 113)—both being different expressions of the same Building.

860 LAKE SHORE DRIVE: A MIESIAN PARADIGM

The twin-towered apartments at 860 Lake Shore Drive (as the compound address is customarily abbreviated) are a landmark in American architecture. Together with his buildings for the campus of the Illinois Institute of Technology in Chicago (beginning in 1939) and his house for Dr. Edith Farnsworth in Plano, Illinois (1945–50), they are most prominent among the buildings inaugurating what came to be called the "Miesian style," which spread so widely in the fifties that some spoke of it as the Second International Style. As already suggested, Mies essentially turned the original International Style inside out after reaching the United States. Whereas in the twenties the frame had been typically boxed within its membrane-like container, after the example of Mies' American work it was as likely to appear on the exterior.

The shift in Mies' own point of view after his arrival in this country is startling.[7] Prior to his immigration, only five of his designs revealed their structural frame on the exterior, all tentatively. Three of them do so in a minor, but significant, manner. These are schemes for glass office buildings in which the supporting columns occur within the box, except at ground level. There they break out of the box to comprise a kind of stilting, not free-standing in the typical Corbusian manner, however, because the glass continues to the ground immediately behind the columns*; the effect is comparable to that of the ground floor of Pietro Belluschi's Equitable Life Assurance Building (Fig. 99), which may, in fact, owe something to Mies' projects. The fourth example of exposed structure in Mies' European work is freakish. For the same exposition in Barcelona (1929) for which he designed his famous Pavilion, Mies also provided a closed cube for the German electrical industry (Fig. 97), one so ominous, despite its elegance, in the unbroken stretch of blank wall down to a low entrance as to suggest that the sole exhibit might well have been an elegant electric chair! The curious structural outrigging along the flanking walls of the cube can only have performed a stiffening function for the basic structure within. Visually, however, it prophesies the structural braille that Mies used on the exteriors of many of his American works. Finally, the fifth work, a projected administration building for the silk industry in Krefeld (designed in 1937, immediately prior to his immigration to the United States) reveals a straightforward industrial frame boldly infilled with windows.† This is nothing more than a dull refinement of the reinforced-concrete-framed factories in America going back to the end of the nineteenth century which Le Corbusier had celebrated in *Vers une architecture,* and a type common in Europe too. However, it should be observed that the routine Krefeld plant, not only in its revealed structure but in its undramatic block, does give a precedent for Mies' later work. Hence it at least raises the question as to how far he might have progressed in his "American style" had conditions been such that he could have continued to work in Germany.

In any event, none of these minor ventures into revealed skeletal structure on the exterior of the building has as much relevance for what was to come as a work by one of Mies' masters. As a young man, between 1908 and 1911, Mies had received part of his training in the office of Peter Behrens, whom the largest electrical company in Germany retained for the design of its factories, as well as for most of its products. The recollection, however tangential, of the walls of Behrens' well-publicized Turbine Plant (1909) in Berlin (Fig. 98) must have meant as much to Mies on coming to the United States as anything in his European career. Indeed, with their forthright exposure, the standard steel

---

* The three projects, all designs of 1928, are those for Leipzigerstrasse and Alexanderplatz in Berlin and for a bank building in Stuttgart. Conveniently illustrated in Johnson, *Mies van der Rohe,* pp. 59, 61, 63. Yet another project of a similar sort for Friedrichstrasse in Berlin (1929), may have been envisioned with a similar treatment at the ground (*ibid.,* p. 62).
† Illustrated in Johnson, *Mies,* p. 128.

FIGURE 97. *Ludwig Mies van der Rohe. Pavilion for the German Electrical Industry at the Barcelona Exposition (Spain), 1929.*

framing elements in the Turbine Plant are closer to Mies' mature skeletal style than is even the boldest framing of Chicago skeletal buildings, clad as it is in masonry or terra cotta, partly for architectural effect and partly for fire protection. The shock of the new environment may have revived the long-submerged image of the turbine factory.

Nothing in Mies' previous professional experience, however, quite accounts for the magnitude of the transformation which occurred in his work once he began to build in the United States. With three minor exceptions, every one of his American designs for a decade and a half—from 1938 until 1954—reveals the structural frame on the exterior of the building, either at the surface of the wall or projected in front of it,

FIGURE 98. *Peter Behrens. Turbine Plant for Allegemein Elektrische Gesell-schaft, Berlin, 1909.*

thereby repudiating the canonical arrangement of the International Style.‡

In addition to providing a prototype for Mies' skeletal style, the twin towers overlooking Lake Michigan have importance in another respect. They are in the vanguard of significant metal-and-glass skeletal skyscrapers which proliferated in the United States after 1950. Once the achievement of the Chicago commercial buildings had faded from consciousness, its memory was only sporadically renewed during the first three decades of the twentieth century by local historians and by a few modern Europeans interested in American technology. Writing for a more general audience, Lewis Mumford did most to keep the Chicago con-

‡ In addition to the above-mentioned project for a concert hall (fig. 96), these exceptions include his unexecuted schemes for the Resor House (1938) and the Museum for a Small City (1942), both of which are composites of the pavilion idea and the curtain wall: illustrated in Johnson, *Mies,* pp. 163, 174–79. Not until 1954 did Mies create his first major American design in which the structural columns occur behind the glass wall in the manner of the International Style; see pp. 256f. below.

tribution alive, in summary, but courageous, remarks in *Sticks and Stones* (1924) and, more especially, in *The Brown Decades* (1931). Not until Sigfried Giedion's *Space, Time and Architecture* (1941) did the early Chicago office buildings receive their due.* In Giedion's influential volume these neglected metal, glass, and terra-cotta structures reappeared as the embodiment of what, since the early twenties, had been a persistent vision of modern architecture.

The "glass" skyscraper was, indeed, the consummate vision of the International Style. Without precedent in the history of architecture before the very last years of the nineteenth century, the skyscraper therefore seemed conspicuously "modern." In Europe, during the twenties, it seemed even "futuristic." As for its material, obviously an "all-glass" skyscraper, as popular parlance would sometimes have it, was an impossibility. Some sort of framework had to support the glass, although the modern European architects of the twenties barely indicated what the nature of the armature might be in their enthusiasm to raise transparent towers in their imagination. In these towers, glass predominated in a double sense: literally and symbolically. Its literal predominance could in fact be said to have been attained years earlier in such extravagantly windowed buildings in the Chicago commercial style as the Reliance† (although the favorite modern effect of the twenties—the "all-glass" wall hung off the edges of cantilevered floor slabs—doubtless did seem more daring to most architects than the glazed infilling of the skeletal frame, even when realized as boldly as in the Reliance). But crystal towers possessed symbolic qualities in European schemes of the twenties which they had never achieved in Chicago. There the frame remained the minimal wall opened as extravagantly as rental concerns made practicable, although as "architecture" this type of design was regarded with considerable embarrassment. In European schemes, these dazzling shafts epitomized the weightless volumetric ideal of the International Style by dramatizing the thrust of space up into space. This effect was of a piece with the scintillant functionalism of the brave new metropolis: light, clean, airy, attuned to that luminous litheness of mind and spirit which the new technology was meant to bring.

In theory which anticipated this aspect of the International Style, glass buildings were initially envisioned as the essence of modern architecture in Paul Scheerbart's *Glasarchitektur* (1914) and in Bruno Taut's

---

* Even he missed the glass wall of the isolated Hallidie Building in San Francisco. See *American Buildings and Their Architects: Progressive and Academic Ideals at the Turn of the Twentieth Century*, fig. 31.

† See *American Buildings and Their Architects: Progressive and Academic Ideals at the Turn of the Twentieth Century*, fig. 20.

Die Stadtkrone (1919).[8] Both of these books probably informed Mies' famous projects for glass office towers in 1919 and 1920.‡ It was Le Corbusier, however, who gave the widest publicity to the fantasy in his versions of the contemporary city which were made during the twenties. These show clusters of glass towers, widely spaced in parks to provide the physical, social, psychological, and symbolic core of the metropolis. Superhighways on viaducts streak past the towers, with primitive aircraft hovering above them, and some cruising at derring-do altitudes between them to risk a landing at the central airport. More than any other monument of the period, the glass skyscraper furnished the dramatic link between the functional and technological aspects of the International Style on the one hand, and its expressionistic aspects on the other. But client skepticism, or even incredulity (witness Willcox's amusement at the mere idea of an "all-glass" building for PSFS*), combined with technical difficulties and the economic crises of depression and war to frustrate their realization. Eventually, just as the dream of the metropolis of separated office towers in gardens was first realized in a large, if partial, manner in the United States with the building of Rockefeller Center, so the glass-towered city also had its premiere in America, although in unplanned circumstances.

Around 1950, four American skyscrapers prominently realized the ideal of the crystal tower. Their wide geographical distribution (it could hardly have been wider!) sufficiently indicates that the pent-up visions of the twenties awaited only a forcing environment to erupt into view. Pietro Belluschi's Equitable Building (1944–47) in Portland, Oregon leads the list. Then, in quick succession, come the United Nations Secretariat (1947–50) from the combined talents of an international team of architects coordinated by Wallace Harrison and dominated by Le Corbusier; Mies van der Rohe's 860 Lake Shore Apartments (1948–51)†; and, finally, Skidmore, Owings & Merrill's Lever House (1951–52) with Gordon Bunshaft as the principal designer (Figs. 99, 100, 101 and 102). These four buildings almost (if not quite) encompass the expressive range of the ensuing spate of metal-and-glass skyscraper design.

The Equitable Building doubtless owes much to Mies van der Rohe's exposure of the metal framing in his earliest buildings at the Illinois Institute of Technology which began to rise in the early forties; but it stands closest in spirit to the old Chicago commercial style, being a

‡ Illustrated in Johnson, *Mies,* pp. 23–25, 27–29.
* See p. 107 above.
† Mies' collaborators on 860 Lake Shore were Pace Associates and Holsman, Holsman, Klekamp & Taylor.

FIGURE 100. *Wallace Harrison* et al. *United Nations Secretariat, New York,* *1947–50.*

frame filled as extensively as possible with glass. Its sleekness, however, attuned to the International Style, makes Belluschi's frame a less assertively structural image than that presented either by the boldest of the Chicago buildings in the commercial style, or by those of Mies.[9] Although Belluschi brought the frame to the exterior of his building, the shallow inset from frame to out-sized plate-glass windows is such that it substantially maintains the early modern ideal of a volume of space lightly enclosed by a membrane skin.

In contrast to the Equitable with its technological inspiration, the more deliberately dramatic United Nations Secretariat (Fig. 100)[10] is the lineal descendant of the *prismes purs* in Le Corbusier's early "radiant cities." As a glazed slab, its skeleton buried behind its window walls, which appear more as an over-all textile of very small elements than a

FIGURE 99. *Pietro Belluschi. Equitable Life Assurance Building, Portland, Ore., 1944–47. (© Ezra Stoller Associates)*

linear grid, it may almost be regarded as a design frustrated from realization for thirty years. Even the enframement of the vast window area by masonry end-walls is vintage Le Corbusier. The billboard thinness of the Secretariat, which the marble enframement exaggerates, and the chameleon changeableness of its glass—alternately perceived as mirror, transparency, and texture in a more dramatic fashion perhaps than is the case with any comparable wall—make it the most immediately spectacular of the four.

To disrupt the chronology of the four buildings by momentarily skipping over 860 Lake Shore, Lever House (Fig. 101) occupies something of a middle position between the Secretariat and Mies' apartments.[11] Its tower is a glass slab in the tradition of early modernism. The articulation of the window walls, however, does not occur as an over-all textured mesh of repetitive units like that of the Secretariat, but as a more deliberate pattern of rectangles created by the opposition of horizontals and verticals—a pattern that is at least nominally Miesian. Expressively, Lever House combines the popularity of the surface drama of the Secretariat with some of the reserve of Mies' perfectionism. This combination of qualities made it, together with Eero Saarinen's low, spreading buildings for the General Motors Technical Center (1948–56) in the Detroit suburb of Warren (Fig. 201), particularly influential in establishing the metal-and-glass image as the corporate architectural norm of the fifties. To Lever House we shall return later. It is enough for the moment to see 860 Lake Shore within this vanguard of prominent metal-and-glass skyscrapers which established the compelling architectural theme for the decade, and simultaneously staked out much of its expressive range.

Coming to 860 Lake Shore (Fig. 102) from (say) Lever House, the average visitor may well be disappointed. The Chicago apartment towers show none of the crisp sheen of Lever House, which is assiduously polished with the Company's products from a motorized janitorial scaffold designed for the purpose as an integral part of the building. The Lake Shore Apartments are more austere than Lever House. The casual spectator may prefer the latter simply because it recalls the gleamingly packaged world of the industrial designer, while being superior to it. Lever's aquatic greens and blues threaded with silver are likely to be more appealing than the dull black and matte silver of 860 Lake Shore. Of the two, therefore, Lever House is the more familiar and approachable image. In the uncompromising severity of Mies' rectangular towers, however, we instinctively feel ourselves at the fountainhead. If Miesian-like formulae are legion, Mies' own greatest buildings reveal the singularity of genius.

The Chicago towers are set on a triangular plot, and at right angles to

FIGURE 101. *Skidmore, Owings & Merrill (with Gordon Bunshaft as the head designer). Lever House, New York, 1951–52.*

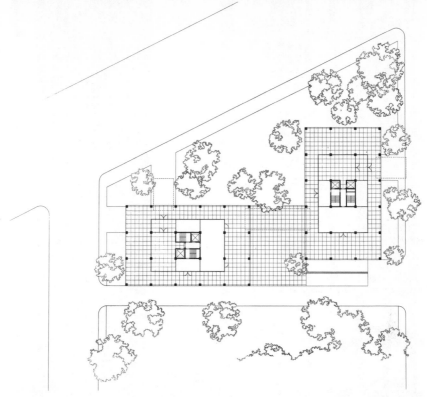

FIGURES 102, 103. *Ludwig Mies van der Rohe. Apartment towers at 860–880 Lake Shore Drive, Chicago, 1948–51. Opposite: general view. Above: ground plan.*

one another across an interval of space (Fig. 103), the one forward of the other. The very thickness of the tower blocks—three bays to five— immediately gives them a classicistic gravity of proportion, comparable to that for the ground plans of temples. Their proportions set the towers at variance with the more vivacious slab preferred by early modernists (and used in Lever House) partly for functional, but as much for expressive, reasons.‡ Had Mies had his way, the proportions of the buildings would have been more suggestive of temple prototypes than they are, and certainly not those of towers. In fact, he recalled that, "When we were about twelve stories high, I said, 'For Heaven's sake, why can't we stop?'" then adding, "When we were twenty-six stories high, it became very thin."[12] But he accepted, as he had to, the com-

‡ On the functional and expressive aspects of the slab, see *American Buildings and Their Architects: Progressive and Academic Ideals at the Turn of the Twentieth Century,* Chapter 1; also pp. 45f. and 93 above.

FIGURE 104. *860 Lake Shore Apartments. Wall detail showing the interval between the towers.*

mercial premises of the building. Although the stilting of 860 Lake Shore traces back to *prismes purs,* it is not obscured so as to make the building volume seem severed from its anchorage with the earth, as was characteristic of stilting in the International Style. In 860 Lake Shore, the columnar decisiveness with which the stilting comes to the ground gives further evidence of Mies' classicistic bent.

The two blocks of the apartment house are lightly coupled above the ground floor by a slab suspended between them as a linking marquee. Like the tense intervals in a painting by Mondrian, the space between the towers plays a far from negative role. The relatively wide breadth of one tower face vies across the interval with the narrowness of the other. The grid seen head on opposes the grid seen in perspective (Fig. 104). The vertical I-beams, welded to the outside faces of the columns and projecting from their surfaces, intensify the changing aspect of the elevations as we move around the towers. "I-beams," the basic elements in steel construction, are so designated because of their I-shaped profile*; the alphabet of commonly used steel elements also includes H's, T's, Z's (right- instead of acute-angled), U's (also right-angled and known as "channels"), and L's (called "angles"). Because of the projecting I's of 860 Lake Shore, the wall which is viewed diagonally appears in marked relief while the wall viewed head on appears with relative flatness. A few steps around the building and this relationship shifts, for the projecting I's are always closing like louvers over the windows of one wall, while opening the grid of the other. More steps around, and the buildings come together across the space. Still more, and they again separate, the wide and the narrow elevations abruptly swapping appearances. There is change, too, in the alternation of lighted and shaded walls as we circle, and in the reflections of one building in the other. As in any glass structure, the accidents of draperies open or closed (here uniformly pale gray, but with an inner curtain track for those who prefer another color), and of furniture or movement within are other aspects of change. Change is constant amid these simple things, which—and here is the paradox—are so elemental in themselves and in combination that they are intellectually perceived as unchangeable.

Unfortunately, the experience of movement around the towers is no longer what it was when, on their completion, and for some years afterwards, they rose in splendid isolation. Most of the adjoining open space has gone to other apartment buildings. They crowd Mies' towers the more cruelly because many of them weakly crib from his esthetic. However much this subsequent crowding has blurred the paradox of flux and fixity which once appeared so vividly in views of the towers seen from a little distance, the same qualities are at least still evident in closer views of the window grid (Fig. 105). The geometry reveals itself as a grid decisively *made,* yet simultaneously as *being made* of its discrete components. Of course this sense of process and realization at 860 Lake Shore is rooted in Mies' early appreciation of the "exploded" nature of Wright's structure and, more directly (it would seem, although Mies has denied it) the fixed-but-dynamic *De Stijl* compositions with their right-angled intersection of lines of varying thicknesses (Fig. 81).† Just

---

* Beams having an I-shape profile are of two types. One type, the most commonly used, has wide flanges, and is technically designated with an interlocked W and F:

$$W\!F$$

The other type has narrow flanges, and this alone is technically designated as an I-beam. For convenience, in this book both types will be termed I-beams, as well as certain I-shaped members custom designed by Mies to simulate their structural counterparts.

† See pp. 196f. above. On Wright, see *American Buildings and Their Architects: Progressive and Academic Ideals at the Turn of the Twentieth Century,* Chapter 3.

FIGURE 105. *860 Lake Shore Apartments. Wall detail.*

as squares and rectangles *result* from the crossing of horizontals and verticals in Mondrian's compositions, so in 860 Lake Shore the window areas *result* from the dynamics of the elements crossing over or behind one another. In this articulation of the window wall Mies elaborates the basic oppositions in frame construction: the rise of the structural columns from ground to roof against the spread of floor-and-ceiling slabs.

One I-beam is welded to the outside face of each of the structural columns; three across the interval between the columns so as to enframe four windows. Having multiple implications—functional, esthetic, and symbolic—these I's illuminate Mies' "less is more." Functionally, they frame the windows as mullions (except for those tacked to the structural columns, which primarily provide visual continuity around the building‡). Esthetically, they provide an element of depth, and hence the animation resulting from their louver-like opening and closing as we circle the towers. They also give a discreet play of light and shadow to the elevation. Esthetically, too, they not only emphasize the verticality of the towers, but furnish the means of relating individual window elements to the full scale of the building. Thus the wall is not simply a pile of identical window units (as are most "window walls"), but a hierarchy of relationships achieving part of their architectural significance in a progression of sizes which records on the elevation the heights of a balustrade, a room and, eventually, the building.

If the projecting I-beams perform specific esthetic functions for this particular design, they also serve in a more comprehensive sense to epitomize a harmonic order. The I-beams are left as unclosed and self-contained elements, abruptly severed top and bottom, much as the black lines are cut by the edges of a Mondrian canvas—not *ended* by a closed composition, but severed by a limited field. Their qualities of openness and discreteness permit the I's to characterize the modern idea of a harmony arrived at through an equilibrium of tensions. Symbolically, finally, the I-beams not only record the technology, but celebrate it. Both the material and the process by which the tower is built become vivid. As specifically "modern" objects, bluntly accepted for what they are, the I-beams intensify our awareness that the building belongs to our time. Because these modern artifacts articulate the walls of the Chicago towers much as pilasters articulated a classical or Renaissance wall, they simultaneously reinvigorate the whole of the great classicizing tradition for present use (Figs. 106, 107). The old stability fuses with the new dynamics; the essence of historical principle with the new functionalism.

In sum, the I-beam *is* the functional member which builds the architecture; it *is* the esthetic member which makes the harmonic order; it *is* the symbolic member which epitomizes a cultural situation. And throughout this gamut of meaning, the I-beam *is* itself—the utterly com-

---

‡ Questioned at the time of the building's completion about the welding of the largely unessential I's to the outer face of the structural columns, Mies replied, "Now, first, I am going to tell you the real reason, and then I am going to tell you a good reason by itself.

"It was very important to preserve and extend the rhythm which the mullions set up on the rest of the building. We looked at it on the model without the steel section attached to the column and it did not look right. Now, the other reason is that this steel section was needed to stiffen the plate which covers the corner column so this plate would not ripple, and also we needed it for strength when the sections were hoisted into place [see Fig. 109]. Now, of course, that's a very *good* reason, but the other reason is the real reason." *Architectural Forum,* November 1952, p. 99.

FIGURE 106. *860 Lake Shore Apartments. Close-up of the wall showing projecting I-beams.*

monplace, banal stock item of the steel mill. In fact, only by being so elementally itself, and only by being so forcefully asserted for such comprehensive effect, can the commonplace present such a nexus of meaning.

As Mies once stated:

> I believe that architecture has little or nothing to do with the invention of interesting forms or with personal inclinations.
>
> True architecture is always objective and is the expression of the inner structure of our time, from which it stems.[13]

Always objective: if the comprehensive nature of the objectivity of the International Style comes to pinpoint-focus anywhere, it does so in the projecting I-beam as Mies used it on the elevations of 860 Lake Shore. Divergent though his work may appear from that of the International Style as defined by Hitchcock and Johnson in 1932,* it maintains the same idealism. Far from moving *away* from the International Style, as some have maintained, Mies has dared to move *into* it, and no small

* See pp. 118f. above.

244

FIGURE 107. *Maison Carrée, roman temple built at Nîmes (France)*, 14 B.C.

part of the authority of his design depends upon his continuing commitment to its objective point of view.

If, as Mies repeatedly asserted, "God is in the details," then his architecture demands closest scrutiny. Looking at the major grid in black steel, for example, we seem to discern a subtlety that may or may not have been a very conscious part of Mies' calculations. The four windows between each two structural columns vary in width so that the two closest to the columns are very slightly narrower than the two at the center; this because the structural columns are of greater thickness than the window mullions. Almost imperceptibly these narrower units accentuate the verticality of the adjacent structural columns, and help to mark the rhythmic "beat" of the structural bays around the building. But this slight change in over-all window size, however much it may have entered into Mies' calculations, is of relatively little consequence compared to the manner in which he has dimensioned the silver aluminum window framing so as to create a contrapuntal reinforcement of the opposition of rise and spread established in the grid of the black steel.

Mies makes the balustrade (bar) across each window thicker than is either the top or the sides of the aluminum framing; the base still thicker. These thicker elements of balustrade and base appear as the

245

boundaries of a horizontal band (or as two strong parallel lines with a stripe between) which seems to run horizontally across the elevation behind the verticals of the projecting I's. Spread is thus reasserted against rise. (Incidentally, the wider bands at the base of the window also visually weight it so that top and bottom are instantly distinguishable, as is frequently not the case in window walls.) But the visual image of the horizontal bands of silver fluctuates. As we continue to look, they seem to change into what they really are: namely, into the boundaries of the double rectangles of the windows. As in a Mondrian composition, the linear emphasis alternately shifts to planar. The horizontal pane of glass at the bottom of the window opposes the vertical pane at the top. Again the vertical remains slightly dominant. But the horizontal forces of the elevation battle, so to speak, to the bitter end, especially since the verticality of the upper window pane is almost countered by its width. Almost, but not quite. If the soaring dimension eventually triumphs, it is by a margin sufficiently narrow that the visual battle perpetually renews itself—up versus across, line versus plane; and withal in the paradoxical fluctuation of components so elemental in themselves, and so clearly, resonantly, and simply related, as simultaneously to seem inexorably fixed.

Different in appearance though the two buildings may be, the manner in which Mies set verticals against horizontals in a forceful equilibrium recalls Richardson's comparable concern in the elevations of the Marshall Field Wholesale Store, where horizontal forces eventually dominate the verticals. (In fact, Myron Goldsmith, a former student of Mies', has recalled that Richardson's Wholesale Store was among the buildings that Mies had most wanted to see when he first reached Chicago. "He was incredulous when we told him that it had been pulled down for a parking lot.") Comparisons between Mies' wall and Sullivan's pier-and-spandrel treatment are more obvious.† Like Richardson and Sullivan, too, Mies did not depend on abstract systems or formulae for his proportions, but rather on empirical and intuitive knowledge. In Mies' case this was often gained from scale models and large-scale mock-ups of structural details, on which he placed special emphasis. Few offices made more comprehensive use of models and mock-ups. Large offices customarily employ professional model-makers, who generally work in some cubbyhole apart from the drafting area, often in another building. In Mies' office, however, anyone on the force might turn on occasion from

† See *American Buildings and Their Architects: Progressive and Academic Ideals at the Turn of the Twentieth Century*, figs. 11, 49; and in the present volume, figs. 25, 145.

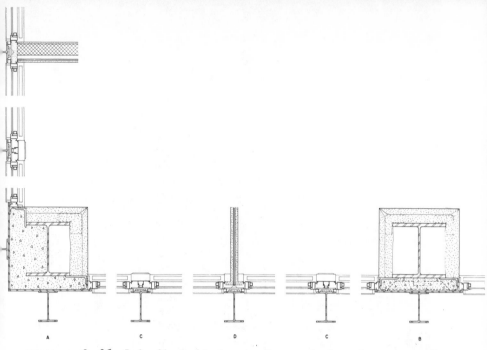

FIGURE 108. *860 Lake Shore Apartments. Structural plan of exterior wall.
A and B are the supporting columns, the dotted areas indicating fireproofing
and insulation around the H-columns. C is a typical window mullion; D
a window mullion with an interior room partition within an apartment unit;
E a window mullion with a thicker partition between abutting apartment
units. Cuts through the glass areas of the windows indicate that their actual
widths are ignored to make the diagram more compact.*

his drawing board to the model-making shop, which was a sizable adjunct
to the drafting space.

A cross-sectional plan of the construction (Fig. 108) reveals the
sense in which the visible grid of the window wall is the surrogate of
the actual structure. Since the metal frames of all multi-storied buildings
must be encased with a fireproof material, the towers' structural columns are necessarily buried. Their fireproof encasement converts the
H-shape at the core of the column to the square shape at its perimeter.
Small L-shaped angle components are welded to the H-beam and also
to other small L's. The latter come through the fireproofing in order
to provide narrow surfaces to which the steel plates that sheathe the
exterior are welded. To these, in turn, the window grids are welded.

The assemblage of the window grid occurred on the roof in sizable,
two-story prefabricated sections (Fig. 109). The projecting I-beams
were welded across the flat steel plates which cover the outer edges
of columns and floor slabs. Derricked down into position, the prefabricated sections were, in turn, welded to the small L's that poked
through the fireproofing from their ultimate anchorage to the H-columns.

247

FIGURE 109. *860 Lake Shore Apartments. Construction process. From the roof top, derricks lower the two-story, prefabricated sections of the facing grid into position for welding to the structural frame.*

(Although known in the thirties, welding in the fabrication of steel buildings became important in the United States only after World War II, which provided much experience in this technology, as well as workmen trained in its skills.). The alternative would have been a framing studded with bolts or rivet heads, which, for example, Mies chose to use and leave exposed in the framing of some of the buildings at the Illinois Institute of Technology.‡ Since even minute irregularities at the joints would have jeopardized the apparent straightness of the projecting I's when viewed looking upward the long perspective of 860 Lake Shore, Mies insisted on their erection on the elevations of the

‡ Actually, the major portion of 860 Lake Shore is bolted, although this is not visible on the exterior.

FIGURE 110. *860 Lake Shore Apartments. Construction process. With the exterior grid in place, workmen attach prefabricated aluminum window units to the mullions from inside the building.*

buildings in the order in which they had been cut from the rolled lengths at the mill. Once the basic grid had been fixed to the structural skeleton, installation of the prefabricated window units occurred from inside the building (Fig. 110). This rapid assemblage from prefabricated parts made the Lake Shore apartment towers economical buildings, costing from five to ten per cent less than comparable apartment buildings. A speculative promoter, Herbert S. Greenwald, who had both the courage and the vision to trust the design to a great architect, commissioned the building with this economic end in mind.[14] Inevitably, the purely technological aspect of Mies' work and the profits to be made from it accounted for the tremendous influence of the Miesian example. In most of the offshoots by other architects and builders, however, neither the "less" nor

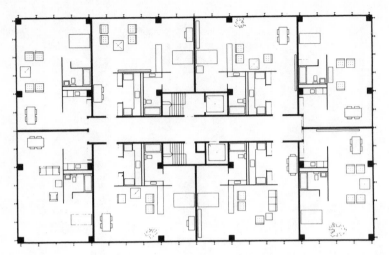

FIGURE 111. *860 Lake Shore Apartments. Projected apartment plans by Mies van der Rohe for the north tower.*

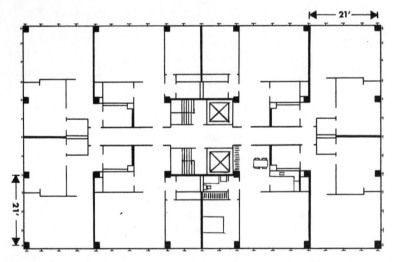

FIGURE 112. *860 Lake Shore Apartments. Floor plans determined by the management and used in the north tower.*

the "more" had much to do with his teaching, except to prove that The Building was as much a prototype as he had intended it to be.

Since the interior plans devised by Mies were deemed too unconventional by real estate experts to provide readily rentable apartments, his design is virtually limited to the shell. His projected plans—each floor in the north tower containing eight studio apartments; each in the south tower four larger units—reveal the consistency with which he would have extended the esthetic of the exterior to the inside. Comparison of them with the typical floor plans that were adopted (Figs. 111, 112) discloses a clarity in Mies' scheme which is remarkable given the tightness and complexity of apartment planning. Each unit echoes the simple rectangularity of the building mass. Within each unit, partitioning continues the rectangular theme. The basic rectangularity of the unit is the more evident since Mies envisioned it as a simple space, where the partitioning recalls (in a very much tighter version to be sure) the kind of conditioning of continuous space with free-standing slabs which he had utilized in the Barcelona Pavilion (Fig. 67). In conjunction with the planar openness of floor and ceiling, such partitioning would have complemented the planar aspects of the floor-to-ceiling windows. But the real estate specialist preferred the privacy of *rooms* (especially with respect to the bedrooms) to the openness of Mies' plans. In further contrast with Mies' scheme, the adopted plans provide corner living rooms for the largest apartments and more space for the valuable corner apartments of the north tower. These advantages come at the cost, however, of increased corridor space, tight kitchens, and spaces kinked with awkward corners.[15] As built, therefore, the plans are at odds with the elevations.

It is the exterior that counts, the opposed towers made of the magnificent bluntness of their enclosing grids.

THE SEAGRAM BUILDING: PARADIGM SUBTILIZED

The Temple of Poseidon at Paestum is to the Parthenon as 860 Lake Shore is to the Seagram (1954–58). The towers seem appropriate in their doctrinaire forthrightness to the Chicago of Holabird & Roche; the luxurious subtlety of the Seagram suggests the New York of McKim, Mead & White, opposite whose Racquet Club (completed in 1918) the Seagram stands at 375 Park Avenue, between 52nd and 53rd Streets.

As Reyner Banham has observed,[16] the gain in refinement over the Lake Shore complex was not wholly to the advantage of Seagram. Whereas the earlier building proclaimed Mies' willingness to accept technological norms, and to make these the basis for "architecture," three aspects of the designing of the Seagram served to threaten this directness. The first, making the others possible, was a sumptuous budget; the second, Mies' choice of lavish materials, and especially his use of bronze for the projecting I-beams comprising the symbolic outrigging; the third, custom detailing to give the matter-of-fact image of structure extraordinary subtlety and elegance. Hence Banham has reason to fear that, in its self-consciousness as "architecture," the Seagram furthers the Miesian myth at the expense of his real achievement. It encourages the view of Mies as too much the devout neoclassicist, too much the perfectionist dealing in exquisite profiles and proportions, too much the Buddha of the profession who polished "almost nothing" to transcendent "truth." As a result, the directness with which Mies confronted the facts of technology tends to be overlooked. To comprehend the essence of Mies' architecture, 860 Lake Shore *is* the better building to study, being the more straightforward in the use of skeletal construction, the more axiomatic, and the less beguiling. But more conspicuously than 860 Lake Shore, the Seagram shows the grander side of Mies' vision. Its austerity of form coupled with its luxuriousness of effect proclaims not only Mies' feeling for the potential of structure to create noble order, in the sense in which it created noble order in the past, but also his conviction that modern architecture of consequence in a period dominated by technology will occur only by facing this truth of its time.

If 860 Lake Shore is a relatively economical building, the Seagram is a prestige building, its cost per square foot of office space coming to roughly twice the average of that for comparable space in midtown Manhattan skyscrapers erected at the same time.[17] Samuel Bronfman, president of Distillers Corporation-Seagrams Limited, wanted a sumptuous building as corporation headquarters. Fortunately, his daughter, Phyllis Bronfman Lambert (who later became an architect herself), had been indoctrinated with high standards of architecture in art history courses at Vassar College. When she saw preliminary schemes of what her father had in mind, she prevailed on him to commission a distinguished architect.[18] From a list of a dozen leading architects supplied by Philip Johnson, by virtue of his onetime position as curator of architecture and design at the Museum of Modern Art, Mies was chosen. He eventually called in Johnson as his collaborator.*

As we approach the Seagram, it is the sheer rise of the dark cliff of dull bronze and gray-amber glass which strikes us first (Fig. 113). Walking along Park Avenue, we come upon it suddenly because the Seagram is deeply set on its plaza, about 90 feet back from the street. (Ideally, of course, the plaza should be strongly enframed by adjacent

* Kahn & Jacobs, office building specialists, were associated.

FIGURE 113. *Ludwig Mies van der Rohe. Seagram Building, New York, 1954–58.*

buildings, as on one side at least it is not: but there is no need to worry this theme further.†) Space in front; cliff behind. The space emphasizes the density of the cliff. Relative to the rise of the building, the space is restricted (however generous by urban standards), and this enhances the looming quality of the building. We look up automatically. As in 860 Lake Shore, the unbroken run of the projecting I-beam mullions through 38 stories encourages the act by which we measure the scale of the building and seize its unity; the more readily because the limited height of the building and the limited space in which to view it make it immediately comprehensible as a whole. The slender window proportioning intensifies the verticality. The horizontals are less emphasized than those of the Lake Shore Apartments (Fig. 114).

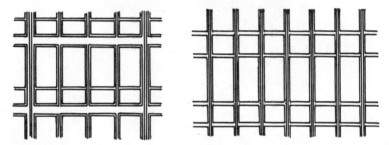

FIGURE 114. *Comparative window proportioning: 860 Lake Shore, left, and Seagram Building, right.*

Fortunately, Lever House is diagonally across Park Avenue from the Seagram. Thus we have an unusual opportunity here to appraise different approaches to curtain-walled skyscrapers in metal and glass where both examples are important in the history of mid-twentieth-century architecture (Fig. 101). Since comparisons are odious as well as revealing, let it be said immediately that, among New York commercial buildings erected in the fifteen years since World War II, certain ones by Skidmore, Owings & Merrill rank with the few which approach the esthetic quality of the Seagram. Along with Lever House, notable designs by this firm erected in New York just before and just after the Seagram Building are the small glass bank for Manufacturers Hanover Trust Company (1953–54) on Fifth Avenue at 43rd Street (see Fig. 47), the Pepsi-Cola Building (1957–59) on Park at 59th Street, the Union Carbide Building (1957–60) a few blocks south of Seagram between 47th and 48th Streets, and the Chase-Manhattan Bank Building in the downtown financial district (commissioned in 1955 and completed

† See pp. 25f. above.

in 1964). These SOM buildings are probably more immediately popular than Seagram, and the last two especially probably provide better corporate standards for office space. All reveal original solutions to the office building, and all have been extensively imitated. None of these commissions, however, was a braver venture than Lever. The earliest of the group, it established a new standard for office buildings after the war, with respect not only to the use of metal and glass but also to the inclusion of a plaza. The first such civic-minded gesture of consequence by private enterprise in New York since Rockefeller Center, the Lever Plaza was doubly justified, despite the disastrous imitations that have followed its lead. Since it was the first in its area, it served as a welcome open space amidst buildings, as plazas should. Then, too, it occurred beneath the building, so that the building line maintained some sense of the street as a corridor, even though the narrowness of the slab did create the first break in the solid front of building that once made Park Avenue a forceful urban corridor. This deficiency in street design notwithstanding, the lesson of the containment of the Lever Plaza within the bounds of the building line may well have been emulated for the great majority of subsequent plazas or, alternatively, of their enframement like the Rockefeller Center plazas fronting on Fifth Avenue. Finally, not the least of these reasons for comparing Lever House with the Seagram Building is the reciprocal, if limited, influence they seem to have had on one another. On the one hand, Mies' approach to design surely conditioned some aspects of the design of Lever House, especially the precise manner in which horizontals and verticals oppose one another in the gridded window wall (so different from the all-over textile-like weave of the glass wall of the United Nations Secretariat, for example, Fig. 100). On the other hand, the well-merited and generally favorable publicity accorded Lever House—among the first corporate skyscrapers in the metal-and-glass idiom that is loosely associated with Mies' manner—surely helped to make Seagram possible.

Whereas the Seagram Building is not seen from a distance, Lever House is visible for blocks up and down Park Avenue. This fact, and the small size of the building (a mere 21 stories), permitted Bunshaft to organize his building as two tautly wrapped packages which are readily perceived as entities. The conception of the metal-and-glass building as made up of weightless packages (juggled in mid-air as a kind of aerial version of Mies' Lake Shore towers) looks back to the volumetric ideal of early modernism. So does the stilting: small in scale, and further diminished by the tendency of its shiny, sheet-metal covering to ripple in the light, it is tucked well under the building so as to intensify the floating sensation of the volumes above (Fig. 115). We experience the stilting of Lever House casually; not decisively, but as a blur. Above,

FIGURE 115. *Skidmore, Owings & Merrill. Lever House. Detail of the stilting.*

the grid of the two glass boxes barely skims the surface of the membrane wall (Fig. 119). As with the stilts, the sheen has a disintegrating effect.

Across the street, the Seagram Building meets the earth firmly, like 860 Lake Shore, on two-storied stilts—2 feet 10 inches square at the base as compared to 24⅞ inches for Lever (Fig. 116). Their prominence and the dark, rigid surfaces give them a visual persistence reminiscent of Greek columns. Although we perceive the stilting in its entirety, each stilt also asserts its identity. The force of the stilting is of particular interest since the Seagram is among the first of Mies' American buildings in which he slightly recessed the columns behind the plane of the projected floor slabs, and concealed them behind the equable screen of his window wall, in contrast to their more exposed placement at 860 Lake Shore. In 1954, less than a year before he received the Seagram

commission, Mies had similarly recessed the columns of the Esplanade Apartments directly across the street from 860 Lake Shore, and thereafter this traditionally modern scheme frequently appeared in his work. As already suggested, the recession of the columns behind the enclosing screen of windows works against the Seagram and in favor of 860 Lake Shore, the latter providing a more visible image of Mies' structural esthetic. In fact, however, in buildings as large as the Seagram, technological considerations rather favor inset columns. Exterior columns must be heavily insulated if they are to expand and contract with temperature changes at the same rate as those in sheltered positions inside. This protection involves extra cost; in large buildings, a considerable increase in cost. Moreover, when the window wall as a homogeneous plane of repetitive units occurs out in front of the structural columns, both the design and the erection of these two elements is simplified by the fact that they can be considered separately (all structure inside, all enclosure outside, and not mixed in the same plane). In commissions subsequent to that of the Seagram, therefore, Mies has tended to use the Seagram formula with its interior columns rather than 860 Lake Shore with its more forthright exhibition as structure. According to Peter Carter, a member of the office, Mies often wished in his late office buildings to return to the directness of the structural statement of 860 Lake Shore; but, realizing that the logic of the technological situation ran counter to his desire for the most vivid expression of structure, he usually resorted to the Seagram formula.[19]‡ Hence, if the build of the building continued as the controlling image in Mies' work, in his late office buildings especially the familiar image is rather taken for granted, and it is the technology of the building process more than the structure itself that tends to condition the design. Not for all commissions of course. In less routinized designs the vigorous structural image of 860 Lake Shore returns, brought back by the fierce attention to the exceptional problem. It reappears especially in the new National Gallery (1962–68) for Berlin, where a vivid sense of structure is wedded to a majestic sense of space—a union obviously impossible to anything like this degree in office buildings. In the Gallery, the spatial emphasis of his Pavilion at Barcelona is mediated by a series of noble pavilion designs dominated by structural considerations, to eventuate in a noble balance of space *and* structure in his final statement of the theme.

In any event, to repeat, the columns are very visibly exposed at the entrance to the Seagram. With respect to their two-story height, they are spaced sufficiently to create voids nearly square in their proportions, thereby providing a stabilizing geometry of compelling clarity as a base for the more intricate window grid above. Assertive at the ground because only slightly recessed, the columns are also clearly visible immediately behind the plane of the windows, and actually break through it at the corners of the building (Fig. 123).

‡ One example is Dominion Center (1963–69) in Toronto, done in collaboration with John B. Parkin Associates and Bregnan & Hamann. Here a preliminary design with structural columns at the surface of the wall in the manner of 860 Lake Shore was discarded for climatic and financial reasons in favor of the inset solution. The cluster of commissions for office buildings in Chicago that came to Mies in the years immediately before his death in 1969—the Everett Dirksen Federal Office Building, the Illinois Center complex, and the IBM Building—are all slightly less subtle variants of the Seagram Building. In Chicago, the most momentously Miesian statement of overt structure in the tradition of 860 Lake Shore is not by Mies. This is Charles Murphy Associates' Chicago Civic Center Court Building (1960–66), in which large columns, very widely spaced, project for part of their depth out in front of the window plane with the spandrel elements stretched bridge-like between.

FIGURE 117. *Skidmore, Owings & Merrill. Inland Steel Building, Chicago,
1956–58. Detail of the stilting.*

If it is somewhat unfair to compare the two-story-high stilting of
Seagram to its modest counterpart across the street and reach an un-
favorable verdict against Lever House, it is surely fair to compare the
Seagram stilting with the much more sizable projecting columns of SOM's
Inland Steel Building (Fig. 117)—not to demean the Chicago skyscraper,
which is among the best office buildings to rise in the Loop from World

War II to the sixties, but to use architecture of exceptional quality in order to indicate the commanding presence of Mies' design.* Not even the bulk of the steel-sheathed fins of the Inland (nor a close-up view taken without the disintegrating dazzle that full sunlight brings) quite saves them from the blur of a discreet slickness. By contrast, Mies' stilting is rigid and resonant in its classicistic command of plaza and entrance. Of the two, Mies' stilting sears the imagination, remaining intensely present in memory.

The column-stilts of the Seagram in conjunction with the plaza establish the entrance as a monumental portal. By comparison, to return to Lever House, its lobby serves a more complex function, and does so admirably, being not only an entrance but also a reception room. The glass-walled lobby sits athwart the plaza, and is so approached from either side that we look through it to more plaza beyond. Columns, planting, pavement, and exhibits provide continuity through the plate-glass barrier, so that indoors and out visually intermingle. The furniture is clustered close to the elevators and behind the outdoor planting, giving a sense of enclosure and semi-privacy, yet enabling those who wait for their appointments to participate in the surrounding vivacity of movement and openness.

No such complexity of function or such spatial *jeu d'esprit* linking inside and out occurs in the Seagram. Space *and* cliff. On bank-ridden Park Avenue, the clients had originally wanted yet another bank in the ground-level space or in part of it; but Mies flatly refused to do the building without the pristine space fronting the pristine portal. The space is formal and empty. Formal in that the front entrance (there are subordinate side entrances opening onto 52nd and 53rd Streets) provides an axial approach to the building. Piercingly empty in that nothing exists on this broad central slab—if we except the flagpole to one side, and clusters of trees flanking the entrance. Aside from these negligible intrusions, nothing but space. There are no planting boxes, no displays, not even benches. Nothing could be further removed from the somewhat over-stuffed, almost too popular, outdoor space at Rockefeller Center. Human figures moving in long diagonals across the pristine, pink granite Seagram slab evoke thoughts of Giacometti figures (Fig. 118). Low fountains in

---

* In view of what has just been said about the requirement of special insulation for exterior as opposed to interior columns, it is worth noting that the office floors of the Inland Steel tower bridge the two rows of exterior columns as slabs unobstructed by any interior supports whatsoever, thus each floor has a completely free space for partitioning (fig. 74). Other factors may also have justified the use of exterior columns here. Inland Steel is not a very large building. A steel company obviously enjoys cost advantages in erecting its own buildings that most companies do not possess. Finally, expenditure for the kind of conspicuous display of its product provided by the projecting columns is also desirable.

FIGURE 118. *Alberto Giacometti.* City Square (La Place), *1948.*

the flanking pools provide the contrast of movement and noise to the empty space. Originally strung out in thin rows toward the edges of the pools, the jets were subsequently gathered in a tight square at their centers. Whether to save pedestrians from wind-swept spray (and on windy days the fountains must still be held down) or to create a concentration of energy consonant with the force of the building, or for both reasons, the change was salutary.† Finally, low, chunky, green marble parapets bound the plaza at either side. To them idlers are banished; regrettably, they must tread a narrow ledge behind the fountain pools to gain their seats. If New York is fortunate in having the plaza of Rockefeller Center as a focus of a kaleidoscopic kind of urban experience, it is equally fortunate in possessing this ascetic space. No American plaza is more uncompromisingly permeated with the spirit of the Italian Renaissance.

The plaza continues uninterruptedly under the building and paves the recessed glass-walled lobby. A slab marquee overhead echoes the plane underfoot as a herald of shelter. The counter-movement of the plaza slab inward and underfoot and the roof slab outward and overhead celebrates the smooth coupling of inside and out, made smoother by the extraordinary refinement of an "astroclock," which adjusts light in the lobby to daylight out-of-doors. This coupling of indoors and out is precisely that. If smooth and easily effected, it is also the collision of two entities, like two railroad cars. Plaza *and* lobby: not the ambiguous flow of one into the other as in much modern architecture (the kind of relationship that Lever House has with its plaza, for example), but more decisive. The sense of this decisiveness is magnified by the intense confrontation of the plaza and the building. Within the lobby the slab ends

† Mies originally intended that the pools have low abstract sculptures set on the existing slabs at water level. The sculptures were never executed. In a sense, the densely massed jets are substitutes.

261

of the elevator shafts (sheathed in a creamy travertine and reflected in the silver mosaic of the ceiling) firmly back up each pair of a double row of stilts. Penetrated by corridors to be sure, the dominating solids nevertheless reassert the density of the building mass. As a result, there is a ceremonial grandeur in the merger of plaza and lobby. Space *and* cliff: the opposition reconciled and dramatized, again as in a Renaissance palace, by the majestically sealed portal.

Towering above the plaza and its portal, the window wall impresses us first by its color. The very darkness of the building gives it gravity. Designers of early metal-and-glass buildings sought a sharp contrast between the metal grid and the window or panel units—usually, as in Lever House, by juxtaposing bright work with dark green or blue glass and panels. (Green and blue glass were the first glare- and heat-resistant glasses available after buildings like Lake Shore had demonstrated the intolerable conditions resulting from the use of clear glass.) In the Seagram, the combination of dull bronze and gray-amber glass is strikingly handsome. Like most glass buildings, however, the Seagram does not take kindly to intense, raking light. In such brilliance the window wall eludes visual grasp more than most, taking on an unpleasantly pale purplish glare. The façade appears to best advantage in late afternoon sun, as shadows climb the lower stories. Then the grid glows with warm browns occasionally burnished to dull gold; the glass, with browns that are violet-tinged toward the ground where it reflects other buildings, and pale blue where it catches the sky. The muted harmony of the color reinforces the solidity of the cliff. The grid never asserts itself at the expense of the wall, never disintegrates into blinding streaks of light, as does that of Lever House.

Whereas Lever House and practically all metal-and-glass buildings previous to the Seagram are designed for a perpetual present, the Seagram itself is the first major metal-and-glass skyscraper consciously designed to age as masonry buildings age—an architectural property as appropriate for Seagram's whisky as sheen for Lever's soap. In time, corrosion of the surface may further the impression of the window wall as a massive entity.

Since the Seagram wall is shadowy, we cannot grasp it all at a glance. We must peer, or miss some of its refinements, much as we must peer at the somber walls of Quattrocento palaces in Florence fully to see the elegant precision which built to such bold effect. Again Mies has used projecting I-beam mullions welded between each of the windows. As in Lake Shore, these projections give depth, shadow, and scale to the wall, while also providing the symbolic pilasters of his builded-art—his *Baukunst* as he refers not only to his specific emphasis in design, but also to the very nature of architecture as he sees it. Even in these projecting

FIGURE 119. *Above left: Lever House. Detail of the window wall.*

FIGURE 120. *Above right: Seagram Building. Detail of the window wall.*

FIGURE 121. *Below right: Seagram Building. Structural plan of the projecting I-beam of the window wall.*

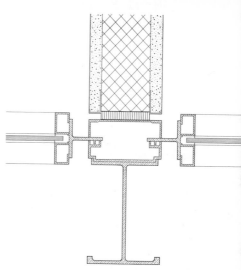

fins, however, refinements appear over the Lake Shore version (Figs. 108, 119, 120 and 121). Whereas the outrigging of the Chicago towers consists of standard items ordered from the steelmaker's catalogue, that in the Seagram consists of custom-designed I's of extruded bronze. Custom-designed, but having the shape of their standard counterparts; nothing more clearly demonstrates the formal and symbolic quality of much of Mies' "prefabrication." Refinements in the I's are not only more appropriate to the Seagram than to Lake Shore, they are also more possible in bronze than in structural steel. Thus their profiling is more attenuated in the Seagram (4 inches across the face and 6 inches in depth, as compared to 5 by 8 for Lake Shore). Right-angled lips edging the underside of the flanges of the outer face of the I's sharpen the shadow.

The close-knit density of the gridded wall derives not only from its color, but from the treatment of the I-beam outrigging. First, in contrast to 860 Lake Shore, there is the narrower spacing of the projected

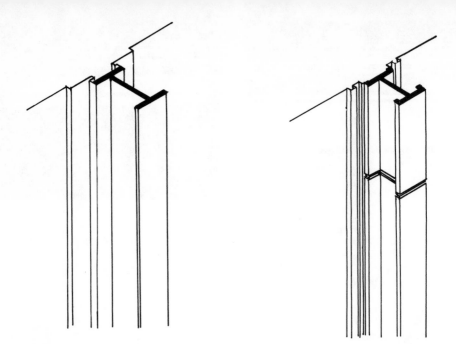

FIGURE 122. *Comparative isometric diagram of the projecting I-beams of the window walls: 860 Lake Shore, left, and Seagram Building, right.*

I-beams. Much as the narrow spacing of the piers gives density as well as verticality to the window walls of Sullivan's Wainwright and Guaranty Buildings (Figs. 145, 25), so the narrow spacing of the Seagram's I's contributes to the wall-like character of what had started as a frame. Mies' design of the spandrel horizontals (in Muntz metal, an alloy containing copper so as to match the bronze mullions) works to the same end. An inset molding runs around the perimeter of each of them (Figs. 120, 123). This inset detail‡ separates the vertical I's from the spandrels (Fig. 122). It also visually draws the I's into the wall. They do not project from a surface, but emerge from slight shadow—a linear shadow, now muffled, now sharp, depending on the light. At Lake Shore, however, it is the contrast in color and material which separates frame from window (the dull black grid abutting the silver aluminum enframement of the clear glass). Furthermore, the projecting I-beams cling directly to the outside face of the horizontals in the Lake Shore gridding.

Whereas other architects had tried to make their metal walls appear as seamless as possible, Mies frankly asserts the breaks occurring between each increment of the I as it mounts Seagram's wall. Thus, even in as minute a detail as the breaks in the I's, he emphasizes the component as

‡ This type of inset was made famous in Mies' detailing in brick for the buildings at the Illinois Institute of Technology.

an entity which builds to the total fabric and, incidentally, again relates his building to the masonry tradition by creating a metal stereotomy for it.*

The Hellenic quality of a *Baukunst*—a building in which each part, whether structural or pseudo-structural, must be a perfect entity—is evident at the corners of the window wall (Figs. 123, 124). In any architectural design with a contained composition like the Seagram, the treatment of corners—where one wall abuts another, or where it touches the ground or meets the sky—is especially indicative of the architect's resourcefulness, or his lack of it. The usual window wall of prefabricated elements simply stops when the client's needs are met, his site is filled, or his pocketbook exhausted. The "architect" adds units much as the butcher slices bologna. Mies' window wall, however, is visibly terminated, and visibly turned into that at right angles to it, and this by means at once decisive, elegant, and economical. Looking across the street again, one sees that the corners of Lever House are also carefully, but differently, conceived. The floating Lever boxes are creased at the corners, like cardboard cartons, and sealed with a metallic *passe partout* in a manner appropriate to the building's weightless esthetic. Of themselves, these corner details disclose how the total form occurs in Lever House by a wrapping around; in Seagram, by a building up. If the corner detail of Lever House epitomizes George Howe's ideal of a modern architecture of impalpable points, lines, and planes,† that of the Seagram begins—only begins—to reassert a sense of physical presences. It does so, moreover, not in the empirical way in which the regional interests of the thirties encouraged palpability—one that largely involved the assertion of "natural" textures, plus the craftsman's pragmatic frankness about structure, as he ingeniously and straightforwardly provided for the miscellaneous comforts and necessities of a building. The palpability of the Seagram involves metaphysical as well as physical considerations in making vividly present as it does the "build" of The Building as its inmost reality, its essential order.

If the visual gravity of the Seagram tower depends on the relation of plaza to entrance and on the density of the window wall, it depends as well on the composition of the over-all mass. In the Seagram floor plan, Mies employed the same 3:5 ratio of depth to width that he had used for his Lake Shore complex. In contrast to the almost 1:4 ratio for the Lever

* The elevations of his Esplanade and Commonwealth Apartments in Chicago, which were roughly contemporaneous with the Seagram Building, are built of stamped aluminum window units. Mies made the breaks between these units even more explicit, in order to assert the prefabricated component that builds to the façade.
† See p. 122 above.

FIGURE 123. *Seagram Building. Corner detail of the building.*

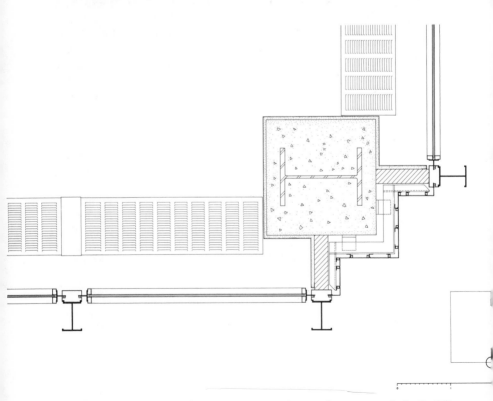

FIGURE 124. *Seagram Building. Structural plan at the corner of the building.*

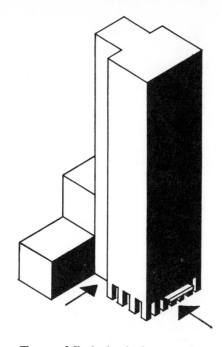

FIGURE 125. *Seagram Building. Diagram of the double-T massing: the T of the tower on its side, the T of the bustle upside down. The area of the notch between the front tower and the bustle is infilled with dark marble slabs to conceal diagonal windbracing. Side entrances at 52nd and 53rd Streets occur at the base of the notch (indicated by an arrow). The height of the tower is 38 stories; of the stepped bustle, 5 and 10 stories.*

Tower, Mies' classical proportions repudiate the exaggerated thinness of the slab, so congenial to weightlessness. Moreover, the Seagram tower is actually a stubby T by virtue of its protruding spine (Fig. 125).‡ Open at the ground, the spine provides the side entrances at 52nd and 53rd Streets—which are protected by glass-topped marquees detailed by Johnson. Toward the base of the building the spine provides a recessed link to flanking wings behind.* The wing element is stepped back from a height of five stories at the lot line to ten stories at the center where it abuts the spine. Hence the T of the tower (a T on its side) abuts the T of the wings-and-bustle (a T upside down). As a geometrical conception this union is elegant, although the linkage of the tower to its bustle is the weakest aspect of the massing.[20] In contrast to the separation of the twin towers of 860 Lake Shore in space, the Seagram congeals into a single complex mass. In contrast to the process of continuous encirclement encouraged by 860 Lake Shore, the Seagram is rigidly frontal.

‡ Mies first used such a spinal treatment in his Promontory Apartments in Chicago (completed in 1949). In these, as Arthur Drexler has noted in his *Mies*, p. 27, he attached two spinal adjuncts to the rear of his main slab. As in Seagram (see discussion immediately below), they are not primarily utility spines.

* As abstract mass, the projection of the upper part of the bustle (floors five to ten) beyond the side planes of the spine would perhaps have improved the articulation of its juncture with the tower, although with a slight complication in the floor plan. Moreover, the visual separation of the two T-shaped masses would have been more in keeping with Mies' discrete treatment of the components overall. As an abstract composition, the tail of the Seagram seems a bit long for the body; but this discord in proportions is not especially observable on the ground.

Arthur Drexler observed at the time of its completion that the building is "bi-laterally symmetrical," adding:

In fact, the Seagram building is the only skyscraper in New York to be so organized while at the same time maintaining distinctly different front, back and sides. The United Nations Secretariat, no less than Lever House or the R.C.A. building, faces two directions at once. Seagram's, no matter from which side it is approached, quite clearly faces one way. Like McKim, Mead and White's 1918 Racquet Club opposite, the Seagram tower is classically and hier-archically composed."[21]

The abstractness of the massing is nowhere more obvious than in the spine at the back. The massings of the slabs for RCA, PSFS, Lever House, and Inland Steel are examples of skyscraper massing dependent in various ways and to varying degrees on functional considerations. This longstanding ideal for modern architecture is partially reversed in the Seagram. Despite the entrance voids at the bottom of the spine, which immediately make evident that the spine does not function solely as a conduit for the elevators and vertical utility stack of the tower in front, we nevertheless half expect that it serves this purpose—especially since the walls of the spine above the entrances are windowless. A close look reveals that marble screens fill the window grid of the flanking walls of the spine, their primary purpose that of concealing diagonal windbracing for the tower. By being the stiffening element in the "back" of the tower, even if not the channel of its nervous system, the spine literally functions as a spine. The basic elevator-and-utility core is housed within the tower, with some overflow into the spine, but only up to the tenth floor (Fig. 126). Above the ten-story bustle, the spine is completely devoted to office space. Hence the marble slabs infilling the sides of this spinal rectangle from the eleventh floor up reduce lighted office space.† Since the Seagram, like the later buildings at Rockefeller Center,‡ reveals the postwar trend toward bulkiness of mass, a considerable portion of the interior space is, by the standards of slab massing, relatively remote from the window wall.[22] This may be less desirable in a rental building divided like the Seagram into many relatively small offices than it is in most of the later Center buildings, which are rented in bulk to single tenants whose files and machines can be relegated to the central space. In Lever House, on the other hand, even the secretarial pool is sufficiently close to the

---

† Although the side walls of the spine are windowless, the back wall of the spine is windowed from the eleventh floor up.
‡ See pp. 49f. above.

view to sense its presence. If the bulky massing frees design from the doctrinaire functionalism of slab massing, the formalism of the Seagram massing has its deficits too.

In the Seagram we find that this formalism is compensated for by the subtlety of the geometry which results from Mies' choice of massing. This subtlety shows in his planning as well; not in the routinely handled spaces of the appendage to the rear, but in the sequence of plans for the tower as they climb the building. The shifts in relationship among the squares of the columnar spacing, the rectangles of floor areas and of elevator/utility pylons, and, finally, the T-shapes of the massing and its echoes within the geometry of the plan are beautifully modulated. The open and interlocked configuration of the scheme at ground level becomes compact and discrete in the upper floors. For planning that is intricate but deals with majestically simple forms, the interlocked rectangles of the lobby floor merit particular study. The progression from the peripheral stilting outside, to the glass enclosure, to the dense elevator core, reproduces in plan the hierarchical quality of the massing.

In contrast to the forthright geometry of the simple squares and rectangles of 860 Lake Shore, and of virtually all of Mies' previous American work, the interlocking relationships of this ground-floor plan are of a piece with the close-knit qualities of the Seagram wall. When these are considered in conjunction with the relative complexity of the massing—the tower as a T-on-its-side juxtaposed to the rear wings as a T-upside-down—the Seagram seems haunted by a number of early works by Mies which depend on *De Stijl* organization of considerable complexity.[23] So clear does the geometry of the Seagram appear until analysis reveals its complexities that it comes as something of a surprise to observe affinities, however distant, with his Liebknecht-Luxembourg Monument in Berlin (1926), and with his initial (and at the time too little noticed) site plan for the Wiessenhof Housing Exhibition in Stuttgart (1927), which called for a densely faceted hillside complex of buildings and terraces (Figs. 127, 128). That the comparison sneaks up on us, further testifies to the abstract, rather than functional, basis for Mies' design. (It should be noted here that these early works by Mies obliquely forecast the in-and-out complexity of sculptural form by other architects which became increasingly popular in the sixties, in opposition to the kind of austere massing that is typical of most of his work.*)

If dignity, elegance, and subtlety characterize both elevations and floor plans of the Seagram, so, too, they describe the interiors. Here Philip Johnson's contribution is especially evident; he is, moreover, wholly responsible for the luxurious design of the Four Seasons restaurant behind

---

* See Chapter 6 below.

269

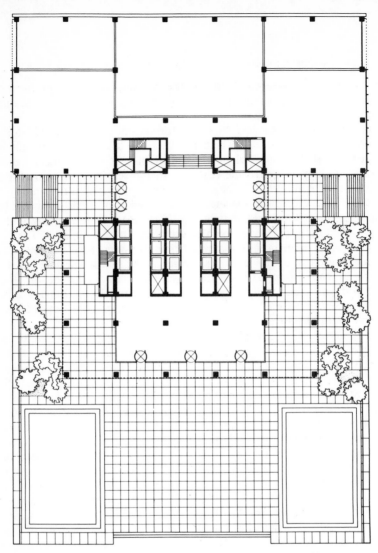

FIGURE 126. *Seagram Building. Plans: plaza and lobby (above); typical floor, 6th to 10th story (opposite, above); typical floor, tower above the 10th story (below).*

the lobby (its fragility, playfulness, and mannered complexity are decidedly un-Miesian).[24] It is impossible to do justice here to the care lavished on the custom design of elevator cabs, lighting, office partitioning, hardware, plumbing fixtures, typography, and similar details.[25]

Many of the custom-designed items for the Seagram interiors have become standard catalogue offerings. Thus custom design and mass pro-

270

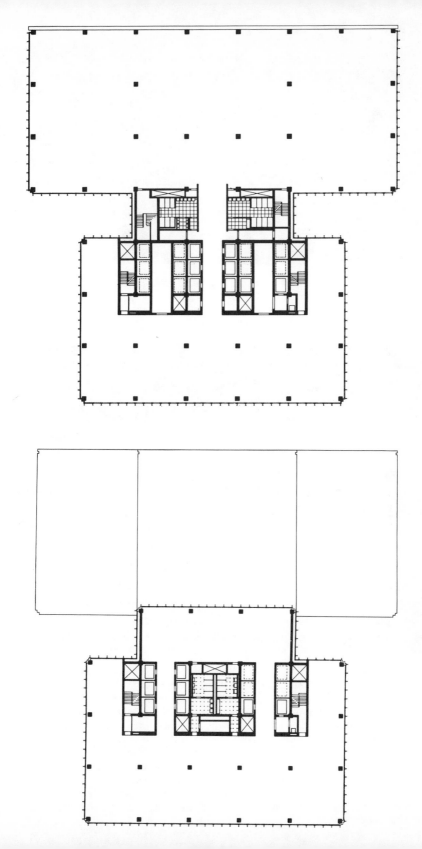

FIGURE 127. *Ludwig Mies van der Rohe. Liebknecht-Luxembourg Monument, Berlin, completed 1926.*

FIGURE 128. *Ludwig Mies van der Rohe. Projected site plan for the Wiessenhof Housing Exhibition, Stuttgart (Germany), 1927. The exhibition consisted of a group of houses and apartment buildings designed by architects working in the International Style. In charge of the exhibition, Mies projected this extraordinary site plan in which a densely configurated scheme of building blocks and terraces are linked together as an undulant super-complex following the contour of the sloping site. It was deemed impractical as a real estate scheme because the interlocking nature of the composition would have hampered sale of the buildings to individual owners after the exhibition. Thus Mies had to settle for a more conventional scheme. It remained for others, in the middle of the twentieth century, to develop the implications of this conception.*

duction merge where the designer keeps the double end in view—as poor Gill tried but failed to do early in the century,† being forced to remain a craftsman rather than become a designer for industry, because he lacked entree to manufacturers, while they lacked interest in his extreme simplification. But there is design for mass production and design which merely *looks* as though it were so intended. The latter may be partially true in regard to the Seagram, since at least one critic[26] complains that when tenants have sought to adapt their own partitioning and furniture (usually based on a four-foot standard, or modular fractions and multiples thereof) to the dimensions of the windows and panel partitioning, they frequently have found difficulties in combining the two. Although custom dimensioning may be regarded as the means of improving the standard, obviously no standard is possible where everyone seeks his own improvement. Again the formalistic element in Mies' design obtrudes. And again, so does the substantially symbolic nature of his image of mass production. In a modular world there will always be artists who break away from the common modules—ironically, some of them, like Mies, will themselves create an intensely modular image, although not so much to standardize it as to explore its esthetic possibilities.

Since close consideration of the interior design of the Seagram is impossible here, we shall indicate the care with which it was done by reviewing certain details of the interior which come to the skin. A specially designed air-conditioning system uses slightly sunken under-window units which project only eleven inches above the floor level; these are set back from the plane of the window to make possible a floor-to-ceiling window comparable to that of 860 Lake Shore.‡ Thus a dream of Mies' (and of other architects) since the twenties of the skyscraper wall without parapeting is finally achieved. Even the bars across the lower parts of the windows of Lake Shore have been removed in the Seagram. As in 860 Lake Shore, exterior framing is integral with interior framing.

There are those who have complained of giddiness at the openness of their aerie,[27] even though the air-conditioning units provide a balustrade, partly physical, partly psychological, blocking contact with the window. The positive quality of the mullions (almost a foot in width between the windows) affords further reassurance, while their columnar-like division of the panorama imposes an order and foreground to the

---

† See *American Buildings and Their Architects: Progressive and Academic Ideals at the Turn of the Twentieth Century,* Chapter 5.

‡ The manner in which the floor-to-ceiling windows are effected in 860 Lake Shore differs from that of the Seagram. In Lake Shore, the major heating elements are in a plenum between the floor slab and the hung ceiling for the apartment below. A single finned tube at the base of the window handles convection heating around the periphery of the exterior wall.

view which the fetish for "picture windows" denies. The mullions also give a tangible framework to which the view can cling. The topaz coloring of the glass warms the harsh New York light, and, at the same time, provides a welcome relief from the underwater effects of the greens and blues which prior to this building dominated heat- and glare-resistant glazing. The topaz wash gives a remote, soft-focus effect to the view, much as a blue-lavender atmosphere gauzes Paris. The city appears an image of itself, somewhat as though it were a photographic mural pasted against the outside surface of the glass.[28] This effect is heightened by a band of lighted ceiling panels (11½ feet wide) immediately behind the windows, which so reduce the discrepancy between light inside and out as to minimize the contrast between in-here and out-there. Thus the view takes on some of the properties of a wall. As a modern equivalent of scenic wallpapers with their magic of vista and containment, the view inside looking out acquires the gentle ambiguities of the view outside looking in.

Hence natural light and artificial light supplement one another to enhance the esthetic and psychic impact of the building. The union of exterior and interior effected structurally also has its environmental dimension. At night the lights in the ceiling panels illuminate the tower, while lights recessed in the ceiling of the entrance area bathe both the lobby and its pavement in the same glow (Fig. 129).[29] It may seem trivial to mention that all the louvers in the Venetian blinds are fixed at a 45-degree angle so that the ceiling lights are visible whether the blinds are drawn or not*—yet what would be gimmickry in another building represents the elaboration of an integrated design in this. Daytime or nighttime, door knob or window wall, building mass or space in front: whatever we examine, we discover that it contributes to this exhaustive design in depth—design that is the complete embodiment of a severely luxurious conception, yet without being a virtuoso end in itself. If a lavish budget permitted a finish and subtlety which Mies had not known since his (much simpler) Barcelona Pavilion, the slightly later Tugendhat House, and perhaps the exterior of the Farnsworth House, this largesse never deflected him from that composite of Hellenic and Renaissance disciplines that makes the Seagram what it is.

His Hellenism of course provides the core of his esthetic: the visually decisive, perfected part combined with other parts in a manner that is actually or symbolically structural. But the peculiarly Germanic quality of Mies' dissecting and purifying temperament completes this Hellenism with the formalistic rigor of the Renaissance. The opposition of plaza

---

* The Venetian blinds have a further refinement in that they can be fixed in three positions only—all the way up, all the way down, or halfway between—for an orderly appearance on the exterior.

FIGURE 129. *Seagram Building. Evening view.*

void and cliff wall, the hierarchical massing on axis, the rigidly rectangular relation of part to part in a geometry of the simplest shapes, the linear and planar detailing, the use of light in ways which are clarifying and subtilizing rather than sculpturally luminous (this latter impossible anyway in the harshness of American light): these are all Renaissance elements. Where the *Baukunst* is Hellenic, the *Formkunst* is Renaissance.

This modern synthesis of Hellenic and Renaissance ideals in the Seagram—and its somewhat less complete manifestation in those of Mies' buildings which immediately preceded it—had extraordinary effect. It certainly influenced Skidmore, Owings & Merrill's Union Carbide Building, just four blocks from Seagram and started even before Mies' building was finished. Like many other American (and a little later, non-American) buildings of the late fifties and early sixties, Union Carbide partakes of the symmetry, the hierarchical massing and the structural feel of the membering of the Seagram.† Whoever would measure the difference between the architecture of genius and the best of the architecture of bureaucracy‡ can do so nowhere more conveniently than here on Park Avenue, weighing the respective virtues of these two buildings. The advantages, especially when both buildings are considered as corporate expressions, are not wholly in favor of the Seagram; but— not to discourage one from the pleasure of making his own analysis by pursuing the matter further here—the Seagram is a greater architectural achievement than Union Carbide. And if Lever House, the Seagram, and Union Carbide be compared with the metal-and-glass competition nearby (ranging esthetically from fair to awful, whatever their functional virtues), then the difference between architecture and minimal investment building, even that in the "de luxe" category, becomes clear.

Shallowly appropriated as prefabricated "styling," incompletely comprehended as a structural esthetic, Mies' architecture is fully understood only if seen as the result of a quest for the inmost essence of irreducible minima which embody functional, esthetic, symbolic, and hence moral meaning. Then his work is revealed as one possible fulfillment of the spirit of objectivity which, grasped with his kind of comprehensiveness, gave the revolution of the twenties its imperative. "I hope you will understand," Mies explained at the time of the completion of 860 Lake Shore, "that architecture has nothing to do with the invention of forms. It is not a playground for children young or old. Architecture is the real battleground of the spirit."[30]

† SOM's small bank building for the Manufacturers Hanover Trust (fig. 47), designed after Lever House and before Union Carbide, provides an interesting intermediary.
‡ See pp. 55f. above.

Is this realm of the spirit, this ultimate "thing in itself" beyond particularity, beyond a sense of place (except insofar as the intensity of Mies' vision makes places of his essentially place-less art), beyond sentiment or analogy from any source outside itself—is this architecture withdrawn in its perfection? Or, to paraphrase Lewis Mumford, if "less is more," can it be that "nothing is even better"?[31] Many, both critics and architects, have attacked the calculated limitations of Mies' architecture in some such manner. It is the mark of his success, however, that if no modern architect has been more ascetic, none has been more influential, and for the very reasons for which he is sometimes severely condemned. His "almost nothing" contains the paradoxical plenitude of an elemental demonstration.

CHAPTER V

The Encompassing Environment of Free-Form Architecture: Frank Lloyd Wright's Guggenheim Museum

> *For a long time, I thought I had "discovered" it, only to find after all that this idea of the interior space being the reality of the building was ancient and Oriental. . . . When building Unity Temple at Oak Park and the Larkin Building in Buffalo, I was making the first great protest I knew anything about against the building coming up on you from the outside as an enclosure. I reversed that old idiom in idea and in fact.*
>
> *[Then] I received a little book by Okakura Kakurzo, entitled* The Book of Tea. . . . *Reading it, I came across this sentence: "The reality of a room was to be found in the space enclosed by the roof and walls, not in the roof and walls themselves.*
>
> FRANK LLOYD WRIGHT, The Natural House, 1954

> *[Of Unity Temple] "The sense of the room is not only preserved—it* may be seen as the soul of the design. *Instead of being built into the heart of a block of sculptured building material, out of sight, sacrosanct space is merely screened in . . . it comes through as the living "motif" of the architecture. . . . But one* motif *may be seen, the "inside" becoming "outside."*
>
> FRANK LLOYD WRIGHT, Autobiography, 1932

THE CULMINATING STATEMENT?

Whatever its faults—and who can unreservedly praise it?—the Solomon R. Guggenheim Museum is a liberating building. It is liberating, first, in the simple sense of being the worthy, unusual scheme that would "never be built" but was. As such it encourages audacity in the future. More than merely unconventional, however, the Guggenheim is liberating in that it represents the boldest American attempt up to the time of its

279

completion to create a building fully expressive of the sculptural freedom possible with reinforced concrete. Designed in 1943–45, then modified, it was only built in 1956–59. Before it was finally opened, it had been preceded in the United States by a few other large-scale demonstrations of the curvilinear drama of reinforced concrete, those with architectural pretension including: Eero Saarinen's Kresge Auditorium for the Massachusetts Institute of Technology (1950–55) and his David S. Ingalls Hockey Rink for Yale University (1956–59); Matthew Nowicki's Livestock Judging Pavilion at Raleigh, North Carolina (1949–53); and Minoru Yamasaki's Lambert Airport Terminal Building for St. Louis (1953–56).* Daring as these buildings were, the Guggenheim is more so. They are merely roofs molding the overhead space. In the Guggenheim, however, the floor plane, too, participates in the plastic conception; indeed, as it spirals upward, the floor virtually establishes the conception. Here, Wright's lifelong quest for the fully sculptural building attains its climax. So does his quest for spatial continuity. As in his Robie House, it is not the spatial continuity characteristic of European modernism—that is, not an open box of space encouraging activity in all directions—but a molded space forcefully conditioned by the path of movement through it.[1] In the Guggenheim, Wright embodies the path of space in a manner which is both monumental and ultimate. Here, as Edgar Kaufmann, Jr., has expressed it, is "space contained by space,"[2] a central well of space created of the space wound around it.

How tragic, then, that this embodiment on a heroic scale of so much that is central to Wright's philosophy of architecture and life should in many ways be disappointing. For all that it is a most personal statement, the Guggenheim is, paradoxically, among his most impersonal buildings.[3] It exists as a mere sketch of what it should be, raw and bare, and in part painfully awkward. Without mystery, it remains a statement of intent, essentially lacking in decorative enrichment, in subtlety of light and shadow, and in the flow of part to part which would have effortlessly fused the whole into the gigantic, resilient entity which Wright had envisioned. Defiant, vital, in many respects crude— and crude, not in the Corbusian sense of something intended as such, but having the inadvertent crudity of something meant to be smoother— the Guggenheim displays the frontier virtues. Like the frontier structure,

---

* The Livestock Judging Pavilion (officially the J. S. Dorton Arena) and the Yale Hockey Rink more properly demonstrate the curvilinear possibilities of suspended cable construction, but in each instance the roofs are suspended from reinforced concrete arches. Nowicki was killed in a tragic airplane crash shortly after conceiving the Pavilion; the engineer of the building, William Dietrick, saw the modified design through to completion. Yamasaki designed the Lambert Airport Terminal Building while a partner in the firm of Yamasaki, Leinweber & Associates.

it had to be "got up" against time, against economic and technical stringencies; in essence, against skepticism. Like the frontier achievement, too, it invites critical comment as much for what it summarizes and foretells as for what it is. Finally, it merits examination as possibly *the* culminating statement in Wright's achievement after World War II, toward the end of a long career.

THEMES OF A LIFETIME

Wright himself wrote extensively about the Museum. In March 1952, shortly before its opening, he explained:

> Here for the first time architecture appears plastic, one floor flowing into another (more like sculpture) instead of the usual superimposition of stratified layers cutting and butting into each other by way of post and beam construction.
>
> The whole building, cast in concrete, is more like an egg-shell —in form a great simplicity—rather like a crisscross structure. The light concrete flesh is rendered strong enough everywhere to do its work by embedded filaments of steel either separate or in mesh. The structural calculations are thus those of the cantilever and continuity rather than the post and beam. The net result of such construction is a greater repose, the atmosphere of the quiet unbroken wave: no meeting of the eye with abrupt changes of form.[4]

So Wright described one of the aims of his building as continuity of mass and space. In addition, the movement within was to harmonize with the dynamics of modern painting; the paintings to be "floated" in the curved space rather than fixed to the walls; and all to be brought about by the "great simplicity" of the in-turned unity.

If the full implications of this experience looked to the future, the formal themes from which the experience derived come from every phase of Wright's long career. Hence the double significance of the Guggenheim: it is a point of focus for what had preceded in Wright's work, and a point of projection for what he believed organic architecture might become. Assertively unique as the Guggenheim is, it emerges from four recurrent themes in his career: the circle; the cantilever; the interpenetrated form; the walled building enclosing a large unitary space surrounded by balconies.

The spiral theme immediately captures the eye. But the spiral emerges, of course, from the circle. The circular theme goes back in Wright's works to those of around 1910 and, behind them, to the

Froebelian ideas with which he was indoctrinated in childhood.† In 1908–9 Wright introduced circular motifs, in the form of floating balloon-like elements, in the abstract patterns of the leaded windows of a play-house on the grounds of the Avery Coonley residence, the most lavish of the "prairie houses" that he was able to realize. The floating circles appear more prominently in 1914 in an abstract mural decoration which he (or possibly an assistant) had designed two years earlier for the Midway Gardens, an elaborate Chicago restaurant and outdoor en-tertainment casino which was demolished in the early twenties (Fig. 130). In fact, in perspective drawings, he even showed balloons floating above the Gardens as festive advertisement. In the very year that Wright designed the abstract mural for Midway Gardens, Vasily Kandinsky in Paris painted what some have called the first purely abstract paint-ings (erroneous, but the mere fact of the myth points up the signifi-cance of Wright's mural). Forty-five years later, the large number of Kandinskys in the Guggenheim collection (Fig. 161) furnished a partial starting-point for Wright's conception of a museum for "an advanced form of painting wherein line, color, and form are a language in them-selves."

In the twenties, the circle all but disappeared from Wright's work, with an important exception which we shall presently discuss. The late thirties, however, saw its reappearance, and subsequently its develop-ment as a formal motif, as Wright increasingly relied on both triangular and circular ground plans in order to free contained space from the last remaining tyrannies of rectangularity. We cannot pursue Wright's variations on circular themes; the point to be made here is that the circle developed into the spiral.

There are several examples. The first, a "Shangri-La," remained unrealized (as did several other almost equally extravagant projects in the twenties for the large-scale integration of architecture and nature). This was the Gordon Strong Automobile Objective and Planetarium proj-ect of 1925 for Sugar Loaf Mountain in Maryland (Fig. 131). Wright envisioned on this mountain site an immense structure of reinforced concrete, fashioned of its own spiral roadway winding to a garden and observation platform. At the time Wright was interested in Mayan ar-chitecture, and his terraced mountain-on-a-mountain was essentially an automotive version of the stepped pyramids with their altars on top. Once the tourist had taken in the view from Wright's platform, he would descend by an automobile ramp within the hollow inverted cone, its walls perforated by a textile-like pattern reminiscent of the surface

† See *American Buildings and Their Architects: Progressive and Academic Ideals at the Turn of the Twentieth Century,* Chapter 3.

FIGURE 130. *Frank Lloyd Wright. Study for the mural* City by the Sea *for Midway Gardens, Chicago, 1914.*

decoration of much Mayan architecture. A vast domed space at the core of the hollow housed the planetarium with a gardened dining terrace supported on its crown. The inner dome also supported the upper portion of the roadway. Seen in cross section, the scheme displays a range and combination of structure in which logic becomes fantasy: a dome; a skeletal frame, partially around it, partially on it; and from

283

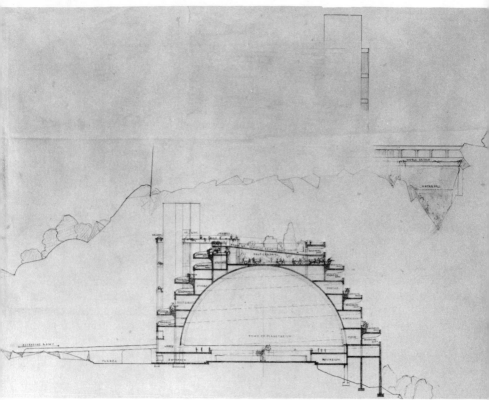

FIGURE 131. *Frank Lloyd Wright. Project for the Gordon Strong Automobile Objective and Planetarium, Sugar Loaf Mountain, Md., 1925. Perspective and cross section.*

the frame, finally, cantilevers that project a good portion of the ascending roadway out into space.‡

With respect to both his personal fame and the number of buildings he was able to realize, the twenties were the darkest decade in Wright's life. It was then, however, that he envisioned a number of his most unusual and ambitious projects, like that for Sugar Loaf. Although forced to store these away (even the existence of the Strong project had been all but forgotten until Arthur Drexler published it in conjunction with the 1962 exhibition of Wright's drawings at the Museum of Modern Art*), Wright produced fresh versions of many of them from the thirties onward. In 1943, after a hiatus of almost two decades, the Sugar Loaf spiral reappeared as Wright's proposal for the Guggenheim. As Drexler suggests, the Guggenheim is the Sugar Loaf project turned inside out,[5] and of course upside down.

Before the Museum spiral was realized at the end of the fifties, however, other spirals appeared. The earliest of these occurred in two Pittsburgh projects, neither of which was built. Both schemes revived the spiral road. In one, for a parking garage (1947), the ramp was largely suspended from cables radiating from a central mast. In the other (also of 1947), Wright envisioned an extravagant community center on the site of what has become the woefully unimaginative Point Park. The scheme was on the order of the Sugar Loaf project: a spiral roadway, with a peripheral terraced garden the whole of its length, provided a gigantic conic hollow. This interior cone of space was partly open to the sky, partly filled with civic institutions housed in dome and bowl shapes, partly spanned by the layers of flooring conventional to office buildings. Wright topped the spiral ascent with a roof-top park and fountain. The cross section resembles nothing so much as that of an ocean liner. Like the Sugar Loaf scheme, this one resembles a boy's fantasy of some machine or building that embraces an omnibus function of stupendous proportion within a single structure. The next two spiral concepts, much more modest than their predecessors, were built: one for the V. C. Morris Gift Shop in San Francisco (1948–50); the other for the David Wright House near Phoenix, Arizona (1952). And while the Guggenheim was rising, Wright once more resur-

‡ It may be that not all of what appears as skeletal framing was in fact intended as such. Possibly some of this construction would have been treated as a continuous box, in which event the project illustrates yet a fourth type of construction.
* Richard Neutra happened to publish the project in his *Amerika, Neues Bauen in der Welt*, 2 (Vienna, Schroll, 1930), p. 73; but it was neglected in subsequent publications of Wright's work prior to Drexler's *Drawings of Frank Lloyd Wright*, figs. 106–13, 270–72.

FIGURE 132. *Frank Lloyd Wright. V. C. Morris Gift Shop, San Francisco, 1948–50. Front elevation.*

rected the Sugar Loaf-Point Park spiral as an Arabian Nights fantasy for a Grand Opera and Civic Auditorium in Baghdad, Iraq (1957).†

† Drexler, *Drawings of Frank Lloyd Wright*, illustrates not only Sugar Loaf but most of Wright's other spiral projects; for the Pittsburgh projects, see figs. 226–30, 277; for the Baghdad project, figs. 260–62. To these might be added the broken spiral in the lozenge-shaped scheme for the Robert Llewellyn House in Bethesda, Maryland (1953), and the square parking base of the "Illinois," or "Mile High," skyscraper project for Chicago (1956), which uses the principle of the spiral road. Spirals also appear in Wright's schemes for Broadacre City, which he developed in a long series of drawings between 1934 and 1958: Drexler, figs. 209, 253, 254, 266, 267. The drawings with spiral structures presumably, but not necessarily, come late in the series.

FIGURE 133. *Morris Gift Shop. Interior.*

Of all these spirals, that for the Morris Shop is closest to the
Guggenheim's (Figs. 132, 133). The front of this shop is completely
closed by a brick wall except where it is pierced by a short, glazed
entrance tunnel. We step into the transparent tunnel and immediately
see the entire interior as a showroom, encircled by the rising coil of
the ramp. On the ground level crystal, china, and silver are withdrawn
to a distance, which enhances their preciousness. The spiral ramp winds
upward past a scattering of circular display niches, around the circular
platter of plants suspended in mid-air, to a small sales gallery immediately
under a ceiling tufted with translucent plastic bubbles. Less a structural
conception than a space modifier, the Morris ramp timidly clings to the
walls, supported in a conventional manner except where a modest bridge
of space occurs toward the rear of the shop.

FIGURE 134. *Frank Lloyd Wright. House for Mrs. Thomas H. Gale, Oak Park, Ill., completed 1909. Perspective.*

Whereas the Morris spiral is boxed (like the gifts), the Guggenheim spiral stands free. Like the chambered nautilus (Fig. 166), the Museum makes its shape both inside and out as it spirals. Unlike the chambered nautilus, however, the Guggenheim winds around a hollow core of space rising from ground floor to dome (Fig. 156). Moreover, each turn is distinguished from the next above on the exterior by a continuous window ribbon, on the interior by one of the projecting balconies which circle around the central hollow. Hence the interior turns of the conch-like spiral become a tier of cantilevers. The cantilever, too, goes back to the prairie houses. We find it, for instance, in the spreading roof of the Robie House, where the wooden structure, stiffened by concealed steel beams, juts out into space, like a rigid diving board anchored at one end and free of supports at the other. The "hovering" effect of the cantilever, as Wright liked to describe it, dramatized the outward thrust of the composition from the fireplace core toward the natural environment. In the same year (1909) the cantilever appeared in the projecting second-story porch and roof slab of the wood-and-stucco house for Mrs. Thomas H. Gale in Oak Park, Illinois (Fig. 134). Wright himself has cited this,[6] the most abstractly composed of all his early prairie houses, as the modest progenitor of the renowned

288

FIGURE 135. *Frank Lloyd Wright. Edgar J. Kaufmann House (Fallingwater),
Bear Run, Pa., 1936–38.*

Fallingwater, at Bear Run, Pennsylvania (1936–38), commissioned by
Edgar J. Kaufmann, Sr. (Fig. 135). Here the structural possibilities of
reinforced concrete are dramatized in the tier of cantilevers above the
waterfall. The levitation of these horizontal boxes is affinitive to the
slide and fall of the water beneath the house. The tensile (stretching)
strength of the steel reinforcing rods embedded within the concrete itself
makes possible the seamless box, where floor and sides (theoretically
at least) are one. Folded and bent shapes are stronger than flat ones,
as the cantilevering of a sheet of paper from the hand readily demonstrates. When extended, the flat sheet sags; folded or bent, especially
into a box shape, it takes on rigidity, as Wright intended for the cantilevers of Fallingwater. If it happens that the parapet as built performs
less of a structural function than Wright envisioned for it, the image
nevertheless calls up the principle. These projecting balconies are sup-

289

ported well back from their outer edges, as a waiter balances a tray on his fingers in Wright's favorite metaphor for this cantilevering. Thus the window bands become mere screens, serving simply as protection against the weather and having no structural function whatsoever. Realizing to a remarkable degree Wright's desire to eliminate the wall, these parapets with window strips between are comparable to, although bolder than, those of the Robie House. The rough texture of the stratified courses of the native stone opposes the smooth surface of the concrete areas. The strength of masonry in compression (that is, in its ability to withstand direct downward loads) opposes the strength of reinforced concrete in tension (that is, in its capability of sustaining the stresses of stretching or spanning). The traditional material opposes the modern. The result is a structure anchored, yet resilient.

In the Guggenheim, Wright gave the cantilevered stack an outward cant. He anticipated this antigravitational swelling of the building toward the top in the wooden cantilevers of a number of houses designed in the thirties, the first an unbuilt project of 1932 for Malcolm M. Willey. An actual example is the hillside house for George D. Sturges in Brentwood Heights, California (1939), in which the outreaching thrust of living room and porch dominates the design (Fig. 136). Here wooden sheathing is stepped outward on an inclined plane to give the characteristic "floating" effect of the cantilever a barge-like solidity and compactness. Enlarge the scale, change the material, bend it, separate each of the boards by an interval of space, and the central motif of the Guggenheim appears. Often in Wright's work, a small motif of this sort in one design combines with other motifs to provide the major theme for a later design.

The first scheme for the Museum, and only a preliminary, appears in an elegant model (Fig. 137). Exhibited in 1945, this model introduced an astonished public to Wright's intentions. Although Fallingwater and the model differ structurally and conceptually, we are nevertheless tempted to see the theme of the famous house—that is, the supporting tower complex and the cantilevers projecting in various directions—as the progenitor of the Museum's. This kinship between the Guggenheim and Fallingwater appears more strongly in the model than in the completed building, for the model emphasizes the reciprocity between the tower cluster and the cantilevers of the ramp. Indeed, the manner here in which the levels of the ramp seem to swing out from the anchoring tower and return is particularly vivid.

This interpenetration of long horizontals by a massive vertical element is another prevalent theme in Wright's career—again witness the Robie House. Forgetting for a moment the vertical webs which cut through the ramp at regular intervals in the Museum as completed (Fig. 156), we find that the composition has two other types of major

FIGURE 136. *Frank Lloyd Wright. George D. Sturges House, Brentwood Heights, Calif., completed 1939.*

vertical penetrations. The first obviously includes the fused cluster of utility, stair, and elevator stacks through the ramp, and the similar tower for the semicircular floor stacks of the satellite administrative precinct (the "monitor," in Wright's terminology, although it no longer wholly houses the functions that he intended for it) [Fig. 138]. The second type of vertical penetration is invisible, yet important, since it provided a generating element for the ramp.

The outward tilt of the exterior walls of the ramp as it rises and its inward taper toward the central core are formed within two invisible interlocked cones (Fig. 139).[7] The cone determining the cant of the outside walls is inverted, its imaginary apex being 180 feet below a base line arbitrarily established well beneath the basement level of the building. Within this cone, Wright inserted another one, narrower and taller, with its imaginary apex 270 feet above the same base line. Since he inscribed the ramp inside the area between the converging and diverging sides of the cones, any horizontal cross section through the structure is automatically

FIGURE 137. *Frank Lloyd Wright. Solomon R. Guggenheim Museum, New York, 1943–45/1956–59. Cross-sectional model of 1945 showing columnar supports toward the inside of the ramp, with the inner parapet integrally curved out of the floor.*

circular. As the spiral comes from Wright's interest in circular shapes, so the invisible cones derive from his triangular constructions. In each instance, what initially appeared in his work as a complicated interlocking of flat pattern, and evolved as a complexly interwoven three-dimensional structure, is here heroically simplified toward a Roman feeling for the grandeur of the basic figures of solid geometry.

As for the visible penetrations of vertical elements through the dominant horizontals, they are only forcefully apparent inside the building. From the exterior they make but little impression (Fig. 138)—at least when compared with the forceful chimney verticals in many of

FIGURE 138. *Solomon R. Guggenheim Museum. View of the administrative "monitor" from 89th Street. The lozenge-shaped spine barely projecting from the monitor roof (and interlocking with the polygonal glass enclosure for the interior light court) provides the principal vertical anchor for the circular office floors around the central void. It also houses vertical communication (elevator and stairs) as well as utility stacks. The big vertical elements behind serve the same function for the exhibition ramp. The one-time parking space to the lower left of this photograph is now occupied by a thin, slab-shaped office block by Taliesin Associates; this addition is similar to a facility envisioned by Wright in his initial designs for the Museum.*

Wright's houses, such as the Robie House and Fallingwater, although even in these works the horizontal elements of the composition dominate the vertical. In the model (Fig. 137), to be sure, the shaft enclosing a tightly wound "fast" ramp (as Wright described this means of quick ascent or descent from level to level of the big ramp) was to have been topped by a spinning plastic bubble designed to enclose an observation platform. As a crown for the central and principal unit in the cluster of vertical shafts (including flanking emergency fire stairs, elevator, toilets, and major utility runs) this spherical dome might have signified on the exterior the thrust of the vertical elements through the turns of the ramp, at least in views from across the street. It was lost to the budget, however. The existing triangular tower for stairs and elevator is a blunter

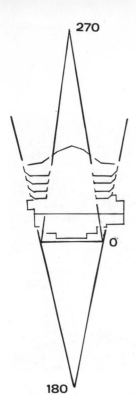

270

180

0

FIGURE 139. *Solomon R. Guggenheim Museum. Cross-sectional diagram indicating the principle of the interlocked cones that determine the opposed pitches of the exterior walls and of the inside edge of the ramp.*

form which Wright chose as more appropriate for the straight flights of stairs demanded by city fire regulations. Together with the rest of the vertical shafts, the entire complex comes through the back of the dome as a nondescript bulk without visual distinction. Inside, however, where it is prominent, this vertical utility complex appears as a relatively dense play of cylindrical and lozenge-shaped elements rising through the tiered ramp, to provide a contrast at every complete turn to the openness of the exhibition area (Fig. 158).

More interesting, although visually even more submerged, is the interlocking of the lozenge-shaped stairs-and-elevator tower with the rings of office floors in the "monitor." This structural motif harks back to one of Wright's earliest works, and thereby movingly links the beginning of his long career with the end. In 1896 he designed a windmill of wood and shingles for his aunts' Hillside School at Spring Green, Wisconsin (Fig. 140), a property which he eventually inherited and made famous as the site of his own house (Taliesin) and school. In the windmill, lozenge thrusts its polygon, polygon embraces lozenge—hence "Romeo and Juliet," the balcony further justifying Wright's name for it. Bracing floors within the hollow polygon strengthened the tower, like the membranes of bamboo. Just so for the monitor (see plans, Fig. 164). The

FIGURE 140. *Frank Lloyd Wright. Windmill, called "Romeo and Juliet," for the Hillside School (later Taliesin), Spring Green, Wis., completed 1896.*

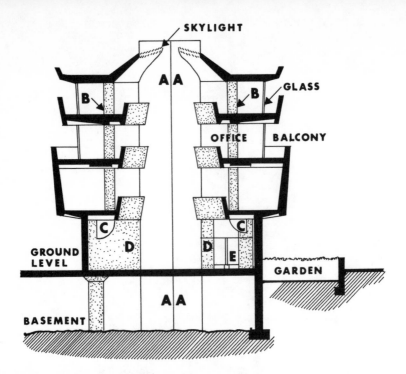

FIGURE 141. *Solomon R. Guggenheim Museum. Schematic cross-sectional diagram of the monitor. The floors are open to a central well with a polygonal skylight above. The lozenge-shaped spine* (A), *projecting from the monitor roof and interlocking with the polygonal skylight* (see Fig. 138), *provides the most conspicuous vertical support for the floors. It is supplemented by a circlet of columns* (B), *from which the office floors are cantilevered in two directions, outward to terminate in the balconies, inward to the vertical light well. The columns, in turn, are supported by brackets* (C). *Finally, these bring compressive forces to the ring wall* (D) *which encircles the ground floor, with the entrance at E.*

rest of the structure for this administrative cylinder is equally ingenious, and may as well be discussed at this point (Fig. 141).[8] A heavily reinforced cylindrical wall encloses the ground-floor reception room. At the top of this, the second floor is cantilevered in both directions, the inside cantilever partially supported on curved brackets. These brackets are, however, principally designed to support the ring of lozenge-shaped columns from which the slabs for the third and fourth floors as well as for the roof are cantilevered in two directions, inward and out. The load of the floors, transmitted to the columns, is brought down to the brackets inside the cylinder, and thence is absorbed by the ring wall at ground level. Above the first floor, all parapets and exterior walls are simply set on the floor slabs. Because they are not integrated into the floor slabs so as to create a continuous folded structure, these parapets contribute to the stability of the structure no more—and possibly less—than those at Fallingwater. The rings of balconied floors are finally stabilized by the big lozenge-shaped stair-and-elevator spine which penetrates the polygonal hollow in the manner of the "Romeo and Juliet" windmill.

In addition to the circle, the cantilever, and the interpenetrating form, one other basic theme from the past remains to be considered: the walled building focused on a large unitary interior space. It was in keeping with Wright's agrarianism, typically American in its distaste for the city, and with his dream of the ideal city as a semi-suburban "Broadacre" spreading through the open countryside, that he frequently closed out the city when he built in it. Where his architecture could not spread in nature, he usually preferred to create his own environment. Four buildings closed around large interiors especially anticipate the Guggenheim: the Administration Building for the Larkin Company in Buffalo, New York (1904–6, and unfortunately demolished in 1950); Unity Church in the Chicago suburb of Oak Park (1904–7), the Administration Building for Johnson Wax (S. C. Johnson & Son, Inc.) in Racine, Wisconsin (1936–37) and the Morris Gift Shop.‡

As a large balconied space lit from above and walled against its surrounding environment, the Guggenheim had its thematic inception four decades earlier in the balconied interior of the Larkin Building (Fig. 142). The Larkin Company was a mail-order and door-to-door sales organization purveying its own brand of household products, but for this client Wright created a building that was more truly a "cathedral of commerce" (a cliché of contemporary publicists) than were any of the early twentieth-century gothicized skyscrapers, such as the Woolworth and Chicago Tribune Buildings (Figs. 2, 26). The interior space of the Larkin Building recalls the central-well type of reading and storage rooms in certain nineteenth-century libraries.* Seated at Wright-designed metal office furniture, some of the clerical workers were stationed in groups in the nave and side aisles of the main floor. Others occupied the broad balconies, both the inner parapet and outer wall of which were lined with filing cabinets containing the customers' records. Whereas a fused continuity is the essence of the Guggenheim, an interwoven fragmentation is the essence of the Larkin Building. The Larkin is the Wainwright

‡ This list might be extended to include the Midway Gardens in Chicago and the Imperial Hotel in Tokyo, both of which enclose a garden precinct. In this connection, too, the Lexington Terrace housing project for Chicago (1909), the Crystal Heights Hotel project for Washington, D.C. (1940), and the aforementioned interior spaces contained in the hollow cores of spiral automobile ramps are relevant.
* Illustrated in *American Buildings and Their Architects: Progressive and Academic Ideals at the Turn of the Twentieth Century*, fig. 140.

FIGURE 142. Frank Lloyd Wright. Administration headquarters for the Larkin
Company, Buffalo, N.Y., 1904–6. Interior.

Building brought indoors, although the density of Sullivan's plaiting of verticals and horizontals has been opened up. Through this loosened plaiting, even the rigidly reticulated and linear elements of the Larkin Building achieve manipulative possibilities permitting a weave of solids to make a weave of spaces. This integral making of space by the inter-locked fragmentation of its structure is the first stage of Wright's life-long quest for an architecture of organic continuity.

Wright made this clear himself. Writing of the plan and the austere, cliff-like monumentality of the exterior massing of the Larkin Building (Figs. 143, 144), he said:

> I think I first *consciously* began to try to beat the box in the Larkin Building—1904. I found a natural opening to the liberation I sought when (after a great struggle) I finally pushed the staircase towers out from the corners of the main building, made them free-stand-ing individual features.[9]

Although the exterior of the Larkin Building is reminiscent of Sullivan's Wainwright (Fig. 145), the strongly enframed pier-and-spandrel wall of the earlier building loses its containing effect in the later one, where there is an incremental "jump" of the corner stair towers beyond the block of the building. These thus appear outside of what were for the Wainwright the containing corner piers; but in the Larkin Building the corner piers, too, appear as semi-independent "towers," by virtue of their projection upward through the level of the roof and outward beyond the plane of the rest of the wall. Each of these piers thereby becomes a nucleus "tower" which, so to speak, spawns another in a cellular fashion beside and beyond itself. As Wright explodes the corner piers of the Wainwright Building into entities that are visually semi-discrete, he transforms its cornice in an analogous manner. In the Wainwright, the decorated cornice band with its projecting slab caps the building like a heavy lid. The decorated capitals atop the piers are capitals in the traditional manner. In the Larkin, Wright enlarges the capital on each pier, and extends it downward the full height of the top band of windows; thus he visually "stops" the vertical piers at the sills of the top windows. The sense of support above is semi-dissolved in the ornament.† This in itself tends to set the cornice slab free of the piers below. Because the cornice slab exists on a plane which is inset from the towers it abuts, it is further freed. The horizontality of the window bands beneath encourages the eye to run across the cornice slab. Hence Sullivan's lid becomes Wright's bridge, spanning the interval between the towers, and seemingly thrusting into them to create an ap-

† Wright employs the same device at the top of the piers inside as well.

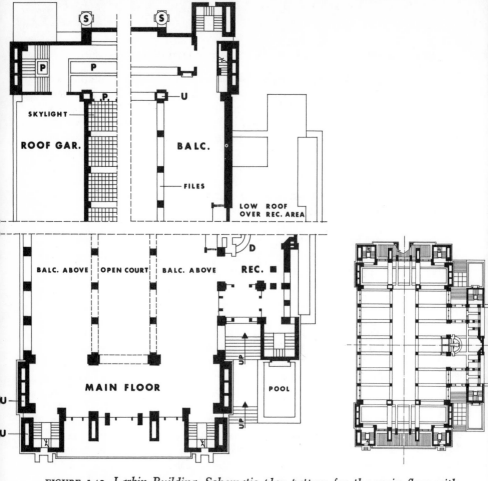

FIGURE 143. *Larkin Building. Schematic plan pattern for the main floor with a three-level plan. Lower half shows the plan of the main floor. Entrance is made from either of two directions into the low adjunct block, up a double flight of stairs, past a pool, through the plate-glass enclosure of a vestibule, and into the reception area* (REC) *with its semicircular desk* (D). *Entrance to the tall clerical block occurs beneath a tier of balconies with a court open five stories to the skylighted roof at its center. Upper right quadrant shows the plan of a typical balcony for clerical workers, with files fitted into the parapeting. The topmost balcony contains a restaurant and other employee facilities. Upper left quadrant shows the plan of the roof garden with planting boxes* (P) *and skylight. The surrounding "walls" of the building also provide hollow tubes for utilities* (U) *and stairs, clustered at the corners of the block and bridged by the rows of windows. The principal interior piers supporting the balconies are also hollowed for utility ducts. Globular sculptural elements* (S) *are attached to the principal front.*

FIGURE 144. *Opposite, above: Larkin Building. Exterior.*

FIGURE 145. *Opposite, below: Louis Sullivan. Wainwright Building, St. Louis, Mo., 1890–91.*

FIGURE 146. *Frank Lloyd Wright. Unity Church, Oak Park, Ill., 1904–7. Perspective. The church cube with its raised central space is to the left; the Sunday school to the right as a comparable block, but lower and spreading as a rectangular mass. Steps to either side of the cube rise to a parapeted entrance terrace that links the two blocks. This terrace is bisected by the corridor-like foyer, lined with entrance doors to either side. See plan, Figure 149.*

parent interlock. A few years later, the principal elements of this compositional complex by which Wright "beat the box" of the Larkin Building—bridge, nucleus pier, and subordinate pier—comprised the bolder motif of the Robie House.‡

As Wright said himself, Unity Church carries the process even further (Fig. 146). It also represents Wright's first building in reinforced concrete. Now the corner stair towers, which give admission to the slightly raised floor level of the auditorium as well as to the interior balconies, are subordinate. It is the cube of the central space, again illuminated from above, which generates the composition. Lifted above the subordinate roofs as a closed block when viewed from the exterior, it throws out subordinate blocks in four directions as window bays. These are also walled at the bottom, and only penetrated toward the top. Their monumental visual thrust outward is intensified by the projecting roof slabs which are again freed of the wall below by the ornamental dissolve of the tops of their pier supports as in the Larkin Building. Such is the force of this outward thrust that it seems to suck the corner stair towers inward (more evident in the completed building than in Wright's perspective). As

‡ Illustrated in *American Buildings and Their Architects: Progressive and Academic Ideals at the Turn of the Twentieth Century,* figs. 84 and 86.

Wright himself went on to speak of Unity Church in telling how he had "beaten the box,"

You will find the sense of the great room coming through—space not walled in now but more or less free to appear. . . . in this simple change of thought lies the essential of the architectural change from box to free plan and the new reality that is *space* instead of matter.

Already a central space is truly the generative core of a top-lighted interior surrounded with balconies (on three sides here) [Fig. 147]. The continuity achieved by the fragmentation of mass into its principal elements, as in Unity Church, is on the way to the continuity achieved through the fusion of the whole, as in the Guggenheim.

The increase of fluidity in Wright's manipulation of forms from the Larkin Building to Unity Church is especially striking in the church interior. The fairly conventional treatment of piers and spandrels in the earlier building he here enlivens by dark stained wooden stripping. The paneling defined by this stripping is so folded around the corners of the piers and spanning elements—which significantly dominate the interior as an interlocked structure instead of the enclosing walls—that what might otherwise appear both inert and blunt becomes immensely dynamic. Wright intensifies the dynamic quality of the interior by the apparent interlocking of these folded panels through their placement at different heights and on different planes. The folding and interlocking results in a three-dimensional visual effect from two-dimensional elements, to enliven the bulky interlocking of the basic structure. Even the balconies are staggered at different levels with respect to one another (an effect not visible in the photograph), and are to this degree closer in feeling to the Guggenheim balconies than to those in the Larkin Building. What is as symmetrical as the canonical Beaux-Arts composition when viewed head on becomes dynamically asymmetrical when viewed from an angle. In angular views it inadvertently prophecies the *De Stijl* composition of the twenties (Fig. 82), but derived, as Wright informs us, from his feeling for the Japanese prints which he collected (Fig. 148). The crisp line; the interlocked planarity transforming flatness to a staccato three-dimensionality; the play between plain and ornamented fields; these characteristics of Japanese prints enliven the interior of Unity Church. Compared to this plastic interaction of piers and spanning elements, the treatment in the Larkin Building seems almost tamely conventional.

One further aspect of Unity Church points toward the Guggenheim. This is its dichotomized plan. The composition is divided between a dominant and a subordinate mass, the entrance occurring toward the

FIGURE 147. *Unity Church. Interior.*

FIGURE 148. *Utamara. Japanese print of an actor.*

middle of the long side of the composition. Wright had already established the theme in the Larkin Building (Fig. 143). From either of the two streets on which the building fronted, one entered the Larkin at one of its long sides by mounting a double flight of stairs. Up a short flight of stairs, across a landing beside a pool, up another flight already embraced by the jogs of the building, through floor-to-ceiling plate-glass doors (a Wrightian innovation now commonplace) to the reception desk. There one turned sharply under the low bridging of the balcony overhead, and stepped into the tall space. Whereas most markedly longitudinal spaces are first viewed from one end, here one comes into the space midway along its axis. In Unity Church (Fig. 149), the complex is more decisively split: the compact cube of the auditorium on one side of a linking loggia; the spread of the parish house on the other.

Elements combined from both of these two early plans and massings subsequently appear in the Administration Building of the Johnson Wax Company (Fig. 150). Again an entrance axis (this one for automobiles as well as pedestrians) penetrates the building complex from side to side. This axis bounds one side of the block devoted to the top administrative and clerical staff of the company. The major block steps down in a low bridging of the entrance drive, and spreads to provide an irregular plateau of roof forms which shelter auxiliary functions; behind this the unique research tower rises. Exactly the same general scheme—entrance beneath the low bridging from ramp and monitor—appears in the Guggenheim.

The Johnson Wax complex also anticipates the Guggenheim in the melting away of prominent right angles, most especially at the juncture of wall and roof in the clerical block. Stopping short of the roof, the wall affirms itself as a merely enclosing (non-supporting) element with the roof lifted above it and set back (Fig. 151). Bands of translucent plastic tubing bent from wall-top to roof-edge eliminate the corner in a band of light, just as Wright had hoped that clerestory lighting for each winding of the ramp in the Guggenheim would do. The horizontal bands of tubing speed the eye across the side of the Johnson clerical block toward the low entrance; here the horizontality is reinforced by the inward curves and diagonals of the banding of the butterfly-shaped container for the executive offices, a mass that penetrates the clerical block and itself is penetrated by the anchoring stair and utility towers. From the gently rounded rectangle of the big enclosure for the secretarial pool, to the penetrating free form of the executive balconies, to the full circle of the cylindrical stair and utility towers: this hierarchy of curvature epitomizes Wright's lifelong preoccupation with "beating the box."

But circular forms come into their own in the interior of the Johnson Wax administrative complex. A winding pathway through a sequence of

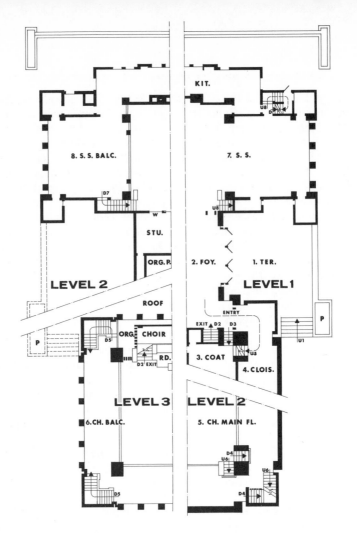

FIGURE 149. *Unity Church. Schematic plan pattern and cross section (oppo-site) with three-level plan which reveals a complex interaction of floor levels, which are linked by many short flights of stairs giving direction, up or down. Lowest level: up stairs from ground to elevated terrace (1. TER), through entrance portals to foyer (2. FOY). Entry to church occurs by moving from foyer past coatroom (3. COAT), which is depressed a few steps below foyer level, and into cloister (4. CLOIS), then up one of several short flights of stairs to the level of the main floor of church (5. CH MAIN FL) at medium level. Other short flights up give access to one of three balconies (6. CH BALC) at the top level. Organ, choir, and reading desk (RD) also appear at level 3. Exit from church down short flights from level 2 to level 1, at front of church beneath elevated section for reading desk and choir. To turn in the opposite direction from foyer is to enter Sunday school room (7. SS) with kitchen facilities. Flights of stairs to either side of two-storied open central section rise to balconies on either side of Sunday school room (8. SS BALC). On the balcony level 2, over foyer, there is a room for organ pipes and minister's study (STU) with windows opening onto upper part of Sunday school room. Skylights decorated with stained glass occur over the centers of Sunday school room and church.*

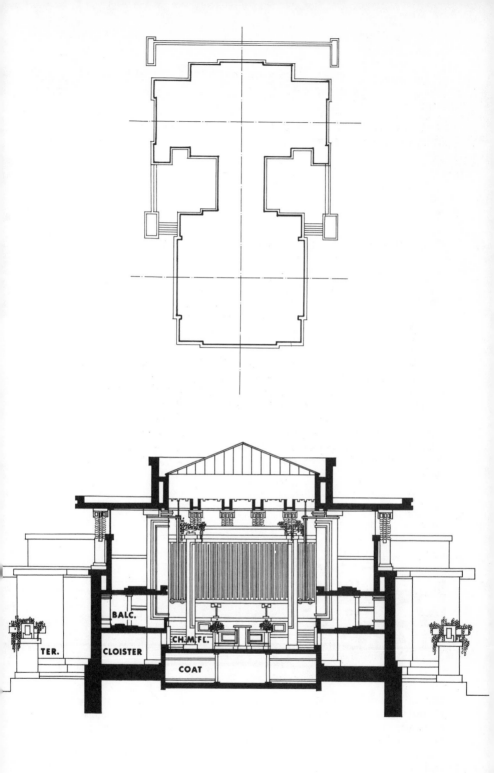

TER.   CLOISTER   BALC.   CH. M. FL.   COAT

FIGURE 150. *Frank Lloyd Wright. Administrative headquarters for the Johnson Wax Company, Racine, Wis., 1936–37; research tower, 1947–50. Bird's-
eye view of the exterior massing showing how the windowless enclosing wall
excludes the surrounding city from the interior of the building. The combined
automobile and pedestrian entrance is at the center. To the right of this
entrance the low block contains the principal office space for clerical staff.
It is interlocked by a curved V-shaped element for stair towers and executive
offices on balconies. A glazed bridge over the entrance roadway leads to an
auditorium and to additional executive facilities. To the left, the research
tower dominates a parking court surrounded by a wall of offices and laboratories.*

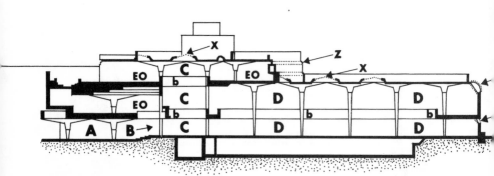

FIGURE 151. *Johnson Wax Company. Cross-sectional diagram through the
clerical block. The automobile entrance (A) leads to steps (B) up to the
entrance; thence to the tall entrance vestibule (C) with executive offices (eo)
on balconies above. The vestibule, in turn, opens under a low balcony (b)
into the principal office space (D) with its dendriform columns. Dotted lines
indicate translucent plastic tubing, as skylights (x) filling the roof areas
between the circular column heads, as cornices (y) bent from wall caps to
roof plane, and as light bands (z) within the wall surface.*

FIGURE 152. *Johnson Wax Company. Automobile entrance (taken from the side of the building opposite to that shown in Figure 150). The translucent bridge to the auditorium passes above the entrance. Executive offices and a stair tower appear in curved enclosure to the left; the corner of the parking and research court to the right.*

spaces with varying qualities (characteristic of Wright's work) brings us from the entrance drive to the administrative hall. The architectural path starts beneath the plastic curves of brick and tubing, which, at this closeness, weigh on the low opening (Fig. 152). From cavernous shadow, a right-angled turn through the plate-glass doors, and we step into the luminosity of the lofty, top-lighted reception lobby. Rising the full height of the butterfly-shaped enclosure, this space preludes the columned clerical hall beyond (Fig. 153). At once solemn and gay (the contradiction is justified by our fluctuating experience), the ranges of reinforced concrete columns in a mushroom profile rise from their light grip of the floor in an inverted taper, to swell at the crown as circular sheltering entities. These crowns are separated each from the other by areas of pearly light from translucent tubing in the roof. This clerical chamber seems to be a modern equivalent of the hypostyle halls of Egyptian temples (compare Figs. 151 and 154).[10] The tightly pressed bulk of the granite lotus and papyrus columns of the Egyptian temple, however, evoke the choked gloom of the life-giving swamp created by the annual overflow of the Nile, with the sky-ceiling mysteriously floated above their capitals by means of concealed blocks. Wright's interior, on the other hand, gives the effect of a walled orchard where trees are set out in

FIGURE 153. *Johnson Wax Company. Interior of the clerical block.*

wide-spaced rows, their tops barely lifted above their enclosure. Hence the ordered solemnity of the temple prototype is countered by the lithe gaiety of the orchard allusion, although there is probably nothing either specific or conscious in the images.

The result, as the climax to the path that led to it, is noble—perhaps a bit too noble. Wright's metaphor seems somewhat pretentious for paper shuffling, the space at once too grand and too cloistered for a secretarial pool. Simultaneously, it seems too unfocused in its regularly spaced columns (which *are* appropriate for a secretarial pool) to quite measure up to the expectation of climax warranted by the approach. Such flaws in one of his most creative works reveal how Wright's magisterial quality as a great "form giver" may compromise the full realization of his "organic" commitment in design, as is more evident in the Guggenheim.

So the themes and ideals of a lifetime disclose themselves in the

FIGURE 154. *Model of the Egyptian Temple of Ammon at Karnak, XIX Dynasty, 1350–1205 B.C.*

Guggenheim in a particularly comprehensive manner. "My Pantheon," Wright once called it in the summer of 1956 on visiting the museum site immediately after a trip to Rome.[11] This seems to have been a casual comparison, yet it *is* tempting to pair the two buildings, not only as domed enclosures of space, but as two temples: the one a temple to all the gods; the other, in a sense, to a career.

THE QUEST FOR STRUCTURAL CONTINUITY

Structurally the Guggenheim went through three major stages.[12] The first appears in the model of 1945 (Figs. 137, 155A). At first glance, one is tempted to forget completely about the nature of the structure, so convincingly does the model suggest the effortless resiliency of the ramp in its boomerang swing, out from the tower and back again. A closer look, however, reveals the ring of columns which provides a major part of the support of the ramp. In the model, these props in the space suggest the architecture of the International Style more than Wright's preference for the drama of structural members which are highly sculptural and vividly evident. To be sure, he had intended that the columns be some-what more sculptural—that is, spindle-shaped, each swelling slightly toward the middle, at the point of maximum bending, and tapered at either end. They took on more bulk than Wright wished, however, owing to the amount of fireproofing which the New York City building code required around them. Because of their clumsiness, Wright rejected them. But he must have rejected them on other grounds too. Incongruous in scale with

311

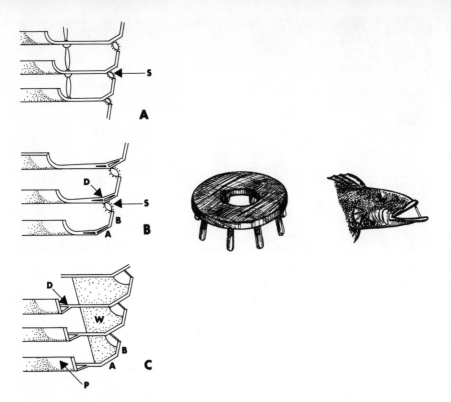

FIGURE 155. *Solomon R. Guggenheim Museum. The three stages in Wright's thinking about the structure for the ramp: (A) columns and struts; (B) struts alone, with the analogies of the multi-legged table and that of the fish; (C) webs—the scheme finally adopted. The ramp folds in planes (a, b) to the outside wall; (s) struts; (d) ducts; (w) webs; (p) hung parapet.*

the grandeur of the tower and ramp, incidental in their relation to the all-of-a-piece curvature of the conception, these columns remain as relics of the skeletal framing characteristic of Manhattan construction, which the Guggenheim as finally built fiercely repudiates.

Even the layman will be aware that the columns alone as seen in the model could not completely support the ramp. Accordingly, the tower of course serves as further support, and so do some piers beneath the lowest turns of the ramp (all evident in the model). The model indicates two other factors of structural consequence in the building. It is at least theoretically possible that the curved and folded cross section of the ramp would stiffen the building structure in an important way. All the more since both curvature and folding are doubled. The ramp curves in plan, as a circle, while its floor plane simultaneously curves up (like the brim of a hat) into a parapet at its inside edge. On the outside, the floor plane of the ramp folds once at an oblique angle (a) so as to separate one turn from the next above, and provide a notch for the ribbon window of the one below. It folds again more sharply (b) to make the gently out-canted wall which, turn by turn, encloses the building. In actuality, the stiffening that results from the profile of the ramp is a minor factor in the structural stability of the building as a whole. Aside from the visible columns in the model, which clearly require supplementation, the other major means of supporting the ramp does not show in the model. This is another circlet of supports (s) concealed within the plane of the outer wall. They bridge the ribbon window interval as short struts from the top of the outside wall of one turn of the ramp to the underbelly of the turn next above. In fact, in the model version, these concealed supports are probably more important than the columns. So much so that, in his second scheme, Wright eliminated the columns toward the inside of the ramp, and depended entirely on an enlargement of the struts to support the bulk of the ramp (Fig. 155B).

In this second scheme the lozenge-shaped steel struts occur at seven-foot intervals in the zone of the ribbon window. The structural function of these struts is clarified by imagining one complete turn of the spiral as a circular table having a hole in the middle and supported on a number of peripheral legs. A series of such tables stacked on top of one another would then crudely approximate the coiling of the Museum ramp. Mendel Glickman, who, with Wesley Peters, did most of the engineering for the building, recalls that Wright used a more vivid analogy when describing this strut scheme, comparing it to wedging a toothpick in a fish's mouth to keep it open. The struts were to have supported a hollow glass tubing inside and out (similar to that used between wall and roof in the administrative headquarters for the Johnson Wax Company), functionally to provide illumination for each turn of the ramp, visually to separate each turn from that above. The scheme was fully calculated and tested with models.

Yet it too was abandoned, Wright feeling that the struts, like the columns, became too bulky when fireproofed. He thereupon adopted the present system of vertical radiating ribs, cutting through the turns of the spiral as planes which semi-partition the ramp into a series of "galleries" (Figs. 155C, 156). To these "webs," as Wright referred to them, we shall return.

At the time of the publication of his 1945 model, Wright compared his conception to a gigantic spring coiled upward on an armature of steel reinforcing rods, although his analogy would perhaps have been even more applicable to the second (or completely strutted) version. "You can see," he told reporters in a serious, if facetious, fashion, "how the ramp, which is coiled in the shape of a true logarithmic spiral, is one continuous piece from top to bottom, integral with the outside wall and the inside balcony. When the first atomic bomb lands on New York it will not be destroyed. It may be blown a few miles up into the air, but when it comes down it will bounce!"[13] Ultimate vanity if literally accepted! Even assuming that the Museum survived the bomb sufficiently that the spring retained its integrity as the coils ripped away from whatever verticals contributed to its rigidity (as might theoretically have been imagined of the first two schemes, but not of the final webbed version), the mere thought of Wright's building bouncing unscathed back to an atomic wasteland is megalomaniacal to say the least. But one of Wright's buildings had already withstood catastrophe. His Imperial Hotel in Tokyo (1915–22) had survived the earthquake of 1923 (while much of the city collapsed around it) only to be junked in 1967 for the usual reason that a wealthy city could no longer afford to keep a masterpiece. The resilience of the Imperial had been a stunning vindication of organic architecture when, at virtually his lowest professional ebb, Wright needed it most. Then, too, his own Taliesin at Spring Green had twice burned to the ground, and had twice risen from the ashes. Now he was arrogantly prepared for larger catastrophes; but with the saving humility of one who works with the natural order of things.

In his extravagant doomsday metaphor, Wright really meant to dramatize the resiliency of the reinforced-concrete curvilinear cantilevers which he had planned for the Guggenheim. And, in a city where all building was ephemeral, he also meant to emphasize the permanence of his monolithic building—one of such unity that the ramp is without a single expansion joint.* Wright was specific on the point, "All is one and as near indestructible as it is possible for science to make a building. Unity of design with purpose is everywhere present and, naturally enough, the over-all simplicity of form and construction ensure a longer life by centuries than could be sustained by the skyscraper construction usual in New York City."[14] Again, as in Fallingwater, he sets the new in the context of the abiding.

In the realization of the building, the addition of the twelve webs at 30-degree intervals around the ramped circle is the most obvious alteration of both Wright's original structural conception and its strutted modification (Figs. 156, and in plan 164.) Four are embedded in different ways within the utility tower, and are not fully visible. Eight are clearly evident around the ramp as segmented triangular elements in the cross section (as

---

* In the conventional "cut and butt" building (to use Wright's phrase) breaks are required at intervals within the structure to accommodate expansion and contraction due to thermal change. The circular continuity of the Guggenheim makes such joints unnecessary, since the building expands and contracts within its skin.

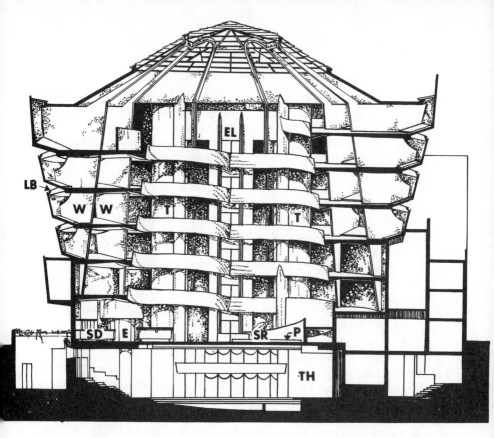

FIGURE 156. *Solomon R. Guggenheim Museum. Vertical cross section of the ramp looking toward the complex of utility towers, as in Figure 158:* (W) *webs;* (T) *toilet and utility stacks;* (EL) *elevator;* (E) *entrance;* (SD) *sales desk;* (P) *pool;* (SR) *start of ramp;* (LB) *double-glazed lighting band around the ramp;* (TH) *basement theatre.*

wall slabs in plan). They become progressively wider as they rise in the building. Almost 22 feet from outside wall to inside edge at the topmost level of the ramp, some of them die away toward the base of the building inside the thick (20-inch) cylindrical wall which supports a section of the lower part of the building. Others assume different shapes at the ground, becoming the lozenge-shaped columns between the basement windows and the triangular elements flanking the entrance to the Grand Gallery, while those to either side of the elevator carry their line to the floor.

We have already observed that Wright changed from struts to webs because, in his opinion, the fireproofing requirements for the struts made them cumbersome. The introduction of the webs considerably modified the unbroken nature of the spiral posited in both the columnar scheme of the model and its strutted revision. Functionally, the webs gave additional wall space, this space vertical rather than tilted, while providing "gallery" units which probably facilitate exhibition arrangement. Visually, the addition of the webs provided rhythmic intervals in what had threatened to be a monotonous corridor of space. Even though these advantages did not initiate his choice of the web scheme, Wright was surely aware of them (in fact he mentioned the webs' functional benefits in his remarks on the building).[15]† If the change to webs brought advantages, it also brought deficits; but these are best discussed in another connection.

Forming a radical building conception and working out the means of engineering it are of course only part of the problem. The actual construction of it, from the wearying process of contract negotiation and persuasion on a dozen fronts to the practical measures of erection, must also be taken into account. It is interesting to note in this regard that when Wright presented his model in 1945, he suggested that perhaps the Museum might be built of steel sheets instead of reinforced concrete. Wartime work in the shipyards was shutting down, and Wright believed that his Guggenheim ramp might well take up some of the slack.[16] (Although Le Corbusier was enthusiastic about ocean liners as a source of inspiration for architecture, he never envisioned any collaboration with shipyards as bold as this!) To get the Guggenheim built, there were innumerable legal, economic, technological, and functional problems to solve. Had Solomon R. Guggenheim not willed its realization (he died in 1949), it surely would not have been built. Had his nephew Harry Guggenheim and the other Trustees not honored this courageous request or had they less respected Wright's genius, the project would have been aborted in the morass of controversy occasioned by the unusual design. Again, had the architect

† For alternative schemes originally suggested to Solomon R. Guggenheim in 1943, and not discussed here, see Drexler, *Drawings of Frank Lloyd Wright*, figs. 190–93, 276; for developments within the accepted scheme, figs. 194–98. The Museum was originally conceived with an apartment for the director; this was later eliminated. Moreover, some schemes show the ramp to the north of the site, rather than to the south where it finally materialized. This reversed composition occurred in certain of the early schemes because, as various drawings make clear, there was some doubt for a while about whether a particular piece of real estate would be included in the site. More interesting than the minor compositional alterations among these schemes—principally in regard to such matters as the projected director's apartment, the monitor, and the fencing—is the handsome skeletal slab building which Wright would have liked to place as a backdrop to the monitor section of the Museum; see Drexler, figs. 197, 198. (Allen Brooks, in a paper presented at a meeting of the Society of Architectural Historians in January 1959, related this proposed slab to Wright's early project for an office building for the Luxfer Prism Company, 1895; see Drexler, fig. 2.) Something comparable to Wright's slab was finally built from designs of the Taliesin Fellowship in 1968–69.

316

been less tenacious, or his collaborators been less dedicated to realization of his vision, the project would have foundered.

Since municipal codes are over-cautious in accepting technological innovation, it is hardly surprising that the preliminary drawings for this extraordinary structure contained no less than thirty-two violations of the New York building regulations.[17] And where architect and authorities could not even agree as to how many stories the ramp contained—some officials said the equivalent of eight or nine; Wright slyly, but truthfully, said one!—it is not surprising that the negotiations were arduous.‡ For months, moreover, it seemed as though no builder could be found for it. With construction booming, most contractors refused even to consider the job. Those who did either submitted fantastically high bids or insisted on a cost-plus contract, which the trustees understandably refused. It was while the discouraging hunt for a contractor was on that Edgar Tafel, a New York architect who had apprenticed at Taliesin, introduced George N. Cohen to Wright. Cohen, who headed the relatively small Euclid Contracting Corporation, called on Wright at his suite in the Plaza sometime in August 1954. As he recalls the meeting, Wright came directly to the point. "Young man," he said, "here are the plans for the Archeseum. They represent twelve years of study. 'Arch' means 'great'. . . . These are the plans for a Great Museum. We have two million dollars with which to build it. If your price is higher than that, then don't bother to come back."[18] By this time Wright had already abandoned the strut scheme of support in the outside walls for the webs of the completed building.

The problem was how to build a curved structure with a technology conditioned to rectangularities, a structure where even so basic a task as measurements had to be handled differently from those in conventional construction. To erect a building of such extraordinary shape as the Guggenheim the ruler is insufficient. Like a topographical map, the drawings must be gridded (in 8-foot squares for the Museum), and measurements which run simultaneously up and across must be treated as being at certain elevations at particular points on the grid. Not that the principle of the grid was exceptional in Wright's work. He had repeatedly used grids comprised variously of rectangular, triangular, and circular units. Having graduated from Froebel weaving games, he believed that such modules ensured an underlying consistency and order to a design, like the warp

---

‡ Since building department officials are notoriously hidebound, it is only fair to add that the Supervising Architect considers that I. M. Cohen, the examiner of the building for the New York City Building Department (and, incidentally, no relation of the contractor), did everything he could within the law to facilitate the approval of plans and specifications.

317

and woof in textiles. For the Guggenheim the grid was practically, as well as esthetically, essential. Moreover, because of the circularity of the ramp, grid controls could be supplemented by polar coordinates measured along radii originating in a mast erected at the center of the circular space.

When submitting his original design, Wright had suggested that the concrete ramp should be formed as a total entity on an armature of expanded steel mesh (a sheet metal perforated and pulled apart in a heavier version of the metal mesh commonly used to support plaster). The steel mesh would be easily bent and folded to the shape of the shell-like ramp, with the layers of reinforcing thicker or thinner, depending on the structural necessity of the cross section, and the whole welded together. Ideally, the ramp would then be poured as a monolithic unit around its freely curved metal armature, even to a continuous triangular channel beneath the floor of the ramp and integrally of it, designed to take the air conditioning. With this unitary method of forming the ramp in mind, Wright conceived both the original columnar scheme and the revised strut scheme. Had either one reached the stage of construction, however, the practical matter of forming the ramp would have come to the fore, and doubtless have complicated Wright's suggested solution. In any event, two obstacles stood in the way of Wright's desire to fabricate the ramp as a unit, one technological, the other legal.

The first was a problem common to all complexly curved structures in reinforced concrete. In fabricating these, or for that matter any shape, in reinforced concrete, so-called "forms," or molds, of wood or other material are built around the metal armatures, and into them the concrete is poured from a mixer or is sprayed under pressure from a hose. It is the construction of this formwork which comprises a major part of the expense of reinforced concrete. Complexly curved forms require highly skilled, hence (in the United States especially) highly paid, labor. To be at all economical, such molds must be struck once the concrete has set and then re-used a sufficient number of times within a large structure to amortize their high initial cost. But Wright's was a continuously swelling ramp. As he originally envisioned the construction of the building, repetitive use of forms would have been limited. Moreover, as a second obstacle to his suggestion for forming the ramp, the code authorities ruled against the use of the expanded metal mesh which Wright had specified. Hence the practical building problem was that of using standard reinforcing rods and pouring techniques in such a way as to make the unusual structure feasible both technologically and economically.

It was obvious that the ramp could be more easily constructed if the curved cross section were broken up into simpler forms, with some of the formwork repeated. The problem could be further simplified if the circular ramp were abandoned for a multi-faceted, near-circular polygon, so that the forms could be made of straight pieces of lumber. Through these basic changes, Cohen believed that he could approximate Wright's design within a little more than the museum's budget.[19] Having scant hope that he could effect a better arrangement, Wright reluctantly concurred with the compromise, and an agreement was signed between the contractor and the Museum. No sooner had he given his consent, however, than Wright regretted the loss of the circle as the ultimate form of the organic ideal. He persuaded Cohen to reconsider the necessity of the polygon. By now fully committed to the conception, and eager to see it realized as Wright wanted it realized, Cohen agreed to try to regain the pristine circularity of the conception. For the courage with which he tackled the problem, the risks he undertook,[20] and the sympathy which he showed for the design once it was put in his charge, the contractor's name is especially deserving of mention on this building. It occurs beside Wright's at the entrance to the Museum.*

The web scheme would seem to have facilitated construction over the earlier schemes—although the engineers insist that had Wright ultimately preferred one of them the means would have been found to construct it. Where large, complexly curved, and constantly changing forms were indicated in Wright's earlier schemes, the webbed version employed simplified construction (Figs. 156, 157). The floor slab of the ramp was poured in units, each of which was that section of the floor spanning the distance between the web supports (which have a fixed thickness of 13 inches). Since the webs become progressively wider as they rise in the building, so does the portion of the floor slab that occurs between them. But the portions of the floor which project beyond the webs as cantilevers around the interior wall of space maintain a constant width of 14½ feet. Hence formwork could bridge from web to web to accommodate the steadily increasing width of the ramp; moreover the formwork for the cantilevered sections could be used over and over. Steel reinforcing rods running in the direction of the ramp predominate in the segment of the floor slab that bridges the intervals between the webs; rods at right angles to these predominate in the cantilevered segment of the slab.

Whereas the deck of the inside of the ramp curls up into a balustrade

---

* For such a unique building, it is appropriate to list others who were preeminently responsible for seeing it through. William Wesley Peters was in direct charge of the project for Wright, supervising the design as well as the execution of the details. As noted above, Professor Mendel Glickman of the University of Oklahoma was, with Peters, primarily responsible for the engineering, after Jacob Feld, originally in charge, had a falling out with Wright. The architectural representative on the job for both Wright and the client was William H. Short. The contractor's supervisor, who devised many of the complex construction procedures, was Charles W. Spero.

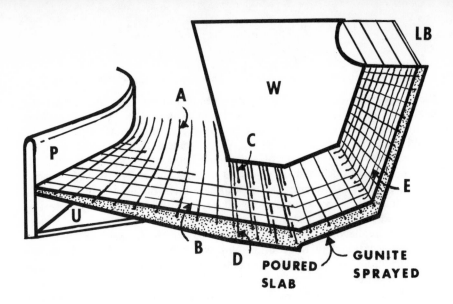

FIGURE 157. *Solomon R. Guggenheim Museum. Schematic structural diagram of the ramp indicating the placement of reinforcing rods and mesh within floor and wall planes. Rods designated as A are ⅜ inch in diameter and about 10 inches apart; B are ⅞ inch diameter and 6 inches apart (and interrupted in the diagram for clarity); C are bars at the top of the slabs in the area of the webs to resist shear stresses; D are ⅞ inch diameter and run continuously at the bottom of the thickest segment of the slab (to the width of the web); E is a lightweight, welded metal fabric made of wires about ¼ inch in diameter and spaced about 5 inches each way. Web (W) is curved away from the glass light band (LB) in order to give the band continuity. Parapet (P) is hung from the edge of the floor slab. Sheets of wallboard hung from the bottom of the parapet and the slab create a triangular duct (U) for utilities.*

in Wright's original scheme, a plaster parapet is simply hung from the edge of the cantilever in the final building. And whereas Wright originally would have cast hollows for air-conditioning and ventilating ducts integrally within the ramp itself located toward the exterior wall, the final plans specified that the encasement of the ducts be fabricated of plaster sheeting and hung so as to produce a triangular hollow beneath the inside parapet of the cantilever. From the other (outer) side of the floor slab, more rods radiating at right angles from those for the section of the ramp between the webs combine with metal mesh (not the sort which Wright had suggested) to fold outward as the armature for the exterior wall. The concrete for the supporting slab and the cantilever sections of the ramp was poured; that for the outer wall was sprayed. Bent plywood sheets temporarily supported outside the mesh provided the formwork, and against it thin layers of concrete, like the successive layers of an onion, were blown from hoses until the requisite 5-inch thickness was attained. With the removal of the forms after the concrete had hardened, the cross section of the ramp was complete.

The realization of Wright's original scheme promised to require very large forms of continuously changing dimensions, complexly bent in two directions. As revised to meet code regulations and rationalized for construction, formwork for the ramp very largely depended on straight pieces of lumber, on repetitive forms, and on single bends (to follow the curve of the plan).

However valiantly conventional technology grappled with Wright's extraordinary conception, it could not quite piece together a structure possessing the visual continuity promised by the model. To carp at these flaws is more than pettiness, since the problems faced in the Guggenheim are difficulties to be surmounted by any designer or builder of structures as boldly curved as this. Interrelated technological problems of many sorts can mar the design of such buildings, and thereby frustrate to some degree the attainment of the organic unity found in comparable structures in nature. For convenience, we shall separate them into problems of shape, surface, components, and structure.

First, there are *problems of shape.* The relative crudities of technology in reinforced concrete make subtlety of curvature and precision of surface extraordinarily difficult in a building at the scale of the Guggenheim. Builders must do mechanically what nature does through growth. In the curvatures of the utility shafts clustered around the elevator, for example, and their awkward melding (collision is perhaps more accurate) with the outer edges of the dome at the top of the space (Fig. 158), the problems of economically forming curved shapes and blending them into other curves is painfully evident. As shapes, they are blunt and boring. They lack the finesse of modeling for light and for transition to other parts which is essential to an architecture that, as here, has luminosity and flow as its very premises. By no means as crude, they nevertheless suggest the sheet-metal ductwork which channels air conditioning.

The very gentleness of the movement from light to shadow on curved shapes at this scale makes them inevitably less decisive in form than they would be as rectangular structures, where two sides of a shape are usually visible—the lighted and the shaded face sharply differentiated. On the exterior of the Guggenheim, especially on overcast days, and in some strong lights, the circling of the ramp goes flat. Of course, the professional photographer does his best to overcome this effect (Fig. 165); even so, compare the way in which the sharp corners of the rectangular balcony around one level of the monitor give a firmness to the shape, which the gradual curve of the level below does not possess. The big curves of the exterior of the ramp especially tend toward flabbiness where

FIGURE 158. *Solomon R. Guggenheim Museum. General interior view looking toward the utility stacks. The entrance and a corner of the sales desk appear in the lower left; the pool and the start of the ramp in the lower right. In order to take in the whole of the space from floor to dome, the camera necessarily distorts the space. In fact, as indicated below, the interior space cannot be seen by the eye as the wide-angle lens presents it here.*

they should be most decisive, by sagging visually as they round the edge of the form. Corners also make depth and thickness more discernible. On the exterior of the Guggenheim nothing is more disconcerting than the contrast between the sculptural form as a whole and the two-dimensional quality of its various curves, as though the building were composed in actuality of the bent sheets of the plywood formwork. Only through complex subtleties of curvature and profile similar to the "optical corrections" of the Greek temples can simple curves of homogeneous material at huge scale take on the organic elegance and resilience for which Wright strove. These are not only expensive, but their precise effect is difficult to calculate before the building rises.

Shaping problems in reinforced concrete blend into a second group: *problems of surface*. These, too, are especially conspicuous on the exterior of the Museum. Despite the care with which they were made, the plywood forms for the outer walls (against which the concrete was sprayed from inside†) inevitably possessed irregularities, and these of course were reproduced in the concrete surfaces. In textureless curves, blemishes of this sort are subject to raking light, which mercilessly reveals them wherever highlight rounds to shadow. A virtue can be made of necessity, as Le Corbusier demonstrated in most of his late buildings by deliberately exploiting the texture of the wooden formwork to achieve surface pattern. Such roughness, however, did not accord with Wright's conception; nor is it compatible with city grime (in fact, much of Le Corbusier's *béton brut*—rough concrete—has become almost too *brut* with dirt).

Because raw reinforced concrete weathers so badly, it is often surfaced with pebbles or chips of a stone which weathers more agreeably. The basic components of concrete are cement, an aggregate of crushed rock or sand, and water; sometimes a special aggregate is used at the surface. This may be a high-grade crushed stone possessing a handsome appearance, such as marble or granite chips. Chemicals added at the surface of the poured form so retard surface hardening that the scum of cement can be brushed from the aggregate after the core has set; alternatively, acids can be used to eat away or pneumatic hammers to chip away the hardened shell of cement in order to get back to the aggregate.

---

† It might have been preferable to have sprayed from the outside inward. The resulting roughness of the interior walls would not have been as vulnerable to the light as the exterior. But the contractor decided that spraying from the outside would be too expensive. It would have required more elaborate scaffolding all around the building. The concrete would have been sprayed against an outwardly canted form—a difficult procedure. Finally, perfection of surface would have required an elaborate screeding operation (that is, a leveling process in which boards or other measuring devices are inserted into the wet concrete).

With his vision of a shell-like purity and luminousness for the Guggenheim, Wright had hoped for a surface of marble chips, even as he had, years before, used the natural colors of a pebble aggregate for the exterior surfaces of Unity Church.‡ Again, too expensive! Unable to have the integral surface of a stone aggregate, he was forced to turn to some such applied surfacing as paint. Here it is a cream-colored plastic skin which expands and contracts with the building, but which also streaks with time. Moreover, the surfacing eliminates almost all sense of substance. This diminished sense of materiality in the curved forms making the exterior of the Museum, taken in conjunction with their wavering surfaces and two-dimensionality, completes the uncomfortable feeling that they might just possibly be made of a thick, fuzzy building board that has been bent, plastered over, and painted. Wright had scornfully dismissed the International Style as "cardboard architecture" and, in some ways, he was right. But the paper-thinness of the surfaces of European modernism is at least appropriate to the architects' intentions of weightlessness and pure geometry. Here the painted surfaces seem too sluggish to be weightless, and too abstract to assert their materiality in a very positive manner. Ironically, in view of Wright's boasts about the permanence of the Museum, the structure appears somehow temporary, suggesting the free-form monument put up for a summer spectacle—something, perhaps, that might have been seen at the New York World's Fair of 1939 had Wright's genius been tapped for that unmemorable occasion.

Difficulties in shaping occur not only in the handling of the reinforced concrete, but merge with perplexities of a third sort: *problems with components.* Components made of conventional materials and designed for rectangular structures and spaces (doors and windows, for example) are integrated with difficulty into such free-form unconventional buildings as the Guggenheim. The closed nature of the Guggenheim eliminated many of these problems; not, however, the awkwardness of wedging near-rectangular panes of glass into the light bands which encircle the ramps above the exhibition space and separate the levels one from another. Wright had to adopt this makeshift arrangement when the local fire code forbade the use of translucent tubing, which he had intended to wind in horizontal bands around the Guggenheim just as he had already done at Johnson Wax. The incongruity of these panes with the curvature of the building is relatively inconspicuous, however, in comparison with the inappropriateness of the rectangles, triangles, and wedges of glass which fill the circle of the dome (Fig. 158).

‡ Since the Unity Church was not cleaned for years, its dingy surfaces do not fairly indicate the qualities possible with exposed aggregate, and of course the technique was in its infancy when Wright used it for this building.

For the dome, too, Wright had originally planned to use translucent tubing. This was to be wound around its inner surface, above a grille of bronze rings which became progressively smaller as they rose to the crown.* Again the Johnson Wax complex provided the prototype; in fact, the domed reception room of the advertising department is a small version of Wright's first scheme for the Guggenheim (Fig. 159). After code regulations had forced its rejection, the dome went through no less than three alternate designs. In these designs, the problems concerning both the nature of the components which might be used for the dome and the manner of their assemblage merge with problems of structure. As we discuss them, we shall return to this succession of schemes for the dome.

Finally, then, *problems of structure*. We have already observed how conventional means of construction were coaxed into unaccustomed effects in making the ramp, however stiffly. We have also seen that the over-all conception remained essentially constant, even though the structural means changed, and changed radically. In other words, despite the structural interest of the building, structure did not determine the form, but (eventually, at least) the form went searching for structure. The less than integral role of structure in making the form appears in the early model, in the unintegrated nature of the inner ring of columns as mere props. Not until the second scheme, which depended exclusively on the struts, did form and structure coalesce (Fig. 155B). Had this scheme been realized, the virtual invisibility of the supports concealed in the wall would have resulted in a structure of mystery. Completely lucid structures were never congenial to Wright. Like much structure in nature, Wright's structure is usually conspicuous, often dramatically so, at the same time that it tends to conceal to some degree the "growth principle" which makes it what it is. The very metaphors that Wright employed for the ramp— that of the shell turning on itself, or that of the unitary curl of a great wave —possess this sense of structure, at once vividly evident, but with a residue of mystery. So the second scheme with the struts seemingly would have provided the structure most consistent with its metaphoric intent. Significantly, when the struts became too bulky, too conspicuous, Wright scrapped the scheme. The alternative which he finally embraced radically altered his structural concept. The horizontal tiers of the ramp remain the dominant visual elements in the composition, just as Wright wished; but now the vertical webs become the dominant supporting elements. As compared to the strut supports, the web supports are much more evident,

---

* In reality the "dome" is a truncated cone (technically, the frustum of a cone) similar to the conic solids used to determine the pitches of the outside walls and inside parapets of the ramp, but of different slope; see figs. 139, 156. For convenience, however, it may be termed a dome, if not for its shape, then because of its function.

FIGURE 159. *Johnson Wax Company. Dome in the reception room of the advertising department showing the bronze grille with translucent plastic tubing like that originally contemplated for the Guggenheim.*

and are felt as important elements in the structure. But as the dominant supports? We cannot be quite certain. They are set so far back of the parapeting as to be lost to view when we enter the building. And when we do see them as we move onto the ramp, they possess the thinness of mere partitions, their structural role ambiguous. We feel the more uncertain about the structural function of these flat planes because they seem to be cleanly cut by the ramp, no curved transitions from the floor and outer walls visually integrating them with the curved realm they inhabit.† To have declared the primacy of the webs over the ramp would of course have completely altered Wright's concept. In realizing a concept so conspicuously structural, it is never a matter of seeing that the structure fully declares itself—of its being, in the nineteenth-century moral imperative, fully "honest" by revealing itself with the utmost lucidity; rather it is a matter of seeing that the premises of the structure are so in harmony with those of the concept that the various elements of the building will impress us with their "rightness," as, for example, we feel the rightness of the cantilevers in Fallingwater. The penalty for the lack of this kind of inevitability between structure and concept in the Guggenheim ramp is our feeling that the concept has raced ahead of its means.

There is another, conspicuous discord between form and structure in the Guggenheim. As already indicated, it occurs in the dome, and again early versions, had they been realized, would have avoided the incongruity. With the plastic tubing eliminated, the dome had to be redesigned. Two more schemes, prior to that eventually used, were tried. One of these vaguely recalled the dome of the Pantheon. A domical shell in glass, with a pattern suggestive of coffering and a circular opening in the center, was dropped below an oculus, making the oculus appear deeply recessed.‡

---

† In fact, the contractor, George Cohen, even argues that the major structural element is the ramp as a continuous spiral beam (or as a spring, to use one of Wright's metaphors), the webs primarily serving as props to hold the coils apart, rather than functioning as the major structural elements. The engineers who worked on the building, Professor Mendel Glickman and Wesley Peters (an architect with engineering training) assert that Mr. Cohen's position is not only factually mistaken, but theoretically impossible. This disagreement immediately following the completion of a building among those involved in its building, and on a purely technical matter of such importance, well illustrates the complexities of determining what actually happened structurally in complexly engineered buildings in the past, where building methods are debatable and where much more of the engineering was empirical and intuitive.

‡ Some idea of what was intended can be gained from a cross section published in *Engineering News-Record*, Dec. 5, 1957, p. 42. Mendel Glickman has informed me that the double dome with the central oculus was designed to function as an air-conditioning device, exhausting the hot air that entered between the two glass domes through the oculus, discharging some outdoors and passing the rest through cooling coils to be recirculated inside.

This scheme briefly replaced a more seriously considered alternative, the most handsome conception of all for the dome. A graduated domical grill of cast concrete circles would have supported glass bubbles, also graduated in size, as they rose in the dome. The scheme essentially converted the two-dimensional design for the bronze grill of the advertising area of the Johnson Wax Company into three dimensions and added something of the effect of the tufted plastic sky of the Morris Gift Shop (Fig. 133). More magnificently conceived than either of its predecessors, and also to more architectural effect, this version had gone as far as shop drawings when estimates of its cost killed it. Only then did Wright prepare the existing dome with its crudely designed panes that infill the hairpin ribs.[21]

Unsatisfactory as it is, the present dome nevertheless reveals the vigor of Wright's conceptual powers up to the very end, since he did nothing less than invent a new motif for one of the oldest of architectural forms. Instead of the usual ribs radiating from a center, he threw hairpin-shaped cantilevers from the tops of every pair of webs. They project out into the space in six independent thrusts, lightly stabilized and linked together by straight ribs just back of the climactic hairpin bend. Or so it appears. The "cantilevers" are really not such at all (Fig. 160). Instead of going up as six independent structures thrust into space off the tops of the webs, and therefore in tension, they went up all at once in the conventional manner for a dome, as a spoked unit, like a rimless wheel, weighing down on the webs, and therefore essentially in compression.

In redesigning the dome in terms of the cantilever, Wright may have intended to echo the cantilever of the ramp. He did so, however, at a price. As Vincent Scully has pointed out,[22] the hairpin-shapes of the pseudo-cantilevers slice the surface of the dome into linear patterns, as do the panes of glass. The rest of the building, on the other hand, is essentially conceived as an enclosure of curved surfaces.* The linear configuration of the cantilevered ribs becomes a quickly apprehended boundary, reducing the apparent size of the interior, whereas a swelling surface of graduated rings, coffers, or bubbles would have enlarged it. Moreover, the projecting ramp awkwardly conceals the supports for the ribs when the view is from ground level. Because of this partial concealment of the ribs by the ramp, the dome seems not so much to swell from the outside walls, thus crowning the full space, as to be just outside it within a spatial compartment of its own.

So technological problems involving shape, surface, components, and structure bedeviled the full realization of Wright's brave conception. To

---

* Except that the ramp in plan is also inconsistently sliced in a linear manner by the webs.

FIGURE 160. *Solomon R. Guggenheim Museum. Diagrams of the structure of the ribbing for the dome. It appears (left) that each hairpin "cantilever" went up separately, projecting out into space like a diving board, and therefore tending to pull away from its supports as a structure in tension. Actually (right) the hairpins went up as a spoked unit with forces radiating equally in all directions down on the supports, and therefore essentially a structure in compression. In the first instance, downward force at T pulls at junction Y where support and hairpin join; in the second instance the downward radiation of forces in all directions at C weighs down on the supports at Y.*

point to these blemishes is not to diminish the achievement. Some cognizance of the reasons for them should, in fact, make us more aware of the accomplishment, and of the lengths to which others must go if they would accomplish as much—let alone more.

THE RAMP AS MUSEUM: SUCCESS AND FAILURE

If Wright's conception presented problems for engineers and contractor, it challenged the museum staff as well. By and large, architects and architectural critics were, if not wholly pleased, at least warmly charitable to the Guggenheim on its opening, recognizing it for the epoch-making architectural achievement that it is. Museum personnel, art critics, and artists were generally hostile, often violently so. No sooner did the trustees announce late in 1956 that Wright's project would be built than a group of New York artists petitioned against it. They disliked the obtrusiveness of the architecture, and especially the tilts of wall and floor planes. Moreover, they were disgruntled that Wright should have anything to do with a museum, when he had repeatedly complained that pictures spoil architecture (although they might have paused in their indignation to recall that Wright's sour remarks on contemporary painting were as nothing compared to his opinions on most contemporary architecture). Surely Wright's instinct for the publicity to be gained from shocking statement must have augmented the fervor of his belittlement of painting, since both James Fitch and Edgar Kaufmann have demon-

329

strated just how often Wright did integrate painting, and more especially sculpture, into his designs.[23] Even so, and despite the radical abstraction of his own painted and sculptural ornament (Fig. 130), Wright's enthusiasm for primitive and exotic arts did not extend to the most progressive work going on around him. He remained particularly suspicious of painting, regarding it as incidental to, yet competing with, architecture, and tending in both respects to disturb the integrated design he sought in his interiors.

It is no secret that James Johnson Sweeney, the first director of the Museum (until his resignation in 1960), thoroughly disapproved of the building in respect to its purpose. Even more than most of those in his profession, Sweeney preferred neutral, flexible spaces for changing exhibitions, where the museum staff could make its own arrangements, and where the work of art could assert itself against the all but non-architecture of the building.[24] In fact, while waiting for Wright's building to rise (he had become Director in 1952, succeeding the Baroness Hilla Rebay), Sweeney, with José Luis Sert, had painted and lighted the interior of an East Side mansion in a shadowless dead white as temporary quarters for the Museum. Sweeney and Wright were decidedly ill-matched and, in a rather intemperate review of the opening of the Museum, Hilton Kramer referred to them as two supremacists, each overpowering the art objects in an extreme and opposite manner[25]: Wright with his spiral; Sweeney with his bucket of paint and stark lighting.

It is difficult not to sympathize with the museum professionals, and especially with respect to Wright's specific ideas on museum display. Many of these were naive. There was merit, however, in his ideas about the relevance of the building for the kind of abstract art which dominated the Guggenheim Collection at the time of his commissioning, most of it paintings by Rudolph Bauer and by the deservedly better known Vasily Kandinsky (Fig. 161). In fact, when Wright began his designs, the official name of the institution was the Museum of *Non-Objective* Art. The Baroness encouraged Solomon Guggenheim to adopt the collecting and exhibiting of such art as its policy. Once Sweeney became director, however, he promptly enlarged the museum's purview and with this expansion of interest, its name became what it is today, a memorial to its founder. Allowing for Wright's customary rationalization for what he wanted to realize, we cannot doubt that he was sincere in envisioning his new kind of museum as especially appropriate for "non-objective" painting. Concerning this, he wrote:

The building was intended by Solomon R. Guggenheim to make a suitable place for the exhibition of an advanced form of painting wherein line, color and form are a language in themselves. . . . in-

FIGURE 161. *Vasily Kandinsky.* Compositions, *1914.*

dependent of reproduction of objects animate or inanimate, thus placing painting in a realm hitherto enjoyed by music alone.

This advanced painting has seldom been presented in other than the incongruous rooms of old static architecture. Here in the harmonious fluid quiet created by this building interior the new painting will be seen for itself under favorable conditions.[26]

Next to architecture, Wright, like many architects, favored music among the arts. The free space of Kandinsky's *Compositions* and *Im-*

provisations, providing skies for constellations of sharply abstract forms or, alternatively, for nebulae from which forms emerge and into which they die, were kindred to Wright's fluid space. And he argued that the curve of the wall would further free them (they were to be unframed) from the mensural environment of rectangular walls. Each painting would thus possess an independence within the space, "much as a jewel set as a signet in a ring. Precious—as itself."[27] Although Wright was certainly ignorant of Abstract Expressionism when he projected his Museum, since, at the time, its leading practitioners were only groping toward what later came to be so labeled, the breadth of the museum's curved space and the mobility it induced already looked toward an environment parallel to "action painting." Not wholly perhaps, since the smoothness of Wright's surfaces, the gentleness of the circle and climb, and its channeled predictability are alien to what is central in Abstract Expressionism. In terms of the blunt "action" of the most violent Abstract Expressionism with its emphasis on human gesture, the qualities of the Museum seem faintly old-fashioned, and closer in feeling to Kandinsky's milder *Compositions* and *Improvisations,* although the intent of certain works by such lyrical environmentalists as Mark Rothko and Philip Guston seems somewhat analogous to the intent of the museum's interior. In any event, granting that the new painting deserved to be viewed in a new kind of architectural space, the Museum was surprisingly "of a piece" with the painting, despite the utterly different worlds from which each derived.

Wright's more specific suggestions on display are most charitably dismissed as the ideas of one who had little sympathy with a great urban museum. Wright would have leaned the paintings against the tilted outside walls—like so many dishes on the plate rails which used to run just below the ceilings of turn-of-the-century dining rooms, and which he himself put to such good use as "banding lines" for the interiors of his prairie houses.[28] Tipped away from the spectator in this manner, so he believed, paintings would be seen as they appeared on easels in artists' studios. (Not all easels are so designed. Artists sometimes tack their canvases on the wall; even unroll them on the floor. And all work knowing that paintings customarily hang perpendicularly. Reasoning of this sort is surely architect's license, transforming fancy into the kind of logic that convinces clients to back the scheme and foot the bill.) According to Wright's original scheme, the paintings would thus have leaned out (or perhaps looked up) to the natural light filtered through the plastic tubing of the banded opening above them. The idea seemingly originated as early as 1919 in the delightfully intimate project for the W. S. Spaulding Print Gallery in Boston (Fig. 162). But the light from the Guggenheim clerestory band would probably have been more in the spectator's eyes than on the surface of the picture. Although we cannot be certain of the effect, Wright's

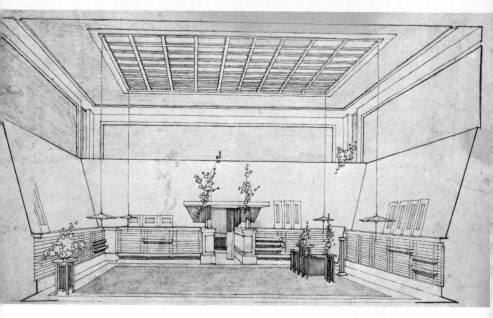

scheme would seem to have entailed the further discomfort of bending over the tilted "do not touch" plane which rises from the floor to the canted outer wall, then bending still farther to look at the tipped-out picture.

Wright even made a few sketches of his ideas about exhibition as a guide for the museum staff (Fig. 163). They reveal how awkwardly a large painting can butt against the clerestory lighting band, whereas a work of extraordinary dimensions (such as Abstract Expressionists made ordinary) would not even have fitted within the modest, somewhat domestic, height of Wright's walls, except in the spaciousness of the Grand Gallery and the topmost turn. In addition to the leaning pictures, Wright's sketches show the ramp partitioned here and there with panels, each containing its own light source and appearing a little too much like bulletin boards to be fully architectural in character. Circular benches of hassock height are seen clustered about the webs, much as Wright used them on the periphery of the heavy clumps of furniture which he designed for his domestic interiors. Here, however, they threaten to encumber the ramp, even though a few have been introduced to good effect. All in all, Wright's ideas on installation were less applicable to the urban museum than to the informal, improvised exhibits of the amateur arts and crafts club. They recall the exhibits in which Wright had participated with other progressive architects during his early days in Chicago, or such as might have been expected in the community centers of his Broadacre City. "I must say," Wright told reporters at the unveiling of the original

FIGURE 163. *Solomon R. Guggenheim Museum. Wright's sketch for a projected display of abstract paintings in the Museum, 1956.*

model, "that I begrudge New York this great gift, which would fit so well in the great Middle West. But where life is most in need of inspiration and culture is where this new impetus should be found."[29]

To be sure, at the time that he began his design for the Guggenheim, Wright envisioned something quite different from the conventional museum. There was to have been an apartment for the director. A skeletal building (initially abandoned for economic reasons) immediately behind the existing Museum as a backdrop was to have provided not only much needed service space for the museum staff, but also studios for artists. In short, Wright originally thought of the institution as a center both for exhibits and for creation, with its director on the premises: a place more akin to Taliesin than to the conventional museum establishment. It is a pity that this more "organic" approach to the Museum could not have been realized, and especially in New York, where its example might have served as a counterforce to the programs of other museums.

Although it would probably have pleased Wright to have been told so, his ideas on museum installation were thoroughly unprofessional. Part of the director's job, beginning with Sweeney, was to find a way of reconciling his own ideas of museum display with the unusual facilities that Wright had provided. Following Sweeney's resignation, portions of the installation were inevitably altered by his successor, Thomas M. Messer, who is more sympathetic to the building. Succeeding directors will make further changes; but a look at the initial installation and then at the early revisions of it by Messer reveals something of the nature of the problems posed by Wright's ramp. On what Sweeney did there were five reactions at the time: some liked it; some liked it considering the building with which he had to work; some detested it for what it did to the building, others for what it did to the works of art, and still others for what it did on both scores. One thing is clear. There is no doubt as to what Wright's opinion of Sweeney's arrangement would have been had he lived to see the opening of his "Archeseum."

First, Sweeney and the paint brush. On all the wall and web areas used for display, Sweeney replaced Wright's warm cream color (lobster bisque, as one critic described it, and none too congenial for the art objects) with white. Brought up on the "natural" colors favored by the picturesque esthetic of the nineteenth century, white was anathema to Wright, and as the characteristic color of the International Style doubly so. Second, Sweeney and the perpendicular. Since the multiple tilts—of floor, wall, and picture—would have made every painting hung on the outside walls appear crooked, he boldly projected the works (first having removed their frames) out into the space on the ends of 4-foot metal rods embedded in the walls. Except for what it did to his scheme for lighting, Wright might just possibly have approved of this effect. It exaggerated his idea of the work of art existing in its own realm, freed from the wall and framed within the curved space of the building. Finally, Sweeney and the lights. For the inadequacies of Wright's "three dimensional experiment" in natural illumination from the dome and the winding lighting band, which artificial light was merely to have supplemented, Sweeney substituted uncompromising and unvarying artificiality[30]—and another aspect of the organic concept disappeared. Intense electric illumination from Wright's clerestory lighting band washed

335

the walls. In fact, as Peter Blake observed at the time of the opening, the light-drenched walls enlarged the architectural space by washing away their palpability.[31]† On this luminescence the paintings floated unframed at the end of their rods. Finally, front lighting from boxed fixtures (another discordant element of rectangularity) balanced the back lighting.

Whether paintings should have been thus disengaged from walls was questioned at the time of the opening. Whether subtleties of paint surface were lost in the intense luminescence was also debated. Whether Sweeney was culpable for not having magnanimously accepted a *fait accompli* with which he profoundly disagreed, or whether he deserved praise for a stunning adjustment to a difficult problem were other matters on which opinions differed. With the flurry of inaugural controversy long past, it may in retrospect appear that the collision between the temperaments of the architect of the Museum and its first director was salutary. Although forced to adapt his ideas to the Museum, Sweeney so positively asserted his position that it has been easier for his successor to adjudicate the demands of the building and those of the first installation. Thus Messer has toned down the white. He has introduced more variety into the lighting.[32] He has moved most works back toward the wall, although he has not hesitated to suspend works, the larger canvases especially, from the ends of Sweeney's poles wherever this arrangement seems best. Where Sweeney had cut a swathe of pristine luminescence across the major part of the ramp used for exhibition, leaving the area around the utility core in Wright's cream color and substantially in shadow, Messer has unified the interior, working both with and away from Sweeney's scheme and part way back to Wright's intention.

The problem of installation is difficult, not only because of the nature of the structure, but because the visual unity of the space requires that new displays be calculated to go up as speedily as possible. Piecemeal barricading of the Museum for exhibition changes is especially awkward in this big, unified interior. As much as possible, shifts in exhibition occur on Mondays, when the Museum is closed to the public. Only extensive preplanning in a scale model of the ramp makes the quick changes feasible. On Mondays part of the exhibition-in-process

† Scully, *Wright*, p. 31, found the glare "compressive" upon the space which demands a "naturally changing and expansive light." The critical discrepancy between Blake's and Scully's points of view probably can be accounted for by differing vantage points. When one was on the ramp, looking at the exhibition, the wash of intense light on the walls did destroy their palpability and thereby tended to enlarge the sense of space within each of the gallery compartments. When one looked up or across the big space, however, the intense bands of light tended to belt it in.

may be temporarily dismantled, and part of the exhibition-to-come may be briefly tested in its place. Works must be considered not only from vantage points close by, but (sometimes with the help of a walkie-talkie) from points across the ramp. For a major show, all is pre-calculated for the hectic Monday immediately preceding the opening. Within this one day, the entire Museum will be transformed: the discontinued show dismounted; walls painted; works installed; lights, plants, labels placed for the opening on Tuesday. It is part of the price of the unity of the big interior.

Cramped, inflexible, and inadequately related working spaces behind the scenes compound the difficulties of the museum staff. Even a casual glance at the original plans (Fig. 164) reveals that the subordinate spaces were simply left over, like the trimmings from a pie crust, once the big circle of the ramp and the small circle of the monitor had been made. There is little point in discussing them, since they have been extensively altered. Most of the changes have been for the good, with the tragic exception of the conversion of the bridge between ramp and monitor into an awkward addition to the gallery space. Whatever difficulties it presented, the monitor should have been devoted to something like the uses which Wright planned for it. Among the renovations subsequent to the museum's opening which have effected conspicuous improvement is a narrow, slab-shaped addition, its window wall rising as a decorative screen, which has been fitted into the one-time parking area immediately behind the monitor. This is similar to the addendum for behind-the-scenes operations that Wright once proposed to augment the space of ramp and monitor.‡ The addition substantially relieved a serious crowding of staff facilities—one so extreme at the time of the opening of the Museum that the topmost turns of the big ramp had to be closed off for storage and conservation.

As for the remainder of the subordinate spaces, only the basement auditorium need detain us. Located immediately under the main entrance floor (Fig. 156), its ceiling is necessarily flat, but coved; seen in conjunction with the dished floor, the plane overhead has the delightfully deceptive quality of a low dome. After the movement and grandeur of the ramp, the critic Walter McQuade found the auditorium a place of rest and shelter, a little like the hearth of the prairie house.[33]

‡ On this administrative slab, designed by Taliesin Associates, see above pp. 316n. and 334f. In proposing the office slab initially, Wright seems to have indicated only vaguely what functions would be allocated to it and what to the monitor. Moreover, he variously suggested that the slab might house studios for artists and facilities for historical research.

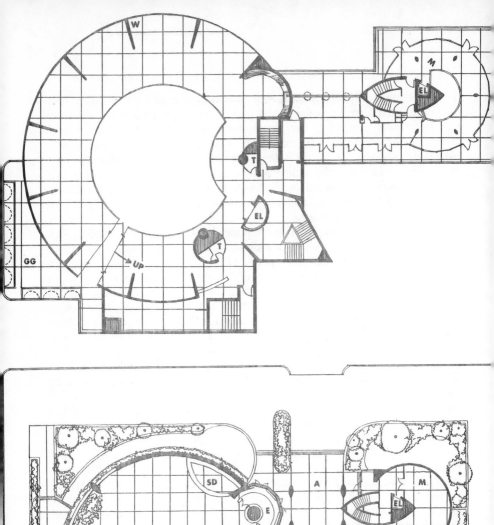

FIGURE 164. *Solomon R. Guggenheim Museum. Floor plans at ground level and at the third level of the ramp.* (A) *Automobile entrance under the bridge to the monitor (as originally intended);* (E) *entrance;* (SD) *sales desk;* (EL) *elevator;* (T) *toilet and utility stacks;* (SR) *start of the ramp;* (C) *original cafeteria (now a work space) immediately below the Grand Gallery at the start of the second level of the ramp;* (M) *administrative monitor;* (GG) *upper part of the Grand Gallery;* (W) *webs. Each square of the grid is 8 feet.*

THE EXPERIENCE OF THE SPIRAL

Walking along Fifth Avenue from downtown, we first encounter the Guggenheim ramp edging from behind the apartment houses as a sinister shape—like some newly landed space craft, although the metaphor has gone limp with repetition. Critics have variously experienced the scale of the building,[34] some saying that the Museum seems large against the neighboring apartment houses which hem it in, some that it seems small. This chameleon-like scale results from the fact that the exterior lacks those devices which would stabilize our comprehension of its size. The Museum looms large as small pieces of it are, by our movement, immediately juxtaposed against the mincing scale of the detail of adjacent apartment houses which bulk larger than the Museum and wall it in. It looms largest—inhumanly so, like a gas tank—as the ramp first comes fully into view when approached from downtown, without any of the rest of the building to contrast with its unrelieved austerity of texture and shape. From this view we cannot measure it against windows, bricks, ornaments, balustrades, or any of the other familiar devices that the eye instantly uses as a scale for judging the size of something else. On the other hand, viewed diagonally from the uptown side, the building tends to appear rather smaller than it is; but, in this view it is large or small depending on how we focus on it: when our attention is poorly focused, the Museum has an odd way of becoming the toy of its environment; when sharply focused, it takes on monumentality.

This vantage point from across the street and somewhat uptown of the building affords the classic view of the exterior (Fig. 165). The monitor mass, with its variety of angles and planes and curves builds upward to the graduated curves of the dominating mass, which now seems less overbearing since it appears in the background of the composition. The windows and parapeting of the monitor and the unhappy leaf ornament of its cornice provide such paltry means as exist within the mass itself for measuring the scale of the ramp. From here, the composition is comparable to that of the Robie House. It is closed to the rear, less important at the ends than that of its famous predecessor, but, like it, predominantly designed for its broadside spread. Like the Robie House, too, the building crowds its site. The Guggenheim especially needs a tracery of trees in front to interrupt its austere surfaces, and as a partial means of fixing the scale of the building. As a one-sided

339

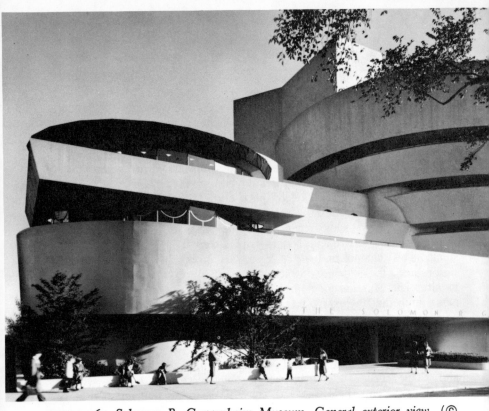

FIGURE 165. *Solomon R. Guggenheim Museum. General exterior view.* (© *Ezra Stoller Associates*)

composition, however, it could not stand free in a park—as some have unwisely wished, suggesting that it might have stood across the street in Central Park.*

The diagonal view across Fifth Avenue also makes evident the familiar Wrightian formula for a closed building: entrance through a tunneled passageway toward the middle of a bifurcated mass. We have already seen this in a sequence of designs going back to the Larkin Building. Equally characteristic of Wright's design is the horizontality of the Guggenheim's exterior. A wide band—at once bridge and plat-

---

* Unwisely, because the location of any public building in a landscape park, other than those needed for park purposes, establishes a precedent. Landscape parks are not "empty space" waiting to be filled with buildings—or, for that matter, with highways, or innumerable athletic facilities. Their primary value is as landscape in the heart of the city, and other uses should be weighed with reference to this utterly unique function.

form—girds the building, to mask a full third of its height. Penetrating through the "bridge," yet resting on the "platform," monitor and ramp spread more than they rise. The dominating horizontals, their visual weight and the substantial support at the ground, all serve to root the building. Cantilevers and bridging notwithstanding, the Guggenheim, like Fallingwater—indeed, like all of Wright's buildings—remains earth-bound.† It thereby contrasts with Le Corbusier's stilted buildings which,

† In this connection, the extravagant void opening into the entrance hall at the downtown corner of the building seems out of proportion with the rest of the base. The square terrace contrasting with the cylinder of the monitor, which did not appear in the original model, is another indication of Wright's instinctive tendency to give horizontal emphasis to the rising element. It is interesting, too, that the outer walls, which are 20 inches thick at ground level need not have been this thick by half; but Wright wanted depth into which he could dig more sculptural openings than thinner walls would have permitted.

FIGURE 166. *The spiral shell versus the crab shell. Le Corbusier maintained that he got his initial inspiration for Notre-Dame at Ronchamp from a crab shell, a photograph of which he reproduced in his book* Ronchamp.

even when heavily supported, oppose the site in the classic sense of the man-ordered entity.

How revealing that major works by these two masters, Wright's Guggenheim and Le Corbusier's Notre-Dame at Ronchamp, have both been compared to seashells, but of divergent kinds (Figs. 166, 167). Le Corbusier, more specifically than Wright, asserted that his inspiration for the basic form of Ronchamp owed its start to a crab shell which he picked up on a Long Island beach during the course of a rare visit to the United States.[85] He translated the angular violence of the crab shell into the heaving, sagging anguish of his chapel, which appears to be miraculously sustained by the towers, the prow-like prop and the upward curve of the collapsed roof at its edges (inside, by a sliver of light between walls and roof so that the sagging canopy overhead seems to float barely free of support). Whereas Le Corbusier emulated the sculptural surface of the crab shell and its plastic enclosure of a unified space, Wright's work is rather to be identified with the process by which spiral-shelled marine life realizes itself. In these very talismans,

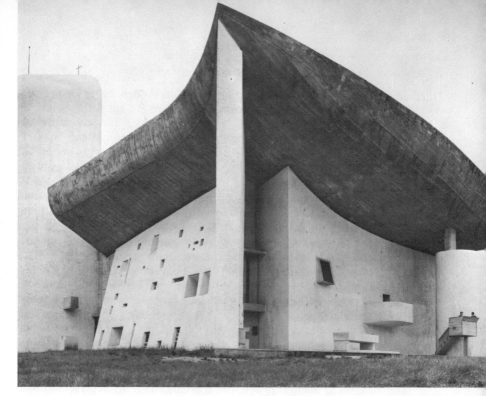

FIGURE 167. *Le Corbusier. Notre-Dame-du-Haut, Ronchamp (France), 1950–55.*

the typical opposition of the humanist and organic positions comes clear. The one contemplates the living entity as the resultant of the life principle: acquiescing to, but struggling against, the titanic forces of its environment, to become what it finally is. The other seizes on the force to which the life principle cleaves and thereby magnifies its potential. Le Corbusier's sculptural image possesses the quality of *having been made* at the conceptual stage, as an *a priori* act of personal will. A conservative structure of masonry walls and concrete beams is almost fully concealed within a turbulent composition of hollow forms tilted and curved, which respects its support only as the armature that lets the sculptural stage set stand. Wright's structural image possesses the sense of *having to be made* through the process of its building. In one instance, the creative act brought the building into being at a blow so to speak, as a total, defiant image; in the other, it was rather the generative act which identified the concept with the processes of its consummation. If Le Corbusier's image is more completely realized than Wright's, he also risked less than Wright, although the dramatic im-

343

mediacy of Ronchamp may make it appear as though he risked more.

How much Wright risked appears even before we enter the building, showing up in those blemishes of surface, modeling, and curvature of which we have already spoken. But free-form buildings present another kind of risk, which Le Corbusier has surmounted rather better than Wright. Free forms frequently bring unwanted images. Critics, as well as the casual observer, have variously ridiculed the Museum as a space ship, an ice-cream freezer, a cereal bowl, and so on. Tedious such taunts may be; yet, even when made with a degree of affection, they suggest that the form does not express its conceptual metaphor in the fully architectonic sense of the chapel at Ronchamp or, for that matter, of Fallingwater. Instead the architectural metaphor is always threatened by interference from representational metaphor of a trivializing or incongruous sort. Indeed the English artist, Robert Hamilton, has counted on the very ambiguity of the Guggenheim image—appearing simultaneously as a building, as an object, and as an abstract form—to create a series of pop images of it. Before the end of the sixties the Pop Art movement in painting and sculpture had come to architecture, and some architects deliberately created designs that depended on ironic oscillations of meaning. But such was clearly not Wright's intention.

The danger of such slippage from architectural to representational metaphor is not only increased with free forms, but possibly further increased by the kind of grandiosely diffuse conception with which the Guggenheim, and so many other of Wright's late works, began. A grand spiral eight or nine stories high wound around a great central space is inherently more difficult to translate into an intensely expressive shape than, say, the hanging roof surrounded by props and towers that Le Corbusier used as his starting point for the chapel at Ronchamp. Extraordinarily large, free-form shapes based on the simplest of geometric figures give the designer relatively less to hold onto in making his forms. Wright's conception for the Guggenheim was quite literally a slippery one. In the free-form works done toward the end of his life, he could not quite develop his forms beyond the point where they ceased to recall shapes more familiar to product design than to architecture. The ambiguous scale of the shapes, their seeming lack of thickness, their textureless surface, the too frequently "streamlined" effect of the curves, all reinforce the unfortunate comparisons. So, too, does his tendency in the late works to apply ornament to surfaces rather than to develop it as the exfoliation of the conception. This deficiency is less obtrusive in such incidents as the stamped leaf forms on the Guggenheim monitor than in his more lavish ornament in other late buildings—for example, his cast concrete repeats and, especially, his screen effects in metal— which bring juke boxes and automobile bumpers unwillingly to mind.

There is an element of pretension in any building which like the Guggenheim forcefully opposes itself to its neighbors as a uniquely monumental edifice, and then—once the impact of first view wears away—reveals itself as consisting of forms no more intrinsically interesting nor more subtly elaborated than those common to industrial design. This "incompleteness" of the museum's exterior massing contributes to the impersonal quality of what is, paradoxically, as personal a conception as any in Wright's career. In fact, many critics have alluded to the Guggenheim as a machine[36]—a characterization unexpected for any work by Wright, and least of all the Guggenheim. But there is more to the paradox: except for the perfunctory embellishment of the monitor, the Museum is (superficially at least) closer to the International Style than any in Wright's career. It is almost as though he wanted to demonstrate here how an organic architecture could appropriate the gamut of elements of the International Style—simple geometry, plain surfaces, the big container of space, ramps, levitation—and "go it one better." Not but that every one of these elements can be found in Wright's other work; hardly, however, in such conjunction. The parallel should not be pushed too far. Yet it is more than perversely whimsical. Close examination of Wright's works done after World War II shows considerable evidence of an unfortunate collision, and perhaps a rivalry that he was not completely aware of, between what was natural to his style and what were alien encroachments from the rest of "modern architecture."[37] One such intrusion occurs with the use of broad, textureless surfaces, which are especially evident in the Guggenheim and tend toward scaleless crudity. Another occurs with his use of sheets of plate glass that are overlarge for the visual weight of his massing. There is even an uncomfortable collisiveness of parts, so congenial to the Corbusian manner of composition, but especially at odds with the hierarchical arrangement of shapes and sizes congenial to Wright's organic approach to design, as this had characterized his earlier works. It is entirely possible that all of these faults can be attributed to haste; but there is a suspicion at least that many of Wright's late designs are, if not influenced by the work of other modern architects, faintly bedeviled by its pervasive presence, just as unassimilated Pop imagery seems to have infiltrated some of his late work without his intending it. The Guggenheim raises questions about both of these apparent influences.

The real experience of the Guggenheim is inside: into the shadow of the entrance walk, through the modestly scaled plate-glass doors, to the climax of the big interior space of Wright's "Pantheon." We are instantly aware of being in a sizable space, of course, but it does not burst upon us with the engulfing unity of its ancient predecessor. The

345

FIGURE 168. *Diagrammatic view of the interior of the Roman Pantheon,* 118–25 A.D., *from the entrance.*

perfect sphere which determines the interior of the Pantheon gives sufficient breadth for the cone of vision to sweep a full hemispheric area from the spacious entrance, up the cylindrical wall opposite and across the curve of the dome to a point just beyond the central oculus, all without any noticeable shift of vision (Fig. 168). In contrast, we view the central space of the Guggenheim as if in a well.[38] From the low entrance, our first view is of the lowest turns of the ramp, which fall like a Venetian blind before us. As we step from under the first turn of the ramp immediately overhead, more tiers of balustrades come successively into sight. Only an uncomfortable tilt of the head, however, brings the dome into view. Whereas the dome of the Pantheon curves as a continuous surface from the cylindrical drum of the walls below, the dome of the Guggenheim is within its own compartment in the topmost layer of space, requiring a separate act of vision. Once the full height of the space has been ascertained, therefore, we find it easier to inspect the curved space immediately before us than to remain looking upward. Moreover, as there is little to hold our gaze in the dome, there is no incentive to prolong the torture of looking up. Only something monumental, making use of this shaft of space, can bring the space alive. In its first dozen years or so of exhibitions two instances only come to mind when artists coped with the problem. Alexander Calder hung a gigantic mobile specially made for the occasion in the space against the rising shapes of a grandiose stabile on the floor (Fig. 170). By placing a carpet of metal tiles in a random checkerboard pattern on the ground floor of the Museum, Carl André solved the problem of the central well of space in another way—making the look down from the ramp to the floor more compelling than the look up to the dome. Yet were the Calder or André to have remained in the central space, the unity of the Museum is such that the featured work would always steal the show.

Viewed from the entrance floor, the cantilevers of the ramp are also devoid of visual interest, being blind boxes relieved only by an occasional hand clutching at the parapet, or by disembodied heads and shoulders bent nervously over it. The decorative quality of the ramp in the Morris Shop (Fig. 133) winding up the cylindrical plane of a wall inset with illuminated circles does not exist here. Whereas the Morris ramp occurs as an S-curve twirling freely around and upward to culminate in a lasso-like balcony, the Guggenheim ramp, when seen from the entrance, appears like a tightly compacted spring. The form is not so much an artistic development of Wright's spiral concept as a literal translation of it; not the positive shape that the Morris ramp became because the Guggenheim design goes too little beyond the crude state of its conception. Again we long for interesting detail, perhaps for occasional punctures of the ramp, even for the sheen of a metal hand-rail. To be sure, such decorative touches would have marred the shell-like purity of the conception. But the organic conception is already blighted by something industrial about these bulky, enigmatic chutes, something that brings to mind the gravity inclines which slide products from the roof to the loading platform of the old-fashioned, multi-storied mill.

And so our eye returns to the horizontal space of the plane on which we stand. It is not so much the circular ground for the grand space which curves around it, as in the Pantheon, but a spreading space of its own. Our eye sweeps around it, and beyond it, out through the plate-glass window to the garden at the corner of the building (Fig. 169). So much is in the classic Wrightian tradition, although the photograph from the door barely suggests a horizontal sweep of space that recalls themes from the prairie houses.

The outstanding feature of the ground floor is the start of the ramp. (To be sure, as we shall observe, Wright spoke of it rather as the *end* of the ramp for those descending it. But obviously on entering the Museum we do not experience it in this way.) For all that the ramp above the ground floor has a somewhat monotonous aspect from below, Wright's solution to the start of the ramp reveals his acumen as a designer. He planned his ramp so that as it begins the

347

FIGURE 169. *Solomon R. Guggenheim Museum. View across the ground level.*

ascent it creates an enlivening counter-movement to the slower curvature above. At a steeper pitch than what follows, the ramp here states
the theme of the building within immediate sight of the entrance, and
it climbs so quickly that it occupies only a relatively small area of
the ground-floor wall which is otherwise needed for doors, windows,
and counters. This initial incline serves as something of a gangplank
to the ramp rather than partaking of it. Hence the major ramp is
grounded neither physically nor symbolically, its first turn incidentally
serving as a perimeter ceiling for the ground floor, as do the horizontal
shelves and "banding lines" which Wright placed below ceiling height
in his houses. Finally, the start of the climb is skillfully located: it
originates near the museum entrance, within convenient distance of
elevator, stairs, and coatroom, and beside a lozenge-shaped pool that
gives a fillip to the off-center start of the climb, much as a newel post
calls attention to the start of a stair. It terminates at the entrance of
the so-called Grand Gallery, the point where the main ramp, for the
spectator entering the building at least, has its true beginning (Fig.
164). In such a detail, where functional, formal, and symbolic qualities
are so interwoven as to be inseparable, the true architect reveals himself, all the more because its unobtrusive appropriateness for the conception disguises the decisions that went into its making.

It is only as the climb begins that the building truly becomes exciting. To repeat: climb. Wright, however, recommended that one take
the elevator and circle downward. "The elevator is doing the lifting,"
as he put it, "the visitor the drifting from alcove to alcove."[39] The
arrangement of most of the museum shows depending on a chronological
presentation have encouraged this procedure by beginning at the top
of the ramp. Such authority to the contrary notwithstanding, the procedure may be ill-advised. Not only does this order reveal in reverse

348

the climactic succession of unfolding tiers of space, but walking down the ramp is a giddy experience. It is difficult to brake before the works of art. Traveled downward, the ramp of the Guggenheim is particularly subject to Robert M. Coates' criticism.

> . . . it has the same defects as the Grande[s] Galeries of the Louvre and other implacably long old-style museum galleries. It is a lengthy parade, lacking intimacy and variety, providing neither the means nor the incentive for pauses and dallying, and not even offering much "backing-away" space for leisurely contemplation. And here all this is aggravated by the fact that the incline, slight as it is, tends insidiously to hurry one on a little. (I'm assuming, of course, that the visitor takes the elevator to the top and walks down; no one in his right mind would do otherwise.)

To interrupt Coates at this point: let each determine for himself who is of "right mind," by trying the ramp in both directions—further evidence, if it is needed, that virtually every critical opinion about this controversial building can be countered by another diametrically opposed. And Coates concludes his observation,

> The whole museum thus becomes, in a sense, a place to "get through," and I can't help feeling that this aspect of the design must in part embody Wright's own probable reaction to the idea of touring a museum—get it over as quickly as possible.[40]

Climbing the easy three percent grade does not wholly eliminate Coates' objections, to be sure. It does, however, project us successively into the galleries. The space curves up in front of us, and we are caught by the webs like a cog in gears. It takes something of an effort to turn away from the pictures (as it should) and enjoy the views across the central well of space. Whatever one's opinion about the wisdom of showing paintings as so many gems in a "signet ring," thus emphasizing display at the expense of contemplation, there is no doubt that seeing paintings in this new way, up close and far away, side by side as well as vertically from tier to tier, has peripheral visual rewards. For one thing, distant glimpses are often surprisingly revealing as to the force of a masterly conception, even when one would not have characterized the work as especially "forceful" in its primary meaning. Since Wright intended that painting should be seen "in a realm enjoyed hitherto by music alone," it is significant that the space repeatedly encourages Baudelaire's test for what he termed the "musicality" of painting. "The right way to know if a picture is melodious is to look at it from far enough away to make it impossible to understand its subject or to distinguish its lines. If it is melodious, it already has a

349

meaning and has already taken its place in your store of memories."[41]
Of course many conventional galleries provide this experience; but here it
is thrust upon us. So is the delight of turning from the inspection of a
single work, to scan the substantial segment of a career or a movement
arcing away from us. Admittedly, for every full composition which offers
itself to distant view, a half dozen are ruthlessly cropped by the architecture, until—particularly when walking down the ramp, and propelled
by its inclination—we can suddenly feel ourselves in the midst of a
gigantic kaleidoscope with colored fragments whirling around us.

And there is always the movement of people, and of fragments
of people, somewhat distracting, but too fascinating an experience for
us to wish it otherwise (Fig. 170). There is the somewhat unnerving
experience of visually colliding with the same people over and over
across the well of space, without necessarily meeting. (What might a
movie maker do with such encounters!) There is the cloud-like clumping
of silhouettes, and abrupt scatter or wisping away into sudden void.
Always there is the ceaseless, random movement, but in the hypnotizing

FIGURE 170. Solomon R. Guggenheim Museum. General views of the ramp, one of them showing Alexander Calder's mobiles and stabiles in the central space.

legato of the Museum, the slow stroll, the shifting stance, the step forward to examine a picture, and the eclipse (or partial eclipse) of the viewer, the step backward and gradual reappearance. Save for the more liberated movement of the ground floor, the groping, tentative movement is always contained by the circular path which spins so surely around the space, and collides with its own swelling, out into the void and over the blue, lozenge-shaped pool below.

For Wright (and how like Sullivan!) the pool was "the oval seedpod containing globular units."[42] Viewed from one of the topmost parapets, the lozenge, its concave-convex permutations in the approach ramp, and its echo the full height of the building with the modular inswelling of the ramp at every level in the area of the utility core, all work together to provide a gentler, more specifically organic arabesque within the larger vortex.

Repeatedly the ramp spins the circuit, eventually to the deepest, beautifully illuminated, topmost level. This is not exactly a climax to the ramp, since it is of a piece with the lower levels. Some sort of observation area overlooking Central Park—part lounge, part cafeteria, part gallery—may someday achieve the climax here that Wright neglected. The small observation globe in Wright's original scheme (Fig. 137) would have furnished a more decisive climax, although it might have become a point of congestion for crowds trying to squeeze into it, and to little purpose. In any event, by the time the building was under way, Wright seems to have given but little thought to an exceptional spatial or functional treatment at the top of his building. Thus an architectural entity, the ramp goes nowhere.‡ Its "beginning" (following Wright's recommendation that the visitor start at the top of the ramp) is at its end; and its "end," back at the entrance—all of which is especially disconcerting in a unified space that makes the path from here to there so emphatic. In this ramp without a sure starting point, and utterly without climactic conclusion, the sense of rotary motion takes on a monotonous insistence.

But invariably? The answer is no, for many of those who initially were distracted by the experience of going round and round the ramp have found (to their surprise) that repeated visits to the Museum so accustom them to the experience that it somewhat recedes from consciousness, thus permitting the works of art to reassert themselves. Repeated exposure to the Museum reveals the unimportance of the element of novelty in the experience. Once the shock of our own unusual

‡ The ramp in the Morris Shop is similarly disappointing. It leads to a circle of shelves around a tight aisle, a destination that is less an upstairs shop than a storeroom.

situation passes, we begin to sense the challenge of the building as a momentous architectural event, in which movement takes possession of a big, unified, molded space, not simply by occurring within it, but literally by making it. Difficult as the space is to work with, Messer has warmed to the challenge because of its exceptional nature.[43] The space does not merely ask for the "make do" of compromise between museum practices and the exceptional character of the building; it forces a reconsideration of old ways of doing things in the necessity of coming to terms with what is. Will it, Messer wonders, ultimately infect the art which it houses, until this lives at ease in the space it inhabits? Certainly architectural space will become more extravagantly sculptural. Surely, then, painting and sculpture will change with it, as contrariwise, modern painting and sculpture have already transformed architecture—and, it should be added, as modern painting, sculpture, and architecture have influenced renovations of the Beaux-Arts museum until not even the Old Masters are seen as they were a few years ago.

THE MEANING OF THE VASE

Such is the experience of the Guggenheim as a space—and as a space designed for the specific function of a museum. Since the Guggenheim is so evidently a culminating monument to its architect and his philosophy, it finally encourages reflection as to its meaning in these respects.

Appropriately enough, the Guggenheim fronts on Central Park (Fig. 171), the first of the great urban landscape parks consciously planned from the start as such (in 1855) by Frederick Law Olmsted with Calvert Vaux. Like Central Park the Guggenheim is informed by the same tradition of nineteenth-century naturalism. In the physical context of Manhattan, the Park and the Museum represent the most conspicuous attempts to counteract what Wright and Olmsted regarded as the evil unnaturalness of the metropolis. Continuity of form, winding path, and enveloping environment: these themes, indigenous to the naturalistic tradition, appear in both. If these themes permeate all of Wright's works, they do so in something of an ultimate sense in the Guggenheim, for in the ramp the three themes become heroically one. Each, moreover, provides a node for diffuse analogy, thereby extending Wright's philosophy of architecture toward his philosophy of life.

In this philosophy, continuity is the overarching theme—its essence, as Wright insisted. His continuity, however, is not that of the box of the International Style, with space diffusely open in all directions, and

FIGURE 171. *Solomon R. Guggenheim Museum and Central Park.*

amorphously extended by plate glass. His is the continuity of nature, of matter expanding as a foliated or crystalline geometry, making its space as it physically occupies space. Whether this interwoven continuity of matter and space radiates from a core (as in most of Wright's compositions) or wraps a central void (as in some of his compositions, including the Guggenheim), the generative principle of form opening to further form persists.

The winding path and the enveloping environment are corollaries of this continuity. Movement along the path constitutes the physical experience of the continuity, literally and figuratively taking us through it and permitting us to act in it. This mobility, intimately related in his mind to the expansive continuity of organic experience, Wright equated with man's freedom in a democratic (or "natural") society. To Vincent Scully the monumental celebration of movement without destination along the ramp epitomizes the expansive, directionless response of the frontiersman to limitless space.[44] The cumulative spread of the typical

354

"prairie house" eventually begets Wright's Broadacre society with its hum of superhighways and commuting hover planes (Fig. 172). In the Guggenheim, lack of focus or climax emphasizes mobility. Winding down the ramp, as Wright prescribed, Scully has noted that the sense of spaciousness at the top disappears at the bottom. As memory of the experience dims, we must return; but to return is again to be lured down the path. Subsequent, and even contemplated, alterations at the top of the ramp do not (or will not) substantially alter the experience. Scully sees the wind of the Guggenheim ramp as another of those pervasive American images of ceaseless movement to no-destination, such as Cooper's Natty Bumppo, Twain's Mississippi, Melville's whaling chase, or Whitman's Open Road.

In the Guggenheim, however, the road turns in on itself, to fashion the all-enveloping environment—a third major theme in Wright's organic philosophy. It serves as the passive counterpart to the action of the Open Road, as the dream of the frontiersman for campfire or hearth as a place in placelessness. Wright repeatedly used another metaphor when speaking of his architecture: that of the vase. The source for it was Lao-tse's aphorism "The reality of the vase is the space inside" —a line that expressed one of Wright's deepest convictions. Lao-tse's vase is the hollow emblem in Wright's architectural philosophy, as the hearth pylon is the solid emblem. In the Guggenheim, he most completely realized the truth of the vase, open at the top, closed at the base, even swelling as it rises in a manner customary to ceramics. In further accord with the potter's tradition, he "laid up" the vase of coils of substance; yet, as Kaufmann reminds us, in a particularly intangible way. Here is "space contained by space."

The analogy of the vase crystallizes sentiments which profoundly and diffusely informed his organic philosophy. Whatever analogies the Guggenheim may suggest to the Pantheon and to the giant scale of the geometry of Roman imperial architecture (which were doubtless unspecific in Wright's conception), the Museum also invokes the exotic strain that runs through Wright's work.[45] Without reference to a particular exotic tradition, it may at one moment call up the spherical mass of the Mayan Observatory at Chichen Itza raised on a massive platform, at another an inverted version of Mayan pyramids and Near Eastern ziggurats, or perhaps the scaleless enigmas of Indian and Oriental stupas and Buddhas. One specific recollection of this type lies concealed: in cross section the profile of the dome and its surrounding roof, in conjunction with the projected prominence of the topmost turn of the ramp, recalls similar profiles in the roofs of traditional Japanese construction (Fig. 156); the wind of the ramp perhaps even the tiering of a pagoda. Wright came to love, and to collect, exotic art as a

FIGURE 172. *Frank Lloyd Wright. Drawing for Broadacre City, on which he worked intermittently during the years 1934–58.*

result of his nineteenth-century conditioning. The exotic strain in the plant-inspired intricacies of Sullivan's ornament may have furthered this enthusiasm, as well as the exotic strand in Sullivan's effusions during those sessions in the drafting room when, the day's work over, he could unburden himself of his thoughts. In any event, for Wright even more than for Sullivan, this exoticism accorded with broader trends in American culture: the negative act of at least partial rejection of Europe, and the positive act of alignment with the strains of exoticism found in Transcendentalism,[46] as this movement impinged on "organic" philosophies of esthetics and morality. With these thoughts we look again at the Guggenheim—the winding strip of lighted space with the tiny figures moving in the vast environment now takes on the quality of a Chinese landscape scroll.

But the encompassing shelter of the vase-like building has other connotations. The spirit of his work simply cannot be grasped without taking into account certain feminine effects on his creativity. A comprehensive exhibition covering sixty years of his work, held at the old quarters of the Museum in 1953, and with the design for the new building as its climax, provided evidence very much to the point. Wright wrote his own captions for the catalogue, and his own dedication.

> To my Mother Anna Lloyd Wright
> Friedrich Froebel, 1876
> Dankmar Adler and Louis H. Sullivan, 1893
> My Wife, Olgivana

First, to his strong-willed, devoted mother, Wright's only parent after his father walked out on the family one day (as Wright was to do in his turn); a woman who had always envisioned her son as an architect. Then, to Froebel, inventor of the kindergarten games by which his mother had trained him for his career after the Philadelphia Centennial Exposition of 1876. So 1876 represented the start of his architectural training, as 1893, the year of his leaving Adler & Sullivan, represented its conclusion. Finally, to the wife whom Wright found after years of marital and extramarital difficulties.

For good reason is Wright without peer in our age as a designer of the relatively modest, privately owned house, since even the largest partake of the fine qualities of the smallest—without peer, in this regard, it seems fair to say, in the history of architecture. It is not merely that he created extraordinary houses in such numbers, throughout a long career, and, in the process, revolutionized house design. It is also that his achievement stemmed from (indeed, depended upon) circumstances so specifically, even so cloyingly, domestic. As *pater familias* of an enlarged family he carried out his professional life at the two Taliesins. So Unity Church makes an enlarged family of the congregation; the administration buildings for Larkin and Johnson Wax "one big happy family" of their working forces, and possibly too much so. Even the Guggenheim, though lacking the quality of Taliesin that Wright originally intended, does what it can to convert the host of visitors into a community (or rather the semblance of a community) within the big shelter provided by the *pater familias.*

So the Guggenheim must be seen, finally, as a monument to certain symbolic themes in his architecture. It may be *the* culminating monument to these themes, *the* climactic monument of his late years, simply because of the directness with which it summarizes Wright's career while achieving in an unexpected manner, and at large scale, a unity and daring which none of the other late works completed after World War II quite possess.

However, in this monument culminating such a long and creative career we sense a certain "social hiatus." It partly results from the fact

357

that Wright, like Sullivan, never filled the gap between the Individual and Democracy, a failure which Tocqueville observed as characteristically American.[47] On the one hand, the assertive ego; on the other, the diffuse conglomerate; in between, no sense of Society, except, and this was surely true of Wright, for the family and communitarian (or family-like) groups. Standing at one of the topmost parapets of the Guggenheim, looking down on the peripheral movement within the funicular void, seeing how "the people" acquiesce to the spiral, knowing how functionaries have labored to complete an environment overwhelmingly given, we may be provoked to ponder the double implication of the Guggenheim as both an act of defiance and a statement of faith. Missing here, and missing in all of Wright's work, is the sense of Society in other than familial or communitarian groupings. Wright's architecture never really addressed itself to the institutional groupings of metropolitan society— more formal, more impersonal, more elaborately rationalized than family or community arrangements. Surely he had his justifications. As an ur-bane man himself, he could not but deplore the lack of urbanity in the American city, nor had he completely failed to indicate ways of over-coming it; witness certain of his apartment complexes and skyscraper schemes of the twenties and thirties. But these had never come to fruition, had never led to further urban commissions. If so, his disillusionment might have been prevented. As for his eventual fame, this did not much change the shocking neglect of his genius by government, big business, and big universities. So it is hardly surprising that the Guggenheim some-what disappoints us as an institutional and urban monument. Wright's original ideas for display prove the point. The cozy circlet of administra-tive offices and library (as they originally existed) confirm it, recalling the facilities for the bureaucracy of a small town rather than those for a major museum.

Finally, as the monument which probably best culminates the last phase of Wright's career, the Guggenheim has an emotional baldness which also cheats us of the depth and complexity of experience that we might have hoped for. To the very end Wright had to "show them." And of course he did. Was it the frontier spirit that impelled him to "show them" long after the need was past? Or the habit of a lifetime of battling against odds? Or the sheer race against time to say all that he had in him, with commissions at last plentiful? Did he mean in the last spill of gargantuan schemes to project his idea of organic architecture beyond his own career, in the sense of showing how much further it could go, and thereby demonstrating its inexhaustibility? Or was it some combination of all these considerations?[48] In any event, he worked to the end of his life with furious energy, perhaps in the last decade at least with some loss of power in design (although none in conception), and perhaps distracted by the very plethora of projects which he tried to push through. If we express some disappointment in the Museum, it is not that we wish to denigrate Wright's virtuosity, rather that we wish his final design could have been marked by greater concentration, serenity, and meditation. From a man who contributed so much, it seems ungrateful to ask more; yet his career is uncapped by those depths of austerity, solemnity, mystery, pathos, quiet, acceptance, that the old-age style of so towering a master with such plastic means at his disposal should have brought. This is the ultimate deficiency of his genius, and perhaps of his world. It is borne home in the Guggenheim as much as in any of Wright's late works. In conjunction with the unavoidable defects of its material realization, its baldness of emotional statement leaves the Museum as something of a sketch of Wright's intention.

Yet what a grand sketch! The Guggenheim is not merely a dazzling structure thrown over a flat floor plane; nor a sculptural fantasy for special effect. To repeat, it posits a curved space making itself into a building out of its climb and curvature, with floors, wall, and roof all integrally of the process. It creates a kind of architectural experience for which scant precedent exists, and none in any such monumental statement. In these respects, no building of the mid-twentieth century more bravely challenges the future. Wright saw to that.

CHAPTER VI

What the Building "Wants To Be": Louis I. Kahn's Richards Medical Research Building at the University of Pennsylvania

Thru the nature—why
Thru the order—what
Thru design—how

One should not be surprised to find, in fact one would expect *to find, an archaic quality in architecture today. This is because real architecture is just beginning to come to grips with a whole new order of artistic expression, growing, in turn, from the new set of tasks which society has set for the architect.*

It must start with the archaic first. The archaic begins like Paestum. Paestum is beautiful to me because it is less beautiful than the Parthenon. It is because from it the Parthenon came.

LOUIS KAHN (1955, 1960, 1961)

SYNTHESIS TOWARD ARCHITECTURAL "REALITY"

A central utility tower radiating three laboratory towers in a pin-wheel configuration, which, in turn, throws out stacks for utilities and stairs: Louis Kahn's Alfred Newton Richards Medical Research Building at the University of Pennsylvania is hardly handsome in an ingratiating way.*

* This essay was originally written before the addition of more towers (shown in the model, fig. 173, in a preliminary scheme for the elevation, fig. 174, and in the completed building, fig. 204, comprising the research center for biology. These are variations of the initial towers, but in my opinion are somewhat weaker both visually and conceptually, and do not overcome various functional deficiencies. To avoid confusion, and because it would add little of substance here, I have eliminated the Biology Building from this discussion. Readers interested in photographs and commentary on it may consult "Kahn's Second Phase at Pennsylvania," *Progressive Architecture*, September 1964, pp. 208–13.

On the contrary, it is a blunt building, a "real" building. That favorite adjective of certain English architectural reformers of the 1840's and 1850's, inspired partly by ecclesiastical and partly by rationalistic idealism, comes to mind when confronting this building. The ideal of architectural "reality" was variously defined in the theory and work of such nineteenth-century architects as A. Welby Pugin and William Butterfield, and was at least peripherally influential for the criticism of Ruskin; but in essence it designated a comprehensive ethics of materials, structure, and function made emphatically apparent in an earnest and solid manner. Kahn's building is real in its tangibility; real in materials and structure; ostensibly, if not literally, real in the inevitability with which the composition unfolds from a functional conception; hence real in its scorn of superficial beauty. If "beautiful" at all, it is so as a dogmatic manifestation of character.

By the middle of the 1950's the forthrightness of the more austere reaches of the regional and folkish concerns of the forties had been reinforced by Mies' use of the blunt I-beam and by Le Corbusier's rugged sculptural effects in his late architecture. The Pop Art enthusiasm of the fifties, with its brash embrace of the laconic and strident aspects of the modern "mass consumption society," worked in part toward the same end. Not that the coincidence of these diverse influences eventuated in a self-conscious program or movement, but rather in a diffuse point of view resulting from shared concerns. Insofar as the point of view became anything like a movement, it did so in the New Brutalism in England, of which Reyner Banham served as principal publicist and, eventually, historian.[1] In effect, except for some of its Pop Art overtones and a lack of religiosity, New Brutalism represented a reincarnation of the sort of attitudes that had polarized around the Old Realism of the mid-nineteenth century. Not only the nature of the reform, but the nature of the discontent, linked the two episodes. In the 1950's, the Angry Young Architects followed at discreet distance the lead of angrier young writers, possibly with some fear of being left behind at a time when postures of indignation among the "concerned" were at least as fashionable as they were justified. To the restless and discontented in the profession, modern architecture had lost its one-time moral impulse and revolutionary zeal. "Will success spoil modern architecture?" asked the title of a popular magazine article of the period. This article articulated the widespread doubt about the superficial sleekness of much of the metal-and-glass building of the period, and questioned the frantic efforts to dispel the monotony of this misused mode with pretty, decorative screening, shallow historical allusion, or outrageous structural exhibitionism.

To Banham, the Brutalist pleas for tougher, more serious, more moral approaches to architecture seemed, for a few years after 1955, on the brink of regenerating modern architecture. In fact, New Brutalist convictions did result in some notable, if indecisive, buildings by younger architects. But the movement, if movement it ever was, flared briefly. In 1966, Banham published *The New Brutalism: Ethic or Aesthetic?* as a self-confessed "survivor" of something that had passed. Something that had been an incipient movement, perhaps; but a set of developments establishing a trend, almost certainly not.

Opposed to what he regarded as the muscular posturing of most Brutalism, Kahn nevertheless appears in Banham's book; although not for his Medical Research Building, which was a bit late for the Brutalist episode. The building, however, was surely informed by some of the same ideas that came to momentary focus in the Brutalist position. It suffices as a preliminary definition of Kahn's aim to call it an effort to locate his building within a large conception of "reality," as this was understood in its old-fashioned sense, but as this old-fashioned sense had acquired fresh relevance. "Reality" provides the context for the moral orientation of his architectural esthetic. It also suggests the Richards Medical Research Building as a synthesis at a time when the state of modern architecture was ripe for such synthesis. Kahn's building represents an initial synthesis of ideas central to the three great masters of the modern movement, Wright, Le Corbusier, and Mies; this, moreover, in a work which is in no sense a pastiche of other men's inspirations, but an authentic creative act.

If the site for the building is unprepossessing except for the botanical garden out of which the rear elevation rises, Kahn has made the most of it. Crowded on three sides by a miscellany of purplish-red brick structures (with which the brick facing of the new building harmonizes), the laboratories do not appear as one sees them in the model or in the elevations prepared in Kahn's office (Figs. 173, 174). In these, they are seen as a spreading silhouette, where the towers for medical research (1957–61) are extended by lower towers for biological research (1957, redesigned slightly and built 1961–64); these preliminaries recall a fortified medieval citadel like Carcassonne, or, more immediately, the towered profile of the Italian hilltown of San Gimignano. Both are favorite images of Kahn's. But when we actually view the laboratories, at ground level, it is only from the rear, across the cramped botanical garden, that we sense the profile of a towered medieval town (Fig. 175). By climbing one of the nearby buildings we get a similar impression—preferably across Cope & Stewardson's turn-of-the-century "Elizabethan" quadrangle immediately fronting the laboratories (Fig. 176). The frothy turrets of this early Beaux-Arts fantasy point up the severe, sterner neo-medievalism of Kahn's towers, although the latter are in fact as close to grain elevators as to medieval prototypes.

FIGURE 173. *Louis Kahn. Wooden model of the Alfred Newton Richards Medical Research Building (the high cluster of towers to the left) and the Biological Research Building (low blocks and towers to the right), University of Pennsylvania, Philadelphia, 1957–61/1961–64. The Richards Building consists of the central service block linked to three peripheral laboratory towers, each with its peripheral utility and stair towers. The entrance to the Medical Research complex occurs beneath the frontmost laboratory tower, as indicated by the pyramidal steps.*

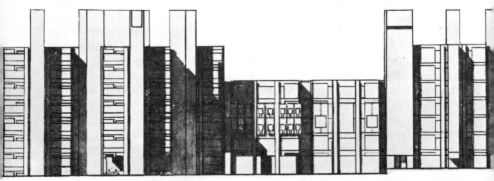

FIGURE 174. *Richards Medical Research Building and Biological Research Building. Preliminary design for the north elevation. Some alterations were made in the biology complex before construction.*

FIGURE 175. *Richards Medical Research Building. South (rear) elevation from the botanical garden.*

Since Kahn's building must be searched out amidst the densely packed urban campus of the University of Pennsylvania, one customarily experiences it first, not as a profile seen at a distance, but as a bulk confronted in the interior of a medieval town. What is lost as silhouette is gained as physical presence (Fig. 177). The masonry towers rise abruptly above one, projecting out from the laboratory platforms and looming over them. The predominating sensation, especially to the uninitiated, is the thrust outward and upward of mysterious blind elements from the stacked window areas. A stack of windows occasionally projects as the dominating entity of a particular view; but always enframed by the towers. In most views, however, the window stacks are inset and cradled. A building, Kahn has said, is a "harboring thing."[2]

Only the cantilevering of the floor slabs, permitting the climactic glazed corners, prevents the voids from losing out in their visual competition with the masses. The physically positive, but psychically negative, element of the blind walls opposes the physically negative, but psychically

FIGURE 176. *Richards Medical Research Building, in the background, with Cope & Stewardson's "Elizabethan" quadrangle in the foreground. The quadrangle was begun in 1895, most of it built in stages through 1907, although various elements continued to be completed as late as 1950.*

FIGURE 177. *Opposite: Richards Medical Research Building. Close view of the laboratory towers. The blind peripheral tower at the center is a utility stack; the tower to the right contains stairs. Entrance to the complex of towers is made from the open "porch" at the base of this tower.*

positive, element of the windows in a staccato counterpoint of solid and void. This forceful opposition of the tangible and intangible has nothing in common with Wright's conception of the building mass as an organic entity, with space permeating it like a tree (Robie House), or with space encircled as in a vase (Guggenheim). Kahn's building possesses something of the stark drama of being and nothingness in Le Corbusier's later architecture (Fig. 178), where solid and void continually shift their roles, relative to one another, as the positive and negative aspects of the composition.

If Le Corbusier comes immediately to mind when one first experiences Kahn's building, it is not only because of its sculptural quality, but also because its sculptural complexity stems from Kahn's comparable concern to break up the institutional lump into human-sized compartments. In his *Unité d'Habitation* at Marseilles, Le Corbusier conceived of an apartment house as a gigantic cabinet into which the apartment units were

366

FIGURE 178. Le Corbusier. *Apartment House* (Unité d'Habitation), *Mar-seilles*, 1946–52. *The free-form spiral structure at the end of the building contains fire stairs from an internal shopping street behind the louvers which are barely visible at the top of the photograph.*

slid like drawers, or—Le Corbusier being French by choice, if not by birth—like wine bottles into a rack (Fig. 179). So Kahn put his building together compartmentally: the "studio" laboratories piled as separate entities against the blind stacks for utilities and stairs. If, however, Le Corbusier's image begins with the *prisme pur*—as the somewhat arbitrary gesture of his sculptural genius with compartments of use encompassed by the larger shapes—Kahn's image is specifically, even dogmatically, alive to its program. In his phrase, the building "insists on what it wants to be." The implications are rather more partly Wrightian and partly Miesian. The Wrightian qualities do not stem from the Guggenheim, but from Wright's early works. Wright's influence is felt in the jointed growth of the building and its crystalline configuration. The laboratory towers radiate from their heart-core as the prairie house from its hearth-core.† Even more, the blind, upended utility towers stiffly gathered around their central spaces recall both the configuration and the function of similar elements in Unity Church and especially in the Larkin Building (Figs. 143, 144, 146, and 149). The fact that Kahn himself has confessed that he was not particularly aware of Wright while creating his building,[3] merely demonstrates how profoundly it comes to grips with modernity through the process of its own integral realization, rather than through eclectic pilferage.

Wright's specific "organic" image, with its metaphoric overtones in nature despite its abstractness as geometry, disappears. Kahn's image is more laconic. It grows as a *building,* as the architectonic thing itself. In this respect it possesses an objectivity which is Miesian, while participating generally in the symbolic objectivity of the modern movement as this was formulated in the twenties.‡ Kahn's objectivity, like Mies', explicitly calls for a certain passivity by the architect in the initial stage of the design. Thus the building for Mies is "almost nothing." For Kahn it is letting the building happen "as what it wants to be," before he intervenes to design what it has become—giving line, before reeling in.

Specifically Miesian is Kahn's definition of architecture in a structural sense, so that the completed building exists in terms of the parts of which it is made. Kahn extends Mies' dissections of structure to other aspects of the building. He also follows Mies' lead in accentuating the discreteness of the parts by combining them bluntly, side by side, much as the I-beam outrigging of 860 Lake Shore appears *beside* the sheathed structural column to which it is welded (Figs. 106, 108). Thus, in his composition, Kahn largely avoids the interweaving of fragmented parts

† *American Buildings and Their Architects: Progressive and Academic Ideals at the Turn of the Twentieth Century,* Chapter 3.
‡ See Chapter 4 above.

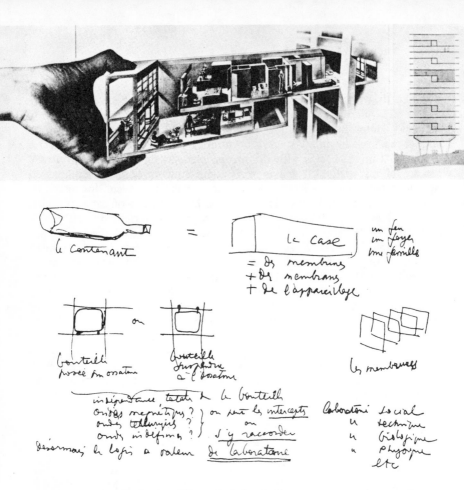

FIGURE 179. *Le Corbusier. The principle of the apartment unit as a drawer, or as a wine bottle placed in a rack. The cross-sectional view of the* Unité d'Habitation *illustrates the standard apartment as being a two-story duplex on one side of the building, with one story running through to the opposite side, and with balconies on both sides. A similar apartment slid in from the opposite direction leaves a corridor between the units to serve both of them on every third floor of the building.*

characteristic of Wright's works (and especially evident in such early work in the prairie style as the Robie House).* On the whole, Kahn's

* The only areas of any consequence in which the parts of the Richards Medical Research Building do interweave in something of a Wrightian sense are the open space-frame ceilings of the laboratories through which ducts and conduits are threaded; see pp. 407f. below.

position depends on additive juxtaposition rather than on fusion. Because the architecture is literally broken down to its A-B-C's, then so assembled that unit-A discretely abuts unit-B, which discretely abuts unit-C (and so on), the composition takes on a didactic quality, and reminds us that both Mies and Kahn have been outstanding teachers. In this sense, Kahn's building merits his own description of it as "archaic."[4] Somewhat impersonal, it appears as the axiomatic demonstration of an intensely personal investigation—so stark, so methodical, and so comprehensive as, like 860 Lake Shore, to provide an "archaic" source of inspiration for further, and suaver, development.

Broadly speaking, however, the elements of which Kahn builds his architecture differ in two respects from those of Mies. As opposed to Mies' preference for the linear elegance of the metal frame, Kahn's preference for reinforced concrete and masonry tends to give his buildings greater bulk and rougher textures. Of course the comparison is not absolute, for Mies also occasionally used reinforced concrete for his structures; the structural members of some of his buildings are very substantial; and even his most attenuated structures possess a visual force which makes the usual metal-and-glass wall seem insubstantial. Even so, Kahn himself distinguishes between the qualities of reinforced-concrete construction and those of metal-frame. "Concrete columns are better," he maintains.

They're real columns! Of course, steel is a marvelous material. You can do wonderful things with it, build great machines, but in architecture you're not building airplanes after all, are you?

A building should be a more stable and *harboring* thing, If you can now put columns as much as 100 feet apart you may lose more than you gain because the sense of the enclosed space disappears.[5]

Real columns! And (by implication) *real* walls! Once more the revival of the old-fashioned nineteenth-century adjective, "Real" implies a palpable presence, a physical actuality. This quality depends, in turn, on declared structure, on substantial girth (and on its corollary, firm relation to the ground), on rugged texture, on revelation of function, on straightforward vigor of conception and execution, on a sense of abiding things which comes from contact with (but not the replication of) historical precedent. Real *columns!* Steel could not appear quite as "columnar" as stone, which had provided columns throughout the history of architecture. This comprehensive meaning of reality as palpable presence in a physical, esthetic, and psychic sense accounts for the different kinds of materials which Mies and Kahn favor (the former more by circumstance than through condition, the latter by preference). It also accounts for the different ways in which they handle the same material. Both have made

371

extensive use of brick. In his American work, Mies habitually preferred a hard-surfaced or glazed material, which he used as paneled infilling for his linear frame. Kahn inclines toward walls of rougher, duller brick, which (as in the Richards Medical Research Building) he characteristically folds into boxes for discrete spaces. Real *walls!* The trend toward such "reality," extending and at the same time opposing the International Style, which is especially associated with the work of Le Corbusier and Aalto beginning in the thirties, and is evident in Breuer's work by the late forties, here attains more comprehensive statement.

These box-like elements together with the stacks of individual studio-laboratories, mark another, and more important, way in which Kahn diverges from Mies. Mies' omnibus container, into which all functions can be dropped, gives way in Kahn's design to a complex mass comprised of particularate spaces that declare their specific functions.

> If I were to define architecture in a word, I would say that architecture is a thoughtful making of spaces. It is not filling prescriptions as clients want them filled. It is not fitting uses into dimensioned areas. . . . It is a creating of spaces that evoke a feeling of use. Spaces which form themselves into a harmony good for the use to which the building is to be put.
>
> I believe the architect's first act is to take the program that comes to him and change it. Not to satisfy it, but to put it into the realm of architecture, which is to put it into the realm of spaces.
>
> An architectural space must reveal the evidence of its making by the space itself. It cannot be a space when carved out of a greater structure meant for a greater space, because the choice of a structure is synonymous with the light which gives image to that space. Artificial light is only a single, tiny, static moment in light and is the light of night and never can equal the nuances of mood created by the time of day and the wonder of the seasons.
>
> A plan of a building should read like a harmony of spaces in light.[6]†

So Kahn amends the Miesian esthetic, which, nevertheless, fundamentally conditioned his own point of view: toward more emphatic struc-

---

† The final sentence in Kahn's statement echoes Le Corbusier's familiar definition of architecture as the "wise, correct, magnificent, play of masses in the light." Kahn significantly shifts Le Corbusier's emphasis on "masses" to "spaces." In other words, interior uses rather than external aspect should determine the sculptural quality of the building.

ture on the one hand, toward the revelation of function through a complex of distinct spaces on the other—the first an extension of Mies' approach to design; the second a break with it.

FINDING THE "FORM" OF THE BUILDING

Since Kahn holds that the spaces containing the activities of the building are its ultimate reality, he starts with these. Merely to provide for the diverse activities sheltered by the building, however, is insufficient. The architect should make them visible, thereby enhancing them for the user and celebrating them for the viewer. Before learning of Kahn's design, the scientists may well have envisioned their laboratory-to-be as a factory-like block, in the typical manner of the International Style, with open warehouse floors for flexible partitioning, and with utility runs for the equipment concealed either in the hollows of double walls, or in those between the ceiling of one story and the floor of the next above. But Kahn drastically altered this standard: "The architect's first act is to take the program that comes to him and change it. . . . to put it into the realm of architecture, which is to put it into the realm of spaces." Everything that subsequently "happened" depended on his redefinition.

He started the commission with his general conviction that architecture consists in giving maximum visibility to what he calls the "life of the building," and with the following three specific premises. First, he argued, the scientist works alone or within a small group, but requires constant contact with colleagues and other small groups. The ideal building for a laboratory is therefore a cluster of studios and not a warehouse. Second, the scientist works in a complicated and potentially dangerous technological environment. Thus, services should not intrude into the space allocated to the studio-laboratory and, above all, noxious fumes should be immediately withdrawn from this work area. Finally, the limited site—a long, narrow plot squeezed by existing buildings—made a vertical building mandatory.

Premises of this sort comprise the "Form" of the building, which Kahn differentiates from its "Design."[7] This differentiation is the core of his architectural philosophy. The full implications of his building, as well as the pedagogical impact of it on the profession, are only to be appreciated in the light of Kahn's philosophy. Form (to begin only with *part* of his definition for this term) is "what characterizes one existence from another." To use Kahn's own illustration, the form of a spoon is a "con-

373

tainer" and an "arm." Hence Form has "neither shape nor dimension." Now it must be admitted that Kahn's use of "form" is to a degree perverse, since giving form to the building has customarily marked the end of the architect's job rather than its amorphous (shapeless and dimensionless) beginning. With some justice, Reyner Banham has complained of Kahn's "willful obscurantism in which 'form' is made to mean 'formless.'"[8] Not quite "formless" however, since a spoon which has attained the conceptual level of container and arm is already outside the realm of chaos, although no aspiring young designer in silver could expect to make much of a career with this discovery. For a complex art like architecture, however, where the basic elements are less automatically given, merely to discern the container and the arm of the problem requires a patient receptivity which the impetuous, flashy, commercial, or matter-of-fact temperament will miss.

Kahn's spoon analogy may give the misleading impression that by form he means a catalogue of functions assembled by ticking off items on the client's program (perhaps slightly altered because of the architect's presumed superiority in organizing the building); then set down in rough diagrammatic form by the architect by way of easing into his design. An architectural diagram in this usual sense is, in short, an inventory of specific items and their logical relationship, more or less in search of a unifying "conception." But this is precisely what Kahn does *not* mean by form. An imaginary comparison may help to clarify his definition. Another architect with Kahn's commission might have begun its consideration something like this, all the while contriving his diagram as he muses. "Let's see, ten scientists . . . allowing so many square feet for each . . . a space about so big . . . now the ductwork will come in from a central stack along the ceiling . . ." and so on. Kahn does not proceed in this manner at all. As his starting point, he seeks to identify what a "laboratory" *might* be as a thing which functions simultaneously in a physical and psychic sense: "a creating of spaces that evoke a feeling of use. . . . [that] form themselves into a harmony good for the use to which the building is to be put." He approaches his task in the spirit in which one would invent a "spoon" were this unknown. Thus, to imagine Kahn's musings over the same problem: "The ideal laboratory is a studio . . . the studio is a cubicle of limited size . . . the studios are surrounded by stacks for utilities . . . the stacks are closed; the studios open . . ." and so on. In the first instance the data tend to be very specific statements of fact; the diagram an abstraction from this specificity. In the second instance the data are general statements of a concrete nature; the resulting schema points to this concreteness, but in a non-specific manner. In Kahn's words (and now a fuller definition), "Form encompasses a harmony of systems, a sense of Order and that which charac-

374

terizes one existence from another."‡ Translating his definition back into the start of his thinking about the laboratories: a harmony of systems (a system of working spaces and a system of utility tubes); a sense of order (cubicles of space in towers with ducts and pipes of an indeterminant shape around them, resulting in an irregular meander of sharply defined geometrical shapes); the characterization of one existence from another (the clearly defined but integrated opposition of work spaces and their equipment systems proclaiming the nature of these two parts of the building, and together proclaiming the nature of this building as compared to others). So the building gets its form.

Accepting Kahn's definition of form, then the form of the building possesses an "existence will of its own." This "existence will" determines "what it wants to be." Form in Kahn's sense is a "total realization of thought and feeling," which the architect discovers only by momentarily discarding his personal psyche to embrace the particular program as the "transcendent act that we share in common." Hence form is impersonal, while design is personal. Where form is "what to do," design is "how to do it." Form is unmeasurable; design is measurable. "A great building," Kahn believes, "must begin with the unmeasurable, go through the measurable means when it is being designed, and in the end must be unmeasurable." In all of this Kahn does not mean to imply an invariable "system of thought and work leading to realization from Form to Design." He believes that, "Designs [can] just as well lead to realization in Form." In fact, "This interplay is the constant excitement of architecture."[9]

The measurable act of design gives tangibility to form in a two-fold sense. First, it makes form visible as a "harmony of systems." These include systems of structure, of mechanical equipment (facilities for utilities, climate control, communication, and the like), of circulation (lobbies, corridors, stairs, elevators), and of use (the organization of activity encompassed by the building). Once the architect begins to chart the flow of movement within the building and to allocate areas for major activities in even the crudest way, the realm of systems merges into the realm of spaces. Each function housed by the building is not only clearly distinguished, together with its relations to other functions, but these occur in a visible hierarchy of "served" and "servant" spaces. Served spaces dominate. They house the principal functions of the building, and are so

‡ In view of what immediately follows, the definition might better have read "harmony of *spaces and* systems"; but, in this instance, Kahn was presumably speaking of "form" in its largest sense. *"Spaces and* systems" would tend to restrict the relevance of his definition to architecture, and to those other aspects of human experience for which space is a primary attribute. On the other hand, in a larger definition of form, "spaces" could be subsumed as one of a number of "systems."

celebrated. Served spaces may have their own hierarchy. The greatest buildings make evident the gradient of importance or impressiveness of use. Servant spaces are subordinate. They include such elements of the plan as corridors, storage areas, bathrooms, and the like.

Form without design is not architecture; design without form (in Kahn's opinion the defect of most architecture, and the disease of most architectural education) must always be superficial. He maintains that "the right thing badly done is always greater than the wrong thing well done."[10] In short—and by way of defining his point of view in a patchwork of his phrases—what he terms the "life" of the building depends on the embodiment of its form as what it wants to be, in a design which makes vividly evident the harmony of systems and the hierarchical harmony of spaces.

From Objectivity to Object-ification

What *it* wants to be: the phrase is worth pausing over to emphasize the agent.* Like Mies' "almost nothing" pertaining to blunt construction, Kahn's phrase ultimately depends on the pervasive spirit of objectivity which gave impetus to the International Style and also comprised its principal continuing legacy to the subsequent development of modern architecture up to (and beyond) the time of the Richards Medical Research Building. Both phrases, but especially Kahn's, posit a potency within the realm of things which the architect must recognize at the outset. The success of his finished building depends on whether we experience what was laconically given at the very beginning as well as what was contributed by the architect himself. In other words, the ultimate design must retain a vivid sense of the primal entities—the elemental "things" of structure, of equipment, and of functional and psychic use—which combined to "make" the building in its pre-design stage. The architect's design never completely subsumes its elemental starting point. The "almost nothing" outside of design, the omnipresent *it* of "what *it* wants to be," exists in a tensional relationship to the design, thereby serving as the primal referent that redeems the design from arbitrariness.

Examining the views of Mies and Kahn, we find that Mies' philosophy of design stems more directly from the objectivity of the

---

* In a very personal way Kahn has explained the "it" in terms of a self-coined word, the "ina." I shall not discuss his philosophy in this sense here. However important as a personal expression of his meaning of architecture, it is rather too personal for consideration in an essay devoted to the larger significance of his philosophy of design. See Rowan, "Wanting to Be," *Progressive Architecture*, April 1961, especially pp. 132f., for a succinct account of this aspect of Kahn's thought.

twenties. His architectural metaphor is more exclusively technological than Kahn's. It is more committed to the idea of norms and standards. It is more generalizing in spirit, proclaiming that the normative technology of the modern world can create a clarifying, harmonic, and noble order of a homogeneous sort which is "functional" while remaining grandly aloof from the particularity of function. Overall, these qualities reflect the spirit of objectivity which permeated the International Style and permitted its development as a community endeavor, the formal principles of which Hitchcock and Johnson eventually enumerated.† Not only did this spirit of objectivity lead to the general principles for the architectural composition of the International Style, but, as we have observed, it also encouraged an enthusiasm for specific *objects* believed to be bluntly expressive of modernity. In buildings actually realized within the International Style of the twenties, these artifacts play but little part in the largest aspects of architectural composition (certain works of Le Corbusier excepted). To be sure, machine-made objects were directly appropriated for use as minor components in buildings, such as fixtures, appliances, hardware, and metal window framing. For the most part, however, machine-made objects (like the liners, airplanes, and automobiles in *Vers une architecture*) served more to reinforce the polemic of the International Style—providing examples of the kind of form, and of the morality toward form, appropriate for modern technology— than to determine architectural composition.

Since the twenties, however, composition which was guided by general principles believed to be objective has, so to speak, been substantially object-ified. We have alluded to the trend in the late work of Breuer, but it was Mies and Le Corbusier who were especially important in initiating the change. Consider, for example, Mies' I-beam—an object which is a particular, definite focus formally, psychically, and symbolically. This standardized component exists at once as a primal source of architecture, as an index of modern technology, as a generator of a comprehensive order, and therefore as a symbol of its "epoch," to use Mies' grandly sonorous term. His omnipresent I-beam nevertheless remains all the while exactly what it is—a commonplace "thing," an everyday "object." Turning now to Le Corbusier, we find that he provided the principal impetus for making parts of the architectural composition object-like. His illustration of modern transportation in *Vers une architecture* make this clear: the views of liners, for example, as "stacks" and "funnels" and "bridges." In *Vers une architecture*,

---

† See above, pp. 118f. In regard to the remainder of this paragraph, see the earlier discussion of objectivity as the central concept of the International Style on pp. 179f. and 217f.; also 244f.

FIGURE 180. *Le Corbusier. Architectural "objects." Above, left to right: a sun screen for a projected skyscraper in Algiers. Rooms as container-like entities on a warehouse floor in the Millowners Building at Ahmedabad (India). A roof drain for Notre-Dame-du-Haut at Ronchamp. Opposite, above: a ventilator atop the Unité d'Habitation. Below: a cross section of the Assembly Chamber at Chandigarh (Punjab, India), with hyperboloid cone for the legislature and tilted water ladle above entrance.*

and in Le Corbusier's buildings of the twenties, the lesson of these objects and their application for architecture is left somewhat ambiguous. Are they simply a grammar of *shapes* for the modern architect, and a syntax for their combination? Or do they suggest that the architect, like the ship designer, should seek out *shapes consonant with their functions* and expressive of these functions? In Le Corbusier's work the decisive step toward the latter position would seem to have been his invention in the early thirties of the sunshade as a deep sculptural grid suspended in front of the excessive glazing favored for buildings in the International Style. With his *brise soleil,* as he termed it, an awning suddenly assumed architectural scale. An appliance became a

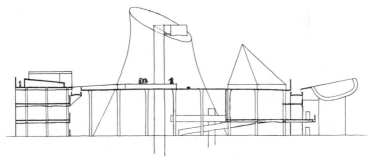

façade (Fig. 180), and yet maintained something of its identity as an appliance suspended off the wall of a building. His almost simultaneous enlargement of the pole-like stilting of his buildings of the twenties to heavy pier-like entities made objects of these structural elements; so did his design of roofs as a series of conspicuous vaults which marked off units of space like so many identical packages ranged side by side.

Le Corbusier's compositions of still later buildings, especially those designed after World War II, bristle with elemental object-like shapes, each proclaiming its functional role. Free-form conic shapes convert commonplace ventilators into roof-top sculpture. Roof drains become immense spouts for dumping water into bowls below. In a number of his buildings rooms exist as independent cylinders and boxes; set into framed structures, they recall crated merchandise on warehouse floors, or the parts of a machine set into its frame. This objectification need not be wholly utilitarian in its allusion. Metaphors involving the history of

FIGURE 181. *Le Corbusier. An architectural "object": roof-top parasol projected for the Governor's Palace, Chandigarh (Punjab, India), c. 1954.*

architecture, hence the history of civilization, are also possible. In Chandigarh, the new capital city of Punjab which Le Corbusier planned and for which he designed the principal public buildings, he raised a columned portico as a free-standing frontispiece in which blunt piers support an entablature conceived as an enormous trencher, its hollow interior serving as a basin to catch the monsoon rains, and its enormous spout spilling the water into a lagoon. Part architecture, part sculpture, part functional appliance, it calls forth all the columned porticoes that have fronted buildings in the past, while dissolving this splendor of allusion in the ironic assertion of what it is. A list that could be enormously extended may be concluded with an object having very complex allusions. Taxed with the problem of providing the Governor's Palace in Chandigarh with a suitable symbol of office—a portico? a dome?—Le Corbusier chose to create a parasol as a reinforced concrete structure on the roof-top terrace (Fig. 181). Parasols had traditionally been held over the heads of those in authority in India, partly for functional, partly for deferential reasons. As projected (it was never built), Le Corbusier's structure serves both ends. But it goes further. The roof of the inverted parasol contains a pool. The pool nestles between slanted planes. Planted, these serve as banks to the pond, which is appropriately lifted up to the sun. At the same time this layer of water and planting is a very practical device for cooling the shade below. Finally, pool and verdant banks lifted into the sky bring together in an intense symbolic confrontation the three basic elements of a garden. So the object interweaves practicality, wit, metaphor, and myth. Yet, there it is; another blunt thing! The laconic object, functioning in a utilitarian sense, conjures up naturalistic, institutional, and cosmic imagery.

Kahn's phrase is only to be understood against this expanded meaning of objectivity as the aim of the International Style into what might be termed a more comprehensive objectification (or, to be playful, an object-ification). What *it* wants to be: the *it* suggests the two-fold implications of this development. On the one hand, *it* implies the concreteness of anything fiercely focused upon, and embodied as an object. (In this respect, the objectification that Kahn sought reinforces those qualities of "reality" with which we began our discussion of his building.) On the other hand, *it* implies an elemental object (a primal entity) outside the whim, and even substantially outside the will, of both the client's program and the architect's design; hence an object imbued with iconic magic. Now, although Kahn's slogan substantially holds to the ideal of objectivity as it had inspired the architects of the International Style, the essential abstractness of their understanding of the concept disappears. The objectivity of the twenties primarily referred to a frame of mind, a mode of approach, that would hopefully bring architecture into rapport with technological and scientific points of view. To recall the implications of George Howe's extreme statement of the goal of modern design: a building would ultimately exist as mere points, lines, and planes in a space-time continuum.‡ In effect, Kahn (and by the beginning of the sixties, other architects too, although he most explicitly) would make the objectivity of the twenties more particularate and more concrete by fashioning the building of object-like entities possessing an immense sense of physical presence, thus making the building as remote as possible from any attenuated state of existence as Howe had described.* In metaphoric terms, the focus of meaning for the most serious expression in modern architecture shifted from an enthusiastic embrace of the technological and scientific idealism of the modern world of the twenties to ironic commentary on the place of man and civilization within the modern situation, the former containing elements of the latter, and making it possible. This enlarged symbolic intent in modern architecture required forms expressive not only of modernity, but of history as well, and, above all, of human kinesthetic and psychic experience. For these reasons "what *it* wants *to be*" is closer to Le Corbusier's position (so well illustrated by the projected parasol) than to Mies' *"almost nothing,"* although the prosaic didacticism of the program for the Richards Medi-

‡ See p. 122 above.
* In this connection it is revealing that, in a major statement of his philosophy published in 1955, Kahn speaks of "order" and "design." Subsequently, he speaks of "form" and "design," with "order" becoming subsumed in his compound definition of "form" (see pp. 373f. above). Apparently Kahn came to feel that the implications of "order" center in abstract configuration, whereas, those of "form" are more concrete and particularate. "Order" is rather more congenial to Mies' aim (and a favorite word of his), suggesting as it does an all-embracing harmony that reveals itself in lucid geometry. The difference in their choice of words is, in fact, the difference in implication between "almost nothing" and "what *it* wants *to be*." Scully, *Kahn,* devotes an appendix to a reprinting of the 1955 statement, plus another of 1960.

cal Research Building and the systematic relationship among the objects that comprise it is alien to both the collisiveness of sculptural form and the metaphoric *élan* in Le Corbusier's work. In this metamorphosis from objectivity to objectification Kahn's forms progressively enlarge and deepen their potential for meaning, from technological and functional allusion increasingly toward that of archetypal human experience.†

So the importance of the Richards Medical Research Building substantially depends on its bringing to focus, both as generalization and as concrete demonstration, many aspects of modern architecture, not, however, in a pastiche, but as a creative action. Hence, by way of summary, in this building and in a way more decisive than that of any of his contemporaries, Kahn amalgamates aspects of the diverse achievements of the three greatest architects of the first half of the twentieth century. His design, moreover, is attuned to that diffuse trend in modern architecture from the twenties to the sixties which we have characterized as the shift from objectivity toward objectification. Going beyond the design of this particular commission, he rather deliberately uses the building to make a comprehensive definition of architecture. He does this in a didactic, almost diagrammatic, manner. Finally, he informs his building with an architectural philosophy which maintains the basic tension in both the buildings and the theory of the International Style: that between the primer of factuality and the mystique of inmost essence—between the *it* and the *It,* so to speak. No wonder this building has taught the profession!

Not only does the Richards Medical Research Building teach within the tradition of modern architecture, it also teaches outside this tradition —reinvigorating aspects of Beaux-Arts theory. Beaux-Arts planning again becomes relevant for its insistence on separate spaces firmly bounded by solid walls, on the differentiation of served and servant spaces, and on the hierarchical treatment of spaces and massing. Its functional basis notwithstanding, the plan of the Medical Research Building does possess an ornamental quality, as though Kahn had not determined its configuration wholly on the basis of the activities to be contained, but had determined it in part as an emblem of the institution, such as a graphic designer might produce (Fig. 188). To speak of the ornamental quality of this plan so thoroughly committed to the logic of its function may seem extraordinary, yet the fact is that Kahn's subsequent planning has often become very intricate as a pattern of shapes. Consider the original

† "Existential" allusion, to cite Christian Norberg-Schulz's term in *Existence, Space and Architecture,* London, Studio Vista, 1971, published as this goes to press. He specifically states, p. 17, that existential form possesses an object-like quality.

scheme for the Jonas Salk Institute for Biological Studies (1959–), in Torrey Pines, California, near San Diego. As yet incomplete, and with some of the geometric complexity slightly reduced in that portion of the scheme which has been realized, the over-all composition of the Institute suggests a blunted version of the grandest sort of Roman ruins (Figs. 182, 183, and 184). (Immediately around and between the buildings there is even a geometry of walls enclosing garden-like areas. The walls are pierced with voids, thus becoming screening devices. Kahn has called them a "ruin of openings."[11]) In plan, the major elements of the complex—laboratories, meeting area, and residences—appear as three clusters of geometry luxuriously spaced in the landscape, and at first sight highly ornamental in quality. Vincent Scully has justly compared the plan to various Roman schemes, such as those for Hadrian's Villa and Diocletian's Palace, or to the shapes in Piranesi's maps of Rome.[12] Closer to home, Bernard Maybeck's grandiose folly for the Panama-Pacific Exposition comes to mind, with its comparable interweaving of building and garden (even to the geometric surround of "ruins").‡ The kind of "cloisonné" planning which Maybeck had likened to a "brooch," however, Kahn transmutes into object-like containers. The relative bluntness of Kahn's geometry, its functional aims, its systematic organization (as much a mode of design as a matter of fact), are qualities that evoke pistons, pipes, chambers, and wheels. By comparison with the dogmatic functionalism of the Richards Medical Research Building, the functionalism of Salk Center becomes more ritualistic. Hadrian and Diocletian accommodate history by vacating their palaces to scientists and technicians.

The grandeur of this planning, reminiscent of the Roman Imperial tradition by way of the more sumptuous reaches of Beaux-Arts projects, epitomizes (however inadvertently) the curious flirtation with academic theory which has persisted within the modern movement in the United States. When the Beaux-Arts theory of design attracted the American profession in the decades around 1900, its appeal substantially depended on its supposed universality of principle. Architectural elements appropriated or adapted from historic buildings of merit and arranged in accord with "laws" of composition provided the basis for design. It was no accident that only an "International" modern style could muster sufficient authority to challenge the "international" academic style. The international and universal implications of Beaux-Arts design notwithstanding, American Beaux-Arts buildings do reveal distinctive characteristics, although those relating to formal properties are more easily felt

‡ See *American Buildings and Their Architects: Progressive and Academic Ideals at the Turn of the Twentieth Century,* Chapter 6.

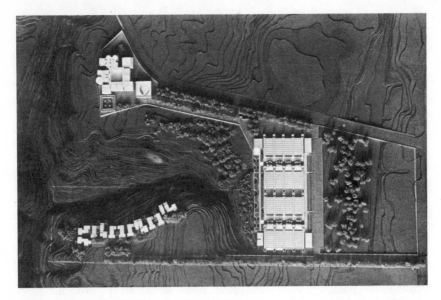

FIGURE 182. *Louis Kahn. Jonas Salk Institute for Biological Studies, Torrey Pines (near San Diego), Calif., begun 1959, first building phase completed 1965. Model of the complete complex as originally projected.*

than specified. Two broad emphases that distinguish Beaux-Arts design in America from that in Europe are pertinent here. In the first place, as Henry-Russell Hitchcock suggests, American Beaux-Arts design strove to be more correct—or better, perhaps, more literal—in its use of the trappings of historical form (especially in designs inspired by classical and Renaissance buildings, since medieval allusion permitted more latitude).[13] Secondly, it has been widely recognized that American Beaux-Arts architecture showed relatively greater concern for adapting historical veneers to practical arrangements and to mechanical convenience. Both tendencies—correctness and practicality—may have been enhanced by the evolution at the end of the nineteenth century of the large-sized architectural office, which, in magnitude and comprehensiveness of organization, was very much an American development.* Group practice on this scale encouraged correctness of detail, since what did not need to be invented was understood by all, and when processed through a tight schedule of deadlines, was guaranteed at least a modicum of "architectural" pretension despite the rush. Group practice also encour-

* See *American Buildings and their Architects: Progressive and Academic Ideals at the Turn of the Twentieth Century,* Chapters 1 and 7.

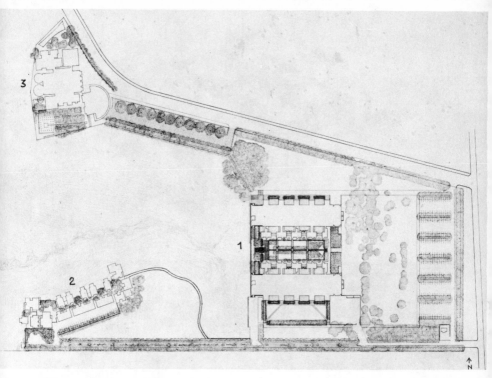

FIGURE 183. *Jonas Salk Institute for Biological Studies. Original site plan, as proposed in 1963. There are three major clusters: (1) laboratories and studies; (2) living quarters, the "Village;" (3) community meeting and conference area, the "Meeting House."*

aged standardization and technical excellence. In fact, mounting complexity and specialization in building technology largely accounted for the establishment of big offices in the first place.

Correctness and practicality have been basic quests in American culture, which seeks a great tradition (even if somewhat prefabricated), but would also strive to have it functional. In all likelihood, this pair of goals explains why Beaux-Arts ideas and formulae associated with Beaux-Arts design as this eventuated in the United States have, from the 1880's onward, haunted not only the academic side of American architecture, but—what is vastly more interesting, and more relevant to Kahn's achievement—even its most progressive side.

Consider merely the roster of buildings already discussed, and chosen without this demonstration in mind. Sullivan's strongly enframed compositions with their "beginning, middle, and end" (in effect, their "base, shaft, and capital," despite his protests at the analogy) so appealed to academic practitioners that they readily appropriated his format, even

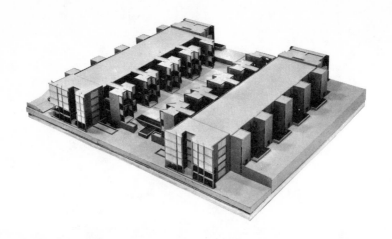

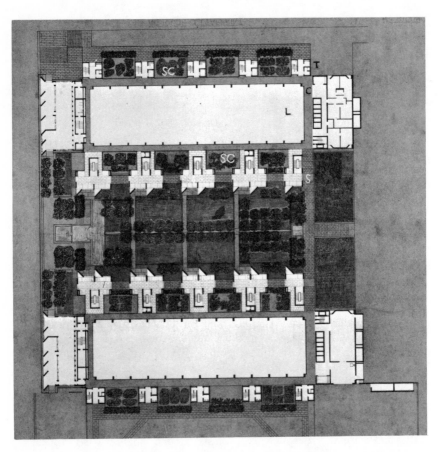

FIGURE 184. *Jonas Salk Institute for Biological Studies. Laboratories and studies. Model and plan:* (L) *laboratories;* (C) *corridors;* (T) *entrance stair towers;* (SC) *sunken courts, because one floor is below ground level, with two above;* (S) *studies. Cross section (opposite):* (1) *laboratories;* (2) *structural ceilings threaded with utility runs;* (3) *corridors;* (4) *one of the sunken courts with a wall of one of the entrance stair towers;* (5) *bridges to studies;* (6) *studies;* (GL) *ground level. The laboratory complex was completed during the first building phase, 1959–65.*

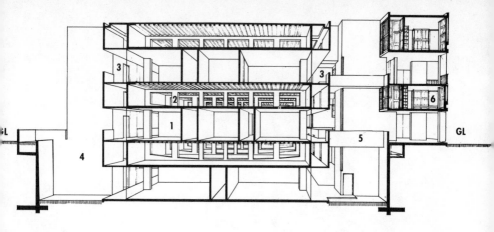

though they usually missed his allusion to the frame beneath and abhorred his idiosyncratic detailing. In Wright's early planning, core focus and the axial symmetries, with their ornamentality radiating outward by means of terracing and parapets, to the extravagant embrace of the landscape, owed much to Beaux-Arts composition. So did Wright's sure sense of hierarchical massing.[14] In addition, Beaux-Arts ideals permeated the most creative pre-World War I work of the Greenes, Gill, and especially Maybeck. But then, the work of all five of these men substantially, and diversely, derived from nineteenth-century points of view. Their work was "progressive" with respect to its past, rather than "modern" in terms of the International Style. Although the Associated Architects responsible for Rockefeller Center did learn from the International Style, the manner in which they kept a footing in one tradition while stepping into another vividly illustrates how most of those who were progressively inclined among the academically trained architects of the day managed the straddle. Even as stellar an example of the International Style as PSFS holds on to Beaux-Arts principles. As for the émigrés from abroad, like Breuer and Mies, once arrived in the States they seem instinctively to have modified their European work in ways reminiscent of classicistic design, which, if not specifically indebted to Beaux-Arts inspiration, are at least congenial to Beaux-Arts ideas and images. Kahn completes our roster. His Beaux-Arts background in Philadelphia paralleled Howe's, although, being of a different generation, it was from the beginning more tinctured with European modernism. Finally—and here we leave our list of buildings momentarily in order to glance at a more literal and more prominent, but architecturally less consequential, aspect of the Beaux-Arts revival which is contemporaneous with Kahn's laboratories—there is Lincoln Center for the Performing Arts (1959–66) in New York (Fig. 185) with its columns and axial organization. Although these formal qualities of Lincoln Center generally characterize all classically inspired architecture, its most immediate pro-

FIGURE 185. *Lincoln Center for the Performing Arts, New York. In order of completion, this general night view shows: right, Max Abramovitz's Philharmonic Hall, opened 1962; across from this, left, Philip Johnson and Richard Foster's New York State Theater, opened 1964; behind the Philharmonic and barely visible, Eero Saarinen's Vivian Beaumont Theater (in collaboration with J. Mielziner) with Skidmore, Owings & Merrill's Library Museum of the Performing Arts, opened 1965; finally, as the focal climax of the plaza, top center, Wallace Harrison's Metropolitan Opera House, opened 1966. (© Lincoln Center for the Performing Arts)*

totypes for American architects are Beaux-Arts buildings. So Lincoln Center brings the tradition of American Beaux-Arts full circle, back to the Court of Honor at the Columbian Exposition of 1892.† Or, a circle within a circle: if Rockefeller Center had marked the arc from Beaux-Arts to modern, so the later Center marks the arc from modern back to Beaux-Arts, with Wallace Harrison among the principal participants in both enterprises.

† Illustrated in *American Buildings and Their Architects: Progressive and Academic Ideals at the Turn of the Twentieth Century,* fig. 32.

Coming late to modern architecture (in the European sense of an architecture fiercely committed to being "modern"), American architects had barely accepted it before substantially reversing themselves. In the middle fifties, and early sixties, Beaux-Arts theory and imagery again became relevant—popping up just as spring bulbs, hidden for a season, but lightly covered, suddenly burst forth. To be sure, the modern movement in other countries had occasionally veered toward an academic point of view. Yet the flirtation of the American modern movement with Beaux-Arts possesses a special character. No mere reactionary or traditionalist eddy (like the porticoed, quasi-modern of Mussolini's Italy, for example, or the classicistic academicism of the later work of Auguste Perret in France), Beaux-Arts theory and formulae have affected the *most progressive* developments in the United States, and they have done so rather *pervasively* and *continuously,* even to accounting for much of the originality of American developments within the modern movement. To prove the point, consider the 1950's, when the decided quickening of American interest in Beaux-Arts ideas and formulae not only was widespread but also anticipated comparable trends in other countries (which seem to have depended on American precedent); this decade scanned the possibilities in Beaux-Arts design, and the results ranged from the stage-set Neoclassicism of the Lincoln Center Plaza to Kahn's profound (if inadvertent) revival of the most creative aspects of academic compositional theory. Whereas Lincoln Center recalls the most perfunctory aspects of Beaux-Arts design in its pompous traditionalistic wrap for the boxed services within, Kahn's incremental compositions are complexly informed by a logic which is partly functional, partly ornamental, and partly ritualistic. Kahn's work thereby gives fresh relevance to the progressive aspects of Beaux-Arts design, which themselves had been sparked by the rationalistic and picturesque ideas of nineteenth-century theory and practice. Surely, to return to the Salk complex, something of this latter emphasis may be discerned in the kind of grandeur that Kahn gave to his functional program.

It is so moving to see a modern work space broadly conceived—its functional, humane, institutional, and monumental aspects alike considered—that it may seem churlish to wonder whether the monumentality of the Salk Center is not slightly overdone. The laboratories already built undeniably provide one of the most impressive, most moving experiences in modern architecture; but a fundamental reservation grows on one who spends time in the complex: are the echoes of Imperial Rome and Virgilian arcadianism, even of Persian gardens, a bit false in this situation? Alternatively, in Kahn's design for the capitol of Bangladesh at Dacca, does his legacy from Roman planning lose itself here in over-elaboration of squares-in-diamonds-in-circles-in-more-squares-and-so-on until the kaleidoscopic geometry appears rather to have generated itself than to have arisen in response to architectural purpose? By comparison, the best of Le Corbusier's late buildings, although embracing programs and values comparable to Kahn's (with a more cavalier attitude toward function to be sure), have a less retrospective monumentality, a more explicit modernity. The very depth of Kahn's commitment to modern architecture, however, keeps the monumentality of the Salk Center this side of pretentiousness. So does his essentially modern view of architectural history as primal building forms primally affecting human experience, in which the forms have come to the history rather than being extracted from it. Yet, for those who would follow the teacher, there is a warning here, as well as a promise.

In any event, the salient which Kahn's architecture opens into the Beaux-Arts tradition is as important as its purview of the modern past. In his awareness of history, Kahn has assimilated imagery equally from medieval and Imperial Roman sources: from castles and fortified citadels for one design; from imperial palaces and fora for another. One cannot be too categorical in this respect. If the Salk complex is Roman in inspiration, the Richards complex is medieval. Again Kahn's career suggests that of Beaux-Arts practitioners adept at making all architectural history grist for their mills, except that Kahn seeks the essence of the past to re-create equivalents, not surface appearances. The abruptness of medieval forms, their combination of glowering bulk and intimate detail, the forceful cluster and scatter of shape in accord with function, apparent in the Richards Medical Research Building, become extraordinarily powerful in a series of schemes for the replanning of central Philadelphia (1952–62) [Fig. 203].‡ The Philadelphia Museum College of Art (1964–), will also forcefully state this medieval theme if the complex is realized, and lives up to Kahn's schemes (Figs. 186, 187). Here, however, the violent interplay of massive solids and scissored spaces brings the design to the brink of staginess—as Kahn's disciples will be wise to note. In addition, a project like this, being much less didactic with respect to Kahn's philosophic position than the Richards Building, is less explicit about "what it wants to be." Designs by other architects have already appeared in which arbitrary shapes in ragged combinations are casually justified by the circular mystique of being what they are because what they are is what they wanted to be![15] But this is the danger besetting the use of any esthetic theory like Kahn's which, superficially interpreted, degenerates into a mystique of "life" in form.

All of which takes us away from the Richards Medical Research Building. Properly so, however, for it is a provocative work, and has much to teach. As no other building at the time, it charted possibilities in

‡ Illustrations are most easily available in Scully, *Kahn*, plates 120–30.

FIGURE 186. *Louis Kahn. Philadelphia Museum College of Art, commissioned 1964. Model for the projected building.*

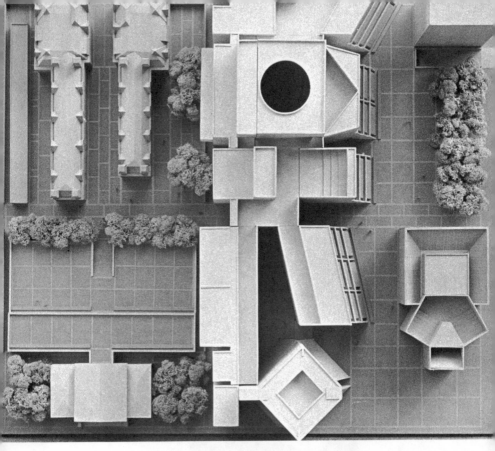

FIGURE 187. *Philadelphia Museum College of Art. Roof view of model and plan pattern, variant versions of the composition.*

many directions, while substantially holding fast to the integrity of its conception.

THE "LIFE" OF THE BUILDING

To search out the life of this building as the form it must take, Kahn began with its division into "served" and "servant" spaces. In accord with his basic premises, which included the limited site, he created a series of windowed studio towers for the laboratories. These are essentially the "served" spaces of the building. Each studio tower abuts two or three utility towers, which are slightly higher and mostly without fenestration. These blind elements are essentially the "servant" spaces, some densely agglutinated into a bulky, block-like unit at the core of the complex building, others isolated as a series of narrow, shaft-like entities around its periphery (Figs. 173, 188). Whereas the "served" towers are emphasized as horizontal tiers of spaces ("floors" conceived as particularate "studios"), the "servant" towers are emphasized, although not exclusively, as continuous vertical elements ("shafts" or "tubes"). These shafts or tubes are of two major types. Some house elevators and stairs for the vertical movement of personnel. Others house utility conduits: lines for electricity, telephone, compressed air, and vacuum; stacks for plumbing and exhaust; ducts for air conditioning and heating, and the like. Schematically (but not precisely), the compacted servant towers at the core of the complex contain the elevators and furnish the utility input for the laboratories. The scattered towers at the periphery of the complex provide exhaust stacks and minor stairways for fire escape, as well as for quick communication between adjacent laboratory floors. In Kahn's revelation of the life of this building, no aspect was more immediately important than that of giving prominence to its mechanical aspects. Because modern technology steadily magnifies the service appliances of a building, they must be provided for in an architectural manner, otherwise the architect must be prepared to relinquish control of an increasingly important part of the building to the mechanical engineer and then blandly veil the result. Kahn feels strongly on this point.

> The mechanics—all those pipes and ductwork, are a *destroyer* of architectural spaces. Most of our columns end up festooned with them, or alternated with fake columns of them. They destroy the clear picture between a column and no-column. . . . I've hated mechanics, but I've learned to respect it because it's a destroyer.[16]

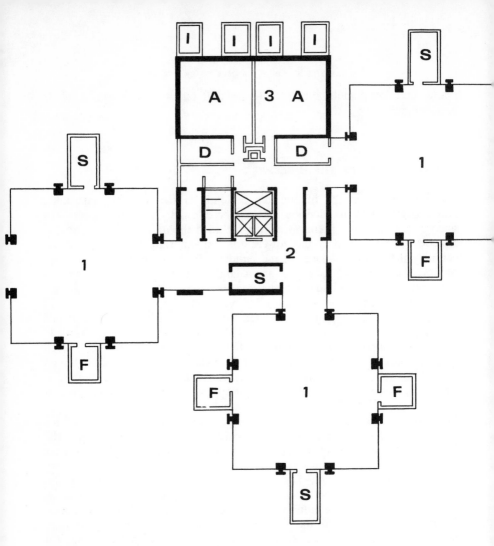

FIGURE 188. *Richards Medical Research Building. Typical schematic floor plan:* (1) *studio laboratory towers;* (2) *corridors and vertical circulation;* (3) *animal quarters;* (I) *shafts for outside air intake;* (A) *animal rooms;* (D) *shafts for the distribution of conditioned air;* (F) *fume exhaust and vertical utility runs;* (S) *peripheral fire stairs.*

If the Richards Building as realized confuses in minor respects the neat allocation of functions to forms premised by Kahn's philosophy, the distribution of these within the logic of the composition makes his intent sufficiently clear.

So much for the over-all scheme. A closer look (Fig. 188) shows that the core partly consists of the utility tubes for elevators, principal stairs, and conditioned air ready for distribution throughout the building. Stacked behind these are the animal rooms (A), centrally located, but separated and insulated from the laboratories. (As it happens, some of these now serve as laboratories.) Together with the corridors, these are the principal exceptions to the verticality of the tubes which otherwise comprise the core. Behind the animal rooms, a dramatic row of four air-intake stacks (I) dominates the rear elevation of the building, which faces the botanical garden. These stacks suck outside air through sizable rectangular openings placed well down on the building. Ducts within the intake stacks bring this air to the top of the building, where it is conditioned for distribution down the forward vents (D). If Kahn could re-do the building, he would no longer bury the distributing segment of the air-conditioning system within the blocky bulk. Instead, he would so divide and rearrange the distributing segment that each of the laboratory towers would have its own stack serving this function, and one clearly revealed where it links with the central core—perhaps as a cylindrical column with passage to either side.[17] In addition to clarifying the life of the building, this change of shape would dramatize the coupling of the laboratory towers to the central block, while incidentally simplifying some of the tightness and awkward runs in the ductwork as it branches from its trunks at the core of the building.

The compacted towers at the center of the complex contrast dramatically with their isolated counterparts on the periphery. In each cluster for each stack of laboratories one of the towers contains stairs (S). The others (F) house flues for exhaust, together with certain other utilities (although the purest revelation of the mechanical system would have distinguished the exhaust flues from other aspects of the mechanical system). Noxious fumes are immediately drawn from the laboratories, to be discharged well above this and neighboring buildings, and far from the air-intake "breathers" placed low at the rear of the core block. (How easy, as late as 1960, to think of the building as a self-contained system!) Unnecessarily bringing the height of his stair towers to that of the exhaust stacks, Kahn has arbitrarily signaled the different function of the former by cleaving their tops into twin vertical slabs (Figs. 173, 176).

Nestled among the dominating utility towers, the stacked laboratory platforms are as completely free of vertical utility runs as are the office floors of the Inland Steel Building (Fig. 74). There are some horizontal runs here, however; located overhead within the latticed ceiling structure, they spread outward from the central core. The size of each platform (45 square feet) is determined partly by plumbing requirements,[18] partly by the need to accommodate laboratory benches 2½ feet wide with 5 feet of working space between them. Towers and supporting columns are so placed with respect to windows as to create a cross-shaped area of relative shadow toward the center of each laboratory studio (Fig. 189). This shaded area can be cubicled for X-ray, photography, isotypes, incubators, cold rooms, and storage, although, as may be imagined, in fact the functions of the laboratories rarely divide so neatly. Major work areas occur in the lighted corners made possible by the cantilevered slabs.

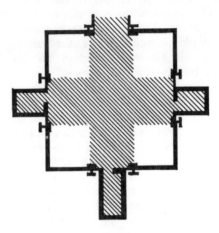

FIGURE 189. *Richards Medical Research Building. Schematic diagram of the shadowed area within the laboratory studios.*

In actuality, these corner windows fail in two respects. Scientists complain of too few walls against which to place equipment and on which to hang shelving. More important, sun control is insufficient. The tinted pale blue panes (Kahn subsequently wished they were gray[19]), in the transom area of most of these corner windows clearly afford inadequate protection against glare and outside heat. Here Kahn fell victim to the fetish of the period for an extreme amount of glazing for laboratories; as a result the windows require not only the countermeasures of Venetian blinds and excessive air conditioning, but often an auxiliary patchwork of insulating board and aluminum foil in order to shield the delicate instruments inside. Metal-mesh screens fitted outside all windows receiving direct exposure from the sun only partially help in deflecting its rays; and they have little effect on the glare. But even if it were fully satisfactory, such screening would fall short of the architectonic solution demanded by Kahn's philosophy for such an important aspect of the life of the building.

So the form of the building as the revelation of its life stakes out the design as a "harmony of spaces" and as a "harmony of systems." In this harmony of systems, the revelation of structure is as important as that of mechanical equipment. The structure of the building becomes fully tangible in a three-fold sense. First, it is fully revealed as the support of the building. Second, it makes and marks out the spaces. Kahn's *bête noir* is the open area with ranges of columns (a standard practice for the International Style), where partitioning follows its own pattern—moving between the columns, or at best uses the columns merely as convenient hitching posts (Fig. 48).

> It was a great architectural event, centuries ago, when the walls parted and columns *became*. . . . You should never invade a space between columns with partition walls. It is like sleeping with your head in one room and feet in another.[20]

Finally, structure also provides the building with an integral sculptural embellishment. Kahn believes that such comprehensive design with structure is only possible with reinforced concrete, and his Medical Research Building demonstrates various techniques in using this material. Here, part of the reinforced-concrete structure is *site-poured;* part of it is *pre-cast.*

Site-pouring is the conventional method of handling concrete (as, for example, in Wright's Unity Church or the Guggenheim). In constructing the walls of a building, steel reinforcing is placed between the formwork for the interior and exterior planes of the wall; the mixing trucks generally bring the prepared cement to the site; it is poured into the forms, compacted by hand or by vibrating machines, and allowed to harden. In the Medical Research Building the central core and the peripheral towers were all site-poured as rectangular tubes and slabs (Fig. 190). "Slip forms" were used in their fabrication. In this procedure, a form for a limited section of each vertical element was set in place and filled with concrete; after the concrete had set, the form was raised and refilled; the process was repeated the height of the tower. Once this work had been completed, the concrete outer surfaces of the tubes and slabs were faced with brick.

The utility containers for the central block (air intake, air distribution, elevators, and stairs) may be viewed as tubular towers, or, alternatively, as gigantic columns become chambers because of their hollowness. Here the utilities do not hang on the columns, like vines, choking them, the arrangement against which Kahn complained; instead, the columns become hollow—hollow bones, in one of his metaphors, accepting the services "as the bone accepts the marrow."[21] We can further describe the Richards Building by revising Kahn's statement on a momentous mythical moment in the history of architecture when "the walls parted, and the columns became," to "the columns separated, and the work

FIGURE 190. *Richards Medical Research Building. View during construction, showing the entrance tower on the north (front) elevation, with the service block behind (taken from roughly the same angle as the view of the model in Figure 173). The tallest element is the core block, site-poured as tubes, slabs, and boxes, with shoring to sustain the most recent pour showing at the top-most level. The small projecting ledges at every second floor will support the brick facing. Around this central block the frames of the laboratory towers are rising, comprised of two kinds of precast reinforced-concrete elements, pre-tensioned and post-tensioned. A typical column segment appears in the foreground with tubular openings for reinforcing cables. After this has been raised into position by the crane in the background, cables will be strung through it for post-tensioning. The site-poured peripheral towers for stairs and utilities will be placed between the paired columns on each face of the laboratory tower, once the framing of the laboratory towers is complete.*

spaces entered" (Fig. 191). In fact, Kahn had once thought of supporting the laboratory platforms from the towers, in which case the service tubes would have literally functioned as hollow columns.[22]

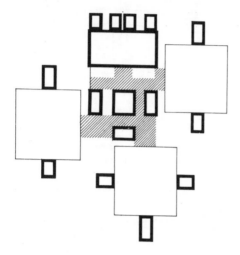

FIGURE 191. *Richards Medical Research Building. The hollow tubular elements in relation to the laboratory working spaces: the "columns" separate and the work spaces enter. The shaded area is corridor space. Compare with labeled plan, Figure 188.*

The poured core element went up first. This then served as a central scaffolding for the erection of the concrete framing for the laboratory stacks. Later, it also served as a vertical storehouse and work area for the plumbers, carpenters, electricians, and other trades as they completed the gangliated laboratory towers rising in a semi-swastika pattern around the core.

In contrast to the poured-in-place solid walls of the utility core, the skeletal frames of the laboratory towers are comprised of prefabricated, pre-tensioned, and post-tensioned reinforced concrete elements, complexly notched and slotted so as to fit together (Fig. 193). Technologically, this frame is the most interesting portion of the structure. The engineering of Dr. August E. Komendant made it possible.

At this point it may be useful to give a brief explanation of the effect of the *pre-tensioning* and *post-tensioning* of concrete members. In the normal reinforced-concrete beam passing over several columnar supports (Fig. 192) the principal steel reinforcing rods are placed toward

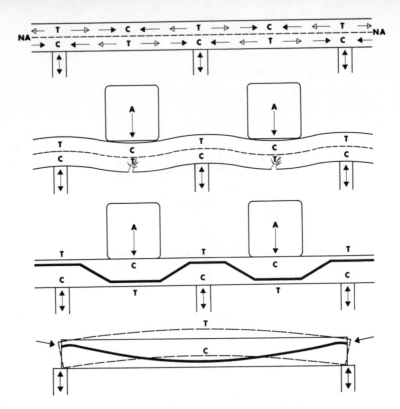

FIGURE 192. *Diagram of the typical reinforced-concrete beam and the effect of prestressing. Top to bottom: alternating compressive (compacting) and tensional (stretching) forces to either side of the neutral axis (NA) within a typical floor beam shown spanning three columns. Extraordinary loads at A can depress the mid-span of the beam to the breaking point, while the beam over the column would be humped. A zigzagged reinforcement alternating above and below the neutral axis counters tensile forces. Pre-tensioning and post-tensioning by means of stretching cable reinforcement bows the beam, thereby inverting the conventional position for tensional and compressive forces at mid-span. Compared with a beam normally reinforced, a mechanically tensioned beam with the same dimensions can span a wider interval.*

the bottom of the beam at the center of its span, and toward the top at the points of support. Although plain concrete has considerable compressive strength (that is, the ability to resist crushing forces, as in a column), it has very little tensile strength (the ability to resist stretching forces, as in a spanning member, like a beam). In plain concrete the tensile strength is in fact less than one percent of its compressive strength. But when it is properly reinforced by rods or mesh of steel—a material strong in both compression and tension—the performance of the concrete member is completely altered.

The reason is apparent in the forces existing in the beam merely from the weight of its own material (its "dead load"), and is increased when load A (a "live load") is located over the center of the spanning beam, between the supporting columns. It is then very apparent that the load tends to make the beam sag in the center. By this action the molecular structure toward the top edge of the beam at its center tends to be compacted (compressed)—forces with which concrete alone can cope—while the bottom edge tends to be stretched (tensioned)—forces which concrete alone can hardly sustain at all. (Within the beam is a plane where the beam is neither in compression nor in tension; this is the neutral axis. It usually occurs about one third down from the top, although both quantity of steel and quality of cement can shift its location.) In an unreinforced beam, a relatively small load at the center of a relatively short span would suffice to stretch the underside of the beam so as to rupture its molecular cohesion and bring about its failure. Hence it is toward the underside of the center of the beam that steel reinforcement is placed to withstand tensile forces.

If load A tends to cause the center of the beam to sag, it also tends to hump that section of the beam over the column, thereby reversing at this point the location of the tensile forces from the bottom to the top of the beam. Hence the reinforcement to counter tension moves from the bottom to the top of the beam as the beam passes over a column. (Theoretically, at least, this is the case, although in actual building practice there are various ways of placing the reinforcement within the beam in order to counter tensional forces, and in the most usual case, where a single beam spans the interval between two columns, the break at each column so minimizes the humping action that, for example, reinforcement for the tension rods may run across the bottom of the beam for its full width with U-shaped upright elements, stirrups, placed toward the ends to counteract such tensional forces as exist over the columns.*)

So much for the action of compressive and tensional forces in beams employing standard reinforced concrete construction. Now for pre- and post-tensioning; *pre-tensioning* first. Under factory conditions it is possible to pour the concrete around a steel cable hung within the formwork in a catenary curve (that is, the sagging curve natural to ropes or cables supported across an interval between two point supports, as in a clothesline or a suspension bridge), and to pour the beam around the cable. At one end, the reinforcement cable is anchored outside the beam; at the

---

* An equally, or more, important function of the stirrups is that of countering shear stresses within the beam, although we need not discuss them in this discussion of pre- and post-tensioning.

other, a mechanical jack goes into operation. As the concrete hardens and binds to the cable, the jack stretches it. When the concrete is sufficiently cured, the cable is severed from the jack. The stretched cable contracts and humps the beam toward its center. Now the traditional location of forces is reversed! Tension occurs at the top of the beam, compression at the bottom. Alternatively, a comparable effect can be realized by *post-tensioning*. At the time the beams are poured, hollow tubes (usually straight at top and bottom of the beam) are inserted in the forms. Once the concrete has hardened the tubes are threaded with cables. The same sort of jacking operation produces the same effect. In either case, if load A is applied at the center of a pre- or post-tensioned beam it must depress the top of the beam from tension to compression at the top before tensional forces ever begin to appear at the bottom. Obviously two possibilities are opened by such mechanically tensioned components. A beam of the same dimension as its conventionally poured equivalent can span wider distances; or a beam of smaller dimension can span the same distance. In the Richards Medical Research Building the mechanical tensioning of the principal reinforced-concrete structural trusses permitted a clear span of 45 feet, thus providing unbroken floor areas for the studio laboratories.

The combination of pre- and post-tensioned concrete members which frame the laboratory towers arrived at the site as prefabricated members, as we have observed, elaborately notched and slotted. The mortise-and-tenoned look of the parts suggest nothing so much as the petrifaction of the membering of some such archaic wooden construction as that for the traditional Japanese house—or perhaps the proverbial Chinese puzzle (Fig. 193).

Explanations of the way in which Chinese puzzles go together are never easy. The Richards Building is no exception. Some sense, however, of the process by which the crane lifted the pieces and fitted them together, and the degree to which the record of this assemblage appears in the completed building, is part of its life. The assemblage of the skeleton, moreover, illustrates the increasing role of the derrick and the prefabricated part in building. Just as the bulldozer has revolutionized building operations on the ground since World War II, the crane has transformed large-scale construction above ground.[23] The application of the first to construction is primarily an American development, growing out of the need to move vast amounts of earth at high speed for military projects; the second (as now used) is primarily a European development of the fifties. Of course both kinds of equipment have pre-war histories in construction; indeed, hoists of various sorts reach all the way back to ancient building. But these machines were hardly as common in construction before the war as they have since become. Moreover, they tended

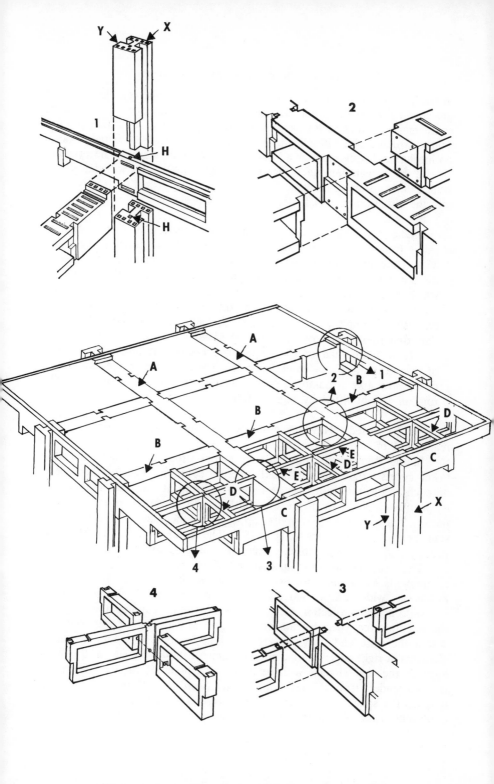

FIGURE 193. *Richards Medical Research Building. Assembly diagram of the skeletal framing for the laboratory towers of prefabricated reinforced-concrete components. References to the letters used on this diagram appear in the text.*

in the past to serve the deferential role of mere tools. By the middle of the century, however, what they can do and the way they do it had become major factors in the very conception and design of buildings, to a degree which Kahn himself was slow to realize. As he originally looked on mechanical equipment as a "destroyer" of architecture, so he originally viewed the gargantuan machinery of modern construction with misgivings. But in both instances he came to realize that what seems destructive often sets the situation in which new creation is possible.

One day I visited the site during the erection of the pre-fabricated frame of the building. The crane's 200 ft. boom picked up 25 ton members and swung them into place like matchsticks moved by the hand. I resented the garishly painted crane, this monster which humiliated my building [by its scale]. I watched the crane go through its many movements all the time calculating how many more days this "thing" was to dominate the site and building before a flattering photograph of the building could be made.

Now I am glad of this experience because it made me aware of the meaning of the crane in design, for it is merely the extension of the arm like a hammer. Now I began to think of members 100 tons in weight lifted by bigger cranes.

To this, he added, "Now the crane was a friend and the stimulus in the realization of a new form."[24]

In the Richards Building, the principal support for each laboratory tower consists of eight reinforced-concrete columns. Two of them occur on each of the four sides where they are placed at the third points (that is, positioned so as to divide the width of the elevation into three equal parts). These columnar supports appear to either side of the peripheral stair and exhaust towers (Fig. 188). The columns have an H-shaped profile, and are more complex than they initially appear.

The columns went up in sections, floor by floor, as post-tensioned components, each stage notched to accept the floors. In cross section the H has one wide and one narrow leg. The narrow leg (X in the diagram) is visible as the projecting element of the column, running the height of the building like Mies' I-beam outrigging. The wide leg (Y) is concealed within the wall, and provides a broad seat for two horizontal structural elements at right angles to one another. One of these (A) sits on the inside edge of the seat aligned with reinforcement holes H on the column. It is a Vierendeel truss, 47 feet long, 3 feet deep, and 22 inches thick, and it spans the space. (A Vierendeel truss resembles a ladder laid sideways; a normal truss, a ladder with diagonals between the rungs.) At each floor pairs of opposed columns received two of these trusses as *pre*-tensioned units (operation 1 in the diagram). Obviously the pair of trusses crossing at right angles to these (B) had to be dropped into place as three pieces (operation 2). Once in place they were *post*-tensioned. Next the stepped cantilever beams (C) around the exterior of the tower were fitted onto what space remained on the seat of the column (aligned with reinforcement hole H; again operation 1). The stepped profile of this perimeter beam reflects the structural nature of the cantilever, which ideally is thick at its columnar support and tapers (or here steps) to its projected outer end (at the corner of the building where two of these stepped perimeter beams meet). Once in place the crossed pair of trusses plus the outer perimeter beams comprised a "space frame"—that is, an interlocked structure of trussed members organized as an *area* structure for the floor slab it supports, rather than as a *linear* structure as is the case for pure skeletal construction. Finally, the nine squares of the crossed Vierendeels became 36 squares with the addition of secondary trusses in a cross-shaped pattern, where, again, one member (D) spans the full distance, while the companion member at right angles to it fits in as two pieces (E; operations 3 and 4). Structurally these secondary trusses serve only a minor stiffening function.†

Once the space frame for one floor was in place, another section of the H-column was hoisted into position. Since, in each section, the outside of the bottom of the column (X) is longer than the inside (Y) by the depth of the space-frame trussing, this new increment locked the space frame below in place, and also provided another flat H-shaped surface for the reception of the space frame above. So the eight-story towers rose. As the columns rose, section by section, reinforcing rods were successively threaded through them, and through the supported ends of the floor trusses. When the roof was reached, jacks fitted onto the tops of the columns *post*-tensioned them into a tight fit with the space frames they supported.

Regarding the complex columnar members of the total skeletal frame in a critical spirit, the carping critic may find the H-shape rather less appropriate for reinforced concrete than for steel, more a sign of gratitude to Mies than the ideal solution for this material. But Kahn has rationalized the notching of what would otherwise appear as an overly bulky member by stating that the cross-sectional shape of the column tends to minimize

† They were important during the erection of the building since they supported forms for the pouring of the floor slabs, thus eliminating the need for shoring in this operation. In the later towers of the Biology Research Building, however, they were eliminated, and the structure simplified. With their elimination, the outermost notch in the perimeter facing beams has been omitted, thus simplifying the visual effect of the fenestration.

FIGURE 194. *Richards Medical Research Building. Interior detail showing the juxtaposition of different kinds of concrete construction frankly avowed: concrete block, site-poured reinforced concrete, and, to the right of the window, a pre-cast reinforced-concrete framing component. Note that the holes through which the formwork was tied together have been retained in the site-poured concrete and that the pitted quality of the surface from defective packing has been deliberately left unpatched; compare with the hard, precise surfaces and sharp edges of the factory-produced member.*

the effect of eccentric loading.‡ The visual and symbolic significance of the notch is more important. The notch here celebrated the jointed nature that Kahn seeks for his architecture. A building, he has said, is "like your hand. The way the knuckles and joints come together makes each hand interesting and beautiful. In a building these details should not be put in a mitten and hidden. You should make the most of them."[25]

‡ The notching of the column tends to suggest this eccentric loading by *visually* isolating the seat for the trusses (Y) from that segment of the total cross section which projects outside the wall as an uninterrupted column (X). Moreover, the truss resting on the inside of the complex columnar member (Y) tends to bend the outside column segment (X) inward. Material removed from the notched area and placed toward the outside (X) increases the cross-sectional dimension of this part of the total member where, threaded through with post-tensioned rods, it counts more in resisting bending. But, to repeat, the particular solution has more visual than structural justification.

The skeletal towers complete, their peripheral stair and utility towers were site-poured like those of the core to finish the three-part operation. Piranesi would have relished the building spectacle: the cavernous site-poured concrete core, around which the crane lifted the giant pre-cast sculptural components of the frame, prior to the site-pouring of the utility towers outside the frame.

The composite nature of the masonry structure is especially evident inside where surfaces are exposed, and in a manner congenial to the "reality" sought in Brutalist thinking (Fig. 194). Here the poured work reveals the impress of wooden forms, the holes where the inner and outer forms were tied together, and the pitted quality typical of site tamping and vibration. On the other hand, the skeletal components reveal the smooth surfaces, sharp edges, and precise tolerances possible only with metal forms, steam curing, and factory control. These two types of concrete, in turn, contrast with the unfinished concrete block of the interior partitions (except where a few adamant scientists have demanded that they be painted), while the purplish-red brick veneer of the exterior shows through the windows. Here, in effect, we also see a hierarchy of prefabrication: the site-prepared portions of the building against the custom-designed, but factory-produced, components; and these beside such standard, universally available items as the concrete block and brick. Even these details, let alone the building as a whole, express the "build" of the structure, much as plan and mass reveal the "build" of served and servant spaces.

Finally, Kahn here realizes his desire to reveal the "build" of the services themselves, and not merely that of the areas which contain them. The vertical runs for mechanical equipment, as we have seen, occur in the big, tube-like towers. From these "trunks" of the system, the "branches" move out to the laboratory towers, floor by floor, as exposed conduits within the lattices of the ceiling space frames (Fig. 195). Through this structural webbing overhead, ducts, pipes, and cables are arranged in grid-like fashion so as generally to align with the right-angled elements of the space frames. The intervals between each of the squares provide convenient bays for fluorescent lighting troffers hung from brackets resting on the bottom chords of the trussing. True to Kahn's conviction that services should be revealed as part of the life of the building, they unapologetically appear as what they are.

THE "HARMONY OF SPACES"—AND SOME DISCORDS

Spaces, structure, services: from "form" to "design" Kahn conceives the Richards Medical Research Building as a revealed "harmony of

FIGURE 195. *Richards Medical Research Building. Reinforced-concrete space-frame ceiling at the corner of a laboratory "studio", with fluorescent lighting troughs hung between the grids and utilities threaded through the structural webbing.*

systems" and a "harmony of spaces," distinctively asserted one from another, yet coordinated to create the totality of the building. In this first definitive embodiment of Kahn's architectural philosophy, which had matured during years of teaching and practice, his intent is clear, however flawed in detail. Some of these flaws we have already observed. Above all, as Kahn confesses, the Richards Medical Research Building lacks the ultimate characteristic of the greatest architecture—a hierarchical har-

FIGURE 196. *Richards Medical Research Building. Detail of the entrance. This stairway, duplicated on the other side of the projecting stair tower to the right, rises to an open porch equivalent to the space of a laboratory unit, Kahn having envisioned that stacks of such "studios" would comprise the work spaces of the building.*

mony of spaces. This deficiency is common to most research centers, for a space hierarchy depends on the ordering of spaces of different sizes and shapes in relation to a dominant space, and in a progression toward a climax, whereas laboratories by their very nature imply repetitive cubicles (Kahn's solution) or, alternatively, open floors capable of flexible arrangement. Although such spaces as auditoriums, classrooms, and libraries in conjunction with laboratory facilities might, in other circumstances, have implemented Kahn's wish for a hierarchy of spaces, the Richards Building is wholly devoted to research laboratories.* And, as it happened, the life of the building in theory and the life of the building in practice have so much diverged that only at the entrance, where one of the laboratory platforms remains open as a porch, does the cubicle of space retain its integrity (Fig. 196). For the rest, practically all of the laboratory studios are extensively partitioned into "areas"—not, as Kahn carefully makes the distinction, into "spaces" (Fig. 198).

---

* The continuation of the Richards Medical Research Building by the towers of the Biology Research Building did offer some possibilities for differential compositional treatment, but very minor ones. Insofar as Kahn took cognizance of them, he did so in a rather arbitrary manner, which does little to illustrate his position.

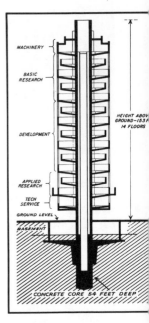

FIGURE 197. *Frank Lloyd Wright. Research tower, Johnson Wax Company, Racine, Wis., 1947–50. Typical laboratory with circular balcony, and cross section of the tower. For exterior view, see Figure 150.*

The very cellular organization of the building which Kahn sought presents the expected problems. Although most of the scientists working in the building appreciate the studio-like spaces in theory (while faculty in non-laboratory disciplines would perhaps be even more enthusiastic with the concept), the 45-foot square is sometimes too large and sometimes too small for specific activities, even though the better than 2,000 square feet of clear space in itself provides for considerable flexibility. More flexibility, surely, than in Wright's famous predecessor for Kahn's stacked laboratories, namely, the research tower for Johnson Wax (Fig. 197). The smaller, 40-foot squares of the Wright tower (alternating with still smaller circular balconies) possess the additional disadvantage of the inflexibility of the central utility core. An inconvenient resiliency occasioned by the bold cantilevering from this core, privacy purchased at the cost of an enforced existence behind translucent tubing, and the impossibility of locating related laboratories in different studios on the same floor are further factors that contrast poorly with Kahn's solution. But the battle over the advantages of enclosing a complex arrangement of spaces within an irregular mass in order to reveal it, or alternatively, to subsume the complexity within an omnibus container with mechanical conditioning to make it viable will never be finally resolved.† In principle, the reason for favoring one over the other is clear: the first is more humanistic in the effort to fit the building to men, the second more impersonal in its emphasis on process. In practice, however, the choice is more difficult, depending as it does on the quality of the space, on the tasks to be performed in it, and on the temperament of those who inhabit it.

In any event, whatever the shortcomings of his overly cubicled space in the Richards Building, Kahn attempted to overcome them in the Salk complex, where, to be sure, the ample site, permitting the low spread of the building, somewhat altered the problem.‡ In the Salk complex the laboratories occur in three-story blocks (one story being below ground level) with broad, open, factory-like floors (Fig. 184). The ductwork for services runs overhead, threaded through the trussing that supports the floors, and spans the space from wall to wall. Logical and convenient this mechanical system may be, but it is substantially concealed and therefore hardly in accord with Kahn's belief that the total "life" of the building be vividly evident.* There is also the question of why laboratories "wanted to be" studios in the Richards complex, whereas they "wanted to be" big flexible spaces in the Salk complex. One suspects that Kahn came to realize that he should never have let the laboratories be what they became in the Richards Building. If this change from one kind of laboratory to another brings some of the hocus-pocus of "existence will" into question, it nevertheless does not seriously invalidate Kahn's phi-

---

† A variant of the same problem led to the dispute over the relative merits of the kind of library represented by the Boston Public Library and that by the Newberry Library. See *American Buildings and Their Architects: Progressive and Academic Ideals at the Turn of the Twentieth Century*, Chapter 7.

‡ The problem was only "somewhat" altered because, even though its site was small, the Richards Building could have been massed as a tall blocky slab with open floors. In short, it could have been designed in the way that most architects would have chosen, rather than as a series of towers.

* Kahn's initial roof scheme showed exposed sculptural forms that combined structural functions for the roof and conduit functions for the utilities in a manner much more vivid than that of the scheme finally used, the latter probably being a gesture as much to economy as to efficiency. A diagrammatic cross section of the early scheme appears in Banham, "On Trial: Louis Kahn," *Architectural Review*, March 1962, pp. 203–6.

losophy. Had he not asked what a laboratory "wanted to be" in the first place, the open floors of the Salk Center might never have been fringed by the series of semi-independent cubicles, bridged to the central laboratory, in which each scientist has his own study above a garden and immediately adjacent to his apparatus. But to return to the Richards Building, it should not have been so uniformly planned for laboratory study units which were at once too large for studies and both too small and too inflexible for some laboratory purposes.

To the visitor unfamiliar with the building, it is immediately apparent on stepping from the elevator that the plan does not work as Kahn intended (Fig. 198; compare with the ideal plan, Fig. 188). Even if it

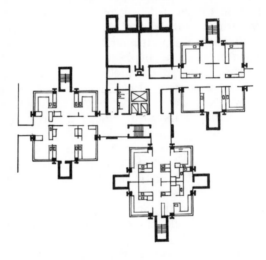

FIGURE 198. *Richards Medical Research Building. Floor plan as typically partitioned in use. (Compare with the ideal plan, Figure 188.) The architectural "spaces" for which Kahn strove have very nearly become the randomly partitioned "areas" which he deplored.*

had, the complexity of corridors angled in three directions from the elevators would, under the best of circumstances, have caused initial disorientation. (Of course the building was not designed for visitors—though it has had many—but for work; and it might be argued that if visitors are disoriented their momentary inconvenience is justifiable penalty for intrusion.) As the plan has worked out in practice, however, our disorientation is compounded by the mélange of apparatus, files, and storage cabinets lining the corridors. Since no space was specifically designed for secretaries, those who do not occupy part of the studio laboratories are inconveniently lodged in the corridors. Desks for assistants and technicians also occur here and there in the halls. Curious this confusion in the hallways of a building so conspicuously informed by the ideal of "servant" spaces accommodating "served" spaces. Surely few laboratories can ever have been more inadequately supplied with "servant" spaces than this, where hollow walls might have lined hallways for storage, and bays might have lodged secretaries.

Although nothing quite overcomes our disappointment that the corridors are burdened in this way, their short runs before turning are a welcome change from the remorseless bureaucratic alley. Moreover, whereas most such hallways are gloomy with shadow or stark with artificial illumination, these show a lively play of natural light and shadow because of the glazing where they couple the laboratory towers to the central block.

In the confusion of corners and apparatus, it is not always easy to be certain where the "corridor" ends and the "studio" begins. Partitioning bisects the studios in order to extend the hallways from the central core into the very heart of the laboratory spaces, and this not only destroys the laboratory studio as a unified space but, by continuing the corridor, also obscures the jointed quality of the building from inside. The corridor extensions are the least of the extensive partitioning which has confused the studio unity that Kahn originally intended. In fact, the kinks of the plan and the kinks of the improvised partitioning, together with the smallness of most of the resulting spaces crowded with paraphernalia for experiments, all combine to give the laboratories something of the effect of the interior of a submarine. Some sense of the jointed quality of the building and of the logic of Kahn's plan can be recovered only by looking from one tower to another, although even in such views Kahn's design seems less a logical scheme than a complex configuration of planar and linear elements harking back to complicated examples of De Stijl-inspired constructivism of the twenties, such as Kiesler's display for the Paris Exposition (Fig. 82).

In addition, two details of the laboratory fenestration (Fig. 199)—the stepping of the perimeter beam, and the folded metal window enframement and flashing—possess the kind of planar complexity that a De Stijl-inspired architect would have relished. It is as though Kahn had deliberately fought shy of a more sculptural treatment of the window detailing in his eagerness to let the building be what it wanted to be. The planar quality is even more evident in the flatness of the juncture of brick parapeting, concrete frame, and window glass. Kahn might have created projections and recessions of elements (at greater economic cost), thus giving them a slight play of light and shadow which would orchestrate the larger pattern of light and shade created by the irregular mass. Since he

FIGURE 199. *Richards Medical Research Building. Window detail of a laboratory tower.*

opted for complete planarity, the wall has a curious effect, being appropriate as a *flat* statement of what the building wants to be, but at the same time an uncomfortably taut one for such a plastic mass. The planarity of all surfaces makes the recall of *De Stijl* the more insistent. Not that Kahn thought of it when designing the building; on the contrary, the arbitrary pictorialism of *De Stijl,* and its too frequent use of structure as a playful *jeu d'esprit,* are anathema to Kahn (although these qualities have not been spurned by his superficial imitators). Kahn orders the kaleidoscopic aspects of his composition with a gravity recalling Mies' approach to the interlocked T's in the Seagram plan and mass†; here, however, the arrangement of elements is a less arbitrary one in that it results principally from functional and structural concerns, rather than from formal considerations. The complex manipulation of discrete elements in folded configurations seems to have awakened ghosts of *De Stijl* inadvert-

† See p. 269 above.

ently. Like the Wrightian overtones of the building (which Kahn does not deny, but which have come as something of a surprise to him) the un-premeditated recall of De Stijl is not an "influence," but another indication of the comprehensive synthesis of the modern movement that Kahn effected in his building.

In views across and through the folded complex, the life of the building—within it, and even around it—attains a climax (Fig. 200). Through the glass apparatus in the glazed corner of one of the upper laboratories we look down the building at people and equipment, at the work going on in other laboratories, at fragments of the surrounding buildings and trees, at those who pass by outside and then, a short time later, magically step as Lilliputians into a cubicle high up on the building and out again. In these views we sense, too, the building as the "harboring thing" that Kahn believes it should be, holding and sheltering human activity. Very occasionally, and especially low in the building where the view out is more oppressive, curtains drawn at windows may testify to the feeling of some that the pleated quality of the building permits too much surveillance. Initially, many of those working in it did feel both exposed and distracted, although most have become immune to the disadvantages, and now seem to enjoy having cubistic vignettes of community endeavor.‡ The disjointed surprise, multiplicity of scale, and unlikely juxtaposition of these views fascinate even more than those of the crowds moving around the ramp of the Guggenheim.

Looking from his corner window at an adjacent tier of cubicles several years after the building's completion, one of the senior scientists admitted that, "We hated the building as a laboratory when we moved into it. I suppose the low point came about a year and a half after we moved. Very little worked in the way that Kahn's plans promised. For a while it seemed that we never would be able to fit ourselves and our equipment into these floors. But we finally did, although not in the way that it was supposed to happen. We improvised. Gradually I've come to like the building, and I believe that many others feel as I do. I've never worked in a laboratory where I was so aware of what others were doing. It's not only that you can look out of the windows and see others at work. It's that I have to wind through all parts of my own section of the lab whenever I leave my desk. Admittedly, it's a rabbit warren, and I'd never recommend that another lab be built like this one. In the biology extension, the spaces were made larger, and the whole plan is more logical; but I prefer this building."[26] Certainly the building has not

‡ Problems of privacy in the cluster configuration have been eliminated in the extension for biology by the in-line arrangement of the towers, although at the expense of the visual pleasure of views from Richards.

FIGURE 200. *Richards Medical Research Center. Views from one laboratory tower to another.*

worked as Kahn planned it. Those virtues that it does have as a place in which to work, however, result from his concern that it be something more than a set of gloomy institutional corridors flanked by files of closed doors opening into the usual factory or warehouse spaces randomly partitioned.

THE "HARMONY OF SYSTEMS"—AND SOME MORE DISCORDS

If, in fact, the "harmony of spaces" of the Richards Medical Research Building falls somewhat short of its theory, the same can be said of the "harmony of systems." We have already mentioned the questionable appropriateness of certain timber-like aspects of the reinforced-concrete framing of the laboratory towers, despite the creative use made of pre- and post-tensioning. But in terms of Kahn's philosophy, another deficiency with respect to the structure, visual rather than technological, is quite as much to the point. As Reyner Banham has emphasized in a critique of Kahn's building,[27] at first glance it appears that the conspicuous peripheral utility towers, rather than the relatively modest columns to either side of them, support the laboratory frame—an ambiguity which may owe something to Kahn's original intention to have them do just this. The flaw here is more than merely the ambiguity of what does what. The prominence given to the mechanical services puts the structure in the shade (and in both senses of the phrase). Without equipment the building may be uncomfortable or unworkable; without structure it does not exist. Relative to structure, moreover, equipment is ephemeral, here today, perhaps replaced tomorrow, and especially in a laboratory building.

Kahn has substantially influenced the profession because of his concern for a visible balance among the spaces, structure, and mechanical equipment of a building. If pressed to emphasize one of these aspects above the others, he would choose spaces as the essence of architecture to those who inhabit it—"spaces," rather than "space," since the plural form of the word suggests enclosure as well as void, boundaries as well as continuity. Then, he would probably give structure second place as the maker of spaces. Despite this presumed order of preferences, it is understandable that he somewhat exaggerated the mechanical services in the Richards Building: the nature of the commission encouraged it. Of more importance, however, Kahn shared in the growing awareness after World War II that mechanical services were among the most neglected elements in building design—a neglect that Banham's *The Well-Tempered Environment* eventually made explicit. Whereas a combination of air conditioning, "daylight" illumination, flexible wiring, conduits for machines and telephone equipment, acoustical treatment, and the like was either exceptional or nonexistent in pre-war architecture, it became commonplace after the war. As the expenditure for this burgeoning equipment rose to a fifth, a fourth, even a third of the building budget (in, say a building wired and conditioned for the most elaborate computers), it became increasingly apparent to many architects that they exerted no control whatsoever over the design of what a substantial part of the building budget paid for, except to bury it. From a more conceptual position, the Brutalist (and his allies) would argue that pipes, ducts, and cables should be frankly expressed. At very least the architect should choose from available forms for these items, and provide for their display in his design. After all, Le Corbusier had made roof-top sculpture of ventilators and drains. Why not equivalent effects from plumbing, wiring, and other mechanical equipment? The result could well produce the kind of visual satisfaction that even the layman experiences when

417

stepping into a handsome engine room with its frank avowal of machinery. At best, the architect might incorporate the mechanical services in a system of conduits and containers that would convey some sense of their functions while enhancing the building design, as Mies had done with structure. Quite apart from any such conceptual considerations, new developments in equipment itself increasingly forced attention to its architectural treatment. If, for example, lighting units are hung at regular intervals from a ceiling, as was the case with pre-war commercial and office buildings, these units are "fixtures" within the space; if, on the other hand, the entire ceiling is an illuminated plane, then the fixtures take on architectural size and architectural function (Figs. 46, 47). In the midst of the profession's discussion about this varied equipment, Kahn came to his conviction about the need to make such "services" a prominent part of the design, as essential "systems" in the "life" of the building.

Of the two places in the Richards Medical Research Building where he revealed its mechanical systems—namely, in the towers and in the ceilings—the towers were both the more original and the more architectural. They of course have their precedents in the exposed equipment systems of various sorts in industrial plants. Many chemical operations, such as petroleum refining, involve nothing but machinery, conduits, and storage facilities completely exposed to the out-of-doors. Some bulk storage operations, such as grain elevatoring, not only flaunt the cubes and cylinders of the massive containers, but often the drama of chutes and conveyor belts as well. The thrust of stacks, transformers, and the like through the shells of factory buildings is even more commonplace. Quite as much to the point, for that matter, are the more hesitantly revealed elevator shafts and (though not equipment) stair wells on building exteriors, as we have already seen them in some buildings within the International Style, in PSFS, and in the Inland Steel Building (see, for example, Figs. 36, 53, 62, and 73). So there is nothing absolutely extraordinary about Kahn's utility towers. In fact, it could be maintained that these towers (except for the ones housing stairs) are rather less expressive of the services they contain than are those in most of our examples. They are certainly less so than the stacks which Eero Saarinen had placed as a functional colonnade outside his well-publicized Dynamometer Laboratories for testing engines at the General Motors Research Center (1945–50) in Warren, Michigan (Fig. 201), which may have inspired Kahn, even as the sculptural vents atop Le Corbusier's *Unité d'Habitation* doubtless influenced both (Fig. 180). Indeed, to those unfamiliar with the reasoning behind the plan of the Richards Medical Research Building, the exteriors of the utility towers very likely possess a largeness, blindness, and mystery wholly inappropriate (as Banham has observed) to the scale, the rationale,

FIGURE 201. *Eero Saarinen. Dynamometer Building, General Motors Technical Center, Warren, Mich., 1945–50. The building was extended in 1956.*

and the matter-of-factness of the utility channels that are boxed inside.*

To dismiss the utility towers on any or all of these grounds, however, is to miss their chief significance. First of all, no previous building with the architectural pretensions of the Richards Medical Research Building had exploited the utility system to such conspicuous and such monumental effect. Secondly, the timing of Kahn's towers was such that they had maximum effect on the discussion as to the role of design with respect to mechanical equipment. Thirdly, Kahn's towers, unlike Saarinen's stacks, were not simply startling incidents—not simply "details" for an especially difficult exhaust problem in a particular part of the building, and without influence anywhere else in the complex. Instead, these utility towers were part of a comprehensive demonstration of what the life of the building required.

In addition to the towers, the exposed utilities in the webs of the space-frame ceilings of the laboratories are another, and more explicit, instance in which Kahn revealed the mechanical systems of his building. As already suggested, elaborately integrated ceiling systems in a modular organization developed very rapidly after World War II. By now, of course, ceilings that incorporate lighting, air conditioning, acoustical properties, and sockets at regular intervals for the attachment of flexible

---

* Early in the design phase, Kahn did attempt to mold the exhaust towers a little more closely to their function. In variant schemes they were fluted and/or stepped out, floor by floor, at the lower levels of the building so as to indicate the progressive enlargement of the area of stack required to contain exhaust vents as these accumulated with the rise of the laboratory tier; see illustrations in Museum of Modern Art, *Louis I. Kahn, Architect Alfred Newton Richards Medical Research Building*. The stepped utility towers recall an early version of PSFS (Fig. 40) which shows Howe's impractical scheme for revealing the different heights of his elevator shafts as a stepped pyramid. Kahn rejected a highly sculptural treatment of the utility towers in his own preliminary designs partly for economic and partly for visual reasons. The sheer towers finally adopted give a bolder architectural effect and bring the building more firmly to the ground.

419

partitioning are commonplace.[28] They are of three types, and the creative aspect of their development (although not consistent of course) has tended toward frankness of expression, in at least partial accord with Brutalist ideals, even if unconsciously so. Most common is the suspension of a ceiling plane from the floor slab above to create a space for the concealment of conduits. A second type makes a lattice of the ceiling, with the conduits above clearly visible through the grid, unless they are "painted out," as frequently happens. The lattice may simply hang from the slab above; alternatively, it may be the lower face of a space frame with the utilities running through the webbing, such as Kahn used for the Richards Medical Research Building (Fig. 195). (It was, in fact, the tetrahedron ceilings in reinforced concrete of the Yale Art Gallery, with the exposed equipment threaded through the triangulated spaces, for which Kahn was best known immediately prior to his commission for the Richards Building.[29]) Yet a third type would seem to be even more consistent with Kahn's philosophy. It eliminates the depressed ceiling plane entirely, whether hung or part of the space frame. This is constructed by corrugating or waffling the underside of the structural floor itself, which not only stiffens the slab, but provides tubes and boxes for equipment systems which are most integral with structure (if somewhat less flexible than the other systems where utilities can be freely altered, and for this reason possibly less desirable in a laboratory).

The medical research staff at the University of Pennsylvania was relatively sanguine about the open ceilings and rough wall surfaces during the early stages of the project, but once in the building some of the scientists had second thoughts about their practicality. In certain of the microbiology laboratories, which must be as nearly dust-free as possible, ceiling panels veiled Kahn's architectural reality as soon as the building was occupied. In certain other laboratories ceiling panels have been installed as much in the interests of privacy as sterility, since complaints are numerous about the lack of privacy in offices with open ceilings, and of noise transmission from one area to another. Then, too, except in the most elegant engine rooms, architects are more likely to applaud pipes, conduits, ducts, and lighting fixtures "in the raw" than non-professionals, to whom exposed equipment is likely to mean an unfinished building, thus arousing suspicion that a limited budget forced the stringency.†

Anyone sensitive to architectural values, however, must feel the blandness of the space in those laboratories where panels have been in-

† In this connection I was interested in the reactions of workmen installing equipment during the final stages of construction. I wondered whether plumbers, electricians, sheet metal workers, and those in other trades, would be pleased to have their handiwork on display in a building of such architectural pretension. Quite the contrary, or so it seemed from my informal poll. The remark of one electrician

serted in the ceiling grid, as compared to the invigorating presence of the latticed interweaving elsewhere. This is not to assert that all of the pleasure of an open ceiling to the person attuned to architecture derives from the sight of the present example, which is very crude. Some of it comes from the thought of what the exposed services presage.

Like so much else about this building, Kahn's solution to the revelation of the mechanical systems is a first step. Like the Guggenheim, the Richards Medical Research Building is also to be completed in the future—"to be continued" so to speak. As the possibilities implicit in the Richards Building are realized, Kahn's building will indeed seem as "archaic" as he himself had described it. Its awkward aspects are already abundantly evident. But these stem from the very comprehensiveness of Kahn's program, both explicit and implicit. His building draws freely and unselfconsciously on the richness of modern developments. It simultaneously opens toward the "grand tradition" of history as understood in Beaux-Arts theory, but with a theoretical commitment to function, plus an awareness of primal building forms and primal human responses to them which Beaux-Arts theory never possessed. In the early 1960's, of all contemporary American architecture Kahn's Richards Building seemed to chart the most comprehensive program for the future. Overpraised at the time it may have been; but of such archaisms new worlds are born.

POSTSCRIPT

This has been a study of architectural philosophies and movements in terms of a few buildings. It deliberately stops around 1960, with Kahn's Richards Medical Research Building, well short of the "present" in which this book appears. During the course of the sixties, the climate of progressive thought on architecture has steadily shifted away from such exclusive concern with *buildings* and toward more attention to *environments*. When the Richards Medical Research Building was rising many events which seem certain to make the sixties something of a watershed decade for the architectural profession were still largely of the future. Barely foreshadowed by events in the fifties, and around 1960 still largely in the future, were second thoughts about monolithic urban renewal schemes conceived as bargain basement versions of Rockefeller Center, reaction against the autocratic ways of the highwaymen, urban riots, hippie

---

typifies the general attitude. Looking up at the ceiling, and shaking his head, he said, "I don't understand it." And then, as though he thought I might be a prospective customer, he added, "If you really want to see the kind of work we do, you should go downtown and take a look at the Sheraton." But of course the work he does is precisely what cannot be seen at the Sheraton!

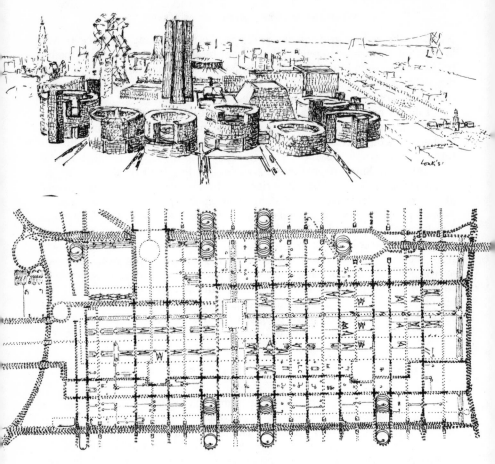

FIGURE 202, 203. *Louis Kahn. Above: perspective sketch of the Philadelphia downtown area showing civic buildings at the center and peripheral parking towers. The cylindrical parking towers serve omnibus functions: parking on the lower levels, with a shopping plaza open to the sky midway up the structure which is walled by a circle of offices and (possibly) apartments. Below: proposed plan for traffic flow in downtown Philadelphia, 1956. Arrows show differentiated volume and direction of traffic flow within the downtown grid. The thickly arrowed arteries at top and bottom are major expressways which provide peripheral boundaries for the area north and south. The Delaware and Schuylkill Rivers provide boundaries east and west. The spirals are movements on cylindrical ramps into the peripheral parking towers. The dotted line signifies staccato traffic movement; small arrows, flow traffic. Curved arrows indicate parking; large arrow heads, garages; crosses are intersections.*

and welfare challenges to establishment ways, appreciation of "pop" phenomena of all sorts, growing recognition that the fullest application of advanced technology implied a far more revolutionary adjustment for architecture than the mere use of new materials on the outside or new equipment in the basement. Finally, for the United States at least, a costly and humiliating war both dramatized and exacerbated these issues. By the end of the decade there were those who scorned the very idea that the principle business of the architect was (or at least should be) the design of individual buildings intended to glorify the client who had paid for them and to demonstrate the prowess of the architect who had conceived them.

Few (possibly none) have denied Kahn's gifts as an architect, both as designer and as thinker. But in the new climate of opinion some have asked whether, in his buildings subsequent to the Richards, Kahn has not been overly concerned with the monumental. Some have wondered whether the mystique of "form" (even though Kahn's meaning is emphatically anti-formal)—and especially in the lapidary epigrammatic manner of his phraseology—sanctifies the act of design as such a momentous act that monumentality is the inevitable result. Such critics, as we have already indicated, are somewhat suspicious of the sybaritic monumentality of Salk Center set off in its privileged setting. Not that they would banish this magnificent complex—especially magnificent if eventually completed as it has been contemplated. On the contrary, most are thoroughly in favor of its completion. They merely question whether monuments of this sort will really chart what is likely to be most relevant in architecture of the future.

But of course, to reply to these strictures, the implications of Kahn's philosophy range beyond the single building. What *it* wants to be: *it* may be a city, for example. Whoever is wary about the implications of Salk Center may see his scheme of 1956 for the center of Philadelphia (Figs. 202, 203) as prophecy. Bounded by expressways north and south, and by the Delaware and Schuylkill Rivers east and west, the grid of the city becomes a field of force for the differentiated energies implicit in differentiated movement. The "form" of the energies has determined the architect's diaphanous "design"; "design" that is almost invisible in the "form" of what the movement wants to be. In the center, the looming buildings are in scale with the energy grid that is the city. They are monuments to be sure, and to be expected from an architect so attuned to the monumental; but they are also of a piece with the whole. On the periphery, like the peripheral towers of Richards, gigantic cylindrical parking towers are even more of a piece with the grid. Kahn himself has compared them to the massively scaled fortifications that ring medieval towns, their beetling scale born of their function, while incidentally providing an exhila-

FIGURE 204. *Richards Medical Research Building. General view of the rear (south) elevation showing the later addition of towers for the Biology Building (left) with the air intake towers for the Medical Building (right).*

rating contrast to the smaller scale of most of what is inside. Here the lower levels of the fortifications have become parking garages ramped off of the expressways. Midway up in the cylinders, plazas, open to the sky, provide shopping areas, encircled by offices, and possibly intermixed with apartments. In this project, therefore, the role of design ranges from the frank monumentality of some of the central buildings, through the acquired monumentality of megastructures housing omnibus activities at the periphery, to the non-monumentality (except as a concept) of cumulative process. So the possibilities implicit in Kahn's conception of architecture as a harmony of spaces and a harmony of systems opens beyond the individual building to the kind of architectural problems that are likely to be of most consequence in the future.

Kahn therefore provides an appropriate stopping point in this series of case studies of buildings. Especially is this true for his Richards Medical Research Building—his "archaic" moment of discovery. Certainly the Richards Building has been his most influential undertaking: in part simply because of its position in time; in part because of the didactic nature of the building, so directly illustrative of the terms of his teaching; in part because of the rounded manner in which he attempted in his design to encompass the entire life of an essentially functional problem; in part because of its rather impersonal quality in comparison with other later buildings, more Kahn's own (and doubtless greater for this reason), but by this very fact less accessible as starting points for other architects.

Whatever the future of monuments and individual buildings in a profession which is increasingly compelled to concern itself with larger systems, the design of the individual building has been the principal concern of the architect during the period covered by these essays. This is not the place to assess the degree of importance that individual buildings may have in the future. Suffice it merely to conclude in a platitudinous vein. Many of the problems surrounding the design of particular buildings also apply to the design of larger architectural systems. More than this, the designer of these augmented systems will hark back to buildings of the past for clues as to how to bring to new situations some of the human satisfactions and meaning that were built into the old ones. Finally, of course, the buildings of the past are—or should be—part of the larger system. Surely they are a vital aspect of environment. So, even in turning away from them in one sense, we return to them in another.

NOTES

The notes contain the following abbreviations.
For the multivolume work of which this book is the concluding volume:

AB&TA   *American Buildings and Their Architects*

For periodicals:

Am. Archt.	*American Architect*
Am. Mag. Art	*American Magazine of Art* (subsequently *Mag. Art*)
Arch. d'Auj.	*Architecture d'Aujourd'hui*
Arch. For.	*Architectural Forum*
Arch. Rec.	*Architectural Record*
Arch. Rev.	*Architectural Review*
Art in Am.	*Art in America*
Eng. N.-R.	*Engineering News-Record*
JAE	*Journal of Architectural Education*
JRIBA	*Journal of the Royal Institute of British Architects*
JSAH	*Journal of the Society of Architectural Historians*
Mag. Art	*Magazine of Art*
Pen. Pts.	*Pencil Points*
Prog. Arch.	*Progressive Architecture*

1. ASSOCIATED ARCHITECTS: ROCKEFELLER CENTER

On the history of the design development and the architectural importance of the Center, a series of articles by Winston Weisman derived from his doctoral dissertation on the Center are most important:

"The Way of the Price Mechanism: the Rockefeller Center," *Arch. Rev.,* December 1950, pp. 399–405.

"Who Designed Rockefeller Center?," *JSAH,* March 1951, pp. 11–17.

"Slab Buildings," *Arch. Rev.,* February 1952, pp. 119–23.

"The First Landscaped Skyscraper," *JSAH,* May 1959, pp. 54–59.

David Loth, *The City within a City: The Romance of Rockefeller Center,* New York, Morrow, 1966, is a popular account, helpful in its historical chapters, although these are largely digests of Weisman and of Fosdick (below). Douglas Haskell, "Unity and Harmony at Rockefeller Center," *Arch. For.,* January–February 1966, pp. 42–47, provides an appreciative and perceptive appraisal. Raymond B. Fosdick, *John D. Rockefeller, Jr.: A Portrait,* New York, Harper, 1956, is the standard biography. Periodical literature contemporary with erection of the Center is legion; the following articles are valuable in respect to general background. For popular accounts of the real estate operation, see Frederick Allen, "Radio City Cultural Center?," *Harper's,* April 1932, pp. 534–45; also M. R. Werner, "Radio City: From Real Estate to Art," *Atlantic Monthly,* April 1933, pp. 463–76. For all phases of the architectural design, organization, and technology, a series of articles in the *Architectural Forum* extending throughout 1932 and early 1933 is particularly helpful; the series opens with Raymond Hood, "The Design of Rockefeller Center," *Arch. For.,* January 1932, pp. 1–12. For the engineering aspects of the Center, see "Planning Rockefeller Center, New York," *Eng. N.-R.,* Nov. 17, 1932, pp. 579–99; the entire issue is devoted to various technical aspects of the complex. On design, see also Henry H. Dean, "A New Idea in City Rebuilding," *Am. Archt.,* April 1931, pp. 32–35+; and L. Andrew Reinhard, "Gardens on the Roofs of Radio City," *Am. Archt.,* November 1931, pp. 34–35+. On the International Building, see "International Building," *Arch. For.,* November 1935, pp. 456–68. The most convenient general source for photographs is the popular tourist album by Samuel Chamberlain, *Rockefeller Center,* New York, Hastings House, rev. ed. 1956. The Public Relations Office for the Center has prepared a booklet (constantly revised) entitled *A Digest of Facts About Rockefeller Center.*

1. For a general discussion of the arcadian aspects of the "city beautiful" movement in America, see Christopher Tunnard, *The City of Man,* New York, Scribner, 1953, Chap. 13. This book and Christopher Tunnard and John H. Reed, *American Skyline,* Boston and New York, Houghton, Mifflin, 1955, provide popular discussions of some of the urban problems that I mention in this chapter, and contain basic bibliography. Jane Jacobs, *The Death and Life of Great American Cities,* New York, Random House, 1961, has much negative comment on the arcadian cultural or monumental center.

2. See Note 7 below.

3. In 1928, a similar scheme had projected hotels where the department stores were located in the revised plan of early 1930; in fact, a series of schemes prior to 1930 contained many suggestions made by a number of firms.

4. Weisman, *JSAH,* May 1959, pp. 56f. This connection between the Promenade and the Plaza had already been anticipated in a scheme by Harvey Wiley

Corbett in 1929 which would have created an inclined ramp from Fifth Avenue to an Opera Plaza above street level, with the entrance to the Opera at the level of the second floor (or *piano nobile*). The vehicular entrance was to have been under this elevated plaza. The raised plaza continued on decks all around the Opera, thus roofing over 49th and 50th Streets on its flanks. See *ibid.*, fig. 3; also Weisman, *JSAH*, March 1951, p. 14 and fig. 6.

5. Information on the early problems of the underground mall from a personal interview with Wallace K. Harrison.

6. Haskell, *Arch. For.*, January–February 1966, p. 45.

7. The plan referred to in Note 3 above might have generated more cross traffic through the plaza area, although this was not its specific purpose. In addition, Hood especially, in 1930, worked on a series of schemes in which he hollowed out part of the lobby floor of the RCA slab into an interior space which he specifically termed a "forum." This was to have been located midway along the length of the corridor through the RCA slab, but it proved too wasteful of expensive store space to be feasible. See Weisman, *Arch. Rev.*, December 1950, 402.

8. Interview with Wallace K. Harrison.

9. How lack of coordinated planning affected the plazas on the Avenue of the Americas is discussed in "Slaughter on 6th Avenue," *Arch. For.*, June 1965, pp. 13–17.

10. Johnson mentioned his enthusiasm for the Ryoanji Garden in Cleveland Amory, "Philip Johnson," *Vogue*, May 1964, p. 189. For other examples of Japanese influence on Johnson's work, see Clay Lancaster, *The Japanese Influence in America*, New York, Walton Rawls, 1963, pp. 165f.

11. Fosdick, *John D. Rockefeller, Jr.*, Chaps. 14 and 19, discusses Rockefeller's zeal for building; so does Loth, *The City within a City*, Chap. 5.

12. Weisman, *JSAH*, March 1951, p. 16; also *Arch. Rev.*, December 1950, p. 401. Todd made the statement at a meeting held on Dec. 6, 1929, as reported in the minutes.

13. Letter by Reinhard published in *Arch. Rec.*, August 1947, p. 20; and in *Arch. For.*, February 1948, pp. 24f.

14. Interview with Wallace K. Harrison.

15. Excellent photographs of the "hatbox" scheme appear in Dean, *Am. Archt.*, April 1931, pp. 32–33. See *Pen. Pts.*, May 1933, p. 387+, for commentary on the hostile reception accorded this preliminary scheme.

16. Hood, *Arch. For.*, January 1932, p. 2.

17. The original zoning act stemmed from *Report of the Commission on Building Districts and Restrictions* (New York, June 2, 1916). This, in turn, was based on the famous *Report on Heights of Buildings Commission* (New York, Dec. 23, 1913).

18. Interview with Wallace K. Harrison.

19. Lewis Mumford, "Mr. Rockefeller's Center," *New Yorker*, December 23, 1933, p. 29. Mumford recommended the alternative of three relatively low slabs parallel to that of the RCA Building.

20. Anson B. Cutts, "From the Sublime to the Ridiculous," *Arch. Rev.*, June 1934, p. 199. Obituary of Raymond Hood, *Arch. For.*, February 1935, p. 132. In a personal interview with the author, Wallace K. Harrison also testified that the gardens were Hood's particular concern. For a general discussion of all garden schemes, see Weisman, *JSAH*, May 1959, pp. 54–59.

21. Photographs of the existing roof gardens appear in Chamberlain, *Rockefeller Center*, pp. 45, 46, 48–50.

22. On the significance of the slab concept in modern architecture and its use for the Center buildings, see Weisman, *Arch. Rev.*, February 1952, pp. 119–23. Weisman, however, exaggerates the primacy of the Center in this respect; see my discussion in Chapter 2 on use of the slab for the office tower of the Philadelphia Saving Fund Society Building. Moreover, Harrison has informed me that his firm designed a slab-shaped building for Pennsylvania Power and Light in Harrisburg, Pa., in the mid-twenties.

23. Allen, *Harper's*, April 1932, p. 539, makes the comparison with the wedge. Hood's statement comes from an interview with Wallace K. Harrison.

24. Information on the early state of air conditioning in the Center from the Public Relations Office. On the Milam Building and pioneer installations of air conditioning in office buildings, see p. 97 below. On the development of environmental technology since 1930, see Reyner Banham, *The Architecture of the Well-Tempered Environment*, London, Architectural Press, 1969, especially Chap. 10 for the development of the mechanical ceiling.

25. On this same point, see Douglas Haskell, "The Lost New York of the Pan-American Airways Building," *Arch. For.*, November 1963, pp. 106–11. For the reference to planning possibilities on the Avenue of the Americas, see citation in Note 9.

26. Interview with L. Andrew Reinhard, *Am. Archt.*, November 1931, p. 76. See also another interview with Reinhard by Douglas Haskell, "A Radio City Architect's Economics," *Nation*, Jan. 25, 1933, p. 102.

27. Hood, *Arch. For.*, January 1932, p. 3.

28. Henry-Russell Hitchcock, "The Architecture of Bureaucracy and the Architecture of Genius," *Arch. Rev.*, January 1947, pp. 2–6; also his introduction to *Architecture of Skidmore, Owings & Merrill, 1950–1962*, New York, Praeger, 1963. Winston Weisman compares the organization of the Center team with other somewhat similar architectural organizations, in *Arch. Rev.*, September 1953, pp. 145–51.

29. L. Andrew Reinhard, "Organization for Cooperation," and Wallace K. Harrison, "Drafting Room Practice," *Arch. For.*, January 1932, pp. 77–80 and 81–84.

30. Interview with Wallace K. Harrison.

31. In 1928 the original lease was signed for 24 years, with options for renewals running to 2015. In 1953 the lease was extended with renewal options to 2069.

32. See especially John A. Kouwenhoven, *Made in America*, Garden City, Doubleday, 1948, pp. 250–52; this analysis of Hood's development exaggerates the depth of a modernity that is almost literally skin-deep, as I indicate in the discussion that follows.

33. Louis Sullivan, "The Chicago Tribune Competition," *Arch. Rec.*, February 1923, pp. 151–57.

34. Mumford, *New Yorker*, Dec. 23, 1933, p. 29.

35. Hugh Ferriss, *The Metropolis of Tomorrow*, New York, Ives Washburn, 1929; the citations from p. 84. Of all the sketches of existing buildings in the book, only that of the Chrysler Building is not literally within the gothicized-modern mode of skyscraper design. With respect to Hood's buildings, Ferriss included blurred images of the exterior massing of the Chicago Tribune and American Radiator Buildings. Of the Daily News Building he showed only the sunken globe in the spotlighted lobby, which seems to have been especially congenial to the quasi-cosmic pretentiousness of his approach to the skyscraper.

36. The plaza and the separated towers do, however, appear in Morris' earliest schemes, with detail and massing simplified under the influence of modern esthetics.

37. Ferriss, *Metropolis of Tomorrow*, p. 80.
38. Ralph Adams Cram, "Radio City and After," *American Mercury*, July 1932, pp. 291–96; reprinted in his *Convictions and Controversies*, Boston, Marshall Jones, 1925, pp. 33–44.
39. Interview with Wallace K. Harrison.
40. Loth, *The City within a City*, p. 94. Louis Sullivan, "The Tall Office Building Artistically Considered," most conveniently available in *Kindergarten Chats and Other Writings*, New York, Wittenborn, 1947, p. 206. On the vexing problem of whether a "skyscraper" is to be defined in terms primarily of height or technology, see Winston Weisman, "New York and the Problem of the First Skyscraper," *JSAH*, March 1953, pp. 13–21, and J. Carson Webster, "The Skyscraper: Logical and Historical Considerations," *JSAH*, December 1959, pp. 126–39. See also pp. 106f. below.
41. Mumford makes these points in his critique: *New Yorker*, Dec. 23, 1933, p. 29.
42. More satisfactory approaches to the treatment of the entrance base of the RCA slab appeared in some of the earlier studies. See Weisman, *JSAH*, May 1959, pp. 56 and 57, figs. 4 and 8; also Fig. 7 above.
43. For representative articles on the murals and sculpture of the Center, see:
   Am. Mag. Art, February 1937, pp. 77–86.
   American Photography, July 1933, pp. 404–8.
   Parnassus, October 1932, pp. 1–3.
   Am. Archt., November 1933, pp. 58–59.
   Architecture, March 1934, pp. 143–46.
   Chamberlain, *Rockefeller Center*, contains a number of illustrations of art works, and the Public Relations Office lists works, their locations, and their meanings, in the brochure *The Art Program of Rockefeller Center and Its Contributing Artists* (revised to August 1953).
44. Interview with Wallace K. Harrison.
45. *Idem*, and information from the Center engineering staff.
46. On the Music Hall and the development of its design, see *Arch. For.*, April 1932, pp. 355–60. On its technology, *Eng. N.-R.*, Nov. 17, 1932, pp. 583–86. For criticism, see Douglas Haskell, "Roxy's Advantage over God," *Nation*, Jan. 4, 1933, p. 11. Loth, *The City within a City*, Chap. 8, gives a breezy historical account of the operations of the Music Hall.
47. Information on the European trip from an interview with Wallace K. Harrison. On Reinhardt and the Grosses Schauspielhaus, see, for example, Dennis Sharp, *Modern Architecture and Expressionism*, London, Longmans, 1966, pp. 55ff. For Roxy's ideas on the Music Hall, see S. L. Rothafel, "The Architect and the Box Office," *Arch. For.*, September 1932, pp. 194–96.
48. Warner, *Atlantic Monthly*, April 1933, p. 472.
49. On the initial promotion of the Center, see *Arch. For.*, October 1934, pp. 292–98.
50. Mumford, *New Yorker*, Dec. 23, 1933, p. 30.
51. See, for example, Montgomery Schuyler, *American Architecture and Other Writings*, W. Jordy and R. Coe, eds., Cambridge, Harvard University Press, 1961, Vol. 2, pp. 556–74.

2. HOWE & LESCAZE: PHILADELPHIA SAVING FUND SOCIETY BUILDING

This chapter is a reduced and substantially revised version of my "PSFS: Its Development and Its Significance in Modern Architecture," *JSAH,* May 1962, pp. 47–83, with an appendix of documents, pp. 95–102. That article also formed the basis for a shorter illustrated appraisal of the building, with Henry L. Wright as co-author, *Arch. For.,* May 1964, pp. 124–29+. The original version owes much both to Robert A. M. Stern, "PSFS: Beaux-Arts Theory and Rational Expressionism," also published in the May 1962 issue of *JSAH,* pp. 84–95; and to Frederick Gutheim, "The Philadelphia Saving Fund Society Building: A Re-Appraisal," *Arch. Rec.,* October 1949, pp. 88–95+.

The most important accounts written at the time of the building's completion are "A New Shelter for Savings," *Arch. For.,* December 1932, pp. 482–98, and "Philadelphia Saving Fund Society," *Arch. Rev.,* March 1933, pp. 101–6. "Philadelphia's Fancy," *Fortune,* December 1932, pp. 65–69+, discusses the building from the client's point of view.

On the technology of the building, see "Building Façade Emphasizes Steel Frame," *Eng. N.-R.,* Nov. 10, 1932, pp. 549–52.

Howe's esthetic and philosophical attitudes toward modern architecture at the time of the design of PSFS appear in three articles:

"What Is Modern Architecture Trying to Express?," *Am. Archt.,* May 1930, pp. 22–25.

"Functional Aesthetics and the Social Ideal," *Pen. Pts.,* April 1932, pp. 215–18.

"Abstract Design in Modern Architecture," *Parnassus,* October 1936, pp. 29–31.

1. Gutheim, *Arch. Rec.,* October 1949, p. 89.
2. Stern, *JSAH,* May 1962, pp. 84–95.
3. *Fortune,* December 1932, p. 68, attributes the remark to James Willcox; but William Lescaze informs me that the attribution is erroneous.
4. *Ibid.*
5. Fortunately, Willcox asked Howe at various times to prepare memoranda on the architects' reasoning behind their design; they are reproduced in the appendix to Jordy article indicated above.
6. Howe's memoranda provide the best statements on the rationale for the design.
7. Although it is true that the banking space can be accounted for in terms of the International Style, except for a monumentality which is akin to that favored by Beaux-Arts design, and of course the specific structural-functional desire to transfer the loads of the office columns to a minimum number of columns within the open space below, it is at least marginally interesting that the treatment of the banking space also shows striking parallels to Wright's Larkin Building. Compare the placement of the entrance and also the flanking rows of piers within the room to the plan and interior of the Larkin Building (Figs. 142, 144). Howe was aware of Wright's work, and, in fact, wrote to Willcox that he had studied modern architecture as it had developed "to the west in America and to the east in Europe"; see *JSAH,* May 1962, p. 96. Lescaze, however, in a personal interview, categorically denied any influence of Wright on PSFS.
8. *Ibid.,* p. 98.

9. Howe, *Pen. Pts.*, April 1932, p. 217.
10. Reyner Banham, *The Architecture of the Well-Tempered Environment*, London, Architectural Press, 1969, pp. 209f. The information on air conditioning which follows derives partly from an interview with Mr. Robert W. Isaacs, who was one of the presidents of PSFS to succeed Willcox and who served as a member of the original building committee, and partly from Gutheim and the article in *Fortune*, December 1932, both cited above.
11. *Fortune*, December 1932, p. 69.
12. "George Howe 1886–1955," *Arch. For.*, June 1955, p. 113. Information for the following biographical sketch is derived from the foregoing and also from;
    Alfred Barr, Henry-Russell Hitchcock, Philip Johnson, and Lewis Mumford, *Modern Architects*, New York, Norton, 1932, pp. 143–55
    Obituary in *Arch. Rec.*, July 1955, p. 20f.
    Interview with Louis McAllister.
13. Discussed and illustrated in Jordy, *JSAH*, May 1962, pp. 57f.
14. Biographical information from an interview with William Lescaze; Hitchcock in Barr *et al.*, *Modern Architects*, p. 144; and *Arch. For.*, December 1934, p. 399.
15. *Arch. Rec.*, November 1928, pp. 417–22.
16. Richard Neutra's more important Ring School project was designed in 1926. For future school design, Howe & Lescaze's Hessian Hills (1931), Croton-on-Hudson, N.Y., is more important than Oak Lane; illustrated in Barr *et al.*, *Modern Architects*, p. 152.
17. For a more extensive discussion of the design process leading up to the model, see Jordy, *JSAH*, May 1962, pp. 63f.
18. For details, see *ibid.*, pp. 68f.
19. Mr. Isaac W. Roberts informed me that Willcox was virtually a one-man building committee in consultation with Howe. The official committee was called upon for nominal advice, suggestions, and approval.
20. *JSAH*, May 1962, p. 98.
21. Gutheim, *Arch. Rec.*, October 1949, p. 89.
22. Banham, *Well-Tempered Environment*, pp. 211f. The principal alteration in the big banking room, for which neither Howe nor Lescaze was responsible, has been the provision for increased illumination. This has necessitated two renovations of the ceiling. Gutheim, *Arch. Rec.*, October 1949, p. 92, discusses and illustrates the first, done shortly after World War II. The initial remodeling produced an all-over pattern of flush rectangles of light in the ceiling plane, which, however discreet in themselves, created a strident pattern of overhead light that reflections in the marble further complicated. The increased illumination from the ceiling made possible the elimination of counter lamps as part of the simultaneous remodeling of counters to permit the handling of more business. In 1965–66, the present fixtures in the banking room were installed; these create a regular pattern of paired circles of light flush with the ceiling plane. *PSFS News*, October 1966, pp. 10–13, discusses and illustrates this later change.
23. *JSAH*, May 1962, p. 101.
24. *Arch. Rev.*, March 1933, p. 104.
25. Together with comparable changes in lighting throughout the building, the colors have been slightly intensified, but basically accord with the architects' specifications.
26. I owe this information to E. W. Bolton, Jr., who was in charge of drawings and specifications for Howe & Lescaze from 1930 onward.

27. For further discussion, see Gutheim, *Arch. Rec.*, October 1949, pp. 94ff. On the development of the mechanical ceiling, see Banham, *Well-Tempered Environment*, Chap. 10.

28. In making this statement I do not include Philip Johnson's design of the Four Seasons Restaurant in the Seagram Building. This was really a separate design commission; one, moreover, which is in many respects out of key with the rest of the building, whatever its merits in its own right.

29. *JSAH*, May 1962, pp. 98, 99.

30. *Ibid.*, p. 96. For more about Howe's conviction that the modern architect must subordinate his individuality in favor of a group style, and about his views as to the nature of the modern world which forced this universalizing role, see the three articles by Howe cited in the introduction to notes for this chapter.

31. The paperback reissue of *The International Style*, New York, Norton, 1966, is especially valuable. In addition to the original text, it contains an afterword by Hitchcock written in 1951, roughly twenty years after the original publication, plus a foreword of 1966 that assesses the other two pieces. In the preface to this book, Hitchcock and Johnson give Alfred Barr, then director of the Museum of Modern Art, credit for the term "International Style." But see Hitchcock's earlier use in the epigraph to this chapter, p. 87.

32. See my article "The International Style in the 1930's," *JSAH*, March 1965, pp. 10–14. This issue of the *Journal* is devoted to a symposium on the architecture of that decade; other articles especially relevant to issues raised here are those by Peter Serenyi, Sibyl Moholy-Nagy, and Vincent J. Scully, Jr.

33. I have adapted this presentation of Le Corbusier's principles, along with his illustrations, from his *Oeuvre complète de 1910–1929*, Zurich, Girsberger, 1956, pp. 128f.; pp. 23 and 77 are also pertinent.

34. Published in *Parnassus*, October 1936, pp. 29–31.

35. For a more extensive discussion of this point, and its broader implications for the whole of the International Style, see my article "The Symbolic Essence of Modern European Architecture of the Twenties and Its Continuing Influence," *JSAH*, October 1963, pp. 177–87.

36. John Summerson, *Heavenly Mansions*, London, Cresset, 1949, pp. 190f., makes a point of Le Corbusier's wit, but without specifically mentioning Dada or Surrealism.

37. *JSAH*, May 1962, p. 98.

38. From "The Tall Building Artistically Considered," conveniently reprinted in Sullivan, *Kindergarten Chats and Other Writings*, p. 205.

39. When he did confront it, in his competition scheme with Adolf Meyer for the Chicago Tribune Tower (1922), he arbitrarily varied the repetitious fenestration.

40. Jordy, *JSAH*, May 1962, p. 78.

41. Another similarity between PSFS and the Chemnitz Schocken Store occurs in the window treatment within the "notch" area of the former and in the roof-top setbacks of the latter. In both, the continuous window band of one floor cantilevered from interior columns is topped by two floors, where the columns come to the surface of the wall and thus rhythmically interrupt the continuity of the window band. It may be carrying the comparison too far, but the projecting roof slab of the Schocken Store may even have helped to inspire the cantilevers of the office tower of PSFS, since the cantilevers in PSFS began in the model as just such a slab.

42. On Howe's dilemma regarding the sign on the early branch bank, see Jordy, *JSAH*, May 1962, p. 55. On the advent of the abbreviation "PSFS," *ibid.*, p. 64 and n. 55.
43. Neutra's Garden Apartments in Los Angeles (1927) are more insistently banded.
44. Although I believe this generalization to be true, it requires much investigation. I have suggested some specific comparisons in *JSAH*, May 1962, p. 78, n. 98.
45. I justify this statement in extended comment, *ibid.*, nn. 99, 100.
46. Howe, *Parnassus*, October 1936, pp. 30f.
47. Winston Weisman, "Philadelphia Functionalism and Sullivan," *JSAH*, March 1961, pp. 3–19.
48. I overlooked this parallel between PSFS and Max Taut's design for the Chicago Tribune Competition in my original article.
49. Interview with William Lescaze.
50. So does the central block of Neutra's project for the Ring School (1926); more literally so perhaps than any of his other early work, because here projecting columns at fairly close intervals support (or seem to) the roof slab which they lightly abut.
51. H. Allen Brooks, "PSFS: A Source for Its Design," *JSAH*, December 1968, pp. 299–302.
52. Vincent Scully, *American Architecture and Urbanism,* New York and Washington, Praeger, 1969, pp. 151, 154, makes a telling comparison between PSFS and Knut Lönberg-Holm's project for the Chicago Tribune Competition of 1922, about which conclusions reached with respect to the Tagblatt-Turm comparison are applicable.
53. Stern, *JSAH*, May 1962, pp. 84–95.
54. General discussions of this tradition of nineteenth-century rationalism include: Henry-Russell Hitchcock, *Architecture, Nineteenth and Twentieth Centuries,* Baltimore, Penguin, 1958, Chaps. 6 and 15.
Peter Collins, *Changing Ideals in Modern Architecture,* Montreal, McGill, 1965, Chap. 3.
Introduction to Montgomery Schuyler, in *American Architecture and Other Writings,* edited by W. Jordy and R. Coe, Cambridge, Harvard University Press, 1961.

3. BREUER: FERRY HOUSE, VASSAR COLLEGE

The principal publications of Ferry House are "For Practice in Housekeeping," *Arch. Rec.*, June 1950, pp. 118–19, and "An Architecture of Energy," *Arch. Rec.*, January 1952, pp. 127–34. The first article covers the initial design; the second one, the completed building.

The most important books on Breuer, all of them containing statements by him, are:

Peter Blake, *Marcel Breuer: Architect and Designer,* New York, Architectural Record, 1949, which contains a bibliography.
Marcel Breuer: Sun and Shadow, edited with notes by Peter Blake, New York, Dodd Mead, 1955.
Marcel Breuer, *Buildings and Projects, 1921–1961,* with introduction by Granston Jones, Stuttgart-New York, Praeger, 1962.

For the situation in modern architecture before World War II, with particular reference to American houses, see Vincent Scully, Jr., "Doldrums in the Suburbs, *JSAH*, March 1965, pp. 36–47.

Several articles of mine traverse ground covered in this chapter:
"Humanism in Contemporary Architecture: Tough- and Tender-Minded,"
JAE, Summer 1960, pp. 3–10.
"The International Style in the Thirties," *JSAH,* March 1965, pp. 10–14.
"Aftermath of the Bauhaus: Mies, Gropius, and Breuer," in Donald Fleming
and Bernard Bailyn, eds., *The Intellectual Migration, Europe and America,
1930–1960,* Cambridge, Harvard University Press, 1969, pp. 485–543, re-
printed from *Perspectives in American History,* Vol. 2 (1968).

1. On Main Hall, see Rosalie Thorn McKenna, "James Renwick, Jr., and the Second
   Empire Style in the United States," *Am. Mag. Art,* March 1951, pp. 97–101.
2. *Arch. Rec.,* June 1950, p. 118.
3. "The New Empiricism," *Arch. Rev.,* June 1948, p. 236.
4. Frank Lloyd Wright, *The Natural House,* New York, Horizon, 1954, especially
   pp. 87–132. He succinctly comments on his use of "Usonian" in *Arch. For.,*
   January 1948, p. 67.
5. The label derives from an exhibition which brought regional developments to
   national attention; see *Architecture of the San Francisco Bay Region,* with
   introduction by Gardner Dailey and Clarence Mayhew plus an appreciative
   essay by Lewis Mumford, San Francisco Museum of Art, 1949. See also
   "Domestic Architecture of the San Francisco Bay Area," *Arch. Rec.,* September
   1949, pp. 119–26.
6. The De Mandrot House (1930–31) at Le Pradet and the Mathes House (1935)
   at Océan, both on the French Riviera, and the E.razuris House (1930) in
   Chile. For illustrations of them, see Le Corbusier, *Oeuvre complète: 1929–1934,*
   Zurich, Girsberger, 1935, pp. 45–52, and 58–62; *Oeuvre complète: 1934–1938,*
   1953, pp. 134–39.
7. See pp. 206f. below.
8. These were the two volumes published by Wasmuth, which I mention in *AB&TA:
   Progressive and Academic Ideals at the Turn of the Twentieth Century,* Chap.
   3, n. 2.
9. See *ibid.,* Chap. 7, n. 30.
10. I discuss the degree to which the principal achievement of the International
    Style had been completed by 1932 in *JSAH,* March 1965, p. 11.
11. In a brilliant, but exaggerated, critical *tour de force,* Vincent Scully, Jr.,
    describes the whole of the esthetic of the International Style as composed
    piecemeal of variants of the Ward Willitts House by Frank Lloyd Wright:
    Modern Architecture: The Architecture of Democracy, New York, Braziller,
    1961, p. 26.
12. Le Corbusier, *When the Cathedrals Were White,* New York, Reynal & Hitch-
    cock, 1947 (originally published in Paris, 1937). The quoted phrase is the
    subtitle of the book and appears repeatedly in the text.
13. The stridently "American" prejudices of editorials by Elizabeth Gordon in
    House Beautiful during the fifties epitomize the type. In fairness, it should
    be added that *House Beautiful* bolstered its American theme in respect to
    modern architecture with issues which handsomely featured the work of Wright
    and of Greene & Greene.
14. Jordy, *JAE,* Summer 1960, pp. 3–10. Scully, *JSAH,* March 1965, pp. 36–47.
15. Reprinted in Blake, *Breuer,* p. 122; also Jones, *Breuer,* p. 257.
16. *Marcel Breuer: Sun and Shadow,* p. 38.
17. See the original plan, *Arch. Rec.,* June 1950, p. 119.
18. *Arch. Rec.,* January 1952, p. 131.

19. Blake, *Breuer,* presents the fullest account of the architect's career.
20. For a more detailed discussion, see Jordy, "The Symbolic Essence of Modern European Architecture of the Twenties and Its Continuing Influence," *JSAH,* October 1963, pp. 177–87.
21. Bernard Berenson, *Piero della Francesca; or The Ineloquent in Art,* New York, Macmillan, 1954.
22. Katherine Gilbert, "Clean and Organic: A Study in Architectural Semantics," *JSAH,* October 1951, pp. 3–7.
23. Reyner Banham, *Theory and Design in the First Machine Age,* London, Architectural Press; New York, Praeger, 1960, makes many illuminating observations which parallel and extend these remarks on the dilemma confronting the International Style: the need for change implicit in advanced technology and the desire for norms implicit in mass-produced standards. Banham eventually uses his discussion in a curiously negative way, as I have indicated in the reference cited in Note 20.
24. Interview with Marcel Breuer.
25. From "Where Do We Stand?" reprinted in Blake, *Breuer,* pp. 119f.; also in Jones, *Breuer,* p. 260, with the changes in paragraphing reproduced here.
26. Plato, *Philebus* (Benjamin Jowett, tr.), sec. 51.
27. Quoted in Bruno Zevi, *Poetica dell' architettura neo-plastica,* Milan, Tamburini, 1953, p. 35.
28. On Breuer's use of color and texture, see his statement in *Marcel Breuer: Sun and Shadow,* pp. 80–99.
29. *Arch. Rec.,* January 1952, p. 131.
30. See especially Vincent Scully, Jr., *Shingle Style,* New Haven, Yale University Press, 1955.
31. Blake, *Breuer,* p. 84.
32. Before reaching the United States, Breuer did a project for a ski lodge to have been built in Obergurgl in the Tyrol. Here he made bold use of stone slabs as end walls, between which he fitted interior arrangements organized as two light wooden boxes—a somewhat discordant combination. Among his early American houses (all done with Gropius), the Haggerty House in Cohasset (1938) and the Breuer House in Lincoln (1939), both in Massachusetts, are the most conspicuous instances of the use of stone slabs and walls with the boxed volume of interior space, but the combination is timidly employed compared to some of his later houses. In the Frank House in Pittsburgh, Pa., (1939) an extensive complex of curved and straight retaining walls prophesies that used to organize the landscape at Ferry House (particularly as projected in his original scheme). The retaining walls for the Frank House, however, seem to have been suggested more by functional, than by formal, considerations, owing to the need to terrace a sloping site.
33. A more overt and formal use of the slab is indicated in his Project for a War Memorial for Cambridge, Mass. (1945); this trend modestly continues in the Geller House in Lawrence, Long Island (1945), and achieves distinction in one of his most important residential designs, the Robinson House in Williamstown, Mass. (1947).
34. After Mies arrived in the United States, two exhibitions of his work which preceded that at the Museum of Modern Art were those at the Art Institute of Chicago (1938) and at the Albright Gallery in Buffalo (1939), but both were limited in scope.
35. See especially Le Corbusier's *Towards a New Architecture,* first English ed., London, Payson & Clarke, 1927; originally published as *Vers une Architecture,* Paris, 1922.

36. The original drawings for Ferry House do show the fireplace as a free-standing element more commandingly placed in the center of the lounge; see *Arch. Rec.,* June 1950, p. 119.
37. See parallel observations by Scully, *JSAH,* March 1965, pp. 38ff. I had written these observations, even to using some of the same examples, prior to hearing Professor Scully's talk on which his article is based. It may be worth mentioning because our independent observations come to such substantial agreement.
38. Paolo Portoghesi, "Marcel Breuer," *Zodiac,* 8, Milan, 1961, p. 55.
39. Baudelaire in a letter to Mme. Paul Meurice, cited in George H. Hamilton, *Manet and His Critics,* New Haven, Yale University Press, 1954, p. 36.
40. See also Jordy, *JSAH,* March 1965, p. 13.
41. Whitney Stoddard, *Adventure in Architecture; Building the New St. John's,* New York and London, Longmans, 1958, discusses the client's program with respect to the initial phases of Breuer's design.

4. MIES VAN DER ROHE: LAKE SHORE AND SEAGRAM

Shorter variants of this essay appeared as "Seagram Assessed," *Arch. Rev.,* December 1958, pp. 374–82, and as a talk prepared for overseas broadcast for the United States Information Service, reprinted as "Mies van der Rohe," *Zodiac,* 8, Milan, 1961, pp. 28–33.
Important publications of 860 Lake Shore during and after its building are:
"Glass in a Steel Frame," *Arch. For.,* January 1950, pp. 75–77.
"Mies van der Rohe," *Arch. For.,* November 1952, pp. 93–103.
"Immeubles à appartements à Chicago: Promontory et Lake Shore," *Arch. d'Auj.,* September 1950, pp. 42–47.
Alfred Roth, "Bemerkungen zu den Wohnhochhausern in Chicago, Lake Shore Drive and Promontory-apartmenthaus," *Werk,* January 1951, pp. 5–9.
Early publications of the Seagram Building are:
"Seagram's Bronze Tower," *Arch. For.,* July 1958, pp. 66–77.
Arthur Drexler, "The Seagram Building," *Arch. Rec.,* July 1958, pp. 139–47.
"Un monumento a New York: il Seagram Building," *Casabella,* January 1959, pp. 3–11.
"Siège de la Société Seagram, New York, 1958," *Arch. d'Auj.,* September, 1958, pp. 90–95.
Lewis Mumford, "The Lesson of the Master: the Seagram Building," *New Yorker,* Sept. 13, 1958, pp. 141–48+.
Thomas H. Creighton, "Seagram House Re-Reassessed," *Prog. Arch.,* June 1959, pp. 140–45. The last is a critique of the above-mentioned articles by Mumford and myself, some points of which I have incorporated in this version; for my reply, see *Prog. Arch.,* August 1959, p. 58+.
The principal books on Mies van der Rohe are:
Philip Johnson, *Mies van der Rohe,* New York, Museum of Modern Art, 1947, rev. ed. 1954; contains bibliography.
Ludwig Hilberseimer, *Mies van der Rohe,* Chicago, Theobald, 1956.
Arthur Drexler, *Mies van der Rohe,* New York, Braziller, 1960; contains bibliography.
Werner Blaser, *Mies van der Rohe: The Art of Structure,* London, Thomas & Hudson, 1965.
The material in the first few pages of this chapter is elaborated in my essay,

"Aftermath of the Bauhaus: Mies, Gropius, and Breuer," in *The Atlantic Migration*, edited by Fleming and Bailyn, Cambridge, Harvard University Press, 1964.

1. Katharine Kuh (reporting an interview), "Mies van der Rohe: Modern Classicist," *Saturday Review of Literature*, January 23, 1965, p. 61.
2. Interview with Myron Goldsmith. The publication to which he referred is George Nelson, *Industrial Architecture of Albert Kahn, Inc.*, New York, Architectural Book, 1939; see especially p. 38.
3. Schuyler, in *American Architecture and Other Writings*, edited by Jordy and Coe, Vol. 2, p. 381; discussed in *AB&TA: Progressive and Academic Ideals at the Turn of the Twentieth Century*, pp. 52f.
4. The quotations from Mies in this paragraph come from the following sources: a recording of a series of statements by American architects issued by the Reynolds Aluminum Company under the title "Conversations Regarding the Future of Architecture"; Kuh, *Saturday Review*, Jan. 23, 1965, pp. 23f.; and *Arch. For.*, November 1952, p. 94.
5. Kuh, *Saturday Review*, Jan. 23, 1965, p. 23.
6. Mies' question occurs in the recording "Conversations Regarding the Future of Architecture." Hilberseimer, *Mies*, compares, as we have, the Temple of Poseidon and the Parthenon, which is the more significant since Hilberseimer was a close professional colleague and friend of Mies.
7. For a related, but somewhat different, treatment of the Americanization of Mies' style, see Jordy, *Atlantic Mig. ation*.
8. On Scheerbart and Taut, see Dennis Sharp, *Modern Architecture and Expressionism*, London, Longmans Green, 1966, Chap. 7; also Banham, *Theory and Design in the First Machine Age*, Chap. 19.
9. The best presentation of the Equitable on its opening appeared in *Arch. For.*, September 1948, pp. 97–106. For an evaluation made twenty years later, see Walter Creese, "The Equitable Revisited," *Arch. For.*, June 1968, pp. 40–45. Creese notes that Belluschi has specifically traced his Equitable Building to a 1943 project for a glass building published in an issue of the *Architectural Forum* devoted to speculation on American architecture in "194X," the "X" standing for some year after the end of World War II: *Arch. For.*, May 1943, pp. 108–12.
10. For basic coverage of the Secretariat on its completion, see *Arch. For.*, November 1950, pp. 93–112, and *Arch. d'Auj.*, September 1950, pp. 73–87. For a more critical account, see Henry S. Churchill, "United Nations Headquarters: a Description and an Appraisal," *Arch. Rec.*, July 1952, pp. 104–22.
11. For the Lever Building on its completion, see *Arch. For.*, June 1952, pp. 101–11, and *Arch. Rec.*, June 1952, pp. 130–35. See also *Architecture of Skidmore, Owings & Merrill*, introd. by Henry-Russell Hitchcock, pp. 22–27.
12. H. T. Cadbury-Brown (reporting an interview), "Ludwig Mies van der Rohe," *Architectural Association Journal*, July–August 1959, p. 40.
13. The statement appears in the prologue to Blaser, *Mies*.
14. *Arch. For.*, November 1952, p. 96. For further information about Greenwald, see David Carlson, "City Builder, Greenwald," *Arch. For.*, May 1958, pp. 118–19+. Greenwald's extensive patronage of Mies' architecture was tragically terminated with his death in an airplane crash in 1959: *Arch. For.*, March 1959, p. 65.
15. *Arch. For.*, January 1950, p. 77, and May 1952, p. 96.
16. Reyner Banham, "On Trial: Mies van der Rohe," *Arch. Rev.*, August 1962, pp. 125f.

17. For the financial aspects of the Seagram, see *Arch. For.*, July 1958, pp. 76–77.
18. For more about Mrs. Lambert's role, see *Arch. For.*, July 1958, p. 77, and "How a Building Gets Built," *Vassar Alumnae Magazine*, February 1959, pp. 13–19.
19. Interview with Peter Carter.
20. Creighton, *Prog. Arch.*, June 1959, p. 145.
21. Drexler, *Arch. Rec.*, July 1958, p. 140.
22. Emphasized by Creighton, *Prog. Arch.*, June 1959, p. 143.
23. Drexler, *Arch. Rec.*, July 1958, p. 140, perceptively, but perfunctorily, alludes to the subtle recollections of *De Stijl* in the Seagram composition.
24. For the design of the Four Seasons, see *Interiors*, December 1959, pp. 80–87+; *Prog. Arch*, December 1959, pp. 142–47; also William Jordy, "The Mies-less Johnson," *Arch. For.*, September 1954, pp. 114–23.
25. *Arch. For.*, July 1958, pp. 73–75, discusses various aspects of the interior detailing.
26. Creighton, *Prog. Arch.*, June 1959, p. 144.
27. *Ibid.*, p. 143.
28. Drexler, *Arch. Rec.*, July 1958, p. 140.
29. Richard Kelly was the lighting consultant.
30. *Arch. For.*, November 1952, p. 94.
31. Lewis Mumford, "The Lesson of the Master," *New Yorker*, Sept. 13, 1958, p. 23.

5. WRIGHT: GUGGENHEIM MUSEUM

The best basic presentation of the Guggenheim is the Museum's own photographic brochure containing statements by Wright on his work, *The Solomon R. Guggenheim Museum*, New York, 1960. The original scheme as displayed in the model of 1945 is most fully described in "The Modern Gallery," *Arch. For.*, January 1946, pp. 82–88. Arthur Drexler, *The Drawings of Frank Lloyd Wright*, New York, Horizon, 1962, contains several alternate designs made for the Guggenheim during the course of its development. Milton Lomask, *Seed Money: The Guggenheim Story*, New York, Farrar Straus, 1964, Chaps. 9 and 10, discusses the Museum in the context of the history of the family. Vincent Scully, Jr., *Frank Lloyd Wright*, New York, Braziller, 1960, discusses the Guggenheim in the context of Wright's career. Presentations and critiques of the building on its completion are legion.

Especially comprehensive and/or perceptive are:

Peter Blake, "The Guggenheim: Museum or Monument?", *Arch. For.*, December 1959, pp. 86–92, which is supplemented by a sampling of excerpts from other critical articles at the time of the Museum's opening.

Henry-Russell Hitchcock, "Notes of a Traveller: Wright and Kahn," *Zodiac*, 6, Milan, 1960, pp. 15–20.

Lewis Mumford, "What Hath Wright Wrought?", *New Yorker*, Dec. 5, 1959, pp. 105+.

Walter McQuade, "Architecture," *Nation*, Nov. 7, 1959, pp. 335–38.

Edgar Kaufmann, Jr., "The Form of Space for Art," *Art in Am.*, Winter 1958–59, p. 77.

"Frank Lloyd Wright's Sole Legacy to New York," *Interiors*, December 1959, pp. 88–95.

"Museo Guggenheim, Nova York," *Habitat*, July 1960, pp. 12–17.

"Le ultime creazione di Frank Lloyd Wright," *Architettura,* November 1959, pp. 472–83.

Carola Giedeon-Welcker, "Zum neuen Guggenheim-museum in New York," *Werk,* May 1960, pp. 178–81.

Articles on the structure and engineering of the Guggenheim are:

"Spiral Art Museum is Built Like a Work of Art," *Eng. N.-R.,* Dec. 5, 1957, pp. 42–45.

George Cohen, "Frank Lloyd Wright's Guggenheim Museum," *Concrete Construction,* March 1958, pp. 9–13.

George Cohen, *Archeseum,* a typescript of the contractor's recollections of the problems of building the Museum.

1. See *AB&TA: Progressive and Academic Ideals at the Turn of the Twentieth Century;* especially pp. 207f.
2. Kaufmann, *Art in Am.,* Winter 1958–59, p. 77.
3. Kenneth Sawyer made this observation in an off-hand manner in the Baltimore *Sun,* Nov. 22, 1959; clipping preserved in scrapbook at the Museum. See also the more specific analysis in text below p. 345.
4. *Guggenheim Museum,* pp. 16f.
5. Drexler, *Drawings of Wright,* p. 300.
6. *Sixty Years of Living Architecture: The Work of Frank Lloyd Wright,* New York, Guggenheim Museum, 1953; caption for illustrations of Fallingwater. The catalogue was issued by the Museum on the occasion of an exhibition of Wright's work.
7. *Eng. N.-R.,* Dec. 5, 1957, p. 44; Cohen, *Concrete Construction,* March 1958, p. 12. The angle of the outside wall of the topmost turn had to be decreased slightly (and fortunately so for the composition) because it overhung the sidewalk.
8. I am indebted to Professor Mendel Glickman, the structural engineer for the building, to George N. Cohen, its contractor, and to William H. Short, Wright's supervising architect on the site, for interviews and letters about the structure of the building. In the opinion of all, the discussion of the structure of the ramp and monitor briefly presented in *Arch. Rec.,* May 1958, p. 190, is erroneous in some details; nevertheless this article is helpful and contains structural diagrams.
9. "The Destruction of the Box," a talk by Wright to the Junior Chapter of the American Institute of Architects, New York, 1952; published in *Frank Lloyd Wright: Writings and Buildings,* edited by E. Kaufmann and B. Raeburn, New York, Horizon, 1960, pp. 284–85.
10. Vincent Scully, *Frank Lloyd Wright,* New York, Braziller, 1965, p. 29, makes this comparison, and also relates the inverted columns of Johnson Wax to Evans' reconstruction of similar columns in the Minoan Palace at Knossos.
11. Interview with William H. Short.
12. I owe the following discussion of the sequence of construction conceptions especially to a series of lengthy letters with diagrams generously provided by Professor Mendel Glickman; but see also Note 8 above.
13. *Arch. For.,* January 1946, p. 82; these words of Wright were widely publicized in different versions, as were most of his remarks on the building. On this statement, see also Mumford, *New Yorker,* Dec. 5, 1959, p. 112.
14. *Guggenheim Museum,* pp. 16f.
15. *Guggenheim Museum,* p. 20.
16. *Arch. For.,* January 1946, p. 85.

17. Cohen, *Archeseum*, p. 3, states that the major objections of the Building Department concerned "absence of stairs for quick egress, absence of fire towers to comply with local laws, cantilever of upper story beyond building line, use of welded expanded metal for reinforcing, use of plastics for domes and skylights, use of cork for walls and floors, failure to provide accurate and proper statement of occupancy, proper height of roof above sidewalk, adequate and satisfactory mechanical appurtenances."

18. Cohen, *Archeseum*, p. 1.

19. Information on the polygonal scheme originally agreed upon comes from interviews with George N. Cohen and William H. Short. Among several schemes which Wright himself submitted to Solomon R. Guggenheim in 1943, there was an unhappy version for a hexagonal mass; see Drexler, *Drawings of Wright*, figs. 193, 276.

20. In addition to the usual contractual arrangements, the Board of Trustees required Cohen to post an especially high performance bond.

21. Letters and interviews with William H. Short and George N. Cohen. According to Short, the X's in the final design (which seem so wrong) developed quickly during a week-end trip which he made with Cohen and Spero to Taliesin West, primarily to discuss several problems about the dome. At one point in the meeting Wright drew X's in each of the areas inscribed by the hairpin ribs. "Do it like this," he said. The pressure of time thereafter was such that the shop drawings were made quickly, and Wright approved, perhaps cursorily. Whether he liked the result or not, Short is uncertain. Wright saw the dome just once after the scaffolding had been removed, immediately prior to his death; but he was too jubilant that the building was nearly complete to quibble at shortcomings, if he noticed them.

22. Scully, *Wright*, p. 31.

23. New York *Times*, Dec. 12, 1956, p. 56; see also Harry T. Guggenheim's reply to the artists, Dec. 24, 1956, p. 2. On Wright's attitude toward painting and sculpture, see James M. Fitch, *Architecture and the Esthetics of Plenty*, New York, Columbia University Press, 1961, pp. 104–23; also Edgar Kaufmann, Jr., "Frank Lloyd Wright and the Fine Arts," *Perspecta*, 8, 1963, pp. 37–42.

24. Sweeney resigned his directorship of the Guggenheim to become head of the Museum of Fine Arts in Houston, Tex. In the addition of Cullinen Hall to this museum by Mies van der Rohe, with its monumentally open space and extensive glazing, Sweeney had another demanding gallery on his hands with qualities almost antithetical to those at the Guggenheim. On the contrast between Wright's and Mies' ideals of museum space, see Blake, *Arch. For.*, December 1959, pp. 89f.

25. Kramer, *Arts*, December 1959, p. 51.

26. *Guggenheim Museum*, p. 17.

27. *Ibid.*, p. 19.

28. On Wright's use of "banding lines" in his early houses, see *AB&TA: Progressive and Academic Ideals at the Turn of the Twentieth Century*, Chapter 3. For the tradition out of which they derived, see Scully, *Shingle Style, passim*.

29. *Arch. For.*, October 1945, p. 9.

30. An account of the original lighting, handsomely illustrated, appears in a brochure issued by the company responsible for it: I. D. Robbins, *The Lighting of a Great Museum*, American Lighting Corporation, 1960. On Wright's scheme

for natural lighting, in which a mirror band and reflected light from the lower of the angled wall planes were subordinate ingredients, see *Guggenheim Museum,* pp. 20, 23.

31. Blake, *Arch. For.,* December 1959, p. 91.
32. The building is wired with a continuous duct for the irregular placement of spotlights which Wright intended as supplemental lighting.
33. McQuade, *Nation,* Nov. 7, 1959, p. 338. Hitchcock, *Zodiac,* 6, p. 20, stresses the treatment of the ceiling.
34. Blake, *Arch. For.,* December 1959, p. 91, emphasizes the point. But see, for example, the observations on scale as experienced outside the building in McQuade and Hitchcock, cited in Note 33 above.
35. Le Corbusier, *The Chapel at Ronchamp,* New York, Praeger, 1957, pp. 89, 94. Wright himself made the comparison with the chambered nautilus, *Guggenheim Museum,* p. 17. For other comparisons of the Guggenheim to seashells of various sorts, see, for example, *Arch. For.* January 1946, p. 82, and December 1959, p. 89; also *Interiors,* December 1959, p. 89.
36. For example, *Interiors,* October 1959, p. 172, specifically states that the Museum is less shell-like than machine-like. Harold Rosenberg has referred to it as a "machine for viewing": cited by Hess, *Art News,* November 1959, p. 48. Both Kramer, *Arts,* December 1959, p. 48, and McQuade, *Nation,* Nov. 7, 1959, p. 336, make the same analogy.
37. On Wright's successful absorption of alien modernism in the thirties, see Vincent Scully, "Wright versus the International Style," *Art News,* March 1954, pp. 32–35.
38. The interior became a little less well-like when Wright flipped over the ramp, which had appeared on the uptown side of the original model, to the downtown side. The acquisition of additional properties at this end of the lot permitted a slightly broader diameter to the ramp.
39. *Guggenheim Museum,* p. 20; and see p. 19.
40. Coates, "The Guggenheim," *New Yorker,* Oct. 31, 1959, p. 168. See also Hess, *Art News,* November 1959, p. 46.
41. Charles Baudelaire, "On Color," *The Salon of 1846,* cited in Jonathan Mayne, tr. and ed., *The Mirror of Art,* New York, Doubleday, 1956, p. 48.
42. *Guggenheim Museum,* p. 43.
43. Interview with Thomas Messer.
44. Scully, *Wright,* p. 31.
45. On the much discussed exoticism in Wright's work, see, for example, Dmitros Tselos, "Exotic Influences in the Architecture of Frank Lloyd Wright," *Mag. of Art,* April 1953, pp. 160–69; also his "Frank Lloyd Wright and World Architecture," *JSAH,* March 1969, pp. 58–72.
46. See especially Arthur E. Christy, *The Oriental Influences on American Transcendentalism,* New York, Columbia University Press, 1932.
47. Wright constantly applied the terms to his architecture and specifically to the Museum in *Guggenheim Museum,* p. 18. On the ambiguous meaning of "Freedom" and "Democracy," at least when applied to the Guggenheim, see Scully, *Wright,* p. 30, and Mumford, *New Yorker,* Dec. 5, 1959, pp. 108ff. On the other hand, for a concise and comprehensive statement of Wright's fundamentally "democratic" point of view, see especially Fitch, *Architecture and the Esthetics of Plenty,* pp. 38–45, 124–32.
48. Sibyl Moholy-Nagy, "Frank Lloyd Wright and the Ageing of Modern Architecture," *Prog. Arch.,* May 1959, pp. 136–42, touches on some of these questions.

443

6. LOUIS KAHN: RICHARDS MEDICAL RESEARCH BUILDING

The original version of this essay appeared in *Arch. Rev.*, February 1961, pp. 98–106.

Important critiques and presentations of the Richards Medical Center on its completion include:

    The brochure issued at the time of an exhibition devoted to the building at the Museum of Modern Art, New York, June–July 1961: *Louis I. Kahn, Architect Richards Medical Research Building*, with an introduction by Wilder Green.

    James Marston Fitch, "A Building of Rugged Fundamentals," *Arch. For.*, July 1960, pp. 82–87+.

    "Art Serves Science," *Arch. Rec.*, August 1960, pp. 149–56.

    "Medical Research Building for Pennsylvania University," *Arts & Arch.*, July 1961, pp. 14–17+.

    Henry-Russell Hitchcock, "Notes of a Traveller: Wright and Kahn," *Zodiac*, 6, 1960, pp. 14–21.

    "Laboratoires de recherches médicales Alfred Newton Richards à l'Université de Pennsylvanie," *Arch. d'Auj.*, February 1962, pp. 76–81.

    Ueli Roth, "Louis Kahn und die Medical Towers in Philadelphia," *Werk*, January 1962, pp. 22–25.

The best account of the building's structure is "Logic and Art in Precast Concrete," *Arch. Rec.*, September 1959, pp. 232–38.

Articles concerning Kahn's philosophy of architecture include:

    Jan C. Rowan, "Wanting To Be," *Prog. Arch.*, April 1961, pp. 130–49, an especially fine statement that makes liberal use of Kahn's own words.

    Walter McQuade, "Architect Louis Kahn and His Strong-Boned Structures," *Arch. For.*, October 1957, pp. 135–44.

    Boris Pushkarov, "Order and Form," *Perspecta*, 3, 1955, pp. 46–49, and "Order in Architecture," *Perspecta*, 4, 1957, pp. 58–65.

    Francesco Tentori, "Ordine e forma nell' opera di Louis Kahn," *Casabella*, July 1960, pp. 2–17.

Articles of a more critical nature are Reyner Banham, "On Trial, Louis Kahn: The Buttery-Hatch Aesthetic," *Arch. Rev.*, March 1962, pp. 203–6; and Sibyl Moholy-Nagy, "Louis Kahn, Doctor Mirabilis," *Perspecta*, 7, 1961, pp. 73–76. The most extensive study of Kahn's work is Vincent Scully, Jr., *Louis I. Kahn*, New York, Braziller, 1962, with bibliography.

1. Reyner Banham, *The New Brutalism: Ethic or Esthetic*, New York, Reinhold, 1966.
2. McQuade, *Arch. For.*, October 1957, p. 136.
3. Personal interview with Louis Kahn. Scully, *Kahn*, especially pp. 24f., 30, has emphasized the similarities between the design of Kahn and Wright; see also his "Wright, International Style and Kahn," *Arts*, March 1962, pp. 67–71+.
4. Fitch, *Arch. For.*, July 1960, p. 86. Rowan, *Prog. Arch.*, April 1961, p. 161.
5. McQuade, *Arch. For.*, October 1957, p. 136. The emphasis is Kahn's.
6. Rowan, *Prog. Arch.*, April 1961, p. 132.
7. For a more complete view of Kahn's architectural philosophy of "form" and "design," the best source, apart from Kahn's own writings, is Rowan. See also Scully, *Kahn*, which has a bibliography of Kahn's writings, and in an appendix reproduces two of his principal statements on his philosophy.

8. Banham, *Arch. Rev.*, March 1962, p. 204.
9. Voice of America, Forum Lectures on Modern Architecture (1960), cited in Scully, *Kahn*, pp. 118, 121.
10. Rowan, *Prog. Arch.*, April 1961, p. 133; also pp. 162f.
11. *Ibid.*, p. 140.
12. Scully, *Kahn*, p. 37. Scully emphasizes the Beaux-Arts influence on Kahn. See also Robert A. M. Stern, "PSFS: Beaux-Arts Theory and Rational Expressionism," *JSAH*, May 1964, p. 95.
13. Hitchcock, *Architecture Nineteenth and Twentieth Centuries*, pp. 398–403, discusses the distinctive qualities of American Beaux-Arts. See also Stern, *JSAH*, May 1962, pp. 84–95, and William Jordy, "Formal Image: U.S.A.," *Arch. Rev.*, March 1960, pp. 157–65.
14. Henry-Russell Hitchcock, "Frank Lloyd Wright and the 'Academic Tradition' of the Early Eighteen Nineties," *Journal of the Warburg and Courtauld Institutes*, January–June 1944, pp. 46–63.
15. For an example of questionable use of Kahn's "wanting to be," see John Johansen's rationale for his library building at Clark University, Worcester, Mass.: *Arch. For.*, February 1966, pp. 64–67. The example is the more telling since Johansen is an architect of distinction, and his building of exceptional quality. Comments on the building and the rationale appear in *Arch. For.*, May 1966, pp. 60–61.
16. McQuade, *Arch. For.*, October 1957, p. 141.
17. Interview with Louis Kahn.
18. Jordy, *Arch. Rev.*, February 1961, p. 103, explains this point.
19. Fitch, *Arch. For.*, July 1960, p. 84.
20. McQuade, *Arch. For.*, October 1957, p. 140.
21. Fitch, *Arch. For.*, July 1960, p. 84.
22. Scully, *Kahn*, p. 28.
23. On the postwar impact of the bulldozer, see:
   "New Approaches to Landshaping," *Arch. For.*, January 1957, pp. 96–103.
   R. A. Miller, "Bulldozer Architecture," *Arch. For.*, August 1950, pp. 84–91.
   G. R. Royse, "Man's Use of Land Form," *Arch. For.*, December 1962, pp. 31–34.
   On the use of cranes in construction, see:
   "Giant Cranes," *Arch. For.*, May 1959, pp. 158–59.
   "Cranes for Building," *JRIBA*, ser. 3, December 1959, sup. 1–6.
   S. Nielson-Eltaft, "Lower Cost for High Building; History of Preassembled Sections by Cranes," *Arch. For.*, May 1960, pp. 140–43.
   "Tower-Climbing Crane," *Prog. Arch.*, June 1962, pp. 132–37.
24. Voice of America, Forum Lectures, cited in Scully, *Kahn*, p. 120.
25. McQuade, *Arch. For.*, February 1957, p. 142.
26. Personal interview with scientist.
27. Banham, *Arch. Rev.*, March 1962, pp. 203–6.
28. On the development of mechanical ceilings, see Banham, *Well-Tempered Environment*, especially Chaps. 10 and 11.
29. For an account of the technology of the Yale Art Gallery ceilings see *Arch. For.*, November 1952, pp. 146–49.

GLOSSARY OF TERMS

AGGREGATE Sand, gravel, or other rock fragments. See CONCRETE.

BALUSTRADE A waist-high enclosure, as the handrail and spindles for a stair, or a parapet whether opened as with a row of colonnettes or closed as with a low wall. Minimally, a mere bar across an opening at waist height. See PARAPET.

BAY The interval between two members, such as a pair of columns or mullions. An elevation is frequently measured by window bays, a skeletal frame by structural bays.

BEAM A structural spanning member of wood, iron, steel, or reinforced concrete. In skeletal metal framing, beams are the smallest horizontal elements bridging the intervals between columns, with girders and trusses as larger components. See I-BEAM and TRUSS.

CANTILEVER A sustaining, projecting element, such as a roof edge or balcony which does not require support at its outer end. The term usually applies to major projections with fairly complex structures, and not to such minor projections as brackets and corbels which are structurally integral with the wall.

CHICAGO WINDOW A three-window unit having a large, fixed area of plate glass in the center and a narrow operable window on either side for ventilation. Inaugurated (or at least popularized) in the Chicago commercial buildings of the 1880's and 1890's, it maximized light for interiors.

CLOISONNÉ Having patterns divided by narrow metal partitions; applies especially to colored enamels, each diked within its compartment and fired.

COLUMN The principal vertical supporting element in a skeletal structure. In classical architecture, a cylindrical support, usually slightly tapered, and consisting of a base (except in severe orders like the Doric) shaft, and capital.

COMPRESSION The stress produced within a member by external forces tending to compact or crush. A member so stressed undergoes molecular de-

447

formation and is shortened. Contrast with the stretching forces of tension, the twisting forces of torsion, the cutting forces of shear.

CONCRETE An artificial stone made by mixing an aggregate (such as sand or gravel) and a binder (cement) with water in specified proportions. The mix is shaped in molds called *forms*. See REINFORCED CONCRETE.

CORNICE A decorative band, often of considerable depth and prominence, at the top of a wall where it meets the edge of a roof.

CROSS SECTION A vertical cut through a building, an architectural space, or component, drawn to show some aspect of its total volume in terms of interior space, structure, and/or mechanical operation.

ELEVATION A geometrical representation to scale of an upright, planar aspect of a building, especially of an exterior or an interior wall. The vertical complement of plan. Sometimes loosely used for any kind of head-on representation of a wall, whether photograph or sketch, whether measured or not. Also used as a synonym for an actual wall.

EXTRUSION A molding, as of metal or plastic, shaped as a ribbon. Also the process of forcing the raw material in its liquid or ductile state through a die shaped to the molding profile.

FAÇADE An elevation or exterior wall of a building, especially the principal, or entrance, front.

FENESTRATION Window treatment: arrangement and proportioning.

FLANGE See I-BEAM.

FLASHING A strip of metal, or sometimes of various flexible compositional materials, placed at roof joints, chimney corners, and the like to keep the weather out. Hence used to designate similar kinds of protective material placed over door and window openings.

FORM A mold into which wet concrete is poured and left until sufficiently cured (hardened).

HUNG CEILING A ceiling suspended from rod-like hangers below the level of the floor above. This flush plane obscures beam projections above while providing a surface for acoustical tiles and such mechanical conveniences as lighting fixtures, and modular sockets for flexible partitioning. The interval between the floor slab above and the suspended ceiling often serves as a space for ducts and utilities and/or a plenum for air transmission.

I-BEAM The term used in this book for all varieties of the most common shape in steel (see qualifying footnote, p. 241 above), although the shape has also appeared in reinforced concrete. Shaped like the letter "I", the vertical segment is known as the *web,* the horizontal end pieces as *flanges.* The shape is efficient: the flanges being at the points of greatest stresses under loads, and at the same time providing flat surfaces for convenient assembly. Steel beams also appear as H's, T's, Z's (the diagonal element a vertical), L's (known as *angles*), and square-cornered U's (*channels*).

MULLION An upright post, or similar member, dividing a wall opening into two contiguous windows, or a window into two units.

MUSHROOM COLUMNS Structural columns in reinforced concrete that flare at the top in order to counteract shear stresses in the vicinity of the column. See SHEAR.

PARAPET A waist-high, solid enclosure for a balcony; the base of a window; or the wall rising above the edge of the roof. See BALUSTRADE.

PIER An upright portion of a wall that takes on a columnar function. Tending to be square-cornered, and typically rather plain, the pier partakes of the aspects of both the wall and the column. It may occur as continuous with the plane of the wall, but may also be distinguished from the plane of the wall to give it a column-like independence. Sometimes capital-like moldings or other embellishment and bases further suggest columns.

PIER-AND-SPANDREL A motif for wall organization utilizing skeletal construction. The wall consists of a double plane of elements: the vertical structural elements (piers) projecting in front of bridging panel elements (spandrels). The spandrels serve both as supporting components for the windows and as enclosing parapets for the intervening window units. The pier tends toward a square or rectangular cross section. See PIER.

PILASTER A shallow, pier-like projection from the wall employing the elements of the classical column. Although largely decorative, this buttress-like thickening of the wall may also serve a stabilizing and stiffening function.

PLAN A schematic drawing representing part or all of the floor of a building as viewed from above.

PLENUM That space within the area between a hung ceiling and the floor above which serves in itself as an air duct, thus eliminating the need to install a metal duct. Adjacent to the plenum may be space for utility runs, although some of these runs occasionally intrude in the plenum. See HUNG CEILING.

REINFORCED CONCRETE Concrete embedded with metal rods or mesh in order to withstand tensile and other forces. See CONCRETE.

REVEAL That part of an opening which lies between the outer face of a wall and the door or window; the depth of a *jamb* in a door, or of a *sill* or *frame* in a window.

SECTION See CROSS SECTION.

SHEAR Any scissor-like cutting stresses within the structure, especially the tendency for heavily loaded floors to punch through columns as the equal and opposite force of the column counteracts the gravity load. In these situations shear faults tend to occur just beyond the perimeter of the column and are prevented by additional reinforcement and/or by mushroom columns. See REINFORCED CONCRETE, MUSHROOM COLUMNS, COMPRESSION, and TENSION.

SPACE FRAME In essence, a series of trusses placed side by side and joined to one another by triangulated rods, pipes, or beams so that the series of linear unidirectional trusses become a planar truss. Especially used in roof structures requiring long spans. See TRUSS.

STEREOTOMY The science of cutting specified solids from sections, such as the units that will make up a carefully fitted masonry wall.

SUSPENDED CEILING See HUNG CEILING.

TENSION The stress resulting from stretching or pulling forces. Occurs within the spanning elements of a structure. The tendency of the molecular structure of such elements to pull apart. See COMPRESSION.

TROFFER A trough-like lighting fixture, especially for tube lighting.

TRUSS   A major spanning element consisting of such linear components as beams, rods, and pipes combined with plates in an openwork arrangement which is usually triangular in configuration. Trusses are the largest spanning structural entities in skeletal construction, and serve as the principal supports of very large roofs or bridges.

VIERENDEEL TRUSS   Named after its inventor, this spanning element is distinguished by its lack of the diagonals found in normal trusses. It resembles a ladder on its side.

WEB   See I-BEAM.

WELDED CONSTRUCTION   The use of electrical arcs, sometimes with chemical compounds, to fuse metal structural components; an alternative to joining them with bolts or rivets. Welding is also used to fuse reinforcing elements in precast reinforced concrete.

Index

Illustrations for buildings are indicated by italicized figures under building or topical entries (for example, under "Guggenheim" and not under "Wright"; or under "Reinforced concrete"). Content breakdown on the works discussed at length is indicated under building entries (for example, under "Guggenheim"), except for some entries relating more generally to architect's career or philosophy. Buildings are also shortlisted under geographical entries (for example, under "New York").

453

Morandi, Riccardo, 174
Morris, Benjamin Wistar, 35–37
Morris (V. C.) Gift Shop, San Francisco, 285–88, 297, 347, 352; *286, 287*
Moser, Karl, 102–3
Mullet, Alfred, 4
Mumford, Lewis, 7, 41, 65, 73, 84, 171, 231–32, 277
Murphy, Charles, Associates, 258n.
Museum of Modern Art, New York, 12, 22–23, 175, 176, 210, 223, 252, 285; sculpture garden, 31–34; *32, 33*
Museum of Non-Objective Art (Guggenheim Museum), New York, 330
Mussolini, Benito, 389

National Gallery, Berlin, 258
Nattibumpo, 355
Neo-Gothic. See "Gothic" skyscrapers
Neo-Plasticism, 195n.
Neo-Platonism, influence of. See International Style
Nervi, Pier Luigi, 174
Neutra, Richard, 88, 102, 144, 153, 154–57, 285. See Lovell House; Rush City Reformed
Newberry Library, Chicago, 411n.
New Brutalism, 362–63, 407, 417, 420
New Brutalism: Ethic or Aesthetic?, 363
New empiricism, 167, 172, 179
New Haven, Conn., buildings. See Yale Art Gallery
New Pioneers, 87
New York, buildings and planning. See Avenue of the Americas; Brooklyn Bridge; Bryant Park; Central Park; Chase-Manhat-

tan; Chrysler; City Hall Park; Columbia Broadcasting; Daily News; Empire State; Equitable Life Assurance; Fifth Avenue; Four Seasons restaurant; Fuller ("Flatiron"); General Motors; Grand Army Plaza (see Plaza); Grand Central Terminal; Graphic Arts Center; Graybar; Guggenheim Museum; Lever House; Hilton Hotel at Rockefeller Center; Lincoln Center for the Performing Arts; McGraw-Hill; Madison Square; Madison Square Garden; Madison Square Presbyterian Church; Manufacturers Hanover Trust Co.; Marine Midland; Metropolitan Life Insurance Co.; Metropolitan Opera; Museum of Modern Art; Pan Am; Park Avenue; Pennsylvania Terminal; Penney; Pepsi-Cola; Philharmonic Hall; Plaza; Plaza Hotel; Post Office (City Hall Square); Racquet Club; Riverside Church; Rockefeller Center; St. Mark's Tower; St. Patrick's Cathedral; St. Thomas' Church; Saks Fifth Avenue; Seagram; Time-Life (see Rockefeller Center); Times; Times Square; Tribune; Trinity Church; Union Carbide; United Nations Secretariat; University Club; Wall Street; Wanamaker's department store; Welfare Island Redevelopment; Woolworth; World; World Trade Center and immediately below
New York City Courthouse, 3
New York City Hall, 2–4

Usonian House, 168
Utamara, *304*

Van Alen, William, 56
Van Doesburg, Theo, 197
Van Nelle tobacco factory, Rotterdam, 131–32, 134, 139, 140, 144, 157; *131*
Vassar College, Poughkeepsie, N.Y., 252. See Ferry Cooperative Dormitory
Vaux, Calvert, 11, 353
Vernacular, influence on modern architecture, 168–69, 184, 188–90
Vers une Architecture. See Le Corbusier
Viollet-le-Duc, Eugène, 183, 184
Voysey, Charles F. A., 185
Voysey, Charles F. A., 185

Wagner, Otto, 185
Wainwright Building, St. Louis, Mo., 48, 68n., 264, 298–99; *301*
Wall Street, New York, 6–7, 25
Walquist, John, 56
Wanamaker's department store, New York and Philadelphia, 11
Warren, Russell, 11n.
Warren (Whitney) & Wetmore (Charles), 7
Warren, Mich., building. See General Motors Technical Center
Washington, D.C., buildings. See Crystal Heights hotel project; L'Enfant's plan of, 12n.
Weisman, Winston, 35, 36, 38, 45, 152
Welding, 248
Welfare Island redevelopment, New York, 54

Well-Tempered Environment, The, 417
"What Is Happening to Modern Architecture?", 175–76
When Cathedrals Were White, 1
White, Stanford, 2. See McKim, Mead & White
Whitman, Walt, 355
Wie Baut Amerika?, 154, 156
Wiessenhof Housing Exhibition, Stuttgart, site planning, 269; *272*
Wilgus, Colonel William J., 7
Willcox, James M., 90, 91, 93, 98, 106–7, 116, 117, 123, 129, 138, 140, 143, 153, 233
Willey House, Minneapolis, Minn., 290
Williamsburg, Va., buildings. See Colonial Williamsburg
Windmill, Hillside School, Spring Green, Wis., 294–97; *295*
Wolf House, Guben (Germany); *129*
Woolworth Building, New York, 5–6, 48, 153, 297
Works Progress Administration, 170
World Building, New York, 4
World Trade Center, New York, 6, 7
Wright, Frank Lloyd, 11, 116, 138n., 152, 168, 170, 171, 177, 183, 193, 208, 210, 211, 213, 215, 223, 226, 279–359, 363, 366, 369, 387, 410; Broadacre City project, 286n.; Museum Exhibition, ideas on, 333–35; themes in work influencing Guggenheim Museum, 281–311; symbolism of Guggenheim Museum, 353–59. See especially Guggenheim